404 f10-95

THE

ECONOMIC MIND

By the same authors

A. Furnham with M. Argyle and J. Graham: *Social Situations* (Cambridge University Press, Cambridge, 1981)
A. Lewis: *The Psychology of Taxation* (Martin Robertson, Oxford/St Martin's Press, New York, 1982)

THE ECONOMIC MIND

The Social Psychology of Economic Behaviour

Adrian Furnham
Lecturer in Psychology, University College London

Alan Lewis
Lecturer in Research Methods in the Humanities and Social Sciences, University of Bath

Wheatsheaf Books

DISTRIBUTED BY HARVESTER PRESS

First published in Great Britain in 1986 by
WHEATSHEAF BOOKS LTD
A MEMBER OF THE HARVESTER PRESS PUBLISHING GROUP
Publisher: John Spiers
Director of Publications: Edward Elgar
16 Ship Street, Brighton, Sussex

British Library Cataloguing in Publication Data

Furnham, Adrian
The economic mind: the social psychology of economic behaviour.
1. Economics—Psychological aspects
I. Title II. Lewis, Alan, *1952–*
330'.01'9 HB74.P8

ISBN 0–7108–0285–4
ISBN 0–7108–0223–4 Pbk

Typeset in 10/12pt Times by Witwell Ltd, Liverpool
Printed and bound in Great Britain by
Biddles Ltd, Guildford and King's Lynn

THE HARVESTER PRESS PUBLISHING GROUP
The Harvester Press Publishing Group comprises Harvester Press Limited (chiefly publishing literature, fiction, philosophy, psychology, and science and trade books), Harvester Press Microform Publications Limited (publishing in microform unpublished archives, scarce printed sources, and indexes to these collections) and Wheatsheaf Books Limited (a wholly independent company chiefly publishing in economics, international politics, sociology and related social sciences), whose books are distributed by The Harvester Press Limited and its agencies throughout the world.

To our families and friends

Contents

List of Tables

List of Figures

Preface

Psychologists and economists until quite recently have had very little to do with each other. Psychologists thought that the economic model of man was simply wrong; economists thought that psychology had nothing useful to contribute. There were a very few exceptions, like George Katona. During recent years however there has been a rapid growth of interest, on both sides, into a wide range of topics of joint interest. A new journal has started, the *Journal of Economic Psychology*. So far that research has not been gathered together in a single volume, and this book is the first to do so.

The book is the product of a most successful collaboration between a social psychologist and a methodologist each distinguished and the author of many successful studies in their own fields. Adrian Furnham is a social psychologist who has carried out much research in the areas covered by the book—for example, with lay explanations of poverty, wealth and unemployment, the economic socialisation of children, attitudes to money and gambling. Alan Lewis is a methodologist who has carried out surveys of attitudes to and knowledge about wealth, taxation and unemployment. They have also done a joint study of lay ideas about reducing unemployment.

For psychologists there is a new field here—'economic psychology'—attitudes and beliefs about money, and how they affect buying and saving, becoming rich and poor, evading tax, and other aspects of economic behaviour. For economists there is also a new field—'psychological economics'—which extends traditional ideas of economic self-interest, to include the effects of economic socialisation, and of the beliefs and values of the public, industry and government, and how they affect economic behaviour.

Some of these issues are of practical importance to policy-makers, for example, in the design of tax systems, the distribution of wealth, the handling of unemployment. Other topics are of theoretical interest. For psychologists there are some basic questions about the psychology of money: Is the need for money based on conditioning, on Freudian symbolism or some other process? Why do people save? Is there really a Protestant ethic? Does being rich make people happier? For economists there are interesting basic questions too: Why do people want to become rich? How do consumers really make choices? Does taxation act as a work incentive? How much do people understand about taxation and government expenditure?

The authors have succeeded in bringing together these and many other issues in a masterly way. They are extremely well informed about a very large area of research, and have added their own original research to it. The book is a very rich source of information on these important issues. And the problems are discussed from several points of view, including politics, ethics and even religion.

Michael Argyle

ACKNOWLEDGEMENTS

This book has gained from the help and advice of many people, principal among whom are: Michael Argyle, David Collard, John Cullis, Peter Kelvin, Jos Jaspars and Bram Oppenheim.

Responsibility for the opinions expressed and any mistakes in the present volume rest, of course, securely with the authors.

Part I:
Introduction

1 The Social Psychology of Economic Behaviour

This book attempts to review and criticise the highly fragmented and diverse social psychological literature on economic phenomena and related topics. The selection of topics and the way they are treated is, of course, somewhat idiosyncratic given that a rapprochement between psychology and economics is still at an early but exciting phase.

Social psychologists are concerned with how the behaviour, cognitions (thoughts, beliefs, attitudes) and emotions (feelings) of one individual are influenced or determined by the behaviour and/or specific characteristics (physical, psychological, demographic) of others (be they individuals or groups). Although there are a number of theories in social psychology (e.g. social facilitation theory, balance theory, equity theory, attribution theory), many of which could profitably be applied to the study of economic behaviour, little or no work has been done in this field. Despite the diversity of topics investigated by social psychologists (e.g. attitudes, bargaining, conformity, etc.) very little work has been devoted to how people comprehend or behave in the economic world.

As the above definition implies social psychology is concerned with social *behaviour*, social *beliefs* and social *emotions*. A social psychological approach to economics would include all three components, though they are, of course, not necessarily mutually exclusive. The sort of questions that a social psychologist would ask (and hopefully research) would be somewhat different from those of concern to a sociologist, anthropologist or experimental psychologist interested in economic behaviour. Consider for example the social psychology of economic beliefs. As in other areas of the psychology of lay beliefs there are a number of topics that may be considered:

1. THE *DEVELOPMENT* OF ECONOMIC BELIEFS

No description of economic beliefs is complete without a full understanding of the aetiology of these beliefs. Developmental psychologists have long been interested in how and when children come to understand the physical world and concepts like time, mass and space, yet they have ignored in large part how the child begins to understand the economic world. There exist very few theories or models of how people come to hold the various economic and related social and political beliefs that they do. An exception is the work of McClelland (1961), who attempted to explain how parents' socialisation of their children leads them in turn to believe in the Protestant work ethic. Similarly, Furnham and Thomas (1984a) have suggested that social class differences in the way in which young children and adolescents are given pocket-money (allowances) may be partly responsible for differences in adult economic beliefs and habits. However there is no systematic work in this field, and no parsimonious theory for guidance. What is of most importance is to establish *which* socialisation experiences (potty-training for the psychoanalyst; early reinforcement schedules for the behaviourist) contribute to the establishment of which specific, consistent and stable economic beliefs. In short what is required is a developmental theory of economic beliefs and habits (Jahoda, 1979). Equally important is to study how these economic beliefs develop. That is, how there is a *social construction* of the economic world.

2. THE *RELATIONSHIP* BETWEEN ECONOMIC BELIEFS

There are at least three equally important, but distinct, topics of research within this category. The first is the relationship between specific economic beliefs within the individual or group. It is important to establish whether beliefs about the causes of poverty mirror beliefs about the causes of wealth. Or it may be that attitudes to taxation are quite distinct from attitudes to welfare benefits. What, however, is most probable is that both global and specific economic beliefs are related in a coherent, relatively stable manner. A second area of interest is the relationship between economic beliefs and other social or political beliefs. Work already done in this field suggests the interesting paradox: 'The issues, then, on which voters and the MPs they have elected agree would be those concerned with taxation, nationalisation and economic power generally. On all other issues there is a clear-cut chasm where "cross-voting" takes place, with electors and elected pulling their different ways' (Eysenck, 1977, p.208). It may be that Conservatives vote into parliament MPs who share their economic but not social and political beliefs in general. Yet other beliefs about justice and control (just world/locus of control) probably do reflect more closely the views of the electors and elected. Finally, and perhaps of most importance in this section, there is the question of the relationship between economic beliefs and economic behaviour. There is a voluminous (and for the simple-minded practitioner, very depressing) literature on why attitudes do not predict behaviour more consistently. Economic, like all other social behaviour is complex, specific and multi-determined, and hence general attitudes may be poor predictors of specific economic behaviours. Yet if specific attitudes *and* intentions are measured over time to specific economic phenomena they may be fairly good predictors of behaviour. Certainly very little work appears to have been done in this area.

3. THE *FUNCTION* OF ECONOMIC BELIEFS

Much of cognitive social psychology is concerned with how people make sense of the social world. That is, various belief systems (locus of control, just world, Protestant work ethic beliefs) serve to make the world a stable, orderly and predictable place. The function of these beliefs is often to establish a cause-and-effect relationship between phenomena, which in turn enables one to apportion blame, praise or responsibility. Economic belief systems may function in various ways: to justify one's own economic position *vis-à-vis* others, to attempt to predict the future of economic trends, etc. Functionalist theories, though somewhat unfashionable, provide useful insights into why people maintain and change various economic beliefs (Gans, 1972).

4. THE *STABILITY* AND *CONSISTENCY* OF ECONOMIC BELIEFS

The question of how and when individual and/or shared economic beliefs change is of considerable interest to psychologists, economists and politicians. The temporal stability of both micro- and macroeconomic beliefs has, of course, very important implications for how these beliefs may be changed. The stability of beliefs refers to their similarity over time, while consistency of beliefs refers to their similarity across situations. The stability and consistency of economic beliefs has implications for how they are measured. For instance, if economic beliefs are fairly inconsistent and influenced greatly by the context in which they are gathered it is important to make reference to the context when evaluating the evidence. Similarly, if they are relatively stable over time, results from surveys and interviews may be safely generalised to predict future beliefs. Perhaps what is most interesting in this area is what factors lead to economic beliefs being stable and unstable, consistent and inconsistent.

5. THE *CONSEQUENCES* OF ECONOMIC BELIEFS

Economic beliefs are not only of importance in the understanding of individual behaviour, but in how groups and societies function. There is likely to be a collective view in certain groups about the nature of the economic world. These collective views may not be explicit or sophisticated as in a school of economic thought, but may nevertheless be important in the way in which groups or societies behave towards themselves and others. That is, belief systems have certain consequences. The idea of unidirectional causality with regard to collective economic beliefs and the state of the economy may be misplaced; it is equally improbable to suggest that 'consumer sentiment' solely determines consumer demand, or that economic forces solely determine consumer sentiment (economic beliefs). Katona (1971) found that public pessimism about the economy showed a sharp decline about 6–9 months *before* each of the major recessions. However, what is not clear is whether public pessimism caused the depression or simply mirrored it. The issue of cause and correlation dogs a great deal of research in this field. But shared economic beliefs do have consequences as to how people perceive themselves and others, who they vote for and who they believe.

6. THE *CHANGING* OF ECONOMIC BELIEFS

Central to social psychological research on attitudes and beliefs are theories of attitude change and consequent suggestions as to the best methods of changing them. There are a number of different approaches including learning and reinforcement theories based on behaviouristic ideas of stimulus–response learning, social judgement and consistency theories which stem from Gestalt tradition and function theories which place most emphasis on human needs. These theories place different emphases on both the causes and methods of change, and are in large part mutually exclusive. Applied research in the area of racism and religious prejudice has revealed the difficulty of attitude change due to the complexity of the process and the number of internal and external factors involved. Yet there are cases of quite sudden and surprising change in beliefs as a result of various happenings. Sudden inflation, the collapse of a bank, increasing unemployment, sudden personal wealth, may each serve to change specific economic beliefs. Economists and planners have to anticipate consumer reaction to specific changes, such as a sudden shortage of petrol. Of equal importance is research on how changes in certain economic beliefs affect changes in other economic beliefs. If economic beliefs form a coherent, balanced, (psycho-) logical system, change in one or more elements is likely to cause changes in other aspects of the system. Extensive research on balance theory is clearly relevant here and may explain why beliefs and attitudes are so resilient to change. That is, to change beliefs about the causes of poverty may involve changing other rather different beliefs about, for instance, mastery over the environment, or postponement of gratification (Furnham and Bland, 1983).

7. THE *MANIPULATION* OF ECONOMIC BELIEFS

Related to topic (6) is how various groups—politicians, advertisers, health agencies—attempt to manipulate beliefs for specific ends. There is a rich yet somewhat atheoretical literature on advertising, and a rather depressing literature on more dramatic means of changing attitudes such as brainwashing. Both may be important in understanding how attempts are made to manipulate the economic beliefs of specific groups or society at large.

8. THE *STRUCTURE* OF ECONOMIC BELIEFS

Studies on the structure of beliefs aim to determine how a variety of economic beliefs are organised along specific dimensions. For instance, Eysenck (1957) suggested that political beliefs could be structured in terms of two (and not one as previously considered) dimensions: Radical-Conservative; Tender-minded–Tough-minded. The same is probably true of economic beliefs in that all lay economic beliefs are probably structured according to a number of specific dimensions. For instance, it is possible

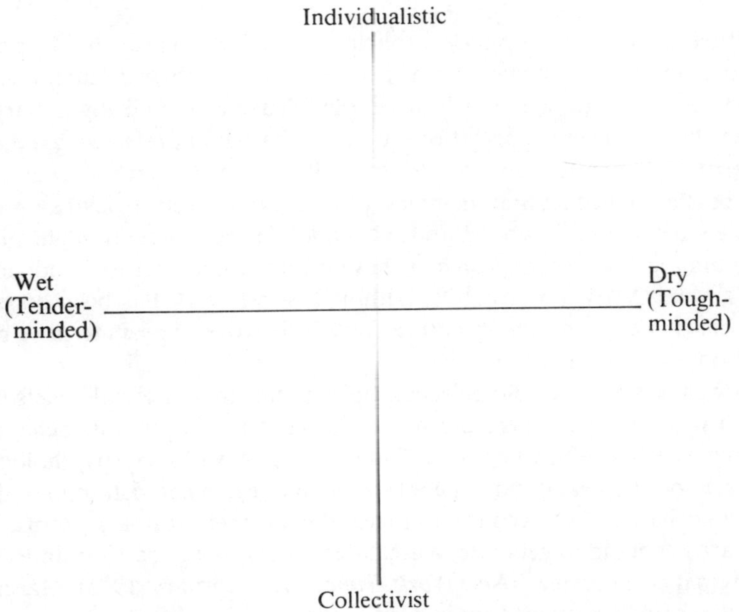

Figure 1.1: A possible structure for economic beliefs

that economic beliefs may be structured in two dimensions: individualistic-collectivistic; tough-minded–tender-minded. The first dimension would reflect right-wing, conservative capitalism, free enterprise beliefs *vs*. left-wing, radical, socialist, state control beliefs, while the second dimension would reflect economic policy implications with tough-minded beliefs emphasising state, legal or political action, while tender-minded beliefs would emphasise passive, consensual or conventional rather than interventionist policies. The terms 'wet' and 'dry', already in current usage in Britain, may be used interchangeably with tough- and tender-minded views to avoid confusion with Eysenck's work. Hence it is possible that economic beliefs are structured as shown in Figure 1.1.

However this is mere speculation based on similar social psychological research on the structure of lay theories and beliefs. Thus empirical studies will be necessary to establish the validity of this model. Furthermore, it may be that economic beliefs are unusual in that people appear to hold ambivalent beliefs simultaneously (apparently contradictory views at the same time).

9. LAY BELIEFS ABOUT ECONOMIC BEHAVIOUR *VS*. ECONOMISTS BELIEFS ABOUT LAY BEHAVIOUR

Whether they are ever made explicit or not, economists hold various theories about mass behaviour of people. Many of their calculations are based on expectations about how people behave economically in varying circumstances. These expectations are often based on previous aggregated evidence and are often fairly accurate. Yet this is not always the case and this may be due to the fact that their view (if there is a collective view) about lay people's behaviour is wrong. Indeed schools of economic thought might differ amongst other things on how they perceive human nature—individual needs, wants, drives and habits. Although some work has been done on politicians' views on human nature, very little work appears to have been done on economists' perspectives.

As well as a number of neglected topics in the area of social beliefs with regard to economics, there are numerous aspects of economic behaviour that have been woefully neglected. There is a paucity of social psychological research on why and how people save money; what determines their gambling habits; how economic issues dictate their voting patterns, etc. Similarly, economics generates a great deal of emotional passion. Indeed in a newspaper interview (*New York Times*, 12 February 1975) Margaret Thatcher said 'the longer I am in politics the more I realise that facts are not the determining thing. Feelings are what count—feelings which are totally out of accord with some of the facts.'

WHAT THE BOOK IS NOT

It would be unfair, either through the title or the introduction, to promise the reader various things that the book does not and cannot fulfill. The book is not a handbook or compendium to all psychological theory as it applies to economic phenomena, partly because it is highly uncertain as to what constitutes the relevant psychological theories and what economic phenomena are to be considered. Topics like inflation, investing, supply and demand are touched on only in passing as psychologists have hardly ever attempted to investigate them. Though the research and theorising of economists, politicians, sociologists, policy-makers, etc. are occasionally mentioned, the focus of this book is social psychological. Therefore the book does not attempt to be a practical manual for the struggling social worker or applied psychologist. Nor is it supposed to provide the economist with a new set of concepts, dimensions or variables which would make his predictions better. This volume is an attempt to offer a comprehensive critique of the (social) psychological literature as it applies to various specific economic phenomena. The latter were chosen primarily to reflect the type of economic issues that social psychologists have concerned themselves with. Of necessity the chapters vary in length and depth, in the amount of theorising and research done in the area, and in relevance and applicability of this research.

Any complete science of economic psychology would not only be able to specify the structure, the aetiology and the consequences of economic beliefs, behaviours and affective states, but also be able to explain the relationship between them. This is, of course, a formidable task.

Perhaps the first task is to review the state of the art so far. This book attempts to do just that.

2 Concepts and Theories in Economic Psychology

ECONOMIC MAN

Economics is concerned with aspects of behaviour which arise from the scarcity of means to achieve given ends (Robbins, 1935). Let us take the consumption of butter as an example. The consumer wishes to buy butter but is constrained by the limitations of income and the price of the good. At its very simplest, consumer demand analysis in microeconomics is concerned with how demand changes (in this case for butter) according to changes in income, the price of the good and the price of substitutes (for example, margarine). All these factors are considered to be measurable, relatively unambiguous and objective.

Choosers, of course, have preferences. These are treated theoretically and axiomatically. And this is the crux of rational economic man or woman.* Our chooser is assumed rationally to pursue his self-interest through utility maximisation. The preferences themselves to be consistent and orderly, i.e. obey a number of axioms such as continuity and transitivity.

In its original form the theory required utility maximisation without exception; the chooser was endowed with perfect information enabling him to choose rationally between alternatives; preferences were presumed to be independent of the preferences of others.

Strict adherence to these assumptions has relaxed over the years and new 'more realistic' assumptions incorporated. Among these are concepts of 'uncertainty', 'risk', 'information costs' and 'expectations'. Economic man, now stripped of perfect knowledge, is uncertain about the future and is 'risk-aversive'. The limits of his knowledge are determined by constraints imposed by information costs (Deaton and Muellbauer, 1980). Nothing fundamentally has changed. Economic man still behaves rationally given the constraints—there are simply new constraints introduced in the model.

Is the economic model realistic? And does this matter? The answers partly lie in the influential essay by Milton Friedman (1953) and economists' enthusiasm for logical positivism. Friedman argues that unrealistic assumptions may be more desirable than realistic ones. Unrealistic assumptions are advocated as they simplify reality in such a way that hypotheses can be derived that apply to economic situations in which predictions are good ones. The emphasis then is placed on prediction of economic consequences based on economic antecedents. The process by

*Henceforth 'economic man' 'socio-psychological' man, etc. will refer to both genders.

which these antecedents are translated into consequences is of no direct interest. The need for parsimony is a central aspect of the posivistic approach: new additions to the theory or model are strongly resisted. However the distinction between parsimony and pragmatism is far from clear (Hollis and Nell, 1975).

Fritz Machlup (1978) has described *Homo economicus* as the 'universal bogey man'. There is something about the concept which upsets anthropologists, philosophers, sociologists, psychologists, and a minority of economists themselves (Sen, 1977). The first of these criticisms concerns whether economic man is a theory at all (Hollis and Nell, 1975). If it constitutes a theory then it should fit the facts, or be amended or rejected in the light of observations. This does not appear to happen. Rational economic man reigns supreme. According to Amartya Sen (1977) there is frequent disagreement among economists as to the status of rational behaviour theory, some accepting that the theory is unfalsifiable, others that it is falsifiable but so far has been unfalsified; whilst a third group feel the theory is falsifiable and patently false.

Other major criticisms concern its 'atomism' or 'individualism' and its 'universality'. Microeconomics is based on individual preferences rather than social preferences. People are viewed like so many blades of grass, albeit of different individual shades, but where the view of the field from a distance is of a uniform green. Furthermore the theory appears to be applicable to all cultures and is relatively untouched by changes in society and by history. For economic anthropologists economic exchanges are viewed as having cultural functions in defining people's status, in maintaining norms, the social structure, and in religious rites: economics is subservient to culture (Herskovits, 1952; Hollis and Nell, 1975; Frith, 1978; Machlup, 1978; Stroebe and Frey, 1980; Farmer, 1982; Lewis, 1982a, Ch. 2).

In a similar vein the theory has been criticised because of its 'determinism'. Because the process whereby economic antecedents are mysteriously transformed into economic consequences is largely ignored it is almost as though man, his thoughts, beliefs, aspirations, morals and so forth, are an irrelevancy. The cause determines the effects and there is next to nothing economic man can do about it. He is imprisoned by his selfishness. But economic laws are surely not immutable: man created economics, not the other way around.

The all pervading motive of self-interest can be viewed as reducing and degrading man. It is a one-motive theory of human behaviour. It allows neither motives of benevolence nor malevolence as such: self-interest and rational behaviour incorporates all human action, it is inescapable in its tautology. Virtually every form of altruism is reducible to self-interest. If I provide money or benefits for others it may be purely because I anticipate reciprocal benefits, or gain in reputation by my generosity. Giving to a beggar may make me feel better, it will also get him off the streets so that I don't have to be upset by him again and reduce my chances of being mugged if I walk the same street at night. Similarly every action is rational: the actions of others need not make sense to me but presumably it must be rational to the actor himself (see Boulding, 1969; Collard, 1978). 'Rationality' becomes confusing as it can mean so many things: it can mean dispassionate, reasonable, logical, explanable, purposeful; it is not always made plain quite what is intended (although Simon, 1976b, does).

Criticising economic theory is a fashionable thing to do. Its tenets appear conspirationally conservative to Marxist commentators (Herman, 1982). But economists enlightened with an 'economic imagination' of which Kenneth Boulding is well endowed, appreciate the ethical responsibility of economics and its place within a cultural and historical context. As science moves from knowledge to control it creates what it knows. Economics can be a self-fulfilling prophecy where the beliefs of politicians, economists and opinion leaders have a major influence on the beliefs and economic behaviour of the rest of us. The methods of economists in part reflect the beliefs and methods of the sub-culture of scientists, and what is acceptable and viable in society at large (Boulding, 1969).

It is useful too to place Friedman's 'as if' propositions on their heads—if economic predictions are good ones it seems probable at the very least that the model of economic man has some truth in it—that it has value in our investigation of the 'economic mind'. As Stigler (1971) has pointed out, the intellectual has a distaste for the market-place and of vulgar men and base motives. Such distaste, should it arise, must not blinker the intrepid researcher too much.

Finally, for all our criticisms, rational economic man provides, if not a unifying theory, a unifying research programme which other social sciences might do well to emulate (Lakatos, 1970; Hollis and Nell, 1975; Farmer, 1982).

SOCIAL-PSYCHOLOGICAL MAN

Modern social psychology, unlike economics, has no grand theory. Yet its subject-matter is even grander, including as it does the whole of social behaviour, of which we argue economics is a part. We must be careful not to be accused of 'psychological imperialism'. Psychology cannot 'explain' economics; neither can economics 'explain' psychology. Although modern economists have shown a tendency to extend the application of the rationality theory to incorporate aspects of marriage, social interactions and crime (Becker, 1976; McKenzie and Tullock, 1978).

Theories in social psychology have been described as systems of thought (Farr, 1980), and 'guiding ideas' (McGuire, 1980) rather than fully-fledged theories. McGuire (1980) offers an informative typology of social psychological theories in a 2^4 matrix which is reproduced in Table 2.1. Most of the theories are directly concerned with motivation. The dimensions used are active/reactive; cognitive/affective; internal/external; stability/growth. The active/reactive dimension articulates one of the crucial differences between economics and psychology: 'active' theories stress that human experiences and behaviour are initiated within the person; 'reactive' theories regard behaviour as a reaction to external environmental forces. Economic theory and the grander theories in psychology (e.g. learning theories and sociobiology) are 'reactive' or, using a similar term, deterministic theories. The two most highly referenced groups of theories in modern social psychology, namely 'consistency' theories and 'attribution theories,' are 'active' theories.

The stability/growth dimension distinguishes between human action motivated to maintain equilibrium, and action which strives towards increased knowledge, complexity, autonomy and personal growth.

The cognitive/affective and internal/external dimensions are referred to as 'end state' rather than initiating dimensions, by which is meant that they describe what terminates action rather than what causes it. A 'cognitive' terminus refers to the establishment of a set of ideas, and the 'affective' terminus to feelings and emotions. The end point for 'internal' is the establishment of internal relations among an individual's personality; 'external' to relationships between the person and the environment (for details, see McGuire, 1980). Using all four dimensions, consistency theories, the darlings of the 1960s, are active stability theories, with cognitive and internal termini. The latter-day fashionable attribution theories are in a similar vogue and differ only in their external termini.

There are three main branches of consistency-type theories, namely Heider's 'balance' theory (Heider, 1958); Osgood and Tannenbaum's (1955) 'congruity' theory; and perhaps the most famous and widely applied, Festinger's (1957) 'dissonance' theory. People are assumed to prefer 'balanced', 'congruent' and 'consonant' states to 'imbalanced', 'incongruous' and 'dissonant' ones, and are motivated to resolve imbalances etc. Balance theory concerns the connection between attitudes and relationships with other people. A balanced condition is one where friends agree on an opinion—say, provisions for private health care, which are of central importance to both of them. An imbalanced state would be one where there is disagreement; a disequilibrium causing a change of position on the issue or in the affective bond between participants. Similarly congruity theory concerns the relationship between a perceiver's evaluation of a source of a message, the evaluation of the message itself and the perceiver's own opinion. Lastly, Festinger has described dissonance as occurring when two or more cognitions have contradictory implications for behaviour—that is, when the first cognition implies you do one thing and a second cognition another.

Consistency theories promised much—it was an attempt by social

Table 2.1: Sixteen guiding-idea theories: partial views of human nature that lie behind social psychological research in the twentieth century

			Initiating dimensions			
			Stability		*Growth*	
			Active	*Reactive*	*Active*	*Reactive*
End-state dimensions	*Cognitive*	*Internal*	1. Consistency (balance)	2. Categorisation (perceptual)	6. Autonomy (control)	6. Problem-solving (utilitarian)
		External	3. Attribution (epistemic)	4. Induction (observational)	7. Stimulation (exploratory; novelty)	8. Matching (teleological; script)
	Affective	*Internal*	9. Tension (drive) reduction	10. Ego-defensive (functional)	13. Assertion (dominance; achievement)	14. Role-playing (identification)
		External	11. Expressive cathartic; acting out)	12. Habituation (behaviouristic; stimulus–response)	15. Affiliative (empathy)	16. Modelling (social learning)

Source: McGuire, 'The Development of theory in social psychology' in*The Development of Social Psychology*, 1980, Academic Press, Orlando, Florida. Reprinted with permission.

psychology to develop a grand theory, and seemed to be suggesting something fundamental about human nature: the needs for equilibrium and cognitive consistency.

Attribution theory also caught the social psychological imagination. There have probably been more journal articles in the social psychological literature concerned in some way with attribution theory than any other single topic in the last 10–15 years. The theory, in its various guises, was outlined by Heider (1958) and developed for example by Kelley (1967); up-to-date reviews and appraisals appear in Kelley and Michela (1980), Hewstone (1983) and Antaki (1981).

Attribution theory is concerned with the way people interpret causes of events. It is not a theory in the proper sense, there are no well-developed and systemised set of assumptions, propositions and deductions, rather it offers general principles for observation, (McGuire, 1980). Man is considered to be a naive psychologist, a naive scientist—he views the world and tries to make sense of it by testing his personal theories against what he observes in the 'outside' world.

The main distinction in attributing causes is between explanations based on personal characteristics and those based on aspects of the environment. Question: 'Why did Johnny Punk kick in the glass of the neighbourhood telephone kiosk?' Answer: 'He is a nasty aggressive person, a vandal (who, incidentally, needs locking up!).' Alternatively, the answer may be: 'He was with a gang, they egged him on, it was a dare, he had to do it or lose face.'

One of the main reasons there has been so much attribution research is that it is so amenable to small-scale laboratory experimentation—still a common method in mainstream social psychology. Scenarios can be prepared which systematically vary, for example, the circumstances, time and continuity of the action in question. People are then asked to offer causal explanations for the vignettes.

Man's needs to explain causes of events is considered fundamental. The discovery of the pattern of these explanations is the main purpose of the research.

Like economics, social psychology is not without its critics both from other disciplines (e.g. sociology) and from 'within' (Taylor and Brown, 1979; Billig, 1982). On the one hand it has been lambasted by positivist experimental psychologists for its lack of scientific rigour; while sociologists have challenged whether social psychology is really 'social' at all. We shall deal mainly with the latter set of criticisms.

The argument continues that psychological laws, should they exist, are like economic laws: subservient to culture and to history. They cannot be immutable, neither can they be universal (Jahoda, 1979). If man has a need to be consistent as the consistency theories imply, who is to decide what is consistent and what is not? Surely it is society that determines what is consistent. If in conversation people are not challenged for pontificating that the role of the state should be reduced while, almost in the same breath, defending increased provisions for the elderly or the sick, there is no inconsistency to be resolved.

Consistency is a relative concept, but the kind of 'inconsistency' we have monitored above may be the norm in western capitalist countries rather than the exception. Thus 'inconsistency' may not motivate cognitive and social change, rather an acceptance of the culture and economic system in which one lives creates an equilibrium however 'inconsistent' that culture or economic system may be. (Similar points of criticism are made by Billig, 1982.)

Criticisms of attribution theory form a familiar pattern. The argument runs that the interpretation of action is culturally determined. The examination of individual preferences is the wrong frame of reference, it is atomistic. Research tends to under-represent the ambiguity and ambivalence so common in ordinary explanations, and like consistency theory treats such attributions as oddities or inconsistencies which require resolution. Because relatively few studies are conducted in the context where people actually go about interpreting events, laboratory studies engender a certain falseness. Often people are restricted in their choices to predetermined categories; rarely is a proper qualitative analysis attempted. Finally, ideological differences between attributors have been largely ignored. The central emphasis of research has been in ascertaining the rules governing stimulus conditions which lead to particular attributions. Recent research on attributions of the causes of wealth and poverty (Lewis, 1981; Furnham, 1982b, 1983e) have indicated major cleavages between supporters of differing political parties, indicating not only that they see causes differently but they impose their view on the stimulus or vignette in question. This latter approach places more emphasis on internal cognitions; the action to which people attribute cause is not 'out there' in the 'outside world', the action itself is perceived differently by people with different beliefs. Thus one's interpretation of the causes of poverty in the USA or Britain depends on perceptions of the extent of poverty, its seriousness, or whether people believe it exists at all!

Looking at social psychology more broadly, Armistead (1974) has subdivided the discipline into 'psychological' social psychology (PSP) and 'sociological' social psychology (SSP). The former he says 'manages to ignore the meaning of the situation to the participants and to depoliticise the social context' (Armistead, 1974, p.16). Armistead clearly favours sociological social psychology with its concern for role theory, reference group theory, norms and conformity. Sociological social psychology (SSP) is further praised for being less deterministic: SSP views social behaviour in terms of man-made forces while PSP sees social behaviour as determined by natural laws which have to be discovered.

Social psychology is a broad church, but the criticism that social psychology is not really 'social' at all is a lingering one (Taylor and Brown, 1979; Semin and Manstead, 1979). Recently there has been a revival of research work on groups rather than individuals. For example descriptions of inter-group relations theory stress the minimal evocation for group formation, how easily 'in groups' and 'out groups' are differentiated, their importance in social identity, and the tendency to credit one's own group members, while disparaging those from other groups especially at times of stress and threat (Tajfel, 1978).

Studies in socialisation in developmental psychology provide a unifying influence in social psychology. And these studies have a prominent place in the ripening field of economic psychology in examining how notions of exchange, saving and economic concepts generally grow.

MAN IN ECONOMIC PSYCHOLOGY

Herbert Simon, a professor of psychology and Nobel prize-winner in economics, has outlined a model of man which bridges the gap between the two disciplines (Simon and Stedry, 1969). Unlike Friedman, Simon argues that realistic models are more informative ones. Simon dedicated the rather cumbersome word 'satisficing' to describe motivation: man is viewed not as a blindly maximising animal, but as a being with a limited capacity for information. This presents a move to the analysis of the 'internal' environment of the person, rather than just the 'external' environment. The quality of a choice, which to an outside observer may seem less than rational, is to be understood not only in terms of information and search costs, but also the cognitive limitations of the chooser. Furthermore 'satisficing' recognises that the aspirations of individuals are variable, people adapt according to what is attainable.

A distinction needs to be made between inductive and deductive methods. In economics the usual course is for hypotheses to be derived from the familiar rationality theory or adaptations of it, and observations made within this framework. As has been mentioned earlier, economic theory is rarely if ever changed in the light of observations—the deductive aspect of the method is strong and the inductive aspect weak. In social psychology generally the opposite is true—often observations are made without sufficient regard to the theory or whether or not they provide an adequate test; the importance of results is commonly overemphasised and the need for further experimentation stressed without proper regard to where it is all leading.

There are probably many reasons for these differences but it seems likely that one of them is the disciplines' varying interest in the internal environment of the person and the external environment. In economics the observations are often in the form of aggregate data collected by people other than the economist (and sometimes for different purposes). 'Failure' in the study can be explained by the inadequacies of the data, or by some external economic factor or constraint overlooked. In social psychology 'failure' is usually explained by weaknesses in the design of the study it is true, but frequently a discussion continues which implies that something about people and social behaviour has been discovered that requires explanation and further testing.

Certainly Simon and the so-called 'Austrian' school of economists (e.g. von Mises, 1978) have given more attention to the internal environment and view man as 'active' rather than a 'passive' pawn of economic forces. In her useful discussion of these and other matters the sociologist Farmer concludes that there is nothing about economics which necessarily excludes examination of the internal environment. Thus much of what follows in the present volume is of interest to those with an economic imagination (see Farmer, 1982).

There are many productive links between economics and psychology, but for the present purposes it is useful to talk of two camps: 'economic psychology' and 'psychological economics', and we recognise, as does van Raaij (1981), that there are overlaps between the two. By 'psychological economics' we refer to work, mainly by economists, that employs psychology to improve and expand the discipline of economics (Duesenberry, 1949; Leibenstein, 1978; Scitovsky, 1976; Maital, 1982). 'Economic psychology' deals more with the extension of the examination and investigation of social behaviour into the economic realm. The present volume leans more heavily on the latter and in particular the importance of this extension of social psychology. We need to say a little more about both psychological economics and economic psychology, beginning with psychological economics.

Duesenberry (1949), in an analysis of consumer behaviour, employed expenditure demonstration effects and comparisons with others. Choices are not independent ones. Purchases are often a function of habit. Income constraints are not only 'objective' but dependent on perceptions of them by consumers and their relative position to other people's incomes and expenditure. In this way Duesenberry's work bears some resemblance to the work in social psychology and sociology on perceptions of equity, reference groups, social comparisons and relative deprivation (Stouffer, 1949; Festinger, 1954; Adams, 1965; Runciman, 1966; Merton, 1968).

Leibenstein (1976) also agreed that interpersonal relationships were important, but in particular emphasised the concepts of 'inertia' and 'x-efficiency'. Both are concerned with 'non-optimal' behaviour. People within the traditional economic units of the firm and the household often do not react to economic changes until the need for change becomes paramount. There is an inertia and sluggishness in decision-making. Economic decisions, say within the firm, are dependent upon negotiation and are constrained by the nature and environment of jobs and occupations, and the structure of the firms themselves. Not everyone is equal within an organisation and firm; it depends where you are on the hierarchical ladder. Leibenstein recognises the cognitive element in decision-making, and recommends future research to examine the degree of 'x-efficiency', by which is meant the difference between maximal effectiveness and actual effectiveness.

Scitovsky (1976) takes issue with the static nature of aspiration and motivation implied in economic theory. Motivation is variable. Borrowing from animal, psychological and experimental psychology (Hebb, 1955; Berlyne, 1960) economic motivation is examined in terms of the need of individuals for optional arousal (a plateau between sluggishness and catastrophic over-arousal) stimulation, and the spur of curiosity.

Much of what we have referred to above is microeconomics, but a considerable amount of interest has also been shown in the use of expectations in research on changes in employment, inflation, exchange and interest rates (e.g. Shackle, 1949; Carlson and Parkin, 1975; Hudson, 1982).

George Katona's book *Psychological Economics* (1975) also included notions of expectations, although of a rather different kind. In the 'index of consumer sentiment' survey respondents are regularly asked whether they feel better or worse off than a year ago, whether they expect to feel better off in a year from now, whether it is a good time for buying things, and whether the next 12 months and 5 five years will be better or worse for the economy as a whole. Aggregated scores are used for short-term forecasts of, for example, expenditure on durable goods. The index has met with some formidable success (Shapiro, 1972). The index is a truly 'subjective' measure of expectations. An abridged version of Katona's thesis states that economic changes, in the short term, are a function of consumer sentiment, rather than economic variables alone: that there are intervening variables between economic stimuli and economic responses.

'Expectations' arise again in a revised form in so-called expectancy-value theories of choice (Edwards, 1961; Fishbein and Ajzen, 1975; Tversky and Kahneman, 1977) and in games theory (von Neumann and Morgenstern, 1944). Generally, expectations are incorporated in terms of the expected utility of outcomes. People are uncertain as to whether given choices will actually succeed in achieving intended ends. Economists prefer to view these choices as rational ones based on probabilistic and 'objective' assumptions. Psychologists combine these with the 'subjective' estimates of choosers. In the theories of games choices are often set up so that they are dependent on the choices of others, 'expectations' are incorporated in the sense that choice is dependent on what choosers expect other choosers will do. The results reveal important differences between 'subjective' and 'objective' expected utility and in the frequent tendency, under certain conditions, for choosers to act competitively rather than cooperatively thereby maximising differences between participants rather than increasing benefits for all. The research, although often conducted in a hypothetical context where participants are asked to simulate their behaviour, tends towards more realistic analysis of choice than that based on assumptions about behaviour alone.

The 'expectancy-value' approach of Fishbein and Ajzen (1975) is more clearly 'social' in its construction. It incorporates not only the evaluation of outcomes and beliefs that given behaviour will lead to these outcomes, but also beliefs about the approval of others and attitudes towards the behaviour itself, i.e. whether or not the act is a good or a bad thing.

Research in occupational psychology falls more clearly in the economic psychology camp. While psychological studies of fair pay, motivation and job satisfaction can be used to improve a firm's efficiency, its main intention is not to contribute to economic theory (Warr and Wall, 1975). Though studies in this area are sometimes prescriptive, many investigators consider their research as purely descriptive; research which gains in validity by studying social behaviour in a social context where many people spend a large proportion of their lives.

Finally, in this brief review, equity and exchange theories deserve mention (Adams, 1965; Walster, Berscheid and Walster, 1973; Homans, 1974; Larwood and Blackmore, 1977). Equity theory bears resemblances to consistency theory in that people are assumed to reduce the inequity where pay-offs are out of proportion to personal contributions (e.g. receiving too much or too little income for a given amount of work effort). Exchange theories are also concerned with what people consider to be fair, but in this context in terms of their 'psychological contract' with others. In giving to others what is it reasonable to expect in return? What does the recipient consider reasonable? and so forth.

The perception of fairness is culturally determined, it is sustained by norms and is of crucial importance in one's adaptation and socialisation. It can also influence more general views about redistributive justice and just deserts.

Exchange theory is of direct relevance to economics and has been expanded through Homans, much as Becker has done for economics, to interpret many social encounters including marriage relationships. And like economic theory it simplifies, and thereby to some extent reduces. The differences lies in exchange theory's interest in social norms and the perceptions of individuals—it is not so much that an individual is maximising self-interest, but bending to the wind of cultural norms and expectations of 'reasonable' and 'fair' behaviour.

To conclude, the present volume is more concerned with economic psychology than psychological economics as we have described it. It has broad themes: an examination of how economic concepts develop and people's concepts of money (Chapters 3 and 4); an examination of people's beliefs and attitudes towards work, wealth, poverty and unemployment (Chapters 5, 6, 7 and 8); consumer perceptions, opinions, attitudes and preferences in the public and private sector (Chapters 10 and 11); spending and saving behaviour especially as it relates to gambling (Chapter 9); and Chapter 12 offers some tentative conclusions.

The book requires little justification for social psychologists given the lack of a concrete review of the literature concerning economic behaviour. It is also justified in a similar way to that espoused by Wright Mills in his book *The Sociological Imagination* (1959), exemplified in his remark that 'It is the political task of the social scientist—as of any liberal educator—continually to translate personal troubles into public issues and public issues into the terms of their human meaning for a variety of individuals' (p.207). Nowhere is this more apt than in our chapter on unemployment (Chapter 7.)

Finally, our book is of relevance to economists with an 'economic imagination' as it explores the inner environment, a realm largely neglected by economists. Although we have to leave to economists the adaption of our review, there is much to be gained thereby. We believe socialisation, lay beliefs, attitudes and perceptions have economic consequences and, to an extent, economic antecedents. We have no quarrel with the notion of man as purposive. Like Stigler (1976) we believe it is possible to assume that people are maximising and given the incorporation of a sufficient number of different goals, economic theory is inescapable. But like Stigler we also believe quite what people are pursuing and how this is understood by them requires proper behavioural analysis. Finally our aim, as Koch (1959) has championed, is to enrich our understanding of man rather than to impoverish it.

Part II:
Socialisation and Money

3 Socialisation and Economics: Children's Use and Understanding of the Economic World

INTRODUCTION

Although there have been a comparatively large number of studies concerned with children's and adolescents' cognitive development relating to the physical world, comparatively few studies have been done on their understanding of the social world. The former studies have nearly all been in the Piagetian tradition and have been concerned primarily with the stages that children pass through in the understanding of physical concepts (Shultz and Coddington, 1981). Related research on social development in children and adolescents has been concerned with such things as political socialisation (Furnham and Gunter, 1984) and moral development.

However the extensive literature on both cognitive and social development has generally ignored the child's understanding of economic relations. Concept growth is very difficult to investigate clinically let alone empirically. One has to be particularly sensitive to which variables, experiences and situations precipitate concept stage growth. Specific examples only hint at the multitude of problems arising from the interaction of the numerous factors which simultaneously influence the development of the conceptual processes. The effect of sex differences, variations in parental and wider societal attitudes, disparate schooling, and all the rest, must be taken into consideration. It is not surprising that, in designing research work, the emphasis tends to be a simplification and elimination of variables. Attempts to isolate factors, however, can be no substitute for the study of the complex interactions themselves.

Hurlock (1972) maintains that money concepts, unlike time and number concepts, tend to lag behind those of many other concepts. Many of the things Hurlock says have not been substantiated by recent research, possibly due to her selection of articles. However more recently there has been a great deal of research in this area. One theme of the earlier work which is still apparant in current research are studies on the developmental stages that children pass through in the acquisition of various economic concepts.

DEVELOPMENTAL STAGES

In a very thorough early study Strauss (1952) studied five boys and five girls at each age between 4½ and 11½ years interviewing them using 71 predetermined questions. Strauss believed that even before four years children have experience of money though they may not realise that it is connected with buying. From his study Strauss drew up *nine* different stages or transformations through which a child passes as he becomes acquainted with money. He argues that as new stages are reached the meanings of old relationships change, become revised and qualified, so that little remains of the initial or early meanings of the concepts. For him insightful learning, conditioning and rewards cannot fully account for cognitive development.

Danziger (1958), in a later article on children's early conceptions of economic relations, maintains that the development of social concepts may follow paths of their own that may not fall into line with the theoretical model elaborated in connection with physical concepts. Using interviews with children 5 to 8 years old he asked them about the meaning of rich and poor, the uses of money, and the position of the boss at work. He found a variety of replies from the fantastic to the fairly accurate, and attempted to codify these into four clear developmental stages:

(a) An initial pre-categorical stage occurs when the child lacks economic categories of thought altogether. There appears to be no special subsection of economic concepts differentiated from social concepts in general.
(b) At a second categorical stage the child's concepts appear to represent a reality in terms of isolated acts which are explained by a moral or voluntaristic imperative.
(c) At the third stage the child becomes able to conceptualise relationships by virtue of the fact that a reciprocity is established between previously isolated acts. However these relationships are isolated.
(d) At the fourth stage these various isolated relationships become linked together to form a system of relations.

Danziger noted that most children were at the lowest of his four levels since most had had the experience of purchasing but not of work. He believed like Strauss that the development in the stages of economic understanding are not simply a consequence of internal maturation, but depend on experience with money and economic exchange. This, it is argued, accounts for class, regional and national differences in the development of economic understanding, a point demonstrated 25 years later (1983).

Later Sutton (1962) maintained that theory and research on the attainment of economic concepts has attempted to answer five questions:

(a) How do children achieve information necessary for isolating and learning a concept?
(b) How do children retain the information from encounters so that it may be useful later?
(c) How is the retained information transformed so that it may be rendered useful for testing an hypothesis still unformed at the moment of first encountering new information?

(d) What are the general features in the growth of economic concepts?
(e) To what extent are the concepts of children a cultural product of the environment?

In his study Sutton asked 85 children randomly chosen from the first to the sixth grade, 12 questions such as 'How do people get money?' 'What is a bank?', 'Why do people save?' etc. The 1020 replies were arranged into six (developmental) categories:

(a) No replies (1%).
(b) Pre-categorical stage where objects are named but with little understanding of economic meaning (63%).
(c) A category of moral value-judgements (good/bad, right/wrong) irrespective of economic function (18%).
(d) Two isolated acts/factors that are economically significant (people save just to be saving) (12%).
(e) Two acts involving a reciprocity which cannot be explained by other economic relationships (if you put money in a bank you get more back) (5%).
(f) The subjective explanation gives rise to the objective—the single act derives its significance from its position in a system of relationships that is no longer conceived in an isolated way.

Sutton found neither age, intelligence nor socioeconomic background variables made any difference in the children's understanding, yet argued that external stimuli were important in understanding the development of economic concepts. Precisely what experiences facilitate or hinder a child's economic growth were however beyond the scope of this study.

Essentially all these early (and later) studies of monetary and economic understanding have isolated three major phases. In the first the child does not understand the role of money in everyday transactions, though he realises that money is required in transactions. In the second phase the child may understand the nature of the immediate exchange but not the network of exchanges within the monetary and economic system, the divisibility of money and its origin. The third stage is characterised by the understanding of most but not all (e.g. profit, investment) types of exchange.

More recently studies into the development of economic concepts have become more conceptually and methodologically sophisticated. Burnis (1983) intervewed 30 4–5, 7–8 and 10–12-year-old children who were chosen as representative of the distinct Piagetian developmental stages (pre-operational, concrete operations and formal operations). The children were interviewed with regard to six basic economic concepts: the commodity (products exchanged in the market place), value (that which governs the production and circulation of a commodity), exchange (economic transaction in the market economy), property (the nature and ownership of property), work (social relations at work) and income (payment from work). Within each area the author found qualitatively different types of responses and significant levels of association between types of response and age levels of the children. For instance, when asked why some people get more money than others for the work that they do, the youngest group argued that it was because some people work more, harder or longer; the next group said it was because some people's work is more important, functional or helpful to others; while the oldest group argued that people get paid more because their work requires more skill, training or education. The results suggest that the younger children tended to represent social phenomena in terms of natural or physical categories (value is identified with physical size; income with the physical quantity of labour). Furthermore the younger children exhibit extreme 'realism' in that they do not understand the conventionality or normativeness associated with social phenomena or institutions—they are accorded the same ontological status as physical laws or objects.

In a similar study using 89 Israeli children aged 7 to 17, Leiser (1983) asked children (by interview and questionnaire) questions about prices, salaries, strikes, savings and investments, factories and banks and the Mint. He found that younger children (8–9) interpret economic transactions from the perspective of individual participants having no awareness of the system of economic forces. Older children integrate their economic knowledge, become aware of conflicts and try to resolve them—for instance, children believe simultaneously that 'government sets all the prices' and yet 'shopkeepers are free to change them'. Similarly once children realise the concept of profit on a fair transaction they are able to resolve the apparent contradiction between 'buying as an exchange of money for something of equivalent value' *and* 'selling goods as a way of earning a living'. Thus when asked how a shopkeeper would feel about a drop in the prices of their goods all the children realised that there would be a diminished profit yet only 25 per cent of the youngest but 75 per cent of the oldest realised that this would probably also be accompanied by an increase in sales. Also when asked what would happen if the economy was suddenly injected with a massive distribution of money 21 per cent of the youngest (8–9), 31 per cent of the intermediate (11–12), yet 89 per cent of the oldest group (14–15) successfully predicted negative economic consequences (rising prices, shortage of goods, people's unwillingness to work). The more abstract and complex the phenomena (e.g. inflation, market forces) and more particularly the more difficult it is to personify, the less children (even up to the age of 15) can understand it. Children, it seems, can understand the motives of individual actors, but not the cumulative or aggregated effect of people's economic actions. It is only when children have some conception of the structure and function of society at large that they can begin to comprehend macroeconomic changes.

THE DEVELOPMENT OF ECONOMIC CONCEPTS

A number of studies have made attempts to trace the development of certain specific economic concepts. Not only have the areas researched been very diverse but also experimental and investigative methods have differed widely. Despite these differences there are coherent patterns of results in the literature.

1. Buying and Selling

Central to any economic activity is buying and selling. Yet for the child these transactions are by no means easy to grasp. Furth (1980) has noted how difficult it is for the child to understand the transaction particularly those of 5 or 6 years who have not even mastered the number system. On the scheme outlined in Figure 3.1 he attempts to explain the various concepts that the child must master.

It can be seen that the child has to master a number of observed and non-observed transactions. He must understand the origin of money, the function of change, the ownership of goods. Children must also integrate the payment of wages, shop expenses and the shopowner's money into the system in order to understand the pricing of goods.

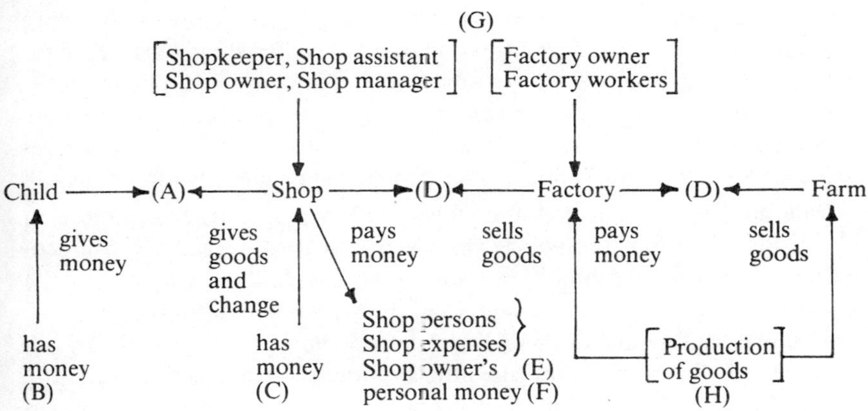

Figure 3.1: Schematic outline of the shop's business.

For Furth (1980) there appear to be four major stages concerned with the understanding of buying and selling: no understanding; understanding of payment of customer but not of the shopkeeper; understanding and relating of both the customer's and the shopkeeper's payment, but not of profit; understanding of all these things.

2. Profit

Jahoda (1979b) conducted two studies—one involving role-playing, and the other semi-structured interviews—in order to investigate 6 to 12-year-olds' conceptions of profit. In the role-playing study children played the role of shopkeeper and the experimenter those of customers and suppliers. The critical test involved the difference in price that the child expected to *buy* the goods from the supplier and *sell* them to the customer. Where the buying price was consistently lower than the selling price, the child was credited with an understanding of profit; when the two prices were consistently identical, lack of such understanding was recorded; and a mixture of responses was regarded as transitional. It seemed that it was not until the age of about 11 that most children began to understand the concept. The interview study showed in more detail the child's development from no grasp of any transaction system to the development of two unconnected systems to an integrated system. Younger children simply accept givens and make up nonsensical answers on being questioned, whereas older children try to make sense of economic relationships but fail to arrive at the correct solution. Children at earlier stages are aware that some people are engaged in the buying and selling of goods, and that people give their work in return for wages. When an adult points out that buying and selling is also a job for which people are paid he draws attention to the relationship between the two systems (mentioned above) and poses the problem for children. Younger children tend to deny that buying and selling can be a job but older children are able to think through the problem and emerge with the answer.

Jahoda (1983) replicated this study with young African children in Zimbabwe. His hypothesis was that owing to their greater exposure to relevant experiences (notably in trading) African children will acquire the concept of profit more rapidly than European children—that is, the traditional 'culture lag' between European and non-European children will be reversed. The results confirmed the hypothesis—being active in trading makes for an earlier grasp of the concept of profit. Indeed the Zimbabwean children were shown to be significantly in advance of British children within the same age range.

Tan and Stacey (1981) in a study of the understanding of socioeconomic concepts of Malaysian Chinese school children found however that developmental trends were 'highly similar to that found among previous Western samples of children studied . . . but there was also a suggestion that there may be (a) less of a tendency for young Chinese children to refer to an imaginary source of money and to refer to parents or work as a source of money, than Western children'. (p. 44).

3. Banking

Jahoda (1981) followed up the study on profit with a study on children's conceptions of banking—a complex and often remote economic concept for children. Eleven, 13 and 15-year-old children were first put through the shop transaction study in order to ascertain whether the subject understood the notion of profit. They were then asked a number of questions about the functions of a bank such as: 'Supposing I put £100 into a bank, and after one year I take my money out again, would I get back more, less or the same?' And 'Supposing I borrow £100 from a bank to pay back after one year. Would I have to pay back more or less or the same?' The responses of the children were categorised thus:

(i) No knowledge of interest (get or pay back the same amount).
(ii) Interest on deposits only (get back more but pay the same).
(iii) Interest on both, but more on deposit.
(iv) Interest same on deposits and loans.
(v) Interest higher on loans (not fully understood).
(vi) Interest on loans (fully understood).

Although there was some evidence of class differences (the middle-class children functioning at a slightly more advanced level) the difference was not significant. However, the developmental trends were striking and highly significant. Only a quarter of the 14-year-olds fully understood the function of the bank and this number showed no increase for the 16-year-olds.

This study was, in fact, replicated by Jahoda and Woerdenbagch (1982) in Holland. They found that while primary pupils in both locations overwhelmingly saw the bank as simply a place that keeps money, twice as many as the older Dutch subjects realised that one borrowed money from a bank compared with the older Scottish subjects.

Ng (1983) replicated and extended Jahoda's (1981) study with 96, 6–13-year-old children from Hong Kong. Although he found much the same developmental trend, a full understanding of the bank emerged at 10 while the idea of profit emerged at 6-years-old. Thus for both concepts the Chinese children were more precocious than the Scottish (and Dutch) sample. As in previous studies Ng examined the dynamics of conflict between schemes in the child. For instance, to induce cognitive conflict the interviewer deliberately asked the child to explain how the bank obtained money to pay its employees, electricity charges, etc. while yet having the same interest charges on money lent and borrowed. Although the impact of this conflict instruction was not significant it seemed to be useful in examining economic development. Ng (1983) concludes:

The exceptional maturity of the Hong Kong children probably reflected their high level of economic socialization and consumer activity, and the business ethos of the society at large. Socially, life would be difficult for them if they did not grasp socio-economic concepts at an early age. Their maturity represents, in short, a case of socio-economic reality shaping (partly at least) socio-economic understanding. (pp.220–1)

4. Ownership

Berti *et al.* (1982) have been particularly interested in children's conceptions of the means of production and ownership. They argued that children pass from an initial stage of complete ignorance about the productive function of means to recognising that various means have to do with work and money and the production of goods. Finally when a coherent and comprehensive view of the network of economic exchanges has been formed the child will understand that the sale of the produced goods permits the owner to realise a profit and pay his employees.

Over 120 Italian children were interviewed in order to determine whether the child recognised (a) the existence of an owner for various objects, who he was, and how he became owner; (b) the existence of agricultural and industrial products, and whose they were; and (c) what advantage the child thought the owner derived from each means of production. From their interviews of who owns such things as factories, five levels were distinguished:

1. The owner is the person found in spatial/temporal contact with the production means (passengers own the bus).
2. The owner is the person who exercises an appropriate use of or direct control over the producing means in question (drivers own the bus).
3. The owner is the one who not only directly uses the producing means in question but also controls its use by others (the boss owns the bus).
4. The owner is clearly differentiated from the employee, in that he has the function of giving orders.
5. The owner is at the top of the hierarchy of command, and the boss at an intermediate position between the owner and worker.

The authors also identified five different levels for the perceived ownership of products. These include a stage where the children believe products are owned by anybody, followed by a stage where they are seen to be owned by those closest to them or using them, and then a stage where product ownership is seen through ownership of the means of production. Only at the final level do children realise that products belong to the owner of the means of production and that the employees are compensated for their work by a salary.

Various statistical analyses showed that children's ideas about different production means develop with different speeds but through the same sequences. Furthermore the parents also had a 'developmental' view of their children in that parents of the youngest children said that they had not been told or asked about jobs and ownership, while the opposite was true for older children.

The authors argue that understandings about the value of money and its use in the act of buying and selling occur at the same time as the development of logical-arithmetic operations. They argue that for children to have a grasp of ownership and other economic relationships they need to be in Piaget's formal operation period. Furby (1978, 1979) has also looked at the concept of possession in children, from a rather different perspective.

5. Labour and Management

Haire and Morrison (1957) set out to measure American school children's perceptions of labour and management to get some idea of the origin and development of these attitudes. They gave 755, 12–16-year-olds five short tests including cards with stereotyped pictures; sentence completion tests 'A union is . . .'; ten statements about union management and labour which they could agree on; a word form test where they were asked to underline two words which best described union, job, etc.; and finally a socioeconomic questionnaire. They found that even by the age of 12 there was a clear distinction between the attitudes of children from high and low socio-economic backgrounds. The former were predictably much more strongly pro-labour, showed more undifferentiated approval of the workers involved, agreed with them on most issues, and tended to identify with them. As the children got older they tended to move in a pro-labour direction; however the basic difference between the class groups remains stable. They also found that where they could differentiate the effect of schools and homes on children's perceptions and attitudes the evidence suggests the school is the major determinant.

Finally they found that lower socioeconomic status groups showed less differentiation in their perceptions of labour-management relations, although this did not prevent their taking sides. Further low SES children tended to describe the union in terms of an economic function, while high SES income groups tended to describe it in terms of a simple aggregate of people. High SES groups tended to see the boss in terms of power, money and intelligence, with unilaterality of action, while low SES children saw him simply in terms of telling people what to do.

In a more recent British study, Patterson and Locksley (1981) tried to determine how a large group of London fifth formers (± 15 year olds) see the unions. Although most students knew who a shop steward was, less than a quarter knew who the 'father of a chapel' was. Just under half the children thought the media treated the unions fairly but generally they were negative toward the unions: nearly a half thought them too greedy, and a fifth too extreme. The majority believed that unions have benefited their members fairly well but were against the closed shop. However the children did not feel that they had been taught enough on the subject of trade unions.

6. Inequality and Poverty

Siegal (1981) set out to determine children's perceptions and evaluations of adult economic needs. Children aged 6–13 were asked to distribute token money to dolls dressed either as a doctor, shopkeeper, bus driver or waiter by the question 'Show me how much money each needs to take care of his children'. They were also asked whether their (unequal) distributions were fair and about the amount of effort required in the various professions.

The results showed that the youngest children did not realise that unmet needs exist, while older children were divided on the issue of equality—some believed that needs should be met regardless of the bread-winner's occupational efforts while others believed that inequality is fair and that effort and ability should be rewarded irrespective of need. These findings are explained in terms of the work ethic in that 'those children for whom work efforts are equated with rewards might be more likely to maintain that inequality is fair than those for whom the relationship between effort and reward is loose and non-existent' (p.301).

Winocur and Siegal (1982) predicted that older adolescents would be more likely to base judgements on equal pay for equal work, while younger children would be more likely to advocate that pay should correspond with family needs. Further they hypothesised that though girls may be more likely to treat male and female workers equally, they would be more conservative in their achievement judgements than boys. Although they found support for the former hypothesis they did not find it for the latter. Thus concern for family needs appears to decline with age, and objective work outcomes takes precedence over need in adolescents' allocations of economic rewards.

In a later study Irving and Siegal (1983) investigated the effect of various mitigating circumstances (including economic need) on children's perceptions of criminal justice. They found that younger children were harsher in their judgements than older ones, but that their leniency and acceptance of mitigating circumstances were highly dependent on the situation. Older children did not consider economic need to be a valid defence.

Leahy (1981) was specifically interested in the development of class concepts (specifically comparisons between rich and poor people) in cognitive developmental terms. Over 700 children in four age groups (mean 6, 10, 14, 17 years) were interviewed and asked to describe rich and poor people and distinguish between them. These responses were classified into categories of person description, including peripheral (possessions, appearances and behaviours) central (traits and thoughts) and sociocentric (life-chances and class-consciousness) categories. The ANOVAs on the content analyses categories revealed numerous significant age effect findings.

Lower- and working-class subjects were more likely than upper-middle-class subjects to mention life-chances and thoughts in describing the rich and the poor, while upper-middle-class subjects were more likely than subjects from the other classes to mention the traits of the poor. As the subjects got older there was an increasing tendency to view classes of rich and poor people as not only differing in their external, observable qualities, but as being different kinds of people. As children got older they placed more emphasis on individual differences in effort, ability and other salient personality traits.

The author offers two explanatory models to account for his findings: a cognitive developmental model and a general functionalist model. As regards the former model, the results are similar to other findings on the descriptions of peers, social roles and sex roles and suggests that later adolescence is characterised by an increased awareness of the nature of complex social and economic systems. Hence, class differences and economic inequality are seen not only in terms of an individual's characteristics but also in terms of his relationship to other classes. According to the second model, socialisation results in considerable uniformity among classes and races as to the nature of the social world. This uniformity retains stability in social institutions while also providing a rationale for the unequal distribution of assets.

Furnham (1982d) sought to compare two groups of adolescent school children's (15-year-olds) explanations for poverty. Public schoolboys (primarily middle-class) tended to offer more individualistic explanations for poverty than comprehensive (primarily working-class) schoolboys who in turn tended to rate societal or structural factors as more important. On the whole public schoolboys tended to blame the poor for their condition. The two most important explanations for poverty among public schoolboys were 'Lack of thrift and proper money management', and 'No attempts at self-improvement'. On the other hand, for the comprehensive schoolboys the two most important explanations for poverty were 'Failure of industry to provide enough jobs for poor people' and 'Low wages in some business and industries'. Curiously one of two items that might have been expected to reveal significant difference did not, namely 'Failure of society to provide good schools'—clearly a salient variable for school children. There were no differences between the groups regarding fatalistic explanations which were by and large considered unimportant. These results have been found with adult samples (Feagin, 1972; Feather, 1974; Furnham, 1982b). Yet it should be pointed out that comprehensive schoolboys saw both individualistic and fatalistic explanations as relatively unimportant in explaining poverty. That is, the major differences between the groups lay in the importance that they attached to societal explanation.

The estimates of the annual incomes of the poor also showed interesting results. With one exception all of the ANOVAs showed significant differences in the predicted direction; namely that public schoolboys gave higher estimates than comprehensive schoolboys. They are interesting for a number of reasons: the first is that by and large the estimates are rather low, in that many people on social security or supplementary benefits earn more money than those estimates. Secondly there appears to be an element of sexism in their estimates—women need less money to be poor than men, and a man supporting a wife and child needs no more money than a man just supporting a child. But both these results probably reflect the adolescents' understanding of the economic world rather than bias or prejudice. It is known for instance that children underestimate both poverty and wealth because of their own experience of money (Danziger, 1958). Presumably adolescents also tend to underestimate, but not to the same extent. Interestingly more comprehensive schoolboys estimated the amount in weekly wages than public schoolboys, who in turn preferred to make estimates in terms of annual amounts. This may reflect what they have learnt from their parents, some of whom are probably paid monthly (middle-class) and some weekly (working-class).

7. Economic Relations and Justice

A few studies have been done attempting to understand how children perceive and understand political and economic relationships. For instance Miller and Horn (1955) were interested in children's perceptions of debt. They chose 20 actual court cases involving debt that would be interesting and easy for children to interpret as well as being representative of a broad area of debt, credit, promises and related contracts. These were given to a panel of adults closely associated with debt or ethics to obtain their opinions concerning the 'best' ethical responses to these cases. They were also shown to 1297 children, ranging in age from 10 to 18 years.

One of the major findings was the lack of agreement between the consultants and the children on 47 of the 129 items. The children of varying ages, sexes and socioeconomic backgrounds tended to disagree with the ethical consultants on the following points which they and the courts had accepted:

1. Debtors ought not to be jailed or forced to labour because of their debt.
2. All acts of the courts should be upheld and respected, despite personal or contingent circumstances.
3. Gambling losses do not constitute legally enforceable obligations.
4. Using credit in making purchases is not morally wrong.
5. Warranties of quality are implied in sales on the open market.
6. Banks and depositors have well-established responsibilities towards one another.

Predictably they found evidence of age differences. Older (14 and above years) showed greater tolerance and ability to differentiate among various kinds of promises as to their cruciality and seriousness. On the other hand the younger children (10 and 12-year-olds) strongly believed that performance of promises should be compelled, and debt-evasion should be punished. Involuntary bankruptcy was also viewed as a legitimate means of collecting debts. The authors concluded that children should be explicitly taught in school elements of debt, credit, promises and simple contract.

Irving and Siegal (1983) were interested in children's perception of justice in relation to crimes concerning assault, arson and treason, each with the respective mitigating circumstances of brain damage, passion and economic need. Seven to 17-year-old children were asked to judge the appropriate punishment given to these various cases. Although younger children were harsher in their judgement than older children, their leniency and acceptance of mitigating circumstances were highly dependent on the situation.

8. Entrepreneurship

For economists, sociologists and informed lay people the entrepreneur is a risk-taking individual, who seeks new markets, promotes new methods of production, has a future time orientation, and is able to fill gaps in services or demands. Though nice distinctions may be made between 'real' craftsmen and 'quasi'-opportunistic entrepreneurs, there is no doubt both that adults recognise the qualities of an entrepreneur and that entrepreneurship is one prerequisite for economic growth. Kourilsky and Campbell (1984) set out to determine children's (938 8–12-year-olds) beliefs about entrepreneurship before participation in an instruction system designed to encourage economic success, risk-taking and entrepreneurial persistence. They were also very interested in sex differences. Results indicated that the stereotypic entrepreneur was male, yet the effect of the instruction and role-playing exercises was to encourage girls to be more interested. Perhaps the most important aspect of this study was however the demonstration that various entrepreneurial behaviours could be taught and measured. Economic success was measured by profit made in a mini-business; risk-taking was measured by exposure to loss and disadvantages; and persistence as the tendency to stick to a task till completed.

MONEY

There are also a few studies on children's use of money. Pollio and Gray (1973) investigated different 'change-making' strategies in children and adults. Five groups of subjects ranging in age from 7–20 years were asked to do mental arithmetic on the giving of change. Whereas the younger children tended to make mistakes, by the age of 13 the children were accurate nearly all the time. Although children of all levels knew the various coin equivalences, younger children used smaller coins by preference when making change while older children used all the coins available.

> This was interpreted to mean that coin equivalences are probably learned as specific-response pairs and that in making change younger children use untransformed base to units such as pennies and dimes, largely because the computational demands placed by change-making operations force them to minimize the number of noncomputational transformations used. (p. 173)

Hitchcock *et al.* (1976) hypothesised that as people in poor countries have greater material need than persons in wealthy countries a country's coinage allows institutional expression of a level of need. They therefore compared 84 countries' gross national product with their mean coin size and found as predicted a negative correlation. This indicates, in their view, the potential usefulness of viewing institutional-level data from a psychological perspective.

In a longitudinal study conducted in Italy, Berti and Bombi (1981) attempted to ascertain 3–8-year-olds' conceptions of money and its value. They showed children a variety of coins and notes which they were asked to identify; asked what (from a chocolate bar to a motor car) they could buy with this money; and took part in a shopkeeper game sequence to determine whether the child would pay for the purchase (as a customer) and give change (as a shopkeeper). From the work of Strauss (1952) and others they hypothesised six stages:

A. No awareness of payment.
B Obligatory payment: recognition of the need for exchange but does not discriminate between various amounts of money.
C. Realisation that not all types of money can buy everything: not all money is equivalent.
D. Realisation that money is insufficient for certain goods.
E. Strict correspondence between money and object.
F. Correct use of change: the realisation that the excessive value of money may be compensated for by the shopkeeper's giving the difference in money to the customer.

As predicted they found a clear developmental sequence in which

> the acquisition of understanding about money can be interpreted as a process of differentiation and articulation which allows the child to construct usage rules that are increasingly more precise and complex . . . the progression through the first four stages is developed around pre-operational thinking and precisely during that chronological period in which such thinking is dominant. In contrast, the fifth and sixth stages imply the use of logical and arithmetic operations. (p.1182)

In an earlier study Berti and Bombi (1979) concluded that the idea of payment for work emerges from a hinterland of spontaneous (and erroneous) beliefs developed by children to explain the origin of money. In effect, the idea of this topic is only acquired in a verbal way: if a child occasionally notices that his parents (and other adults) take part in extra-domestic activities, this is not defined as work and the child cannot have any direct knowledge of payment. Verbal information about this constitutes initially a strange body in childish thought, in which predominate the spontaneous ideas of the origin of money. Only when the understanding of work is substantially developed does it support the spontaneous beliefs about the origin of money.

It was also established that the links between money and work is initially understood asymmetrically. Children affirm that parents work for earnings but do not understand that there is a need for money which can be obtained through working. This indicates the existence of systems of ideas that are relatively independent, although they possess certain facts in common. In fact, the ideas that we found can be divided into two heterogeneous categories, the one containing spontaneous and fantastic ideas about the origin of money, the other containing information about the work of parents.

More recently in an investigation of incentive effects Witryol and Wentworth (1983) found that seven-year-old children confused the two American coins (a dime and a nickel) yet by 9–12 years none chose the nickel over the dime.

ECONOMIC SOCIALISATION: POCKET-MONEY

The paucity in the literature on children's understanding of the social world is matched by a dearth of reviews on economic socialisation. In a review of this literature Stacey (1982) has divided the research into four different areas: money, possessions, social differentiation and inequality, and socio-economic understanding. He concludes thus:

> the most early experience of economic socialisation appears to revolve around possessions which take on social characteristics involving inter-personal control and power over possessions. Between the ages of four and six children acquire monetary understanding by associating money with buying, but it is not until the age of about ten that the numerical value of money, and the functional understanding of money transactions is developed.

At about the same time children begin to develop ideas of poverty, wealth, income, property and class differences. In early adolescence, teenagers are able to give 'near-adult' explanations of economic events and relationships. Finally the literature led Stacey to conclude that

> in the first decade of life, the economic socialization of children does not appear to be strongly influenced by their own social backgrounds, with the exception of the children of the very rich and possibly of the very poor. In the second decade of life, social differences in the development appear to be more pronounced. (p.172)

Perhaps the most important way in which parents socialise their children in monetary and economic matters is through their pocket-money—a weekly or monthly allowance given either unconditionally or for some work. Almost no research has been done in this area although market research over an eight-year period in Britain has attempted to determine changes in pocket-money patterns. On average in 1982 5–7-year-olds got 64p, 8–10-year-olds 74p, and 11–13-year-olds 113½p. Girls tended to get less than boys at all ages, and pocket-money was often supplemented by part-time jobs, as well as gifts. It is also noted that children's spending power is almost £640 million a year on pocket-money alone, and in excess of £780 million if earnings from jobs and gifts from relatives are included. However, as is the case with most opinion-poll studies, no effort is made to analyse the cause or consequences of these differences, which are presented simply in terms of percentages (Walls, 1983).

On the other hand books and articles have been written to guide parents in the economic socialisation of their children. Rarely, if ever, do they present data but are nearly always forceful, moralistic and middle-class in their advice:

> The allowance should be paid weekly—on the same day each week—to younger children, and monthly to kids as they approach their teens. The shift to a monthly payment is not for your convenience but is for the purpose of encouraging more careful attention to budgeting and planning ahead on the part of your teenager. The important thing is that the payment should represent a predictable source of income that the child can count on. (Davis and Taylor, 1979)

However, much less work has been done on how children come to acquire these various economic concepts. Fox (1978) has argued that even by the time children enter school they already have experience of working, buying, trading, owning, saving, etc.: 'Research on children's informal economic learning indicates that early economic instruction in the classroom needs to take into account these unprocessed experiences, economic attitudes and children's cognitive capacities' (p. 137).

Through primary and secondary socialisation children acquire knowledge of money and economic concepts. Marshall and Magruder's (1960) study appears to be one of the few studies specifically investigating the relationship between parents' money education practices and children's knowledge and use of money. Amongst the many hypotheses examined were: 'Children will have more knowledge of money use if their parents give them an allowance' and 'Children will have more knowledge of the use of money if they save money'. They found as predicted that children's knowledge of money is directly related to the extensiveness of their experience of money—whether they are given money to spend; if they are given opportunities to earn and save money; and their parents' attitudes to, and habits of, money spending. Thus it seems that socialisation and

Table 3.1: F levels from the sex × age × class ANOVA on all items in the pocket money questionnaire (abbreviated items)

Questions	*Sex*	*Age*	*Class*	*S × A*	*S × C*	*A × C*	*S × A × C*
1. How much pocket money do you get each week?	0.27	15.26_a	1.08	0.93	0.03	1.63	2.18
2. Do you get your pocket money regularly?	0.03	1.30	2.40	0.22	0.15	1.51	1.21
3. Are you usually given money as a Christmas/Birthday present?	0.04	1.74	0.11	2.39_d	5.02_c	0.79	0.18
4. If yes how much money do youget at Christmas?	0.40	27.58_a	2.64	0.20	0.46	6.87_b	0.02
If yes how much money do you get on your birthday?	0.09	40.23_a	0.04	1.15	0.11	0.09	0.65
5. Do you have to work around the house for your pocket money?	0.41	0.08	5.05_c	0.01	0.00	0.84	1.56
6. Do you have a regular part-time job, that you do for money?	1.42	1.52	0.68	0.18	2.81_d	0.05	0.30
7. Do you go shopping alone for your parents?	0.01	5.78_b	0.10	1.28	0.21	0.42	1.84
8. Do you save any of your pocket money?	2.56	1.42	0.71	1.40	0.15	0.16	1.33
9. Are you encouraged by your parents to save your pocket money?	2.21	2.78_d	0.21	0.07	0.45	1.16	1.20
10. How much money have you saved?	1.73	4.11_b	1.25	1.21	0.13	1.16	0.80
11. Why do you save money: To buy something special?	4.91_c	1.11	2.59	1.00	1.49	0.28	0.21
In case you need money in the future?	0.30	7.72_b	0.15	0.55	1.74	0.38	0.23
Because your parents want you to?	0.13	2.36_d	1.34	0.06	0.68	0.08	1.96
12. Where do you put the money you save: Money box?	0.99	0.47	0.39	0.33	4.08_c	1.46	2.77_d
Savings account?	1.16	7.65_b	2.25	3.30_d	1.95	1.02	1.84
Parents look after it?	0.13	0.22	4.41_c	1.39	0.17	0.31	2.48_d
13. Would your parents give you more money if you had spent it all?	4.64_c	1.43	1.96	2.14	2.71	1.53	0.23
14. Do you ever lend money to your friends?	0.21	1.88	0.48	0.29	0.10	1.04	0.03
15. Do you ever borrow money from your friends?	0.96	0.52	0.01	1.96	0.01	3.16_c	0.82

Source: Furnham and Thomas (1984a).

Note: $^a p < .001$, $^b p < .01$, $^c p < .05$, $^d p < .09$.

education would have important consequences on a child's or adolescent's understanding of economic affairs. However, they did *not* find any evidence for a number of their hypotheses. These were: children will have more knowledge of money use if their parents give them an allowance: if children are given allowances, less of the family's money, rather than more, will be taken for children's spending money; if children are given opportunities to earn money, they will have more knowledge of money use than children lacking this experience; children will have less knowledge of money use if money is used to reward or punish their behaviour; and children will have the attitudes about the importance of money and material things that are expressed by their parents.

In an extensive study of over 700 seven-year-olds Newson and Newson (1976) collected data on children's pocket-money. They found that most of their sample could count on a basic sum of pocket-money, sometimes calculated on a complicated incentive system. Some children appear to be given money which is instituted for the express purpose of allowing the possibility of fining (confiscating); others are given as a substitute for wages; while some have to 'work' for it. Over 50 per cent of the sample earned money from their parents beyond their regular income but there were no sex or social class differences in this practice. This means that it is difficult to determine how much money children get per week as it varies. They did however find social-class differences in children's unearned income and savings. Middle-class children received less (18 vs. 30p) than working-class children, and saved more (90 vs. 48 per cent). That is 52 per cent of class V children *always* spend their money within the week, whereas only 10 per cent of class I or II children do so. The authors conclude: 'Having cash in hand is equated with enjoying the good life: the relationship between money and enjoyment is specific and direct . . . the working-class child already begins to fall into this traditional pattern of life in his use of pocket money' (p.244).

Furnham and Thomas (1984a) set out to determine age, sex and class differences in the distribution and use of pocket-money. They predicted age

Table 3.2: Amount (in pence) of pocket-money received by the three age groups

	Years 7–8	Years 9–10	Years 11–12
1. How much pocket money do you get each week?	57.32	76.43	97.93
2. How much money do you get at birthdays?	353.86	712.72	1417.95
Christmas?	257.69	480.88	940.97
3. How much have you already saved?	1498.60	2320.41	3845.13

Source: Furnham and Thomas (1984a).

differences: older children would receive more money and take part in more 'economic activities' such as saving, borrowing, lending. And class differences: working-class children would receive more but save less than middle-class children. They tested over 400 7–12-year-old British children and confirmed many of their hypotheses.

Table 3.1 shows that there were many more age, than sex or class differences. Older children received more money, saved more and were more likely to go shopping than younger children.

Middle-class children reported more than working-class children that they had to work around the house for their pocket-money and tended to let their parents look after the pocket-money that they had saved. Overall, however, there were surprisingly few class differences. The authors point out that the questions that did not reveal significant differences are as interesting as those that did.

Fox (1978) has drawn a number of conclusions from her review of studies on economic education: 'For example, we might consider the optimal timing for instruction in economics . . . Second, we might try to determine what economic misconceptions are corrected by maturation and life experience and which ones tend to persist' (p.480).

More recently Furnham and Thomas (1984b) investigated adults' perceptions of the economic socialisation of children through pocket-money. Over 200 British adults completed a questionnaire on their beliefs concerning for instance how much and how often children should be given pocket-money, as well as such things as whether they should be encouraged to work for it, save it, etc. There were a number of differences based on sex, age, social class and children (i.e. whether the subjects did or did not have children) differences. Sex differences that existed showed females more in favour of agreeing with children in advance on the kinds of items pocket-money should cover, more in favour of giving older children pocket-money monthly, and also more in favour of an annual review of a child's pocket-money, than males. Thus, all of these differences show females more willing to treat children as responsible individuals. It is possible that this is due to the tendency for women, both at work and in the home, to have greater contact with children and therefore a better understanding of their capabilities.

The age differences showed, as expected, that older adults were more likely to expect children to spend less on entertainment and more on reading materials, than younger adults. Further, as expected, older adults disagreed less than younger adults that boys should be given a little more pocket-money than girls. Younger adults were also more in favour of pocket-money being linked to the performance of household chores. Younger adults tend to view pocket-money more as a contractual arrangement between adult and child than older adults. Middle-class adults were more in favour of giving children pocket-money and of starting to give pocket-money at an earlier age than working-class adults. Over 90 per cent of the middle-class adults believed that by the age of 8 years children should receive pocket-money, while just over 70 per cent of working-class adults believed that children of 8 should receive pocket-money. All middle-class adults believed that by the age of 10 the pocket-money system should be introduced, yet only 84 per cent of working-class adults agreed. Indeed some working-class respondents did not believe in the system of pocket-money at all. A similar class difference was revealed in the question concerning when children should receive their pocket-money. Whereas 91 per cent of the middle-class believed children should receive it weekly (and 4 per cent when they need it) only 79 per cent of working class adults believed children should receive their pocket-money weekly (and 16 per cent when they need it). Furthermore significantly more working-class adults believed that boys should receive more pocket-money than girls.

These class-difference findings are in line with previous studies on childhood socialisation (Newson and Newson, 1976) and with figures on class differences in general. That is, working-class adults introduce pocket-money later and more erratically than middle-class parents. However the study of Furnham and Thomas (1984a) revealed far fewer class differences which may be the result of the fact that a greater range of ages were considered in this study.

Certainly the research on pocket-money or allowances seems a most fruitful avenue of research, especially as so many researchers have reported that experience plays such an important part in the understanding of the economic world in children and adolescents.

CONCLUSION

The literature on children's and adolescents' understanding of the economic world is highly diffuse and of varying quality. Most of the research has attempted to describe the stages through which children pass in their understanding of a specific concept. There is, however, a good deal of disagreement about the number of stages, the points of transition and the exact understanding in each stage. Considerably less work has gone into describing those factors which speed up or slow down the transition from one stage to another or individual differences within the various stages. Social class, exposure to the economic world and parental practices seem most important determinants of children's knowledge and use of money, though there well may be other important determinants.

The importance of this area cannot be underestimated as it seems that habits of using money (spending, saving, gambling, etc.) are established in childhood. Studies on children's pocket-money for instance suggest that class attitudes towards money are established even before adolescence. This is in accordance with the literature on the Protestant work ethic (see Chapter 8) which suggests that early socialisation in gratification postponement, internal locus of control, and need for achievement leads directly to later success in the adult world.

One of the more interesting applications of research on children's acquisition of economic concepts is the teaching of these concepts in schools. For instance there have been studies on the 'Kinder-economy' of the 'mini-society' which involve classroom discussions of economic concepts like scarcity, opportunity cost, production, specialisation, distribution, exchange, and so on followed by a long-term role-play. For instance Kourilsky (1977) using 96, 5- and 6-year-olds, attempted to answer four important questions:

1. Is the child's success in economic decision-making and analysis related to instructional intervention or to increased maturity inherent in the passage of time?
2. To what extent and degree, through instructional intervention, are children able to master concepts that, psychologically, they are considered too young to learn?
3. What type of school, home and personality variables are predictors of success in economic decision-making and analysis? For example, does initiative predict success in economic decision-making? What part is played by the parents in their day-to-day discussions with their child of his economic activities?
4. What are the parents' attitudes toward the teaching of economic decision-making and analytic principles as part of early childhood education?

Her results seemed to indicate that the children's understanding of economics was most strongly influenced by the intervention programme even at this early age (5-years-old). From their answers children appeared to be able to master concepts that, developmentally, they were considered too young to learn. Yet the analysis also showed that parental factors were the best predictors of economic mastery—more so than the cognitive, social or verbal development of the child. Finally, parents seemed very positive to the intervention programme—some even reporting that they found it embarrassing to find that their 5-year-olds knew more about economics than they did!

Certainly, the widespread ignorance about economics in children, adolescents and adults suggests the importance and relevance of the teaching of the subject even in kindergarten.

4 The Psychology of Money

INTRODUCTION

Despite its importance as the primary medium through which goods are exchanged, there is a considerable paucity of research into the psychology of money. A surprisingly diverse and very unrelated series of studies have been done on such things as the perceptions of coins and notes, and a few on people's attitudes towards money. There are also various theories as to the origins of beliefs and behaviour concerning money and a few studies of its symbolism. There is, however, no coherent theory or body of research on the psychology of money; this chapter will attempt to review that work which has been done so far.

Economists, anthropologists and historians have pointed out that as people went from barter societies to more advanced economies money had to be invented. Galbraith (1977) has noted that money has been an everyday fact of life for at least 2500 years. There were tremendous abuses of coined money (in terms of weight, metal content, etc.) until the nineteenth century. Given its functions, almost anything will serve as money, though of course it is preferable for money to be durable, portable, consistent and inherently valuable. Coins, now largely redundant, were for centuries the main source of money. Many characteristics and terms still associated with them, served interesting functions: coins have milled edges to prevent people shaving away a little of the valuable metal from which the coin is made; the term 'debasing the currency' came about because of the practice of adding base metals (lead, iron) to gold and silver to increase the number of coins made. In Europe coins were the major form of transaction until the creation of banks, which because they could lend money, could 'create it'. Coins were invented by the Greeks but it was the Italians, Dutch, French and British who developed banks. Paper money (notes, bills) which were promises of real money (gold or silver), came from America and was popularised by Benjamin Franklin.

Of course, other disciplines—particularly economics and to a lesser extent anthropology and sociology—have taken a great deal of interest in the origins, functions and use of money. Economists argue that money in any form, fulfills a number of functions:

(a) A medium of exchange, to avoid the necessity of finding the double coincidence of wants.
(b) A unit of account: a way of simplifying and summarising the worth of goods that are exchanged.

(c) A standard of deferred payment, to be used to separate in time the exchange of a good or service and the payment for goods or services.
(d) Store of value: to be able to receive payment at one moment and postpone purchase until a later date.

Apart from its obvious and above-stated virtues, economists have also attempted to define the reasons why money is desired. These include:

(i) Transactions: to be able to make planned transactions.
(ii) Precautionary: to be able to cope with unplanned expenditures and circumstances.
(iii) Speculative: to be used as an asset to accrue more money.

Furthermore, there are a number of different economic definitions of money. These include *currency* (fiat money); *demand deposits*, which are the amounts people and organisations have in their various accounts; *narrow money*, which is a combination of hard currency and demand deposits; and *near money* which are moneys which pay interest to the owner.

There are many theories concerning the value and importance of money. For instance Fisher provided a simple formula which determines the value of money:

$$P = \frac{MV + M^1V^1}{T}$$

Where P = prices, M = the quantity of ordinary money/cash in circulation, M^1 = bank deposits, V and V^1 are the velocity or speed at which these two kinds of money are spent, and T is the number of transactions.

Monetarism and related monetarist policies are currently popular theories based on the quantity of money in circulation or the cost of credit. Ways of controlling the money supply include central bank's lending rate as well as government control over lending. It is, however, debated by monetarists whether priority should be attached to the quantity of money or the cost of credit though the two are obviously related. As well as macro-economic theories of money, there are microeconomic theories concerned with such things as what economic factors (bank rates, inflation) affect individual saving, investment, etc.

It is, of course, impossible to do justice to the range and complexity of economic theories of money in a single chapter. Economists differ from psychologists on two major grounds, though they share the similar goal of trying to understand and predict the way in which money is used. Economists are interested in aggregated data at the macro level—how classes, groups and countries use, spend and save their money under certain conditions. To this extent economists have more in common with sociologists than with psychologists who are interested in individual and small groups differences. Thus, whereas economists might have the goal of modelling or understanding the money supply, demand and movement for a country or continent, psychologists would be more interested in understanding how and why different groups of individuals with different beliefs (e.g. in the Protestant work ethic) or different backgrounds (e.g. middle vs. working class) use money differently. Whereas individual differences are 'error variance' for the economists, they are the 'stuff' of social psychology. Secondly, whereas economists attempt to understand monetary usage in terms of rational decisions of people with considerable economic knowledge and understanding, psychologists have not taken for granted the fact that people are logical or rational in any formal or objective sense, though they may be subjectively rational or self-consistent. Indeed it has been the *psycho*logical, rather than the *logical*, factors that induce people to use money the way they do that has, not unnaturally, fascinated psychologists.

There are as such no psychological 'theories' of money although various psychological paradigms or traditions have been applied to the psychology of money. These include psychoanalytic theories which are discussed later in this chapter, Piagetian developmental theories which are covered in Chapter 3 on socialisation, and behaviourist learning theory.

Behaviourist research has been concerned with how money becomes a conditioned reinforcement and hence a valued and meaningful object. Research in this tradition has been limited to studies on animals in which animals of various sorts (rats, chimpanzees, cats) perform a task in order to get tokens (poker chips, iron balls, cards) which, like money, can be exchanged for desirable objects such as food. Hence money is valued because it represents or is associated with various desirable objects. However it should be pointed out that in most experiments of this sort money is not strictly a generalised conditioned reinforcer but a specific reinforcer or a symbol of a specific reward. Hence animal studies do not fully test or prove behaviourist theories.

As well as animal studies there is a vast literature on 'token economies' which is effectively the application of behaviourist 'monetary' theories to clinical populations such as mental patients (particularly schizophrenics), disturbed adolescents and recidivists. The idea is based on the well-established principles of operant conditioning—behaviour followed by positive consequences tends to occur more often than if followed by negative consequences. A token economy is a self-contained economic system where clients/patients are paid (reinforced) for behaving appropriately (socialising, working), and in which many desirable commodities (food, entertainment, cigarettes) must be purchased. Thus luxuries (indeed necessities) must be earned. Token economies are based on various principles (Ayllon and Azrin, 1968) which include:

(a) Specifying the target behaviours that are rewarded so that reinforcement is consistent.

(b) Specifying the 'token' which is a medium of exchange and a representation of more primary reinforcers.
(c) Specifying the back-up reinforcers which are the goods and services for which tokens are exchanged and which must be desirable over time.
(d) Specifying the exchange rate which is the number of tokens necessary for each good or service and which are realistically priced to maximise performance.

Numerous studies have shown the benefits of token economies (Ayllon and Roberts, 1974) but have also received various criticisms on clinical grounds. These include the fact that as there is little comparative research (only a no-treatment control condition) it is difficult to establish whether token economies are better or worse than other conditions; that token economies are often aimed at institutional rather than individual needs; that token economies violate many individual rights in total institutions; but perhaps most importantly that conditioned behaviour does not generalise to new environments where the token economy does not operate (Bellack and Hersen, 1980).

Finally, it should be pointed out that there is a fairly large literature, in the behaviourist tradition, on the effects of monetary incentives on various cognitive tasks (Eysenck and Eysenck, 1982). Most of this work has demonstrated that motivation (through monetary reward) controls attention and hence learning which in turn affects memory.

THE PSYCHOLOGY OF MONEY USAGE

There have been a few empirical studies on the psychology of money. Wernimont and Fitzpatrick (1972) used a semantic differential approach to attempt to understand the meaning that different people attach to money. In their sample of over 500 subjects they had such diverse people as secretaries and engineers, nursing sisters and technical supervisors. Factor analysis revealed a number of interpretable factors which were labelled shameful failure (lack of money is an indication of failure, embarrassment and degradation); social acceptability; pooh-pooh attitude (money is not very important, satisfying or attractive); moral evil; comfortable security; social unacceptability; and conservative business values. The subjects' work experiences, sex and socioeconomic level appeared to influence their perceptions of money. For instance, employment status showed that employed groups view money much more positively and as desirable, important and useful, whereas the unemployed seemed to take a tense, worrisome, unhappy view of money. They conclude that money does have a good deal of symbolic value and means quite different things to different people which may go in developmental stages. Important individual differences factors which may affect one's attitude to money include sex, associates, economic status and personality.

Some researchers have looked at personality and money. Luft (1957) found, for instance, that a person's weekly income determines how he is perceived. Hypothetically rich men were seen as relatively healthy, happy and well adjusted, while the poor person was seen as maladjusted and unhappy. Rim (1982) looked at the relationship between personality and attitudes towards money. He administered the Eysenck Personality Inventory and a number of questions concerning money, and found that over half showed significant differences on the extraversion factor, and a third on a neuroticism factor. Predictably, stable extraverts seemed more open, comfortable and carefree about their money than unstable introverts. Rim's pilot study appears to be the only one concerned with individual differences but is completely atheoretical. It was, in fact, based on another large-scale survey which attempted to measure Americans' attitudes towards money.

Rubinstein (1980) devised a money survey for *Psychology Today* to investigate readers' attitudes and feelings about money, to get an idea of its importance in their lives, what associations it evokes and how it affects their closest relationships. Although over 20,000 responses were received from a moderately well-distributed population, the results were only analysed in terms of simple percentages and few individual difference variables were considered. Some of these questions were later combined into a 'Midas' scale but no statistics were presented. They found that spenders, as opposed to self-deniers, were healthier and happier. The Midas respondents (self-deniers) were more unhappy about their finances, personal growth, friends and jobs. They are more pessimistic about their own and the country's economic future, and appear to have more psychosomatic symptoms than spenders. She found that people were still secretive about money: 57 per cent of the sample believed it prudent to conceal one's income from family and friends. As regards disclosing one's income, 97 per cent of men were prepared to disclose the amount to their spouse, 52 per cent to their parents, 44 per cent to their friends, 29 per cent to their co-workers and 18 per cent to their siblings. The proportion of respondents who concealed their financial worth increased with income. Also with two-income families money appears to be a frequent source of friction, and over 40 per cent agreed that money made them envious, aspiring to material goods beyond their means.

On the basis of a number of questions (e.g. how rich or poor they feel; how often they think about money; how unhappy they are with their financial situation) respondents were divided into the money contented and the money troubled. The troubled want things they cannot afford, are in debt and have saved little. They believe their friends to have more money than them; that they deserve more; that they lack financial control over their lives. They also lacked a secure sense of self and were more dissatisfied than others with friendships. Unhappiness at work and at home was also associated with money discontent.

Over half of the sample associated the following negative emotions with money: anxiety, depression, anger and helplessness. Finally half of the sample were pessimistic about the future of the economy which was independent of their income.

A study such as this has, of course, major problems: the representativeness of the sample, the analyses performed, the applicability of the questions, etc. Perhaps the most important criticism of this work is that there is a confounding of correlation and cause. That is, it is not certain whether one's attitude to inflation, material possessions, happiness, etc. is a cause or a consequence of one's income.

Goldberg and Lewis (1978) considered the numerous paradoxes, hypocrisies, inconsistencies and lies surrounding money. They suggest that the main symbolic factors associated with money are security, power, love and freedom. They claim that people who turn to money for security inevitably become alienated from others and their fear about being hurt or rejected by others manifests in a paranoid fear that they will deprive them of their money. Among the security collectors that Goldberg and Lewis describe are the compulsive saver, the self-denier, the compulsive bargain hunter, the fanatic collector, all concerned with the safety-first syndrome. That is, the security collectors are primarily concerned with safety rather than happiness, success or productivity. Power-oriented people are greedy for money which is power they never had during infantile omnipotence. The power-grabbers fit into various categories: the manipulator, the empire-builder, the godfather—all aggressive attempts to build barriers between them and a threatening world. Others give and withhold money and gifts as tokens of love. People both attempt to buy and sell love. Finally, there are those who perceive money as bringing freedom for themselves but as a possible enemy of freedom for others because of its power over them.

Each of these 'clinical' types is illustrated by a number of case histories which are interesting and convincing. However rich these case histories might be, the empiricist is no doubt frustrated by the lack of coherent evidence for the typology outlined. Furthermore, important questions are neglected, such as how easy it is for each of these money types to change in their beliefs and behaviour; the incidence of these types over different groups, cultures and societies, etc.

Some studies have however attempted to do more systematic research in this field. Yamanchi and Templer (1982) attempted to develop a fully psychometrised money attitude scale. A factor analysis of an original selection of 62 items revealed five factors labelled power-prestige, retention-time, distrust, quality and anxiety. From this a 29-item scale was selected which was demonstrated to be reliable. A partial validation—correlations with other established measures such as Machiavellianism, status concern, time-competence, obsessionality, paranoia and anxiety—showed that this questionnaire was related to measures of other similar theoretical constructs: 'The correlations are in agreement with ostensibly suggested motives such as power and prestige. And the evidence is viewed as congruent with less surface psychodynamic formulations such as the relationship of money retention to the obsessive-anal character structure' (p. 528). Most interestingly the authors found that money attitudes were essentially independent of a person's income.

While Yamanchi and Templer's (1982) study is to be welcomed it did appear to have a number of shortcomings. Although the authors obtained a large and fairly heterogeneous sample they failed to investigate any demographic differences (age, sex) save income. Secondly their partial validation seemed too concerned with psychopathological correlates of money attitudes rather than on normal social beliefs and attitudes. Finally the study makes no attempt to trace the aetiology of these beliefs.

More recently Furnham (1984a) attempted to overcome these shortcomings in an empirical study in Britain. The study had three aims: (i) to develop a useful, multifaceted instrument to measure money beliefs and behaviour in Britain; (ii) to look at the relationship between various demographic and social/work beliefs and people's monetary beliefs and behaviour; and (iii) to look at the determinants of people's money beliefs and behaviour in the past and the future.

The importance of the demographic and belief determinants of money beliefs and attitudes lies mainly in the clues it gives to the aetiology of these beliefs. Primary and secondary socialisation and later experience have important effects on people's monetary habits and beliefs. Parental factors such as income and education, as well as social and political conservative beliefs and Protestant work ethic values no doubt determine certain child-rearing practices of independence, saving, achievement, motivation, etc. (Furnham and Bland, 1983). Studies of children's pocket-money and allowances suggest that factors such as class and age have very important effects on children's spending and saving habits, even before they reach the age of 10 (Furnham and Thomas, 1984a).

First, the study aimed to investigate subjects' perceptions of the way in which they had experienced money in the past and anticipated using it in the future. Although there may be various memorial and attribution errors involved in such a procedure—so casting doubt on the usefulness of this approach to collect valid information about the past—a number of very interesting findings emerged. Predictably older, less well-educated people believed their early childhood to be poorer than younger better-educated people, reflecting both the average increased standard of living and the class structure of society. Overall there were few differences in the subjects' perception of money in the past, but a large number regarding money in the future. Older people were more worried about the future than younger people, and richer people were more concerned about the future than poorer people. Conservative voters believed that the country's economic future was bright, while Labour voters and those with high alienation and those with conservative social attitudes believed that it would get worse. Although these questions may seem vague they are not trivial because presumably people act on their beliefs about future trends (Rubinstein, 1980). That is, if one believes that future economic trends mean that one might be substantially worse off one might take steps to avoid this.

A copy of the factor analysis of this scale is found in Table 4.1.

Table 4.1: Factor analysis (Varimax) of the money scale.

Factor	Items	Mean	Loading	Eigenvalue	Variance
(1)	2. I put money ahead of pleasure.	2.67	.46	7.49	12.5
	10. I feel compelled to argue or bargain about the cost of almost everything that I buy.	2.27	.49		
	17. I often feel inferior to others who have more money than myself, even when I know that they have done nothing of worth to get it.	2.32	.48		
	18. I often use money as a weapon to control or intimidate those who frustrate me.	1.71	.52		
	19. I sometimes feel superior to those who have less money than myself regardless of the ability and achievements.	2.10	.46		
	20. I firmly believe that money can solve all of my problems.	2.25	.57		
	21. I often feel anxious and defensive when asked about my personal finances.	3.10	.48		
	22. In making any purchase, for any purpose, my first consideration is cost.	3.85	.46		
	24. I feel stupid if I pay a little more for something than a neighbour.	3.56	.46		
	28. I feel that money is the only thing that I can really count on.	2.29	.71		

	36. I believe that time not spent in making money is time wasted.	1.83	.51		
	43. I would do practically anything legal for money if it were enough.	3.37	.57		
	45. I am proud of my financial victories—pay, riches, investments, etc.—and let my friends know about them.	2.19	.58		
	50. I believe that a person's salary is very revealing in assessing their intelligence.	2.11	.48		
	55. Compared to most other people that I know, I believe that I think about money much more than they do.	3.19	.53		
	56. I worry about my finances much of the time.	3.23	.47		
	57. I often fantasise about money and what I could do with it.	4.09	.41		
	60. In Britain, money is how we compare each other.	4.46	.44		
(2)	3. I sometimes buy things that I don't need or want to impress people because they are the right things to have at the time.	2.67	.52	3.97	6.6
	15. If I have money left over at the end of the month (week) I often feel uncomfortable until it is all spent.	1.87	.42		
	16. I sometimes 'buy' friendship by being very generous with those I want to like me.	2.15	.53		
	25. I often feel disdain for money and look down on those who have it.	2.62	.41		
	35. I often give large tips to waiters/waitresses that I like.	3.55	.45		
	38. I often spend money on myself when I am depressed.	4.51	.41		
	41. I prefer not to lend people money.	4.28	–.47		
	58. I very rarely give beggars or drunks money when they ask for it.	4.75	–.42		
(3)	1. I often buy things that I don't need or want because they are in a sale or reduced in a sale or reduced in price.	3.16	.41	3.00	5.0

	4. Even when I have sufficient money I often feel guilty about spending money on necessities like clothes, etc.	3.34	.59		
	7. I often say 'I can't afford it' whether I can or not.	3.75	.64		
	9. I often have difficulty in making decisions about spending money regardless of the amount.	3.69	.58		
	17. See above.	2.32	.41		
	26. I prefer to save money because I'm never sure when things will collapse and I'll need the cash.	4.24	.42		
(4)	8. I know almost to the penny how much money I have in my purse, wallet or pocket at all times.	3.26	.50	2.62	4.4
	13. I prefer to use money rather than credit cards.	5.27	.40		
	14. I always know how much I have in my savings account (bank or building society).	4.34	.64		
	23. I believe that it is rude to enquire about a person's wage/salary.	4.71	.48		
	26. See above.	4.24	.42		
	32. My attitude towards money is very similar to that of my parents.	3.94	.46		
	34. I always pay bills (telephone, water, electricity, etc.) promptly.	4.27	.40		
	59. I am proud of my ability to save money.	3.37	.59		
(5)	27. The amount of money that I have saved is never quite enough.	4.84	.58	2.12	3.5
	42. I am better off than most of my friends think.	2.99	–.53		
	46. I am worse off than most of my friends think.	3.51	.56		
	49. I often argue with my partner (spouse, lover, etc.) about money.	3.12	.42		
	52. Most of my friends have more money than I do.	3.71	.61		
	56. See above.	3.23	–.42		
	59. See above.	3.32	–.42		
(6)	33. I believe that the amount of money that a person earns is closely related to his/her ability and effort.	2.75	.45	2.02	3.4

51. I believe that my present income is about what I deserve, given the job I do.	3.51	.67
53. I believe that my present income is far less than I deserve given the job I do.	4.35	–.60
54. I believe that I have very little control over my financial situation in terms of my power to change it.	4.48	–.58

Scale: Agree 7 6 5 4 3 2 1 Disagree
Reprinted with permission from *Personality and Individual Differences*, 1984, Furnham, 'Many sides of the coin: The psychology of money usage', Pergamon Press.

The results were not dissimilar from related American studies (Rubinstein, 1980; Yamanchi and Templer, 1982). Attitudes towards money are by no means unidimensional: factor analytic results yielded six clearly interpretable factors that bore many similarities to the factors found in Yamanchi and Templer (1982) such as power, retention and inadequacy, as well as the hypothetical factors derived from psychoanalytic theory (Fenichel, 1947). Whereas some of the factors were clearly linked to clinical traits of anxiety and obsessionality, others are more closely related to power and the way in which one obtains money. Also some factors more than others proved to be related to the demographic and belief variables: obsession with money showed significant differences on sex, education and income and all the belief variables (alienation, Protestant work ethic, conservatism), whereas the inadequacy factor revealed no significant differences on either set of variables.

Other results showed an interesting and predictable pattern of results with age, education and the Protestant work ethic values discriminating most strongly. These differences would not have been predicted by psychoanalytic theory. It should also be noted that feelings of alienation did not discriminate very clearly so casting doubt on a narrowly clinical approach to money beliefs and attitudes. From a social psychological perspective these results are quite sensible—as one gets older and one's needs change so money takes on new meanings. Furthermore, as one might predict, education makes a difference to one's beliefs about money (see Chapter 3).

The canonical correlation yielded three significant variates which described the relationship between the independent (attitudes to money) and dependent (demographic belief) variables. The first two significant variates both showed a relationship between specific independent variables and two of the dependent factors, namely obsession with money, and beliefs about whether one gets money through ability or effort. Females more than males, high Protestant work ethic scorers rather than low, low rather than high income-earners and less rather than more alienated people tend to be obsessed by money and to believe that the accumulation of money is due to effort and ability. The third significant variate showed that age, education and sex were related to conservative monetary beliefs as well as feelings of inadequacy about money. Case studies on people with money obsessions indeed point to the importance of the above factors (Goldberg and Lewis, 1978).

EXPERIMENTAL STUDIES ON COINS AND NOTES

One experiment published in 1947 has meant that considerable research has been done on the psychology of coins from various countries. Bruner and Goodman (1947) argued that values and needs play a very important part in psychophysical perception. They entertained various general hypotheses: the greater the social value of an object, the more it will be susceptible to organisation by behavioural determinants (i.e. perceptually accentuated) and the greater the individual need for a socially valued object, the more marked will be the operation of behavioural determinants. Rich and poor 10-year-olds were asked to estimate which of an ascending and descending range of circles of light corresponded to a range of coins. Another control group compared the circle of light to cardboard discs of identical size to the coins. They found, as predicted, that coins (socially valued objects) were judged larger in size than grey discs, and that the greater the value of the coin, the greater is the deviation of apparent size from actual size. Secondly, they found that poor children overestimate the size of coins considerably more than did the rich children. Furthermore this was true with coins present and from memory.

Because this experiment demonstrated that subjective value and objective needs actually affected perception of physical objects, this study provoked considerable interest and many replications have been done. Studies have been done in different countries (McCurdy, 1956; Dawson, 1975) with different coins (Smith *et al.*, 1975) and with poker chips as well as coins (Lambert *et al.*, 1949) and found that although there have been some differences in the findings, the effects have been generalisable. Tajfel (1981) noted that about 20 experiments have been done on the 'overestimation effect' and only two have yielded unambiguously negative results. Nearly all the researchers have found that motivational or valuable stimuli had effects on subjects' perceptual judgements of magnitude as well as size, weight, number and brightness.

Tajfel (1981) has made some important observations and criticisms of this work. He notes that two aspects of this experiment need to be considered: the *inter*-serial effect (the perceived relationship between any stimulus of the value series and the neutral stimuli) and the *intra*-serial effect (the relationship between the stimuli of a value series as compared with the corresponding relationships in an objectively identical neutral series). He thus stresses the accentuation of differences as an explanatory device which suggests that polarisation effects should operate systematically at either extreme of the response continuum.

Two other, methodologically different studies have looked at the value size hypothesis. Hitchcock *et al.* (1976) compared 84 countries' per capital income and the average size of the currency to determine whether 'persons in poor countries have greater subjective need than persons in wealthy countries, and that a country's coinage allows institutional expression of the level of need' (p. 307). They found a correlation of –0.19 ($p < 0.05$) between GNP per capita and the mean size of all coins minted for a country, and a correlation of –0.25 ($p < 0.025$) between GNP per capita and the size of the least-valued coin. They conclude that this data indicate the potential usefulness of viewing institutional-level data from a psychological perspective.

Furnham (1985a) did an unobtrusive study on the perceived value of small coins. It was assumed that the finder's behaviour (either picking up the coin or not) is an index of the perceived worth of the coin at the time. Specifically it was hypothesised that the value of the coin would be linearly related to the number of times that it would be picked up. The four smallest coins of the country (England) were dropped in the street and observers recorded how people who saw the coins reacted. In the study 56 people who saw the smallest (½p) coin ignored it, 44 ignored the 1p coin, 16 the 2p coin and 10 the 5p piece. It was concluded that because of the fact that money is both a taboo and emotionally charged topic unobtrusive measures such as these are particularly useful, particularly in times of high inflation, unemployment, or where there were changes in the coinage.

The psychological factors associated with actual coins and notes have received some attention. Bruce *et al.* (1983a) were interested in the introduction of two new coins into British currency which were small relative to their value compared with other coins present in the system. This was done because small coins are cheaper to produce, easier to handle, and brings British coinage into line with the coins of other nations. A number of studies were done on members of the public. In a preliminary series of studies they found that it was not the colour of a coin (gold vs, copper vs, silver) that made it appear more valuable, but rather its thickness and elaborate edge. Further in Britain, 'seven-sidedness', rather than a purely circular coin is seen as more valuable. In the main study they found that their adult subjects appeared to apply specific 'rules' about the value-conferring features of coins. These rules refer to the shape, colour, edge and sidedness of the coins.

In a second series of studies Bruce *et al.* (1983b) looked at the extent to which the new British £1.00 coin might be confused with existing coins. In a series of studies they found that the new coin could easily be confused with a coin $\frac{1}{20}$th of its value and a different colour, but a similar circumference. Where coins have the same shape and circumference it is most important that the thickness of the more valuable is sufficiently great to make the weight difference between the two coins very easily detectable. They concluded that more ergonomic work is needed before coins are introduced into circulation in order to establish problems of confusion in the public.

Both of the Bruce *et al.* (1983 a and b) studies were concerned with how natives recognise their own currency. However some work has also been done on how people identify coins they are not familiar with. Furnham and Weissman (1985) showed all the British coins to over 60 Americans (in America) who had never been to Britain, nor previously seen British currency. Only one subject was able to rank order the coins correctly according to worth. Whereas over half of the sample could identify the relative worthlessness of the two smallest coins (1p, ½p) less than a third correctly identified the rank of the top five coins. In a second study the authors asked 4–5 and 9–10-year-old children various questions about British coins when showing them all the coins of the realm: e.g. 'Which coin can you buy most with?'; 'Point at the 10p piece'. They found that whereas the 9–10-year-olds were accurate in their answers (90 per cent or more) in each case the 4–5-year-olds were often wrong. The 4–5-year-olds seemed to be operating on much the same principles as the American adults had done. That is, given the choice the children (and foreign adults) assumed that size was positively correlated with worth (circumference, not volume) and that silver coins were more valuable than copper or gold-coloured coins.

Two studies have looked at the effects of inflation on the perception of money, one using coins, the other notes. Lea (1981) showed that subjects tended to overestimate the sizes of identical coins as a function of inflation. That is, subjects made bigger estimates of coins given their old pre-decimalisation names (2 shillings) than their new name (10 pence). Although there are some alternate hypotheses that may be entertained the most satisfactory explanation appears to be that because inflation has reduced the actual worth of the same sized coin, they are perceived as smaller. Furnham (1983 c) found evidence of the same phenomena when considering notes. Subjects were asked to identify rectangles corresponding in shape to a £1.00 note withdrawn from circulation in 1979, and a £1.00 note currently being used. The notes differed slightly in colour, shape and design but were broadly similar. As predicted subjects tended to overemphasise the size of the old note (10.714 cm vs. 9.692 cm) and underemphasise the size of the new note (8.243 cm vs. 9.045 cm).

Together these studies provide evidence for the value/need money perception hypothesis and the effects of inflation on the perceived size of money.

MORALITY AND MONEY

Many religions and philosophies have considered the benefits but also the dangers of money, and the accumulation of wealth. It is far beyond the scope of this chapter to consider them all in any depth. However some of the more salient aspects of Christian teaching on money will be considered.

There is no shortage of biblical teachings on money or indeed of commentaries on these teachings (Fuller and Rice, 1966; Barclay, 1972). Many writers have been impressed by the fact that the apparent wealth of a country is often associated with increased, rather than decreased, social problems such as mental illness, drug and alcohol addiction, delinquency.

There are a number of parables concerning money:

1. The Rich Man and Lazarus (Luke, 19–31): the rich man was punished in the world to come for being complacent and doing nothing to help the poor. The sin was not so much the possession of wealth but the diminished sense of responsibility for those less fortunate.
2. The throwing of the money-changers out of the Temple (Mark II, 15–16): Jesus threw the money-changers out of the Temple because they were exploiting honest pilgrims' credulity, trust, and more importantly their basic needs.
3. The rich young ruler (Matthew 19, 16–30). Jesus tells a rich young ruler to give all of his considerable wealth to the poor. The sin of the rich man was not his money *per se* but his possessiveness.

It is not money that is condemned but a particular attitude towards it.

The more money a person has the more temptations he has and thus the more he needs God. The dangers of money are manifold: it creates a false sense of independence and invulnerability; it can be most easily acquired immorally and hence encourages bad habits; the more people possess in this world, the more difficult it becomes for them to leave it; and paradoxically instead of satisfying people that they have enough, it does the opposite making people more greedy.

Barclay (1972) concludes with five general principles which supposedly save people from the dangers of wealth:

1. Money should be honestly acquired so that it harmed or injured no one, but helped and enriched the community.
2. Money should be regarded as something to be shared, not hoarded. It should be used to help others.
3. Money should not be used selfishly but given away.
4. People are more important than things; men are more important than money; workers are more important than machines.
5. Sometimes giving money is not enough but an evasion of a greater responsibility—a gift of self.

THE PSYCHOANALYSIS OF MONEY

In an essay entitled 'Character and Anal Eroticism' Freud (1908) argued that character traits originate in the warding-off of certain primitive biological impulses. In this essay he first drew attention to the relationship between adult attitudes to money as a product of anal eroticism. Many psychoanalytic thinkers have developed these notions. For instance Ferenczi (1926) described the ontogenic stages through which the original pleasure in dirt and excreta develops into a love of money. Freud (1908) identified three main traits associated with people who had fixated at the anal stage: orderliness, parsimony and obstinacy with associated qualities of cleanliness, conscientiousness, trustworthiness, defiance and revengefulness.

The child's first interest in his faeces turns first to such things as mud, sand, stones, thence to all man-made objects that can be collected, and then to money. Essentially the Freudian thesis may be spelt out thus: children all experience pleasure in the elimination of faeces. At an early age (around 2 years) parents toilet train their children—some showing enthusiasm and praise (positive reinforcement) for defecation, others threatening and punishing a child when it refuses to do so (negative reinforcement). Potty or toilet training occurs at the same stage that the child is striving to achieve autonomy and a sense of worth. Often toilet training becomes a source of conflict between parents and children over whether the child is in control of his sphincter or whether the parental rewards and coercion compel submission to their will. Furthermore the child is fascinated by and fantasises over his faeces which are, after all, a creation of his own body. The child's confusion is made all the worse by the ambiguous reactions of parents who on the one hand treat the faeces as gifts and highly valued, and then behave as if they are dirty, untouchable and in need of immediate disposal.

If the child is traumatised by the experience of toilet training, he tends to retain ways of coping and behaving during this phase. The way in which a miser hoards money is seen as symbolic of the child's refusal to eliminate faeces in the face of parental demands. The spendthrift, on the other hand, recalls the approval and affection that resulted from submission to parental authority to defecate. Thus some people equate elimination/spending with receiving affection and hence felt more inclined to spend when feeling insecure, unloved or in need of affection. Attitudes to money are then bimodal—either they are extremely positive or extremely negative.

Evidence for the psychoanalytic position comes from the usual sources—patients' free-associations and dreams. However Freudians have attempted to find evidence for their theory in idioms, myths, folklore and legends. There is also quite a lot of evidence from language, particularly from idiomatic expressions. Money is often called 'filthy lucre', and the wealthy are often called 'stinking rich'. Gambling for money is also associated with dirt and toilet training: a poker player puts money in a 'pot'; dice players shoot 'craps'; card players play 'dirty-Girty'; a gambler who loses everything is 'cleaned out'.

Families, groups and societies which demand early and rigid toilet training tend to produce 'anal characteristics' in people, which include orderliness, punctuality, compulsive cleanliness and obstinacy. Hence one can be miserly about knowledge, time and emotions as much as money. These effects may be increased or reduced depending on whether the child grows up in a socialist or capitalist country, in times of comparative expansion or depression, or whether one is part of a middle- or working-class family. Parents' belief in the Puritan or Protestant ethic may also alter money beliefs and habits.

Psychoanalytic ideas have inspired a good deal of empirical work (Beloff, 1957; Grygier, 1961; Kline, 1968). Although there are a number of measures that have been constructed to measure dynamic features Kline (1971) developed his own test of the anal character. Examples of this scale include:

1. Do you keep careful accounts of the money you spend? (Yes/No)
2. When eating out do you wonder what the kitchens are like? (Yes/No)
3. Do you insist on paying back even small trivial debts? (Yes/No)
4. Do you like to think out your own methods rather than use other people's? (Yes/No)
5. Do you find more pleasure in doing things than in planning them? (Yes/No)
6. Do you think there should be strong laws against speeding? (Yes/No)
7. There's nothing more infuriating than people who don't keep appointments. (Yes/No)
8. Do you often feel you want to stop people and do the job yourself? (Yes/No)
9. Most people don't have high enough standards in what they do? (Yes/No)
10. Do you make up your mind quickly rather than turn things over for a long time? (Yes/No)
11. Do you think envy is at the root of most egalitarian ideals? (Yes/No)
12. Do you like to see something solid and substantial for your money? (Yes/No)
13. Do you easily change your mind once you've made a decision? (Yes/No)
14. Do you disagree with corporal punishment? (Yes/No)
15. Do you regard smoking as a dirty habit? (Yes/No)

This scale has been used in Ghana as well as Britain.

The empirical research into the anal character has been reviewed by Hill (1976) and Kline (1972). Both reviewers were critical of the methodology of studies done in this area, but came to the conclusion that the evidence for the existence of the anal character as described by the psychoanalytic thinkers is poor.

THE SYMBOLISM OF MONEY

The fact that money is emotionally charged and highly symbolic has already been mentioned. There is a great deal of speculation about this but comparatively little empirical work in this field. For instance the introduction and/or removal of a coin from circulation causes a great public outcry. The use of credit cards as opposed to cash has also altered the way in which people use and perceive money. For Lea and Webley (1981):

> The essence of money is that it carries meanings. It involves multiple symbolisation. It is not simply a symbol of *ordure* (Freud), nor only a symbol of what it has bought in the past (Skinner); neither only a symbol of what it could buy in the future (as indicated by some anthropologists), nor only a symbol of the most valuable objects in a society (as other anthropological data suggest); nor is it only a symbol of the world of dehumanised salaries and payments (as Deci says, or some Marxists). Money symbolises *all* these things, and furthermore many others. (p. 12)

Consider for example two areas in which some research has been done: The use of *tips*, and more importantly the exchange of *gifts*. It has been suggested that the word 'tip' stands for 'to insure prompt service' and is given for services in such places as hotels and restaurants, barbers and hairdressers. A tip is often a symbolic gesture of satisfaction with service, though it may be a requirement in some organisations. Tips usually relate directly to performance and are rewards for specific services though there are norms for the amount of tips (e.g. 10 per cent of the bill). Shamir (1983) has pointed out two interesting features of the tip: first, in that a tip is a tangible form of feedback from clients, workers who receive tips may be thought of as more highly satisfied and motivated compared with workers who do not get tips. Secondly, people who receive tips are often put in conflicting roles between the management/superiors and the customer but that they are more likely to side with the latter as opposed to the former which would be more true of those who do not receive tips. In a study it was demonstrated that tip recipients experience more conflict yet were more favourable to their customers, but were less satisfied than those not receiving tips. The author suggests that his results provide more support for the boundary role perspective (conflict between roles) than for the motivation theory perspective. The dependence on the customer is probably more a source of stress for occupants of subordinate service roles than a source of reward or satisfaction.

The exchange of money as a gift reveals most clearly the symbolic nature and psychological quality of money. Webley *et al.* (1983) set out in a series of four studies to investigate the unacceptability of money as a gift. They found that money or a cheque was less acceptable than a gift token or a selected present as a gift to the subjects' mother. A third study considered why the gift of money was inappropriate. The top three reasons were: that a gift ought to be something one would not usually buy for oneself and hence chosen by the giver, whereas with a cheque this cannot be the case; a cheque involves no thought devoted to choosing the present; money given as a gift would be used for general expenses. In the fourth study of students' mothers' reactions to gifts the researchers found that the mothers indicated that a cheque would be less acceptable than a selected present or gift token, but that they did not expect more to be spent on a cheque than on other gifts. Money, therefore, is not acceptable as a gift-giving medium, as a gift is an expression of thought and effort of the giver not only the absolute worth of the gift. The results 'suggest that modern, Western money is like primitive moneys in that there are taboos on its use. Whatever the institutional position, therefore, in psychological terms money does not meet the economist's definition of being a *universal* medium of exchange' (p. 237).

ECONOMIC ANTHROPOLOGY AND PRIMITIVE MONEY

Unlike psychology, anthropology has long been interested in economics and consumption (Douglas and Isherwood, 1980). Economic anthropology is concerned with the economic aspects of the social relations of persons. Indeed there are a number of standard textbooks on economic anthropology (Thurnwald, 1932; Herskovits, 1952; Dalton, 1971). Although there have been a number of well-established authorities in this field, Polanyi's work is perhaps the best known. Anthropologists have long been aware that nearly all economic concepts, ideas and theories are based on only one type of economy—industrial capitalism. Some have argued that these modern economic concepts (maximising, supply, demand) are equally applicable to primitive societies while others are not convinced.

One of the major tasks of economic anthropology is to detect economic universals in human society by sampling the many forms in which they are manifest across cultures. For instance, whereas the deferment of wants, through saving and investing, may be considered good for some cultures, most primitive cultures dictate that resources be expended.

First, it should be pointed out what all economies share in common. Dalton (1971) has noted three features: a structured arrangement with enforced rules for the acquisition or production of material items and services; rules whereby natural resources, human cooperation and technology are combined to provide materials and services in a sustained, repetitive fashion; and the existence of superficially similar institutional practices in the form of market-places, monetary objects, accounting devices and external trade. However, he is much more impressed by the differences in economies in terms of their organisation, performance, change, growth and development.

Anthropologists have been concerned with all aspects of economic activity including barter, the market, distribution of goods and wealth, ownership and property, etc. There are certain similarities between primitive societies' economic behaviour. For instance, Thurnwald (1932) noted that a characteristic failure of most primitive economies is the absence of any desire to make profits either from production and exchange. Many studies have looked at the symbols of value and money—stages of evolution of money, and the diverse number and type of object used as units of barter, including shells, dogs' teeth, salt and copper bracelets. Various distinctions have been made such as objects which are treated as treasure and hoarded as such or an article of daily use; whether the object is regarded as capital capable of yielding profit; and also whether the object is the potential source of others of its own kind. Certainly what is interesting about anthropological studies of money is not only the range of objects used as money but the fact that primitive money does not fulfill many of the functions that current money does.

Whereas economists seem concerned with only non-social aspects of money, such as its worth, divisibility etc., anthropologists look at money which is used in reciprocal and redistributive transactions, in terms of the personal roles and social context of what occurs. The exchange of whatever serves as money—be it armbands, pigs' tusks, shells or stones—as well as its acquisition and disposition is a structured and important event that often has strong moral and legal obligations and implications and which might change various status rights and social roles. Because money is a means of reciprocal and redistributive payment used fairly infrequently to discharge social obligations in primitive societies its portability and divisibility are not very important. The introduction of western-style money does more than just displace indigenous money; it has inevitable repercussions on the social organisation of a people. This is because western-style money allows both commercial *and* non-commercial (traditional) payments to be earned with general-purpose money earned in everyday market transactions. Hence patrons, elders and heads of families and clans lose some control over their clients and juniors who can earn their own cash and dispose of it as they wish.

The essence of the anthropological message is this: money has no essence apart from its uses which depend on the traditional transactional modes of each culture's economy. Money is what it does and no more.

CONCLUSION

Psychological research on money is diffuse and varied. Yet there appears to be a consistent theme running through all the literature from studies on perception through to psychoanalytic observations. Money is not simply a convenient medium of exchange, it is a complex and richly imbued symbol.

To understand how and why people spend, save and perceive money as they do requires some understanding of the sociological, economic and historical nature of the society in which they live (i.e. post-industrial, liberal capitalism is pre-industrial, peasant economy) *as well as* a knowledge of the personal development of the individual. For whereas there are culturally shared beliefs, taboos and symbols surrounding money there are also individual patterns of beliefs and behaviours.

Each of the different branches of psychology has something to contribute to the study of money: developmental psychology (how and when money concepts and behaviours are learnt); experimental psychology (distortions in the perception of familiar and unfamiliar money); occupational psychology (the use of money as a reward and incentive for labour); personality psychology (individual differences in the use of money); and social psychology (individual, group and societal attitudes to money).

Perhaps the psychological significance of money is seen most clearly when it changes, i.e. when coins and notes appear, disappear or are inter-changed; at times of inflation; when the use of money is being replaced by other tokens such as cheques and cash cards. Governments can radically alter the way in which people use and perceive money by changing its form: changing the name of the currency (and little else), by decimalisation, but perhaps most commonly and effectively by changing notes into coins. Another innovation is the payment of wages and salaries directly into bank and building society accounts which has an influence on and hopefully leads to less immediate expenditure and saving. Inflation is another important factor in the understanding of money. Epstein and Babad (1982) found that variation in income was not as relevant as people's subjective appraisal of the threat of inflation in predicting their expenditure.

The future of money in many advanced western countries however appears to be in doubt. That is, with the introduction of more and more 'plastic' money in the form of credit cards, cash in the form of notes and coins appears to be being used less and less. However, as the work on token economies has shown, there is no reason to suspect that the psychological significance and symbolism of present-day coins and notes might not be equally appropriate to the understanding of money substitutes.

As has been stressed before, this is a rich and neglected area of research made all the more interesting by rapid changes in the use of money and its substitutes. For the economic psychologist it would be very interesting to see whether the use of credit cards increases expenditure; whether credit cards are used for some interactions rather than others, and why; whether the credit card reduces guilt and/or changes attitudes about being in debt, etc. It is already apparent that credit cards have assumed a disclosive/display role in that the colour of the card (e.g. gold vs. green) indicates one's credit limit which is itself an indication of annual income. Thus a credit card enables one to disclose more about one's income than was allowed by simple cash or cheques, and hence they may take on a more important psychological role. Individual preferences for cards, cash or cheque books may also be a useful indicator of socialisation experience (class).

Part III:
Social Issues and Social Problems

5 Poverty: Aspects of the Psychological Literature

INTRODUCTION

In contrast to many of the other social sciences—anthropology, economics, political science, sociology—psychology has not paid particular attention to poverty. Why is poverty important? Is it merely a result of uneven distribution of wealth? Why does poverty exist in a rich country? Can it be prevented? All these questions (which clearly have major social policy implications) have not caught the imagination of psychologists. Paradoxically, in times of economic expansion (the 1960s) and in rich countries (USA) psychologists appear to have taken most interest in poverty (Allen, 1970).

Suffice to say that some of the most important topics in poverty research have been almost totally neglected by psychologists. These include the definition, measurement, incidence and characteristics of poverty; the life of the poor; the causes of and remedies for poverty; and politics, social policy and poverty. Poverty for the psychologist is a sort of Pandora's box—the obvious problems are immediately apparent. Poverty is a comparative, economic concept that can rarely be isolated from more general questions of inequality. Because the definition of poverty is problematic and many of the questions concerning poverty are structural involving macroeconomic or political factors, psychologists have been hesitant to apply psychological concepts to poverty. Furthermore, others have been convinced that any psychological analysis would be a fundamental attribution error in that one would erroneously focus on individuals and their behaviour rather than economic and industrial organisations and institutions.

Poverty can be defined both relatively and absolutely. In absolute 'objective' terms it can be defined in terms of total (weekly or monthly) earnings which are insufficient for a maintenance of basic physical and mental health. A minimal amount may be specified by government agencies and all falling below this amount may be said to be poor. Alternatively, an 'objective' definition could be the 10 (or so) per cent of the population who earn the least. That is, one can have a relative objective definition. It is also possible to make some 'subjective' (non-economic) definition of poverty in terms of people's experience. Townsend (1979) has however agreed that

> definitions which are based on some conception of 'absolute' deprivation disintegrate upon close and sustained examination and deserve to be abandoned. Poverty has often been defined, in the words of an OECD review, 'in terms of some

absolute level of minimum needs, below which people are regarded as being poor, for purpose of social and government concern, and which does not change through time.' In fact, people's needs, even for food, are conditioned by the society in which they live and to which they belong, and just as needs differ in different societies so they differ in different periods of the evolution of single societies. Any conception of poverty as 'absolute' is therefore inappropriate and misleading.

The second conclusion which might be drawn is that, though the principal definitions put forward historically have invoked some 'absolute' level of minimum needs, they have in practice represented rather narrow conceptions of relative deprivation and deserve to be clarified as such. Thus Seebohm Rowntree's definition amounted in effect to a conception of nutritional deprivation relative to the level believed to be required for members of the manual working class at the turn of the century to function efficiently. That definition corresponded with contemporary Liberal interpretations of the rights and needs of labour in industrial society and was a class standard. The US Social Security Administration Poverty Index is similar in basic respects. It is a stringent view of nutritional deprivation relative to the minimally adequate diets achieved by low-income families in 1959 who were managing their budgets economically. (p. 39)

Townsend (1979) insists on the distinction between subjective, collective and objective definitions of poverty and suggests that to understand poverty properly it is important to document all public and private resources which contribute to actual standards of living but which are inequally distributed. Nevertheless he admits that definition of poverty must involve value-judgements but feels it is important to make the criteria for the definition as objective as possible.

Notwithstanding serious problems in the definition and measurement of poverty there exist a number of theories for the causes of poverty. These theories—because they come from different disciplines—focus on different factors, operate at different levels of abstraction and are made explicit by people with different values and axioms. Sullivan *et al.* (1980) have attempted to classify how three classic perspectives on social problems view poverty:

From the *functionalist* perspective, poverty becomes a social problem when it no longer performs this function of motivating people to make productive contributions to society. This might occur if there were large numbers of poor because the system was unable to reward all those who performed important tasks; or it might occur if, because of some inequalities in the system, the performance of important tasks only carried a small likelihood of moving up in the stratification system. ... Poverty becomes a social problem, from this perspective when the poor are no longer able to adapt to their plight and thus pose a threat to the functioning of society...

For the *conflict* theorist, it is not the breakdown of the culture of poverty that constitutes a problem; rather the culture of poverty itself is a social problem because it inhibits the ability of the poor to struggle with other groups over scarce resources. ... From the conflict perspective, poverty becomes a social problem when some group feels that the existing distribution of resources is unfair and unjust and that something can and should be done about it. ... For the conflict theorist, the emphasis is on more relative criteria. One is poor relative to what other groups have.

Rather than establishing absolute cut-off points, one must think in terms of relative inequality...

For *interactionists*, poverty is a matter of shared expectations—and the poor often share the negative definition of themselves that is held by others in society. Those who are the objects of such labelling are stigmatised and may begin to behave in accordance with those expectations. The interactionist emphasises that poverty is not just a matter of economic deprivation, but involves the person's self-concept. (pp. 376–8)

Of course there are both orthodox and radical economic theories. Orthodox theories have not tended to look much at the distribution of personal incomes preferring to look at aggregate data. (Townsend, 1979). However where they have, it is assumed that there is a strong positive relationship between income and productivity, the latter of which is determined by such factors as ability, education, skills and expertise. Thus the focus of these theories is on the individual differences in school achievement, education, etc. rather than on institutional or government factors. Other more radical economic theories have stressed various other forces which determine wage levels and the demand for labour, such as the influence of trade unions and government. These radical theorists see the labour market divided by class into primary (stable, well-paid) and secondary (unstable, badly-paid) sectors which determine both a worker's productivity and his income. These radical theories are proposed by both economists (Gordon, 1972) and sociologists (Coates and Silburn, 1970; Townsend, 1979) and are heavily influenced by Marxist ideas. However there are other sociological and anthropoligical theories which are much more sociopsychological in nature. Three will be considered, the last of which was probably attracted most attention.

1 MINORITY GROUP THEORY

This represented an early attempt by Rowntree (1901) not so much to discuss the ultimate causes of poverty, but to describe the characteristics of the poor. His 'theory' has three interesting facets. First, there was a distinction between primary and secondary poverty which had different causes:

Primary poverty	*Secondary poverty*
Death of wage-earner	Drink
Incapacity of wage-earner (accident, illness)	Betting and gambling
Chief wage-earner unemployed	Ignorant/careless housekeeping
Chronic irregularity of work	Irregularity of income
Largeness of family	
Lowness of wage	

In a sense this represented an attempt to distinguish the deserving from the non-deserving poor. Secondly, Rowntree hinted at, but never fully explored, the concept of a cycle of poverty with certain categories of people descending into and unable to escape from poverty. Thirdly, and related to the above, this early theory began to typologise the poor into various groups—the old, the unemployed, the sick, etc. The idea of a minority group was to have an important influence on how others saw the behaviour of the poor.

It is perhaps incorrect to describe the minority-group approach as a theory but it clearly had important ideas in it. Indeed running through a good deal of the social psychological studies on poverty is the idea of *labelling* which has been applied to all minority groups.

2 FUNCTIONAL ANALYSIS OF POVERTY

Functional analysis—the sociological idea that persistent social patterns and structures fulfill important basic functions—has also been applied to poverty. Gans (1972) has argued that poverty fulfills a number of important functions for special interest or socio-economic groups, though of course it is dysfunctional for others. He lists 15 functions which include the economic, social, cultural and political:

1. The existence of poverty makes sure that 'dirty work' (dangerous, temporary, undignified, menial) is done.
2. The poor, either directly or indirectly, subsidise many activities that benefit the affluent such as consumption and investment in the private economy (by virtue of the low wages that they receive), and through paying regressive taxes.
3. Poverty creates jobs and markets to serve the poor such as social workers, prostitutes and peacetime armies.
4. The poor buy products (second-hand clothes, stale food) not wanted by others and consult professionals too old or poorly trained to attract more affluent clients.
5. The poor may be labelled and punished as deviants in order to uphold the legitimacy of dominant social norms regarding, for instance, work and health care.
6. The disabled or unlucky poor provide the better off with opportunities for emotional satisfaction in the form of charity, compassion and patronage crucial in the Judeo-Christian ethic.
7. The poor also offer the rich vicarious participation in the uninhibited sexual, alcoholic and drug-taking habits that they are supposed to have.
8. Poverty helps to guarantee the status of the non-poor—they remain a reliable, relatively permanent measuring rod for status comparison.

9. The poor assist the upward mobility of the non-poor because being denied educational and other opportunities they enable others to obtain better jobs.
10. The poor help the economic viability of various businesses and professions such as middle-class civic organisations and the churches so justifying their continued existence.
11. The poor perform cultural factors such as providing their labour on various great building projects or providing the surplus capital to create 'high culture' (e.g. build art monuments).
12. The poor have low culture—artefacts, music, poetry—which becomes adopted and then 'owned' by the rich.
13. The poor serve as symbolic constituencies or opponents for various political groups: vanguards of the revolution for the Left; the spendthrift and dishonest for the Right.
14. The poor, being unable to do otherwise, can be made to absorb the economic and political costs of technological and economic change.
15. Because the poor vote less and participate in politics less than other groups, the political system has been able to ignore them.

The thesis of the functionalists is not that poverty should or must exist but that it does exist because it is useful to a number of groups in society and that many of the functional alternatives to poverty would be quite dysfunctional for more affluent members of society. He concludes:

> That social phenomena which are functional for affluent groups and dysfunctional for poor ones persist; that when the elimination of such phenomena through functional alternatives generates dysfunctions for the affluent, they will continue to persist; and that phenomena like poverty can be eliminated only when they either become sufficiently dysfunctional for the affluent or when the poor can obtain enough power to change the system of social stratification. (p. 288)

Some studies have considered the functional perception of poverty in India. Pandey *et al.* (1982a) asked rural and urban, male and female North Indians the extent to which they believed in the functional nature of poverty. Although the trends were in the predicted direction, none of the analyses reached significance, yet all believed poverty to be functional in India.

Functional theories have however been criticised on a number of grounds. Theories are sometimes presented entirely speculatively with no verification or data in their support.

It has been objected that functional theories are teleological, and thus incur the logical error of placing the cause of an event after it in time. However, this takes place in any self-regulating system with a negative feedback loop. For example, in a thermostat the behaviour of the system leads to the goal of a certain temperature being attained, though the goal was actually set before his temperatue was reached. Homeostatic processes, whereby the body maintains the constancy of its internal environment, operate in a similar way. Teleological explanations are also given in biology to explain the existence of parts of the body in terms of their contribution to the working and survival of the organism. The process behind such functional relationships is natural selection acting on spontaneous mutations in the genes.

It has been objected that functionalism encourages or reflects a conservative bias by emphasising the positive functions of every aspect of the *status quo*, from the class system to the Royal Family. Advocates of social change can try to bring about alternative institutions to meet the same needs, or to meet them better, and to avoid areas of dysfunction in society (e.g. groups of people whose needs are not being met).

Coser (1964) objected that functionalists see conflict as dysfunctional, and argued that conflict can have positive functions: for example duelling can allow the free expression of pent-up hostile feelings, and thus preserve the group. Groups can define themselves through struggling with other groups; and conflict can bring about what may be beneficial social changes.

Whether or not functional theories are either necessary or sufficient to explain the perpetuance of poverty in different cultures at different times, they do provide a clear picture particularly of some of the latent or hidden functions of poverty.

3 THE SUB-CULTURAL THEORY OF POVERTY

The anthropologist Lewis (1951, 1965) elaborated, clarified and popularised a view that had been in existence for some time. He pointed out that the poorest sections of many societies (English, American, Mexican, French) shared very similar values, interpersonal relations, a family and community structure and had similar spending patterns and concept of time. That is, there appears to be a distinctive pan-cultural, self-perpetuating culture of poor people. The poor form a unique society within society: their beliefs, attitudes and values are passed on from one generation to the next and their life proceeds with different expectations at a different rhythm. The poor are separate and different, not only economically but also intellectually and emotionally.

Part of the appeal of Lewis's work is the careful detail and vivid description. He writes of the characteristics of the poor thus:

> the lack of effective participation . . . in the major institutions of the larger society . . . they have a low level of literacy and education, usually do not belong to labour unions, are not members of political parties, generally do not participate in the national welfare agencies, and make very little use of banks, hospitals, department stores, museum or art galleries. They have a critical attitude towards some of the basic institutions of the dominant classes, hatred of the police, mistrust of

> government and those in high position, and a cynicism which extends over to the church ... [they] are aware of middle-class values, talk about them, and even claim some of them as their own, but on the whole they do not live by them ... on the local community level, we find poor housing conditions, crowding, gregariousness, but above all a minimum of organization beyond the level of the nuclear and extended family ... [although] there may be a sense of community and *esprit de corps* ... people with a culture of poverty are provincial and locally oriented and have very little sense of history. They know only their own troubles, their own local conditions, their own neighbourhood, their own way of life. (Lewis, 1968, p. 26)

According to this poverty theory, poor families are likely to be unstable, often headed by females who are less able to respond to the needs of the children. There is usually considerable discontinuity in family life, with marriages dissolving and the make-up of the family changing. These families do not provide the supportive and stable environment that helps children to acquire the skills, education and motivation so that they might work their way out of the cycle of poverty. The poor are also isolated from the centres of decision-making about their lives and do not involve themselves in political activities or join groups that might exert political influence.

Because of these experiences, the poor feel cut off from the sources of power in society. The poor tend to be fatalistic believing quite correctly that they have little control over what happens to them and thus become resigned to the degrading and unpleasant conditions in which they live. The culture of poverty is also marked by a present-time orientation—a tendency to seek gratification in the present and not worry about the future. Long-range plans and goals are secondary to pleasurable pursuits in the present.

Despite the popularity and intuitive appeal of the culture of poverty theory, it has come under considerable attack. Some (Coward *et al.*, 1974) have provided data which suggest that the characteristics of the culture of poverty are less common among the poor than suggested by the theory, and that these characteristics may be part of the culture in numerous groups in society rather than simply a result of poverty. Others (Ryan, 1971) have objected to the individualistic, 'blame the poor' aspect of this theory which ignores the lack of opportunity, the discriminations and the prejudice that causes much poverty.

Townsend (1979) has pointed out five problems with Lewis's theory and work:

1. The research method was individual-oriented and uncontrolled.

> Because behaviour was described almost wholly through unstructured individual self-histories, it was inevitable that the patterns of elaborate social organization and in particular the influence upon individuals and communities of values, beliefs and institutions which are nationally or regionally controlled, should have gone largely unexamined and even unremarked. He concentrated on the family and not the subsystems and forces of the wider society as the principal unit of analysis. (p. 67)

2. Many of the criteria of poverty—apathy, fatalism, inferiority, despair—were formulated in terms of middle-class values, and chosen to contrast with them.
3. The criteria used to distinguish the sub-culture of poverty were ambiguous, inexact and unquantified. Lewis distinguished between those who belonged to the sub-culture of poverty and a larger class of those who lived in poverty, but did not state the non-tautological reasons for this separation.
4. The evidence from a number of studies failed to confirm Lewis's findings: 'Much of the evidence presented by Lewis was inconclusive. He emphasized the limited parochial interests and the lack of class-consciousness of people with a culture of poverty, and yet large parts of the testimony in his books suggest the contrary' (p. 69).
5. The theory is inconsistent because on the one hand it suggests that poverty is perpetuated by socialisation and social control, but suggests that many of the supposed values of the sub-culture are not accepted by its members. That is, because it can be shown that certain features continue from one generation to another, it does not imply that they have internal (within-group, socialising) causes but could equally be external.

Lewis correctly reported many of the stresses and penalties of life for the poor which affect styles of living. But what he did not do was to distinguish clearly between working-class culture and a sub-culture of poverty and relate these to the 'structure' of deviance in society. Neither did he begin to disentangle the effects upon behaviour of a simple lack of resources from other cultural influences. (p. 70)

The three theories outlined above—minority group, functional and sub-cultural—though hotly debated, have contributed most to social psychological ideas and research. This has occurred mainly because each has specified various *behaviours* which are characteristic of, or describe, the poor and may or may not be responsible for the cause and perpetuation of poverty. This is particularly true of the last theory which, because it appears to point out cognitive and behavioural universals in the poor, seemed highly crucial to psychological variables in causing poverty.

Psychologists are also interested in taxonomising and forming typologies as a necessary stage in the description of behaviour. Much of the literature concerning poverty consists in describing deprivation in terms of housing, health, education, work and general life-style. More interesting for the psychologist are attempts to differentiate minority groups living in poverty. Townsend (1979) has identified 13 minority groups as such for a British study:

1. One-parent family. Households in which there was a child, one of whose parents was not resident.
2. Woman and adult dependent. Households in which there were two or

more adults one of whom was an unmarried, separated, divorced or widowed woman who was partly or wholly supporting the other(s) (usually related to her), none of whom was in employment, by means of either income from employment or an unearned income which was larger than that of the dependent(s).

3. Large family. Households in which there were four or more dependent children belonging to the same family.
4. Unemployed. Households in which there was an adult of under 65 years of age who had been unemployed for 8 weeks or more during the previous 12 months, consecutively or altogether.
5. Households affected by the long-term sickness or injury of an adult under 65. Households in which there was an adult under 65 who had been ill or injured for 8 weeks or more and off work during the previous 12 months, consecutively or altogether.
6. Households in which there was a disabled adult under 65. Households in which there was an adult scoring 5 or more according to a special index of disabilty, or scoring 1 or more and having a disablement condition: epilepsy, mental handicap, breathlessness or pain in the chest; difficulty in physical movement; having a severe nervous condition (such as depression, inability to concentrate or sleep); inability to read; inability to hear or join in ordinary conversation.
7. Households in which there was a 'borderline' disabled adult under 65. Households in which there was an adult scoring 1–4 according to a special index of disability, or having a disablement condition (as listed above), or having disability only for certain times of the year.
8. Households in which there was a disabled child. Households containing a child of under 15 years of age who, through illness or disability, had been continuously confined to bed or to the house for at least 8 weeks; those with a disablement condition (as listed above); and those attending a special school, training centre, club, day or occupation centre, out-patients' department etc., for reason of long-term illness or handicap.
9. Households in which there was a severely handicapped adult over 65. Households in which there was an adult of 65 years of age or over scoring 9 or more according to a special index of disability, or had been confined to bed or the house continuously for 8 weeks or more.
10. Households with low-paid female earners. Households in which women aged 21–59 were earning less than £8 gross per week for at least 30 hours' work. This figure was about two-thirds of the median for women.
11. Households with low-paid male earners. Households in which men aged 21–64 were earning less than £14 gross per week for at least 30 hours' work. This figure was a little lower than two-thirds of the median for men of this age.

12. Households in which there was a non-white person.
13. Households in which there was someone born in Eire.

Other sociological writers have attempted to describe different categories of the poor, e.g. the welfare poor, the marginal poor, the working poor. Some have looked at rural dwellers, minority ethnic groups, the young and the old. However underlying nearly all these classifications and typologies is the idea of the difference between the deserving and the undeserving poor. Matza and Miller (1976) in attempting a 'sub-employment' conception of poverty have tried to distinguish the reputable from the disreputable poor. The former consist of:

1. Unemployed individuals who are willing, able and currently available for work and who have taken definite steps in the last month to find a job.
2. Discouraged workers who want jobs but are not looking because they think no work is available, lack the necessary experience or schooling, are too young or too old, or have other personal handicaps making them unattractive to employers.
3. Currently employed family heads and unrelated individuals whose earnings in the previous 12 months were inadequate to lift their households above the poverty threshold.
4. Other currently employed household heads earning less than a poverty income during the preceding year because of intermittent employment, less than full-time work and/or low wages.
5. Workers employed part-time during the survey week not included in the previous category, who want full-time jobs but cannot find them, have been laid off during the survey week, or have some other economic impediment requiring part-time employment.

The disreputable poor include the dregs (such as beggars, tramps, criminals and prostitutes who have been born into poverty and never left it), the immigrants and newcomers (who, because they have no useful employable skills or financial resources to avoid gravitating to slums), skidders (addicts and perverts who have fallen from higher social niches) and the infirm (those who have moved downwards because of age, injury or illness).

Others have drawn up similar typologies but have failed to explain where the types are similar and where different with regard to the causes and consequences of their poverty. These taxonomies have been based either on economic or government classification schemes or sociological concepts and are of not great interest for the psychologist who is more interested in behaviour differences.

PSYCHOLOGICAL THEORIES FOR THE CAUSES OF POVERTY

There are many reasons why the obvious joke about psychological theories of poverty being poor theories in psychology are true. First, poverty is a relative economic concept which is too broad and heterogeneous a concept for psychologists. The poor include children, the aged, the unemployed, the handicapped, mentally ill people, migrants etc., some who have always been poor, others who have recently become poor. That is, there are quite distinct poverty groups like the welfare poor, the marginal poor and the working poor. Because of some (seemingly arbitrary) cut-off point they are all classified as poor yet have very little in common psychologically. Secondly, poverty is almost always a consequence of (or at least a correlate of) some other variable such as socioeconomic class, intelligence etc., or some other set of variables which psychologists are more experienced at measuring and theorising about. Psychologists are highly sensitive to moderating and intervening variables that come between individual and group differences and poverty. Thirdly, and perhaps most importantly, psychology (even social psychology) is not aimed at analysing macro-sociological variables such as poverty and has neither the appropriate level of theoretical and conceptual analysis nor the most appropriate methodological tools for analysing poverty. Social psychology is concerned with the individual and the social and economic system within which he is enmeshed so that it may be useful in explaining why some individuals from poor homes remain poor while others do not, but cannot explain the existence of mass poverty over time. Psychology theories and variables have indeed been applied to the poor with a moderate degree of success but they are of necessity never sufficient (and possibly not even necessary) to explain poverty however it is defined. Few, if any, psychologists would be as naive or arrogant to suggest that poverty can be fully understood or eradicated by psychological factors alone. By concentrating on beliefs, expectations, values and motives, psychology is not asserting the pre-eminence of the behavioural over the economic, political or sociological factors, but merely suggesting that they too have an important role to play.

Poverty has either been conceived of as an independent or dependent variable. When used as a dependent variable psychologists attempt to isolate psychological phenomena characteristic of the poor and thought to be a consequence of the deprived conditions under which they have lived. This will be discussed under the heading 'The behaviour of the poor'. When used as an independent variable, psychologists attempt to ascertain which beliefs or behaviourable variables contribute to an individual's poverty in some theoretical way. However, to establish that a particular behaviour pattern or belief system is associated with poverty does not imply direction or causality. It may be that, as with so many other aspects of human behaviour, there is bi-directional causality between poverty and various psychological phenomena.

There is no shortage of potentially useful psychological variables (individual differences) which may be used partially to explain the existence and maintenance of poverty. It should be pointed out that none of these variables was constructed specifically to explain poverty but other more general aspects of social behaviour, and seemed pertinent to the problem of poverty. Some of the 'theories' seem self-evident, even tautological, while others offer a unique perspective both in the way they explain poverty and in the way they offer insights as to how to 'remove' it. There has also been some attempts to taxonomise poverty. For instance Rainwater (1970) has offered five perspectives on the poor based on two dimensions: the poor being characterised as weak or strong; and evaluated as virtuous or evil. These taxonomies—such as the deserving and the undeserving poor—are more helpful when it comes to social policy rather than to theorising.

A good deal of psychological research and theorising on poverty has concerned children, as early socialisation and learning experiences have been stressed as very important determinants in understanding the psychology of poverty. The primary (parental), secondary (schooling) and tertiary (peer group) socialising agents are thought to play a central role in shaping how poor people think, act and feel. It has been argued that because a child's academic performance depends heavily upon his internalised mechanisms of emotional self-evaluation (Katz, 1970) and that poor children are more self-critical, they tend to under-achieve at school. But a good deal of the debate in this area has concerned the hereditability of various traits and skills among the poor. For one school (Jensen and Reynolds, 1982) the role of hereditary factors in determining difference in intelligence is both paramount and proven, other schools of thought have maintained that individual differences in mental abilities are determined primarily by the environment. Although the argument has been applied specifically to intelligence and race, some have attempted to consider whether genetic factors contribute to poverty (Crow, 1970; Vandenberg, 1970). Suffice to say that there is no agreement about the importance of genetic factors in determining poverty though it is quite reasonable to assume that they have some effect. Part of the problem with the heredity—environment literature (apart from its complexity and political overtones) is the fact that while it may be shown that either or both genetic and hereditary factors determine certain traits and abilities (intelligence, dexterity, strength) it is yet another conceptual step to explain how these traits and abilities relate to poverty.

Perhaps the most interesting pyschological work has been done on personality correlates of poverty. A number of factors—many of which are related—have been isolated.

1. Time Perspective and Delay of Gratification

A number of researchers since and before Oscar Lewis (1961) have pointed out the present-time orientation and short-time perspective in the poor. Allen (1970) has argued that 'the literature review indicates that the assumption that the poor have shorter time perspective is rather untenable in the light of empirical findings' (p. 247) because of confounded variables (age and ethnic origin with class), weak methodology (projective techniques and story-telling) and equivocal results. Allen (1970) is also disparaging of the more extensive research on postponement of gratification which is a concept akin to impulse control and ego strength. A person's ability to postpone gratification (delay immediate, less valued goals for the sake of later, more valued goals) is supposed to reflect a more mature personality orientation in which the pleasure principle is superseded by the reality principle. In a recent summary of the extensive literature (much of it his own work) Mischel (1981) notes:

> Two contrasting patterns of delay and impulsivity have been conceptualized as extreme poles. On one end is the individual who predominantly chooses larger, delayed rewards or goals for which he must either wait or work. This person is more likely to be oriented toward the future and to plan carefully for distant goals. He also is apt to have high scores on 'ego control' measures, high achievement motivation, to be more trusting and socially responsible, to have a high level of aspiration, and to show less uncontrolled impulsivity. This extreme pattern resembles what has been called the 'Puritan character structure'. Socioculturally, this pattern tends to be found most often in middle and upper (in contrast to lower) socioeconomic classes, and in highly achievement-oriented ('Protestant ethic') cultures. This pattern of high ego strength is also related to a relatively high level of competence, as revealed by higher intelligence, more mature cognitive development, and a greater capacity for sustained attention.
>
> At the opposite extreme is the individual who predominantly prefers immediate gratification and declines the alternative of waiting or working for larger, delayed goals. Correlated with this is a greater concern with the immediate present than with the future, and great impulsivity. Socioculturally, this pattern is correlated with membership in the lower socioeconomic classes, with membership in cultures in which the achievement orientation is low, and with indices of lesser social and cognitive competence. (p. 47)

As ever, not all the published studies confirm the association between delay of gratification and poverty but the theoretical formulation seems sound and the results encouraging.

2. Need for Achievement

Since the work of Murray in the 1930s various researchers have been interested in achievement motivation (McClelland, 1961). Achievement is considered an individual motive that includes concern for meeting and excelling various social standards of performance. There is a rich and fairly complex literature on need for achievement. For instance researchers have distinguished between the motive to achieve success (as measured by TAT stories) from the motive to avoid failure. At the very outset of this research investigators stressed the relationship between this personality disposition and actual behaviour in a variety of settings over time. McClelland (1961), however, extended the concept to a societal level and attempted to find relationships between the achievement level of a society (as measured by, for instance, children's stories) and the economic development of that country.

Many studies done on children and adolescents have shown as predicted that the need for achievement is lower in the poor and the working class (Rosen, 1959). Similarly achievement motivation appears to be correlated with upward social mobility. Although the literature in this field is fairly clear (albeit slightly tautological) three problems are apparent. First, there is the ever-present problem of mediating variables such as intelligence, age and race, which have been demonstrated to mediate between achievement motivation and socioeconomic states. Secondly, there are very real problems in measuring achievement motivation by the unreliable, and often biased, projective techniques most often employed. Thirdly, although McClelland (1961) has offered an aetiological account of the origin of achievement motivation (see Chapter 8) there is very little work that attempts to assess the direction of causality when it comes to the relationship between poverty and the need for achievement.

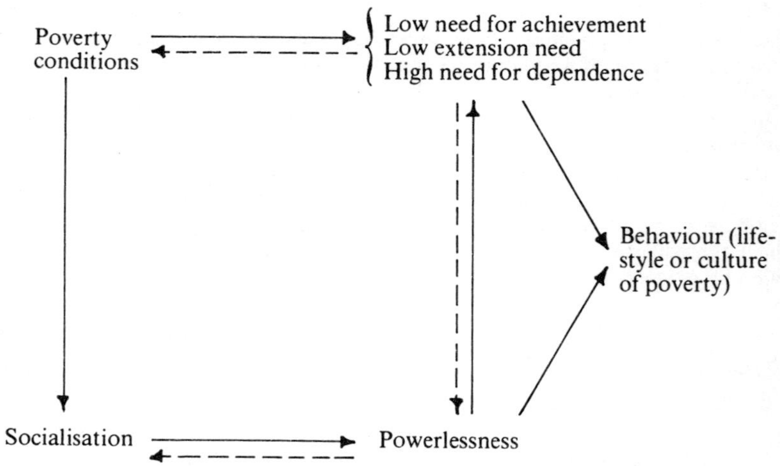

Figure 5.1: A representation of the culture of poverty

Reprinted by permission of the publisher from Pareek, in Allen: *Psychological Factors in Poverty*, Markham, Chicago, 1970.

Pareek (1970) has attempted a conceptual relationship between motivation and poverty. He provided a paradigm for the culture of poverty, reproduced in Figure 5.1. He also noted some of the consequences of low need achievement: disproportionate risk-taking (very low); interest in chance not control; lack of interest in feedback; seeking the company of friends not experts; and lack of activity and initiative.

Research in various parts of the world—e.g. India (Singh, 1983), West Germany (Ray and Kiefl, 1984)—continues to be done on the relationship between achievement motivation and poverty though the literature is highly equivocal indicating that achievement motivation is often high in poor countries (e.g. India) and low in rich countries (e.g. West Germany)

3. Locus of Control, Just World and Related Beliefs

One of the most popular concepts in cognitive social psychology is that of locus of control—general expectancies regarding one's ability to control one's life. People who believe that most life-events are consequent upon their actions (behaviour, personality) are said to have an 'expectancy of internal control' while people who believe events in their lives to be controlled by luck, chance, powerful others or powers beyond their control or comprehension have an external locus of control. Numerous studies in the 1960s showed that poor, ethnic, lower socioeconomic and other deprived groups had greater external locus of control beliefs than 'normal' groups. However, as in so much of this research, it is unclear whether these beliefs are a cause or consequence of poverty. What is most likely is that there is bi-directional causality and a spiralling effect whereby poverty leads to external control beliefs which in turn help to maintain and increase poverty. Gurin and Gurin (1970) have reviewed the not inconsiderable research on beliefs about expectation and poverty. They conclude:

> Perhaps the overall impression from the expectancy literature we have reviewed is one of complexity, contradiction and tentativeness of our knowledge in this area.... Success experience and reality changes in opportunities probably can be used to raise the expectancies on low expectancy people. Second studies consistently stress that this be done under conditions where a person feels that the successes come from his own skill and competence. The literature on internal and external control indicates that effects of success and failure are not very reliable when a person feels they do not depend on his own actions. (pp. 97–8)

A related concept is 'just world' beliefs which relate to the idea that the world is a predictable and controllable place in which people get what they deserve. People who hold just world beliefs tend to blame the victim for his fate irrespective of the factors causing the problem. Thus the non-poor with just world beliefs see the poor as lazy and undeserving. Furthermore if the poor themselves have just world beliefs (which is a cultural norm; Lerner, 1980) they would tend to derogate themselves with the probable consequence that they lose face and develop a poor self-concept. Once again the direction of causality between just world beliefs and poverty is not clear.

There are other related beliefs like anomie, the Protestant work ethic (see Chapter 8) and conservatism, which overlap with locus of control and just world beliefs and which operate in much the same way. That is, it may be expected that external locus of control, unjust world, anomie, low Protestant work ethic and non-conservative beliefs contribute to the maintenance of poverty in the poor, while those with the opposite belief system may escape poverty.

4. Self-Concept, Self-Esteem and Self-Worth

Phenomenological theorists have long stressed the importance of the self-concept (a product of social learning) in the determination of social behaviour. Developmental studies have attempted to determine what factors lead to the development, stability and change of the self-concept. Most studies have hypothesised that people from disadvantaged groups (the disabled, the poor, ethnic minorities) will have a more negative self-concept than the general population because of a number of factors—defence against anxiety, admission of inadequacy, reference groups. For Allen (1970) the results remain equivocal. However a review by Burns (1981) on the psychological literature on the self-concept suggests that it may be a very

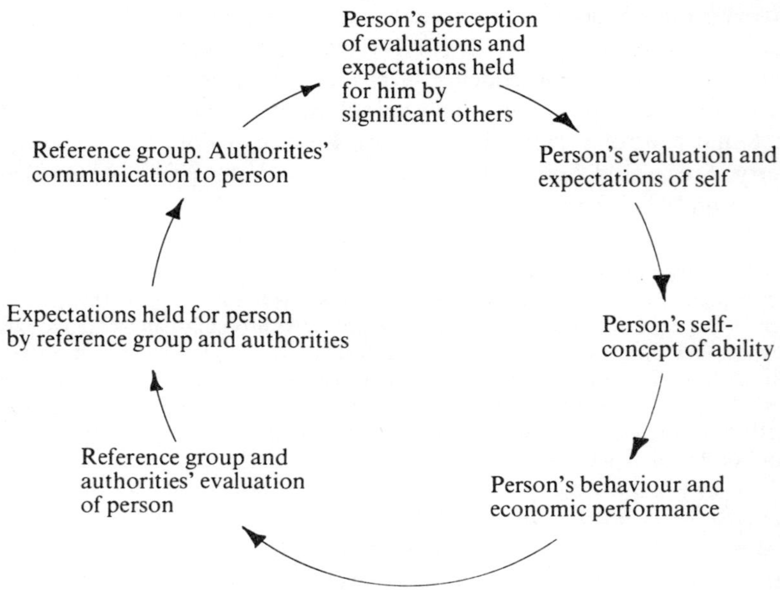

Figure 5.2: The circular process of self-concept, behaviour and feedback

Reprinted by permission of the publisher from Burns: *The Self Concept*, Longman, Harlow.

important factor in helping to explain the origin and maintenance of poverty. For instance, work on the relationship between school children's self-concept and their manifest behaviour perceptions and academic performance shows that successful students are typically characterised by self-confidence, self-acceptance and stable feelings of adequacy, personal competence and personal regard, while unsuccessful students tend to have feelings of uncertainty, low self-regard, self-derogatory attitudes and strong inferiority feelings. The research points strongly to a circular or feedback process which may be generalised to explain poverty. For instance the process may be represented as in Figure 5.2.

Overall the psychological theories are interesting, perhaps necessary, but certainly not sufficient. Most are individual personality theories rather than social psychological theories, which are perhaps not appropriate for understanding the interdependence between the individual and the social and economic system, and the specification of intervening processes. Personality dispositions are clearly important in determining some aspects of poverty, while situational variables clearly predominate in other areas. Most importantly psychological theories need to take into account the well-established problems in social psychological theorising: bi-directional causality, confounding and intervening variables, and the non-linearity (curvilinearity, bi-modality) of variables.

EXPLANATIONS FOR POVERTY

As well as explicit, coherent theories for the causes of poverty found in a variety of disciplines (economics, sociology, political science, psychology) there is a fairly considerable literature on lay or everyday explanations for poverty. Some studies are fairly simplistic national surveys where people are asked to attribute poverty to internal or individualistic causes vs. external or societal factors. For instance, a 1945 Opinion Research Survey in America asked a representative sampling 'Why are some of the people always poor?' Relatively few people mentioned economic, political or structural factors such as employment conditions or educational differences; most spoke of lack of effort and initiative, money mismanagement, weak character, or related causes. Other studies have been more restricted in their scope, sample and methodology but have shown similar results.

Perhaps the most thoughtful and careful work on poverty has been the studies of poverty in America. Feagin (1975) asked over 1000 Americans to rate the importance of 11 reasons why some people were poor in America. Table 5.1 shows his results.

More importantly Feagin categorised these explanations into three groups:
Individualistic (which places responsibility for poverty on the behaviour of

poor people); structural (which places responsibility on extreme society and economic forces); and fatalistic (which places responsibility on luck and fate). Furthermore, the results showed various socio-religious, racial, regional, age, income and educational differences. Groups with the largest concentrations of persons giving high priority to individualistic explanations were:

White Protestants and Catholics,
Residents of the south and north-central regions
The over-50 age group,
The middle-income group,
Groups with middle levels of education.

In contrast, the groups with the largest proportions ranking high on structuralism were:

Black Protestants and Jews,
The under-30 age group,
The low-income group,
The less well-educated.

Feagin (1975) argued that as long as Americans tend to individualise their economic and social problems, attempts at redistributive reform will be

Table 5.1: Reasons given for poverty by 1000 Americans (per cent)

	Very Important	*Somewhat important*	*Not important*
1 Lack of thrift and proper money management by poor people.	58	30	11
2 Lack of effort by the poor themselves.	55	33	9
3 Lack of ability and talent among poor people.	52	33	12
4 Loose morals and drunkenness.	48	31	17
5 Sickness and physical handicaps.	46	39	14
6 Low wages in some businesses and industries.	42	35	20
7 Failure of society to provide good schools for many Americans.	36	25	34
8 Prejudice and discrimination against Negroes.	33	37	26
9 Failure of private industry to provide enough jobs	27	36	31
10 Being taken advantage of by rich people.	18	30	45
11 Just bad luck.	8	27	60

Americans' explanations of poverty

Importance	*Individualistic*	*Structural*	*Fatalistic*
low	7	18	11
medium	40	60	71
high	53	22	18

impossible. He argues that individualistic views reflect 'false consciousness and mesh well with establishment attempts to maintain the *status quo*, whereas structural interpretations lend themselves to attempts at counter-ideologies and at structural reforms in this society' (p. 126).

Feagin's work was important for a number of reasons. First his *a priori* classification of explanations into three groups has received fairly considerable backing from factor analytic studies (Feather, 1974; Singh and Vasudeva, 1977; Furnham, 1982b). Secondly, his study has been replicated in a range of countries: India (Singh and Vasudeva 1977), Israel (Rim, 1984), Britain (Furnham, 1982b,d), and Australia (Feather, 1974). Thirdly, the variables that apparently discriminated between explanations for poverty (e.g. religion, age, education) have proved equally discriminatory in other studies. Those variables which have shown most discriminatory power with regard to beliefs about poverty have been income and social class, age, rural/urban background, education, ideological beliefs, religion and to a lesser extent, sex. Fourthly, he found that explanations for poverty are systematically linked to attitudes to welfare so suggesting that people hold coherent theories about both the causes of and cures for poverty. Consequently, Feagin's work inspired a great deal of further work in the field concerned mainly with which other variables determine explanations for poverty.

Feather (1974) who replicated this experiment in Adelaide, Australia, was interested in both a cross-cultural comparison and generational differences between parents and their children. He found that Australians were generally less likely than Americans to blame poverty on individualistic reasons, though the pattern of explanations was fairly similar. There were some significant differences in the 11 explanations for poverty offered by the subjects, who were differentiated according to religion, sex, occupation, education and income, though the major differences were between the two age groups (over 75 per cent of the explanations). Younger subjects were less likely to blame poverty on individualistic factors and did not obviously support the Protestant work ethic. However, Feather suggests that other values and beliefs as well as macroeconomic factors should also be considered in attempting to predict people's explanations of the causes of behaviour.

> In affluent societies, however, members may believe that there is plenty to go around and that, even though the poor have brought misfortune upon themselves, they should have some part of the plentiful resources that are available. One's reactions to inequalities would therefore depend upon the sometimes harsh economic and social realities of how much is available and whether it can be increased, as well as upon the dominant values, attitudes and modes of causal attribution that have emerged as complex products of one's socialization. (p. 215)

The idea that socialisation is important in explanations for poverty was demonstrated by Furnham (1982d) who found that English public schoolboys (traditionally from richer middle-class homes) found individualistic explanations for poverty more important than comprehensive schoolboys (from poorer working-class homes) who in turn found societal explanations more important. This is consistent with other studies looking at the effects of schooling on values.

A study by Singh and Vasudeva (1977) in India and a very extensive EEC study on the 'Perception of Poverty in Europe' (Commission of the European Communities Report, 1977) by and large substantiated the findings of Feagin (1975) and Feather (1974) on demographic factors associated with explanations of poverty. The Indian study considered similar age, education and income-related differences but few religious differences. The European study considered how people in the EEC saw and explained poverty. Overall the most common causes of poverty were believed to be—in rank order—poor luck, laziness and lack of willpower, injustice in society. However as Table 5.2 shows, there were considerable differences—the Italians and French tended to blame societal factors, the British and Irish the poor themselves, and Danes fate. Overall the better educated, and the better off most often blamed social injustice, while the less well educated and non-leaders tended to blame the poor.

The percentage in brackets after the country's name refers to the percentage of people in the respective countries who maintain that they have seen people in poverty.

Others have related intelligence and personality to explanations for poverty. Rim (1984) found that extraverts and neurotics and the more intelligent prefer societal and fatalistic explanations for poverty in Israel, while introverts, non-neurotics and the less intelligent prefer individualistic explanations.

Another variable which has received some attention is political beliefs and poverty explanation. Many have suggested that left-wing people (and post-materialists) are more inclined to put down poverty to social causes while the right-wing are more likely to blame the victims. As predicted Furnham (1982b) found Conservative (right-wing) voters found individualistic explanations for poverty more important than Labour (left-wing) voters, who in turn found societal explanations more important than Conservatives, though fatalistic explanations showed no difference between the groups and were not rated as important in explaining poverty. Using a simpler questionnaire concerning the attribution of poverty but a more elaborate measure of political beliefs, Pandey *et al.* (1982a) found as predicted that those politically neutral and right-wingers attributed poverty more to individual habits and ability as well as fate than the left-wing activists, who in turn attributed poverty in India more to governmental policies and the economic dominance of the few in society. Williamson (1974a and b) has proposed an ideological self-interest theory which predicts a negative cor-

Table 5.2: Percentage of people rating explanations for poverty in their own country.

Italy (59%)		*Luxembourg* (50%)		*France* (40%)	
1. *Deprived childhood*	63%	1. Drink	55%	1. Old age and loneliness	50%
2. *Lack of education*	47%	2. Laziness	39%	2. *Deprived childhood*	44%
3. Too many children	36%	3. *Deprived childhood*	30%	3. *Ill health*	38%
4. *Ill health*	31%	4. *Lack of education*	29%	4. *Lack of education*	37%
5. Laziness	29%	5. *Ill health*	27%	5. Chronic unemployment	36%
6. Old age and loneliness	28%	6. Old age and loneliness	23%	6. Drink	31%
7. Lack of foresight	19%	7. Too many children	19%	7. Too many children	26%
8. Drink	15%	8. Chronic unemployment	13%	8. Laziness	15%
9. Chronic unemployment	9%	9. Lack of foresight	10%	9. Lack of foresight	15%
Germany (39%)		*Ireland* (36%)		*Belgium* (31%)	
1. *Deprived childhood*	47%	1. Drink	65%	1. Old Age and loneliness	46%
2. *Ill health*	42%	2. Chronic unemployment	56%	2. *Ill health*	43%
3. *Lack of education*	41%	3. *Ill health*	42%	3. *Deprived childhood*	39%
4. Chronic unemployment	38%	4. *Lack of education*	32%	4. Drink	29%
5. Old age and loneliness	32%	5. Old age and loneliness	31%	5. Laziness	28%
6. Drink	31%	6. Laziness	25%	6. Chronic unemployment	26%
7. Laziness	30%	7. Too many children	23%	7. *Lack of education*	24%
8. Lack of foresight	18%	8. *Deprived childhood*	16%	8. Lack of foresight	20%
9. Too many children	17%	9. Lack of foresight	8%	9. Too many children	13%
United Kingdom (27%)		*Netherlands* (18%)		*Denmark* (14%)	
1. Laziness	45%	1. *Deprived childhood*	43%	1. Drink	49%
2. Chronic unemployment	42%	2. *Lack of education*	33%	2. *Ill health*	46%
3. Drink	40%	3. Chronic unemployment	33%	3. *Lack of education*	44%
4. *Ill health*	36%	4. *Ill health*	32%	4. Chronic unemployment	42%
5. Too many children	31%	5. Drink	29%	5. *Deprived childhood*	42%
6. Old age and loneliness	30%	6. Old age and loneliness	24%	6. Old age and loneliness	14%
7. *Lack of education*	29%	7. Lack of foresight	22%	7. Laziness	14%
8. Lack of foresight	21%	8. Too many children	16%	8. Too many children	10%
9. *Deprived childhood*	16%	9. Laziness	11%	9. Lack of foresight	7%

Source: EEC Report (1977, p. 70).

relation between socio-economic status and the perceived motivation of and support for aid for the poor.

Most, but not all, of the studies in this area have considered the causes of poverty among unspecified groups. Furnham (1982b) has argued that as different groups in a society are differentially likely to experience poverty, various explanations become salient in explaining these differences. This is also true of different historic periods. Thus Huber and Form (1973) asked a sample of Americans why they thought people went on social security during the Great Depression. Only 4 per cent cited individualistic explanations, yet asked why people had taken social security during the previous six years, 54 per cent cited individualistic reasons. Similarly Furnham (1982b) asked his subjects to imagine a poor person from one of four groups: black/white; middle/working class and then explain why they were poor. It was established that explanations that may seem salient for one target group are not necessarily so for another. Although there was considerable agreement on the causes of poverty among those groups most susceptible to it, people began to differ radically in the causes of poverty ascribed to groups not usually thought of as poor.

Finally, although it is not always easy to do so, some attempts have been made to verify public beliefs as to the causes of poverty. Feagin (1975) pointed out that figures available indicated that the public were wrong—or at least vastly overestimated—the amount of people lying about or having illegitimate children to increase their social security payments. Similarly Goodwin (1973) found that the middle class tended to underestimate the work values (ethic) and life aspirations held by the poor. Indeed a considerable amount of psychological (Allen, 1970) and sociological (Davidson and Gaitz, 1974) research has demonstrated few differences in attitudes, beliefs and values between the poor and those not so badly off. Goodwin (1973) did a path analysis on the relationship between education, age, the work ethic and the perceived motivation of and support for aid to the poor. Naturally those who believed in the work ethic believed the poor to be badly motivated and did not want to support them. They conclude that the work ethic is a fundamental element in popular ideology and that its change could lead to numerous important results.

ATTITUDES TO THE POOR AND THOSE ON SOCIAL SECURITY

A number of studies have attempted to explore both the range, structure and determinants of beliefs about the poor as well as which individual difference and demographic factors best predict these beliefs. Most of the studies have shown a predictable pattern of findings. For instance studies have shown a weak but noticeable relationship between class and images of the poor, the middle class being more negative than the working class (Rainwater, 1968). Similarly Williamson (1974 a and b) noted that older subjects were more negative about the poor than the young, although this could reflect cultural and historical changes. Osgood (1977) noted that rural dwellers had more negative beliefs about the motivation of the poor and were less likely than urban dwellers to support welfare programmes. Some evidence suggests that religious beliefs are related to attitudes to the poor—the more religious the more negative, and Protestants more than Catholics are negative about the poor (Feagin, 1975). Other variables which may relate to attitudes to the

Table 5.3: Just world beliefs and attitudes towards poverty

	Just world beliefs			
	Low	*Mid*	*High*	*F level*
1. By pouring money into poverty programmes we are destroying the very thing that made this a great and prosperous country—competition.	6.14	5.87	4.64	10.63_c
2. Though I know that their condition is not always their fault, I find poor people unpleasant to be with.	5.35	5.75	4.80	3.83_a
3. I can't understand why some people make such a fuss over the disadvantaged state of the poor. Most of them could improve their condition if only they tried.	6.32	5.70	4.75	10.42_c
4. In this country almost everyone can make it if they try hard enough.	6.28	5.62	4.10	20.25_c
5. Some people feel that extreme poverty in this country is largely the fault of the poor. By and large, this is true.	6.42	6.29	5.08	12.00_c
6. Stealing is more excusable among lower-class children than it is among children from middle-class homes.	4.92	5.02	4.67	0.48
7. Somehow I can't blame a poor man for hurting a rich man as much as I blame a rich man for hurting a poor man.	3.92	4.56	4.35	0.79
8. Although we don't like to face it, most people on social security are lazy.	6.17	5.62	4.83	5.89_b
9. Pouring money into poverty programmes is crippling the national economy and asking too much of people who have worked hard to get what they have.	6.35	5.54	4.70	9.19_c
10. To solve the population problem and to make life more pleasant for the poor, they should not be permitted to have more than a couple of children per family—that is, there should be compulsory birth control based on income level.	6.07	5.81	4.77	6.57_b
11. I am in favour of a government-guaranteed minimum annual income—that is, nobody would receive less than a certain income per year.	2.14	2.97	2.78	1.64
12. Kindness, generosity and love are characteristics found more among the poor than among the wealthy.	3.75	4.54	4.35	1.17

$_aP < 0.05$; $_bP < 0.01$; $_cP < 0.001$.
These scores are the mean on a 7-point agree–disagree scale: 1 = agree; 7 = disagree

poor include self-esteem, anomie, inter-personal trust and authoritarianism (Davis *et al.*, 1984).

A number of studies have been based on the Attitude to Poverty scale developed by MacDonald (1971). For instance, attitudes to poverty have been shown to relate to the Protestant work ethic (MacDonald, 1971a), political affiliation (Wagstaff, 1983), birth order (MacDonald 1971b) and just world beliefs (Furnham and Gunter, 1984). Thus people who believe in a just world tend to be negative in their attitudes. The results of Furnham and Gunter (1984) are given in Table 5.3.

In a review, Davis *et al.* (1984) have pointed out three major shortcomings of the literature on attitudes to the poor. First, most studies have considered how people explain poverty or how the poor behave, but not how respondents felt about appropriate remedies for poverty. Secondly, studies have looked at demographic determinants of attitudes to the poor rather than the influence of personality and general attitudinal variables on specific attitudes and behaviour relating to poverty. They also believe an important gap in the literature concerns the link between prejudice towards minority groups and attitudes towards the poor which has important implications for how beliefs might be changed.

In an attempt to rectify this omission Davis *et al.* (1984) examined attitudes towards poverty among a large representative sample (N = 2359) in Ireland. They examined the relationship between personality characteristics (e.g. self-esteem, anomie), general social attitudes and beliefs (religiosity, national pride, state efficacy) and attitudes and beliefs about poverty (fatalistic causes of poverty, belief in lack of ambition). In contrast to previous results, poverty was more likely to be attributed to fatalistic causes than to individual traits of the poor. General social beliefs and attitudes to poverty were related to the demographic variables where age was the best discriminator, and personality variables where social alienation and authoritarianism were the best discriminators.

> Overall, there was a tendency for those who endorsed dispositional causes of poverty also to express more individualistic or dispositional beliefs in general. Thus they were more likely to indicate prejudice towards travelling people, belief in innate tendencies, national pride and national deprecation ... The common poverty was seen to be the greater the likelihood that it was attributed to social, structural, or fatalistic causes. Conversely, the less common it was seen to be, the greater the likelihood that it was attributed to dispositional causes. (p. 160)

Overall, the respondents were very positive about improving social welfare benefits. Those with more fatalistic beliefs about the causes of poverty were more likely to consider improving social welfare to be important and familiar, though most respondents believed the idea of improving benefits difficult.

Despite a great deal of public debate and media coverage on the topic, very little empirical work appears to have been done on the (British) public's attitude toward social security (welfare) recipients. For instance, Golding and Middleton in a thorough, content-analytic study, noted that although welfare news is more extensively covered in the 'quality' media, it is given more prominence in the 'populars', and suggest that it gets widest coverage when meeting news values which stress the importance of crime or political dispute. Furthermore abuse of social security, either by fraud or excessive claiming, is a major theme of news coverage being given considerable attention.

Some British empirical work has however been done. Runciman (1966), as part of a large survey on social inequality, asked people about their attitudes towards government help. He found, as predicted, that both skilled and unskilled Conservatives felt government help in general was sufficient while both Labour and Liberal voters thought that it was not.

Two more recent British studies are worth mentioning. Furnham (1983b) examined the effect of sex, education and voting pattern of over 170 normal subjects' attitudes towards (unemployed) people receiving social security benefits. Both education and vote (but not sex) appeared to be important factors in predicting people's attitudes. A factor analysis of the 12-item questionnaire revealed three clear interpretable factors which indicated that attitudes centred on the difficulty of coping with the amount of benefit provided; beliefs about people being dishonest about their needs and abusing benefit payments; and the loss of self-esteem and stigma associated with being on social security. The results showed that in Britain, just as in America, people not on social security tend to have negative attitudes toward those that are, although they may appreciate some of the problems of the unemployed on social security.

Golding and Middleton (1982) reported on a study concerned with social security benefits and claimants in Britain. They found that people generally feel that benefits are too high and too easy to get. Over 60 per cent of the general population and over 50 per cent of those with experience of receiving benefits believed that people on social security can manage quite well. Over half agreed that there is a stigma attached to claiming benefits, yet they thought too much was spent on social security, while less than a quarter believed too little was spent. Nearly half of the sample believed that it would be better to pay low rates and taxes and let people pay for services as they want them. Older, lower-income groups tended to believe that the British welfare system was something to be proud of, yet approximately three-quarters thought that too many people depended on welfare and that welfare made people lazy. Finally, they found that older people and manual workers were most anti-welfare, 'showing the extent to which living on the edge of the welfare state induces fears that are easily aroused by economic recession and that are most easily articulated in terms of the most readily available mythologies' (p. 168).

Furnham (1985b) aimed, in another study, to investigate simultaneously the effects of eight independent variables (five demographic and three 'psychological') on social security attitudes in order to determine empirically which of the independent variables relate to which dimension of attitudes towards social security. Each of the eight independent variables was chosen according to its salience given previous literature: age, sex, education, vote and income; Protestant work ethic beliefs; conservative beliefs and feelings of anomie/alienation. A factor analysis of the attitudes to social security scale revealed four factors similar to those in previous studies. Analysis of variance showed that vote, Protestant work ethic and conservative beliefs most differentiated subjects' attitudes to social welfare. Furthermore, a canonical correlation analysis revealed three significant variates which showed Protestant work ethic beliefs were associated with beliefs about recipients' dishonesty, age with beliefs about the difficulty of coping, and also with the stigma attached to being on welfare.

Not only are factors similar from different studies but so are the misconceptions surrounding social security. As Coughlin (1982) found in America, there is a widespread misunderstanding in the distinction between social insurance and public assistance which may account for some of the more draconian views expressed. However he also found a paradox in that while there is widespread belief that social security payroll taxes are too high, at the same time a majority of people think the benefits should be maintained or increased. That is, people can be in favour of reduced taxation and improved social security benefits simultaneously; just as some can and do believe that whereas many social security recipients are idle and dishonest, they may experience both stigma and shame on the dole. Thus people appear to be making in the latter case a distinction between the deserving and the undeserving poor. However, this questionnaire—like all those upon which it is based—does not allow for this distinction to be made. Future work in this field may do well to specify in items the *target* of social welfare benefits as this may allow subjects to make the distinction between whom they see to be deserving and who not.

Nevertheless there seems to be a universal dislike and distrust of those on social security who are distrusted, stigmatised and patronised. This is most clear in the consistent attacks on 'scroungers' in the media who are seen as the most undeserving of the poor (Deacon, 1978). But one should not imagine that there is no demand for social welfare (Whiteley, 1981). Taylor-Gooby (1983) has attempted to study the contribution of moralism and self-interest to attitudes to social security. He notes that one should distinguish betwen the various facets of social security. Whereas the general public are in favour of education, a health service and benefits for deserving groups, they tend to be against unemployment benefits and council housing. It has been suggested that these values represent the dominant ideology of the society. In a study of 240 British subjects Taylor-Gooby found benefits for the retired, widows, the sick and disabled, care for the elderly, the National Health Service and education receive strong support, while the unemployed, single parents, the low-paid, those in need of day-care for children, child benefits and council tenants receive little support. Although various other beliefs—the work ethic, beliefs in social justice—related to welfare attitudes, social class, income and age were more closely related to welfare beliefs.

THE BEHAVIOUR OF THE POOR

There is no shortage of findings that have demonstrated that the poor hold different beliefs and behave rather differently from the non-poor. But the establishment of a relationship between poverty and various behaviours is of little importance if it can not explain how specific economic conditions produce which psychological phenomena that may account for the maintenance of the psychological condition. As yet this literature is rather speculative though the pattern may be changing. Traditionally research has considered five correlates of poverty: education (where the poor perform badly), housing (where the poor are inadequately housed and over-crowded), families (which are large and unstable), health (where the poor have worse mental and physical health) and crime (where the poor are disproportionately represented).

Mental and Physical Health

Perhaps one of the most consistently researched topics in this area is the relationship between poverty and mental health in adults (Orford, 1976) and children (Langner *et al.* 1970), as well as poverty and physical health. Reid (1977) reports data showing that there is a linear pattern with regard to health and social class. The lower one is on the social class scale (and hence the poorer) the more likely one is to report long-standing illnesses; take 'illness-days' off work; suffer from tuberculosis, diabetes, influenza, pneumonia and bronchitis; lose all one's teeth in mid adulthood; consult a doctor; commit suicide and smoke cigarettes.

Cochrane (1983) has recently reviewed the literature on class differences in mental health. Studies of individual patients admitted to mental hospitals as well as community surveys on the epidemiology both point to the fact that the lower one's social class the more likely one is to suffer mental illness. Two hypotheses for these findings are considered: social causation—social class is correlated (confounded) with a whole range of other variables (work stress, financial strain) which contribute to the higher rate of psychological disturbance in lower social groups, social selection—psychiatric impairment prevents people from maintaining the socioeconomic position of their family of origin and they decline into poverty. Despite attempts to do the crucial test between these two hypotheses the results remained equivocal

(Dohrenwend and Dohrenwend, 1969), yet the evidence appears to favour the social selection hypothesis. Of course, a major difficulty in this area is diagnosis as it may be argued that the perception of adjustment and maladjustment is relative and evaluative, and often based on the acceptable behaviour patterns of the middle class.

Linguistic Codes

Another area of research first popularised by Bernstein (1964) concerns the use of language. It has been suggested that the poor have a different linguistic system compared with the non-poor. Essentially the linguistic code of the poor is restricted rather than elaborated—it is undifferentiated, simple, implicit, lacking in modifiers and aimed at reflecting and reinforcing social structure and routines rather than at conveying information. Although there has been some criticism of this work (Argyle, Furnham and Graham, 1981) a great number of studies have shown a difference in the use of language between the poor and non-poor.

Personal Relationships

It has been suggested that many of the interpersonal relationships (family, work, public authorities) among the poor are perceived and structured in terms of power and authority (Hess, 1970). This stress on power probably reflects the poor's position in society where they have little or no opportunity to make decisions affecting their daily lives. To have rank or status is to have power. Thus poor parents tend to equate goodness in their children with passive compliance, silence and respect. Techniques of control are based on appeals to norms, rules and status rather than on rational arguments or future consequences of behaviour.

Dependency

There is a fairly extensive sociological literature on the relationship between poverty and dependency (on public facilities and welfare). The poor become dependent on welfare for a number of interrelated pressures: unemployment, illegitimacy, few occupational skills. Burgess (1970) has noted an adult behaviour pattern including child neglect, illegitimacy, promiscuity, abandonment, marital conflict, drinking and criminal behaviour which characterise the deprived and makes them dependent on welfare benefits. More recent studies have shown that the sex of the head of the family on social welfare is a major conditional variable with regard to poverty (Osmond and Grigg, 1978).

Work Behaviour and Attitudes

One of the simplest explanations of poverty is that the poor work less hard than the non-poor. However studies of both work behaviour and attitudes have yielded few, if any, significant differences (Friedlander, 1966; Cook,

1971; Goodwin, 1972). In attempting to control for other variables—such as ethnic group and sex—Davidson and Gaitz (1974) compared the work behaviour and attitudes of urban poor and non-poor in America. Contrary to the popular view and in accordance with previous literature, the poor were as work-oriented as the non-poor.

Crime

Strong individual and aggregate level correlations between poverty and official measures of crime are perhaps among the most firmly established of social science empirical generalizations. However calculated, official crime rates are almost always higher among the poor, and poor people are more likely to be arrested and convicted for a wide variety of offences. Yet the precise mechanisms linking poverty to crime remain elusive. (Berk *et al.* 1980, p. 766)

Part of the problem lies in problems of definition (of poverty and crime), part in making causal inferences from aggregate data, and part in the large number of intervening and confounding variables.

In addition there are a whole range of findings regarding the behaviour of the poor which attest, in some sense, to the idea that there is a culture of poverty. Studies have shown, for instance, that the poor have a deficit of social skills (Beiser, 1965), greater pre-marital sexual experience (Kinsey, 1948) and a lack of financial savings with an inefficient pattern of consumption (Schneider and Lysgaard, 1953).

CONCLUSION

What is often error variance for the economist and sociologist (individual differences) is the focus of interest for the psychologist. Thus whereas economists explain and describe poverty in terms of macro- and microeconomic forces, and sociologists focus on class, institutional and social policy aspects of poverty, psychologists have traditionally looked at such things as attitudes to and explanations for poverty, as well as attempting to isolate factors that discriminate between the poor and the non-poor. Whereas the literature on attitudes and explanations is fairly consistent, coherent and complete, research on behavioural differences has been much less successful.

Behavioural variables that psychologists have focused upon (delay of gratification, locus of control belief) are to be found in the anthropological and sociological literature and appear to be necessary but not sufficient variables to be taken into account when explaining poverty. The problem with the research is essentially threefold. First, the findings from the research have often been inconclusive and contradictory, making it difficult to be certain about the relevance of each variable considered. Secondly, because so few of the studies are longitudinal in nature it is not clear whether the discriminating factors found are a cause or a consequence of poverty. What is most likely is that there is reciprocal causation. Thirdly, it may be argued that psychological research operates at an inappropriate level when it comes to poverty in that it focuses on individual behavioural variables and neglects wider contextual and structural variables which are much more important in explaining poverty.

Nevertheless psychologists have an important role to play in poverty research, which until now they appear to have sadly neglected. The sort of questions that would interest a psychologist include: Why is it that some people from identical socioeconomic backgrounds, with similar educational experiences, etc. remain in poverty while others escape it—indeed even become rich? Why is it that some comparatively well-off people sink into poverty while others do not? Why is it that people with identical incomes define themselves quite differently—the one poor the other not? How can we change attitudes to and beliefs about the causes of poverty and the nature of the poor themselves? What simple behavioural measures can we use to encourage people with unwise spending habits to budget more carefully?

There is no limit to the psychological questions that one can ask with regard to poverty. It has already been explained why psychologists feel uncomfortable with the concept of poverty. Nevertheless their contribution is both relevant and important in understanding a serious social problem.

6 Wealth and Affluence

INTRODUCTION

Whereas there appears to be a wealth of social science (if not psychological) studies on poverty—its causes, consequences, definition, explanations (see Chapter 5)—there has been a comparative poverty of studies on wealth and affluence. This is no doubt due to the fact that whereas poverty is considered to be a major social problem, wealth is not. This is despite the fact that many recognised social problems—drug and alcohol abuse, family disorganisation—are associated with increased wealth (Merton and Nisbett, 1976). Of course since Mill and Adam Smith, economists have been interested in wealth and welfare (Carter, 1971), though all have pointed out the difficulties in defining wealth.

Those studies that have been done on the rich appear to have been done primarily by sociologists (Rubinstein, 1974; Abrahamson, 1980) and economists (Galbraith, 1958; Carter, 1971). There have been countless popularist books on the rich and manuals on how to become rich (Biggart, 1983) some more popular and analytic than others (Veblen, 1953).

There is surprisingly almost no psychological, and particularly social psychological, research in this area. Even economic psychologists (Katona, 1977) have devoted very little attention to the rich, or top asset holders as Katona calls them. The only psychologists who have ventured into this area are psychoanalysts who have been intrigued by the desire to amass wealth.

Table 6.1: Two different but similar estimates of wealth distribution at different periods of time.

Distribution of personal wealth

% of wealth owned by:	*England & Wales* 1923	1938	1950	*United Kingdom* 1966	1971	1978	1979	1980
	%	%	%	%	%	%	%	%
most wealthy 1 per cent	60.9	55.0	47.2	33.0	30.5	23	24	23
most wealthy 5 per cent	82.0	76.9	74.3	55.7	51.8	44	45	43
most wealthy 10 per cent	89.1	85.0	—	68.7	65.1	58	59	58
most wealthy 25 per cent	—	—	—	86.9	86.5	83	82	81
most wealthy 50 per cent	—	—	—	96.5	97.2	95	95	94
least wealthy 50 per cent	—	—	—	3.5	2.8	5	5	6

Source: Noble, Structure and Change in Modern Britain (1981), reproduced in *New Society*, 6 October 1983 from 'How Much Inequality', Institute of Economic Affairs.

Wealth ownership, 1911–13 to 1970 per cent of total personal wealth (based on mortality rates corrected for social class)

Proportion of adults		*England & Wales Adults aged 25 and over (as presented by Lydall and Tipping)*				*Great Britain Adults aged 15 and over (estimates from Inland Revenue)*		
		1911–13	*1924–30*	*1936*	*1951–6*	*1960*	*1965*	*1970*
	%	%	%	%	%	%	%	%
Top	1	66	60	56	42	39	34	31
	5	86	83	81	68	64	62	56
	10	90	90	88	79	76	75	70
Bottom	90	10	10	12	21	24	25	30

Source: 1911–13 to 1951–6: Lydall and Tipping (1961, p. 92). 1960 to 1970: estimates from *Inland Revenue Statistics* in: Polanyi and Wood (1974).

There is, of course, considerable popular interest and writings about the rich who fall into a number of categories, a few who made their wealth in entertainment and the media (pop and film stars, novelists), entrepreneurial or corporate wealth attainers, and the landed wealth owners. Statistics about the rich reveal how few there are.

Table 6.1 shows two different but comparable estimates. To consider the more recent estimate (Noble, 1981), it seems that in 1980 the top 1 per cent of people owned 23 per cent of the marketable wealth and the top 5 per cent, 43 per cent of the wealth. Although the pattern of distribution has changed over the last 50 years it is not so much between the rich and the poor, but between the top 1 per cent and the top 5 per cent of the rich. This perceived inequality has led to considerable debate as to how to change this relationship.

THE REDISTRIBUTION OF WEALTH

Although social stratification and economic inequality have long been topics of interest for sociologists, there have been comparatively few empirical studies on people's perceptions of a fair wage and the distribution of wealth. That is, although there are numerous demographic and econometric studies on the actual distribution of wealth and the factors which determine that distribution, there is much less on what people believe to be fair and equitable.

Some studies have shown consistent but predictable differences across cultures (Robinson and Bell, 1978) in beliefs about equity and distributive justice. Indeed equity theory—the relationship between inputs and outputs—is central to a good deal of social psychological theorising. Similarly, the nature and concept of distributive justice is well known in philosophy and ethics. Most researchers in this field have attempted to find general rules of distributive justice in a society while also looking at individual differences in preferences and the rationalisation of observed inequalities.

Alves and Rossi (1978) set about investigating the consensual normative framework for judging the fairness of distributions of earnings in the USA. A large sample were asked to judge to what extent people in certain jobs and households with specific salaries were either under, over or equitably paid. Predictably not all characteristics play equal roles in justifying earnings: occupational attainments count more than educational attainments, and husbands' characteristics count more than wives'. As with other findings in this area subjects tended to judge the very richest as over-paid and the very poorest as under-paid irrespective of all other factors. Low income is thought of as unfair despite low levels of merit (occupationally/ educationally) while the highest wages could not be justified on any ground. 'Need' therefore appears to play an important role in judgements. Married persons and those with children tend to be rated as underpaid more than unmarried or childless people with identical characteristics and income:

> In sum, respondents were both more generous and more democratic than public policy and the empirical income distribution. The ceilings in earnings represented by the computed social maxima are well below the earnings of the affluent. At the same time fair earnings for persons on the bottom of the occupational and educational pyramid are set higher than poverty-level definitions. Implicitly respondents define an equitable earnings distribution that has a higher mean and a lower variance (Alves and Rossi, 1978, p. 557)

Analysis of individual differences of the respondents showed that higher-status respondents allowed more earnings for additional increments in education and occupational attainment of the hypothetical target people, while low-status respondents give considerably more earnings for each additional child. Thus high-status respondents 'stretched out' the inequality in what they believe to be a fair distribution of earnings while low-status respondents 'shrunk' that inequality.

In a Belgian study aimed at devising a mathematical model to predict attitudes towards the redistribution of wealth (via incomes), Overlaet and Lagrou (1981) found very much the same results as Alves and Rossi (1978)—namely, a desired decrease of the incomes for occupations with 'high' pay, and an increase in income for 'low'-pay occupations, but a maintenance of the income structure. From their study of 161 individuals' judgements of the fair (equitable) income of 12 occupations they were able to devise a regression model which allowed for the calculation of how much each individual favours redistribution, the extent to which an alteration in the income structure is desired, and the reference point used to determine which incomes have to be moderated and which not. Some of their more interesting results suggested that the more a person earns the higher he draws the line between high and low incomes. There is a 'preference drift effect' such that as people get used to a high standard of living they consider this level a minimal welfare level. Furthermore the mean income subjects' estimate for themselves is somewhat higher than for the mean of the population as a whole. People then do not use the same criteria in evaluating fairness for themselves and fairness in others.

By and large, studies on the perceived equitable redistribution of wealth are fairly consistent. People appear to favour a reduction in the range (the rich get less and the poor more), an increase in the mean income, but a higher than average income for themselves. Idealism then, does appear to be tempered by some desire to improve one's lot. Precisely how one may redistribute wealth to fit these many noble sentiments is, of course, not at all clear.

ATTITUDES TO THE RICH

Whereas there have been lots of studies on attitudes to poverty (see Chapter 5), there have been very few studies on attitudes to the rich. Those that have been done have nearly always been a response to debates over taxation.

Lewis, Sandford and Pleming (1979) completed a survey in two cities in Britain (Bath and London) of over 200 people in each on their perception of wealth and the wealth tax. Asked whether a wealthy person was one who earned a high income, owned a lot of property and had substantial savings, or both, most people chose the second option (property and savings, rather than income). This result seemed independent of age, sex, social class and political preference. They found that 44 per cent of the respondents said that to be rich a person needed an annual income of £15–30,000. However, when asked the question: 'What would the total value of a person's savings and possessions need to be before you considered them to be wealthy?' nearly 80 per cent believed it less than £100,000. This is much the same result as that found by Furnham (1983e). Items considered part of a person's wealth included land, antiques, jewellery, stocks and shares, but national savings certificates, life assurance policies and pension funds were not considered part of a person's wealth.

Asked what their attitude to a wealth tax was, 27.5 per cent thought it a very poor idea and 18.5 per cent a fairly poor idea, while only 8.5 per cent thought it a very good idea. This response was independent of age, class, sex, marital status, income and home ownership, but not party political preference. Predictably Conservative supporters thought the wealth tax a poorer idea than Labour supporters. The respondents were also asked that if a wealth tax were introduced, it should be in addition to, or a substitute for, top rates of income taxation. Most respondents believed that it should be a substitute, but replies depended on whether people were in favour of the wealth tax, and least evident for those in favour. Overall it seemed that the an additive tax but this trend was most evident for those who were against a wealth tax, and least evident for those in favour. Overall it semed that the respondents felt that the wealthy had not worked harder than others, although they were perceived as more skilfull, luckier and having had the benefit of help from others.

Respondents who considered a wealth tax a good idea, or were uncertain about it, were *more convinced* that people who inherit wealth should be taxed more heavily. Respondents who thought the wealth tax a poor idea were *largely undecided.* Those people who considered a wealth tax a poor idea consistently and accountably agreed that the wealthy should keep their wealth and *disagreed* that there should be a more even distribution of wealth in the UK.

People who considered a wealth tax a good idea or were uncertain *agreed* there ought to be a more even distribution of wealth in the UK. People who considered a wealth tax a poor idea *disagreed* more that inheritances of property or large sums of money were unfair. People who were uncertain whether a wealth tax was a good idea, or were convinced that it was not, *agreed* more that people should be able to pass on their wealth to their children without it being heavily taxed. People who thought a wealth tax a good idea, or were uncertain about it, felt *more strongly* that people who spend their money on lavish entertainments should be taxed more severely than those who save and invest. People who thought a wealth tax a poor idea *agreed* more that the lower paid would not benefit from a wealth tax. The authors conclude:

> Public opinion is notoriously conservative, in that it is resistant to change. It would be very surprising indeed if this survey were to record a demand for the introduction of a new and radical policy especially one relating to an increase in taxation. Consequently some reviewers of the public opinion and attitude literature argue that it is the Government's role to lead public opinion rather than follow it. Nonetheless the Labour party would do well to heed the findings of this investigation as it provides evidence germane to specific proposals such as the wealth tax threshold, whether the new tax should be in addition to or a substitute for the top rates of income tax and an indication of what forms of wealth people feel most strongly should benefit from concessions or better still be outside the wealth tax base altogether.... Similarly the Labour party should note that the introduction of a wealth tax, should it occur, would not only be met by the customary degree of indifference but also with antipathy, a reaction which would not be restricted solely to the wealthy. (p. 54)

Attitudes to the rich may of course differ from one country to another. For instance in a study of equality, success and social injustice in Britain and America, Robinson and Bell (1978) found that the belief that a person has the standard of living that he deserves reduces egalitarian attitudes more in

Britain than America, This may be due to the British belief that British society is just in that social arrangements reflect fair rules of competition. Further, while of no importance in Britain, the cultural belief in monetary success reduces egalitarian attitudes in America and functions as the belief in the just society does in Britain.

PSYCHOANALYSIS AND WEALTH

As it is pointed out in Chapter 4, psychoanalytic writers have long been interested in money. But some have attempted to explain the drive or need to amass wealth. Fenichel (1944) considered both normal and abnormal drives to become wealthy. He suggests a number of quite different motives:

1. The rational motive which argues that the more money one possesses, the better one can satisfy ones needs.
2. The power motive which argues that wealth is a source of power sought by those who are fearful of impoverishment and loss of love: 'The original instinctual aim is not for riches, but to enjoy power and respect, whether it be among one's fellow men or within oneself' (p. 96).
3. The possession motive which suggests that one accumulates money to regain in fantasy those possessions which one has (faeces) or might lose (genitals).
4. The self-preservation motive which suggests that one needs wealth to generate wealth and eliminate competitors and hence one consistently strives to keep ahead.

The essay relies a great deal on the association between the anal period experiences (i.e. potty training) and subsequent attitudes to and habits of money usage. Because money is equated with faeces one can explain terminology such as 'stinking rich', 'filthy lucre' and understand why the discussion of money and money-related matters are considered indelicate. Furthermore the anal obsessions (cleanliness, orderliness, time-keeping) of famous rich men (such as Howard Hughes) becomes understandable.

All rational and irrational attitudes to money are seen as arising from unsolved anal erotic conflicts:

> One thinks of kleptomaniacs, or of the women who drain men of their resources, to whom money, which they are always striving to take away, symbolizes a whole series of introjected objects that have been withheld from them; or of depressive characters who from fear of starvation regard money as potential food. There are too those men to whom money signifies their potency, who experience any loss of money as a castration, or who are inclined, when in danger, to sacrifice money in a sort of 'prophylactic self-castration'. There are, in addition, people who—according to their attitude of the moment towards taking, giving, or withholding—accumulate or spend money, or alternate between accumulation and spending, quite impulsively, without regard for the reality significance of money, and often to their own detriment

(sometimes unconsciously desired). In the unconscious mental life money can represent not only possessions but everything that one can take or give; therefore it can represent relations to objects in general and everything through which the bodily ego feeling and with it self-regard can be increased or diminished. (pp. 99–100)

Like all psychoanalytic thinkers Fenichel (1944) draws heavily on medical, anthropological and historical examples. Every psychological event (such as the accumulation of wealth) is explained as the resultant interplay between biological structures and environmental influences (social institutions). But because environmental influences change over time, the drive to accumulate wealth exists only in certain definite social epochs.

Other psychoanalytic ideas are to be found in the chapter concerning the psychology of money.

TYPOLOGIES OF THE RICH

Although psychologists have not paid much attention to the rich there appears to be an insatiable curiosity among the general (western) public about them. Galbraith has in fact noted that wealth has never been a source of honour in itself as it must be advertised through obtrusively expensive goods. Hence there are a number of journalistic articles and books about money, the rich, etc. Some of course are much better (more insightful, better documented) than others. Many have attempted to classify the rich either according to their motives or their habits recognising that as a group the rich fall into many quite distinct categories.

Wiseman (1974) classified money types into eight different categories which he describes and discusses at some length. However he does note that it is only the predominant characteristics of a person that means he goes into one category or the other, and that overlapping may occur.

All the categories that I am postulating are open-ended and fluid, but I believe it can be shown that there are patterns in people's money behaviour which can be related to their character make-up, and that there is a sufficiently constant correlation between character and behaviour to justify speaking of money types. (p. 74)

1. The Romantic

The romantic idealises and overestimates his favourite love—money: 'To him money is applause, vindication, approval, the expression of fate's favouritism' (p. 74). These types derive the sort of satisfaction from accumulating wealth as others get from art, religion and scholarship. He is, according to Wiseman, the visionary inventor or pioneering entrepreneur.

2. The Company Man

This type denies the joy of making money, and does so anonymously on behalf of others. They claim they are skilled at making money (for others) and do so out of duty or responsibility. There appears to be guilt when talking about money.

3. The Collector
Collectors enjoy the mathematics of their money. They enjoy the investing and accounting aspect of money watching it reproduce itself. Closely aligned to Freudian conceptions of the anal personality, this type also denies the source of interest in money.

4. The Hustler
The hustler does not suffer guilt about his desire to accumulate money. They are enterprising, energetic, aggressive often unethical, pursuers of money. Heros to some, but swindlers to others, the hustler is somewhat emotionally and socially unstable.

5. The Double-Dealer
As the name implies they are clever amoral, confidence tricksters. Although not all may be rich, they are psychopathic individuals whose joy is often as much in the defrauding or stealing from another as it is in the money itself.

6. The Criminal
As the name implies, this person is simply a criminal and a misanthropist. He will do anything for money and appears to be quite unmoved by acts of cruelty or revenge.

7. The Gambler and Loser
The gambler has a real expectation of winning and risks sums, the loss of which would hurt him. This person has the repetitive compulsion to lose (either consciously or not) and so sees rapid rises and subsequent falls in wealth.

8. The Non-player
This person may have wealth thrust upon him as he does not seek it and indeed often shuns it.

The variety of uses, abuses and symbolism of money makes such typologies useful. Wiseman has noted some of these as well:

> There is blood-money and bride-money, conscience money and stolen money, easy money and money that has been earned by the sweat of the brow, money to burn and money as the prize of merit; there is money that is a king's ransom and money that is a whore's pay; there is money to squander and so much money as will make it difficult for its possessor to get into heaven; there is the mistress's allowance and the wife's due; pocket-money, spending money, hush money, and money in the bank; there are the wages of sin and the bequests of rich uncles; there is the price that

everyman has, and the pricelessness of objects, and the price on the outlaw's head; there are the forty pieces of silver and also the double indemnity on one's own life.

Behind its apparent sameness lie the many meanings of money. Blood-money does not buy the same thing as bride-money and a king's ransom is not the same kind of fortune as a lottery prize. The great exchangeability of money is deceptive; it enables us to buy the appearance of things, their physical form, as in the case of a 'bought woman', while what we thought we had bought eludes us. (pp. 13–14)

WEALTH AND HAPPINESS

Psychologists, sociologists and economists, as well as moralists and theologians, have been interested in the relationship between wealth and individual happiness.

There are, of course, many famous biblical quotations warning one about the dangers of materialism and wealth accumulation, e.g. (1) 'The righteous man will flourish, but the man who trusts in riches will wither' (Proverbs 11.28); (2) 'Keep life free from the love of money' (Hebrews, 13.5); and (3) 'Woe to you that are rich' (Luke 6.24). There are also various teachings about money and the rich which are discussed in Chapter 4 on the psychology of money.

There are two sorts of studies that are relevant to wealth and happiness: there are studies looking at the relationship between income and job, as well as life, satisfaction. The literature on pay and job satisfaction is by no means unambiguous. Certainly better-paid workers are more satisfied, but pay is confounded with type of job, social status, intrinsic nature of the work, etc.

Studies done in America have found no relationship either cross-sectionally or longitudinally for a strong positive relationship between money and happiness (Campbell, 1981). Lane (1983) has proposed three principles to explain this relationship:

1. *Adaptation level theory.* Thus although one might feel 'happier' by a recent increase in the standard of living, one soon adapts to this and the positive relationship disappears.
2. *Social comparison theory.* This theory suggests that people's standards of wealth are determined by comparisons with kin, peers etc., and thus if they all rise together (over time) the relative difference disappears and so as people get wealthier over time they do not become any more happy.
3. *Declining marginal utility of money.* As the supply of money increases other values like freedom, true friendship become relatively more valuable.

Thus the power of any increment of money decreases with affluence. Lane noted that there is always a much stronger relationship between income *satisfaction* and life satisfaction, than between *actual* income and life satisfaction. Furthermore the aspirations and expectations of people, as well as their perceived position with regard to others, is important in predicting happiness. Of course, there are many other social, cultural and economic factors which affect life satisfaction hence making comparative studies of income and happiness difficult. Thus education which is associated with greater consciousness of self with particular emphasis on weaknesses and lesser concern for objective circumstances tends to be associated both with increased income (better-paid jobs often require considerable training) but less satisfaction with self and a special sensitivity to missed opportunities.

Money may make one less worried about some things but more worried about others.

> But the main effect of income is in changing the nature of worries. There is a difference between those who worry about things over which they think they have control, such as their work, and over those things which are less controllable, such as death. Those who worry about relatively controllable things are happier than those who worry about the uncontrollable. Increased income is associated with shifting worry to the more uncontrollable elements of life, perhaps because income is associated with a sense of control over one's fate. Equally important is the shift that income brings in another aspect of substantive worry: from financial, job and health problems to interpersonal and characterological problems, the kind of person one is. As it turns out, this shift helps to explain some of the waning power of money to buy happiness in rich societies. Over the 1957–76 period, the concerns of Americans shifted from role identities, greatly affected by income, to 'a more personalized self-consciousness', where income is less relevant. An increase in national income, like an increase in personal income, shifts the axis of worry to interpersonal dimensions where money has less power to relieve worries. In this sense, personal and national income first buy happiness through relief of some major worries, but increased income also alters the dimensions of worry toward a field where income loses its significance. (Lane, 1983, pp. 25–6)

Thus Lane's conclusion is that happiness or life satisfaction is most closely related to self-esteem and belief in one's own effectiveness, neither of which is necessarily related to income. Although money may reduce material worries, concerns with psychological matters, 'Happiness and life satisfaction are too various to be captured in money's golden net' (p. 27).

Others have gone further. Fromm (1980) has argued that the pursuit of wealth and happiness is based on two fundamentally mistaken psychological principles: radical hedonism—the aim of life is maximum pleasure which is the satisfaction of any desire or subjective need a person may feel; and that egotism, selfishness and greed, as the system needs to generate them in order to function, lead to harmony and peace. Fromm distinguishes between the mode of having and the mode of being, the former of which confuses material possessions, power and wealth with the latter mode which leads to growth, creativity and satisfaction. Central to this religious/ascetic view is the idea that 'Security, sense of identity, and confidence based on faith in what one *is*, on one's need for relatedness, interest, love, solidarity with the world around one, instead of on one's desire to have, to possess, to control the world and thus become the slave of one's possessions' (p. 167). Fromm freely admits that his ideas are not new but found in religious, philosophical and political writings in many countries over various historical periods. The theme of this work is not that money never leads to happiness but that the sole pursuit of money can never lead to happiness. One consistent piece of evidence cited by people who do not believe that wealth necessarily brings happiness and that is the observation that wealthy men—such as Lord Nuffield in Britain—attempt to attain public honour and social esteem by lavish gifts to universities, etc. which is something the accumulation of wealth alone cannot bring but which is clearly very important.

A second source of information on the relationship between wealth and happiness are studies on people attaining sudden or unexpected wealth. There is in the sociological literature the concept of the anomie of affluence. Simon and Gagnon (1976) have extended Merton's formulation of the causes of anomie thus. Anomie results when culturally prescribed *goals*, such as education or material wealth, are disassociated from acceptable *modes* for realising these goals, such as availability of schooling or employment. Basic to any notion of the anomie of success is too easy access to the modes or avenues of achieving the societally determined goals. More people than ever have the possibility of access to these legitimate modes, which leads them to question both their commitment to these goals and the gratifications that they bring. Hence they see the rejection or moderation of the achievement motive (and the desire to accumulate wealth) as an expression of the transition from the anomie of deprivation to the anomie of wealth. Like Merton (1938) they devised a typology of adaptive responses to the anomie of affluence. Briefly they are these:

1. *Optimal conformist.* People committed to the major goals of society and experience their realisation as gratifying (upwardly mobile, Conservative).
2. *Detached conformist.* People who find the sources of gratification associated with achievement adequate but are not particularly committed to the goals.
3. *Compulsive achiever.* People totally committed to achievement but lacking a capacity for experiencing the congruent gratifications.
4. *Conforming Deviant.* People who have acquired the means of gratification seek out new (and often illegitimate) modes of gratification.
5. *Detached People.* People who have an dispassionate rejection of both the values of achievement and the gratifications attending it.
6. *Escapists.* People who reject the values of achievement and accept innovative and possibly deviant styles of gratification.
7. *Conventional reformed.* People who combine a desire to replace the major goals of society with an acceptance of the qualities of life that constitute the content and style of a successful life.

8. *Missionary.* People who wish to replace the major goals of society but also reject the qualities of life associated with current views about success.
9. *Total rebel.* People who desire to replace both the goals of the social order and the quality of life associated with success within that order.

Diagrammatically this typology may be summarised as in Table 6.2.

Table 6.2: Typology of Adaptive Responses

Type	*Commitment to the goals of society*	*Gratification by goal, achievement*
1. Optimal conformist	Plus	Plus
2. Detached conformist	Minus	Plus
3. Compulsive achiever	Plus	Minus
4. Conforming deviant	Plus	Innovative
5. Detached person	Minus	Minus
6. Escapist	Minus	Innovative
7. Conventional reformer	Innovative	Plus
8. Missionary	Innovative	Minus
9. Total rebel	Innovative	Innovative

Source: Simon and Gagnon 'The Anomie of Affluence: A Post-Mertonian Conception', *American Journal of Sociology*. 82, The University of Chicago Press, 1976.

Abrahamson (1980) examined the effects on lottery winners in American state lotteries. He tried to establish the amount of anomie experienced by the winners a year or so after their win, and also their general commitment to strive for future attainments. He found, as predicted, a positive but small relationship between size of winnings and anomie, however the larger, indirect effects of large winnings appear to be anomie-reducing. The magnitude of winnings are positively related to gratification permissiveness, and inversely related to future aspirations: 'Thus increased desires do not seem so brutalizing: the appetites, when whetted, do not seem to result in detachment. High anomie is, rather, the price that is paid by those who resist a readjustment in their consumatory styles' (p. 56). It is argued that sudden wealth only leads to alienation or anomie when the society is prudist, restrained and respectable and the failure to restrain indulgent impulses may eventually produce a sense of bondlessness and detachment.

In a somewhat atheoretical but interesting study of pools winners in Britain, Smith and Razzell (1974) asked 89 winners a number of questions. They found that people spent their money on such things as property, cars, consumer durables and travel. Nearly 60 per cent invested more than half of their winnings. Of the 70 per cent in full-time employment before their win only 17 per cent remained in full-time employment after. The questions on problems and happiness resulting from the win revealed rather ambiguous results. Winners reported that people in general were more hostile than their relatives and friends to their win (16 per cent vs. 8 and 6 per cent, respectively), while relatives were most positive (47 per cent) and other people least (24 per cent). Compared with a control group, twice as many separated from their spouse, (8 per cent) and five times as many divorced (14 per cent). However it is possible that the greater incidence of divorce amongst pool winners is that they can afford to legalise a separation which previously would have been beyond their financial means. When asked if they ever felt lonely, the pools winners tend to be at extremes—more of them claimed never to experience loneliness or to feel it often, while people in the control group tended to cluster in the middle ranges. Thus while a number of winners suffer acutely from the effects of the win, the vast majority adapt themselves successfully to their new situation. Indicators of health suggested that, if anything, the pools winners were healthier than the control group, possibly because of the security that the money brought them. Of course it should be pointed out that most of these winners in fact came from working-class groups where financial insecurity is probably greater.

LAY EXPLANATIONS OF WEALTH

Despite the paucity of psychological research into wealth and the wealthy there have been a number of studies on lay perceptions of financial success. Although these have been done in different countries and with very different populations the results are remarkably similar.

Younger *et al.* (1977) asked a group of Canadian undergraduates to account for how a certain person 'got to be who and what he is'. In the financially successful condition he was described as earning $100,000 per annum; in the average condition he was described as earning $12,000 per annum; while in the failure condition he was described as unemployed. The students viewed the financially successful person as least responsible, and the failed person as most responsible for their condition. The successful person was seen as luckier than either the average or failure person but not more hardworking than the average person. The subjects did however believe that if the 'target' person were asked to account for his own success or failure the successful would attribute his achievement to personal and/or situational factors, while failures would attribute their circumstances primarily to situational factors. The authors point out that as the subjects come predominantly from an 'average' background their explanations may serve a self-protective function:

> If one assumes that a high level of observed success functions as a threat to the subject's self-concept or self-esteem, then a conceivable strategy would be to attribute the performance to extrapersonal causes. Such a defensive posture would no doubt serve to minimise feelings of one's own inadequacy or that of one's family. (p. 513)

In an American study of over 1000 male workers Vecchio (1981) found that people who expressed external locus of control beliefs were themselves less wealthy, less well-educated, less satisfied with their job, and more likely to be black than workers who expressed internal locus of control beliefs. However a study such as this could not determine whether locus of control beliefs were the cause or consequence of wealth and poverty.

In a large British study, Lewis (1981) looked at the relationship between political beliefs/voting patterns and attributions for wealth. Overall the respondents felt that the wealthy had been luckier than others (54 per cent agreement), had received more help from others (60 per cent agreement), rather than having worked harder (26 per cent agreement), although they generally made more skilful use of their opportunities (52 per cent agreement). However as predicted, more right-wing voters (Conservatives) as opposed to left-wing voters (Labour Party supporters) believed that wealthy people make more skilful use of their opportunities or generally worked harder.

In a similar study on a group of British subjects Furnham (1983e) hypothesised:

1. Conservative voters would find individualistic (effort and ability) explanations for wealth across the general population as more important than Labour voters, who would find societal factors more important.
2. A different pattern of explanations would emerge depending on the social class and race of the group from which a wealthy person came.
3. Definition of wealth would differ according to the sex, education and voting patterns of the subjects.

Fifteen explanations for wealth were offered, and subjects were requested to rate them on a 7-point scale.

The results support the hypothesis that Conservatives would find positive individualistic explanations for wealth, more important than Labour voters, who in turn find societal factors that maximise inequality more important than Conservatives. Thus Conservatives believe that rich people are more hard-working and thrifty (have more effort and ability) than do Labour Party supporters. However the latter believe the rich to be significantly more ruthless and determined than do Conservative voters. That is, Conservatives support individualistic explanations when they portray the wealthy in a positive light, whereas Labour Party supporters support individualistic explanations for wealth when they portray the rich in a negative light.

Similarly Labour voters believe that the rich had better opportunities, and are more favourably treated by the tax and economic system than Conservatives. Yet Conservatives believe more than Labour voters do that society rewards those who work hard and take risks. Liberal and other voters varied considerably, rating explanations similarly to the Con-

*Table 6.3: Means of the three voting groups for the general expectations for wealth in Britain**

Explanations	*Conservative*	*Labour*	*Liberal/other*
Individualistic			
1. Careful money management throughout life	2.62	3.59	3.20
2. Hard work and great effort among the rich	1.89	2.78	1.76
3. Being very intelligent	3.78	4.35	4.58
4. The rich are ruthless and determined	4.41	3.17	4.44
Societal			
1. Very high wages in some businesses and trades	2.34	2.25	2.58
2. Being sent to certain schools and universities	3.91	3.60	3.61
3. Better opportunities for people from certain families	3.49	2.57	3.15
4. The taxation system favours the rich	5.25	3.34	4.69
5. Strong trade unions that get higher wages	4.61	4.78	4.37
6. The economic system automatically creates inequality	4.28	2.85	2.62
7. Society rewards those who work hard and take risks	3.19	4.54	3.84
Fatalistic			
1. Inheriting wealth from parents or relatives	1.44	1.09	1.22
2. Good luck in winning money at gambling	5.43	5.21	5.84
3. Having a lucky break	2.88	3.10	3.28
4. Being born with good business sense	2.50	2.95	2.78

*Low scores indicate high importance, i.e. the 7-point scale 1 = Important, 7 = Unimportant

Reprinted with permission from *Personality and Individual Differences*, 1983, Furnham, 'Attributions for affluence', Pergamon Press.

servatives in the individualistic explanations 2 and 4 and similarly to Labour voters in societal explanation 6, and midway between the two in individualistic explanation 1, and societal explanations 3, 4 and 7.

These explanations differed for different groups, however. Thus it was that there appeared to be very little difference between subjects in explaining wealth among blacks, while there was a considerable difference in explaining wealth among the whites. There were only three significant differences (one sex, and two education effects) in explaining wealth among working-class blacks, and no significant inter-actions. All the subjects believed that luck, business sense and intelligence were the most important factors to account for wealth among working-class blacks. Yet there were a number of differences between the subjects in their explanations for wealth among the middle-class whites, arguably the group most likely to achieve wealth. Apart from one significant sex and two education main effects, there were seven significant vote effects. They paralleled almost exactly the pattern of significant differences found in the explanations for general wealth—namely, Conservatives found positive individualistic explanations more important than Labour voters, who in turn found societal explanations more important than Conservative voters.

Two other results were of interest. A factor analysis of the scales revealed the same three economic explanation diversions that had occurred earlier: individualistic, societal and fatalistic. Although there were no significant differences in the estimates of the annual income of the rich the results are interesting in themselves. However the figures in Table 6.4 indicate that subjects appear to believe that the annual income of rich people is about ten times that of the poor, and those able to 'live decently' about 2½ times that of the poor. Similarly the subjects seem to discriminate on a sex basis, though these results are not significant.

Table 6.4: Estimates of the approximate annual income of different categories of people

	Estimated annual income (£)		
	Poor	Live decently	Rich
Single man	2103.00	5349.00	21.666.00
Single woman	2022.00	5156.00	19.965.00
Man, wife and two children	3719.00	9215.00	31.500.00
Single parent and one child	3007.00	7082.00	26.218.00

Reprinted with permission from *Personality and Individual Differences*, 1983, Furnham, 'Attributions for affluence', Pergamon Press.

These estimates are, of course, crude indices of perceived wealth. Many other variables associated with the target person—age, age of their children, nature of their accommodation, financial commitments, savings, etc.—may be important in estimating their annual income. Yet there appeared to be relatively little variation in the subjects' estimates.

Forgas *et al.* (1982) did a similar study in Sydney, Australia, though with a larger sample and somewhat different analysis. The first part of this study was based on a content analysis of the answers to the free-response question 'Indicate the six most important reasons, in order of importance, why you think some people are better off financially than others'. They found that by far the most important explanatory category used by subjects were family background variables (inheritance, good schooling), social factors (strong taxation), individual effort (hard work, savings) and luck (gambling).

Subjects made a total of five sets of attribution judgements for wealth, with the target being (1) a person in general, (2) a native-born working-class person, (3) a middle-class person, (4) a migrant middle-class person, and (5) a working-class person.

Attributions to external/social causes such as taxation and the economic system were not affected by the target's class and ethnicity: these explanations applied uniformly to all target characters. It is interesting that attributions to internal/individual causes, such as thrift, hard work and business sense, were significantly more likely to be made when the target was a migrant, rather than a native-born Australian. This tends to confirm the common Australian stereotype of migrants as being particularly hard-working and motivated, in contrast with the easy-going, *laissez-faire* attitude of native-born Australians. The third attributional category, family advantages (inheritance, good education, etc.), was significantly more likely to be used as an explanation of wealth in native-born rather than migrant, and middle-class rather than working-class targets. The interaction of class and ethnicity on this variable indicates that family background was mainly seen as an important cause of wealth in native-born middle-class targets. Finally, the fourth attributional category, luck/risk-taking, was significantly more likely to be seen as a cause of wealth in working-class rather than middle-class targets, irrespective of ethnicity.

Certain individual differences in attributions for wealth were also found. The most powerful deterrents were voting preferences, nationality and education. Finally Forgas *et al.* (1983) found that Australians estimated the necessary income of a 'wealthy' person to be considerably higher than the British estimates of Furnham (1982b). British subjects believed that considerably less income was sufficient for decent living than did Australians, while about twice as much income is necessary to be considered wealthy in Britain than in Australia.

These studies have important implications. What is particularly surprising is the significant and consistent differences between migrant and native-born subjects found here. Migrants to countries like Australia come from a variety of backgrounds, yet they appear to be unified in their belief that individual effort is a significant source of wealth. Migrants are also more likely to be seen by others as having acquired wealth through individual effort, and they have more limited estimates for income levels necessary to be 'wealthy'. The ideology of individual achievement is of course a well-known component of the migrant experience. It is still interesting to note that the Protestant ethic finds its most devout followers not among the predominantly Anglo-Saxon native population, but within the heterogeneous migrant community.

CONCLUSION

A surprisingly large number of people have as their primary hope and desire becoming rich. What they define as rich, and how they wish to spend their wealth are very variable. Despite this there is a surprising dearth of psychological interest in wealth. Those studies that do exist are simply applications of standard social psychological theories—attribution theory (lay explanations of wealth), equity theory (the distribution of wealth)—to the acquisition and distribution of wealth. Those studies which have considered individual differences have usually restricted themselves to demographic factors (age, sex, class, income) rather than considering any psychological factors (social beliefs, attitudes). The fact that wealth is not a social problem does not mean that it does not merit good research.

7 Unemployment: An overview of the Social and Applied Psychological Literature

INTRODUCTION

Research into the psychological consequences of unemployment, like unemployment in the western world itself, tends to be cyclical. The two major periods of research activity followed periods where unemployment increased dramatically—the 1930s, and the 1970s and the 1980s. Most of this research has been done in Britain, Europe and America but there are exceptions (Feather, 1982 a, b). The fact that research has been done in two periods nearly 40 years apart means that interesting and important comparisons can be made. Jahoda (1982) has noted

> If it were found that modern unemployment was psychologically less disturbing now than in the past one would conclude that the standard of living to which the unemployed were then reduced—subsistence level and often below—had a greater weight in shaping their experiences than the absence of a job, which would emerge as a matter of secondary importance. If, on the other hand, the modern unemployed showed similar psychological disturbances under unquestionably better living conditions than in the past, economic deprivation would count for less and the absence of employment for more in explaining their experiences. (pp. 15–16)

What is perhaps most striking about the literature is that studies have revealed a substantial amount of similarity whether focused on physical or mental consequences of unemployment; irrespective of where conducted, at what period of time or with what specific population.

This chapter will attempt an overview of the major findings in the unemployment literature. Though diverse in terms of where, when and how research was conducted, an attempt has been made to address the topic under broad general headings.

EARLY RESEARCH IN THE AREA

Although there has been sporadic research into unemployment for a very long time (Rowntree and Lasker, 1911) the psychological literature dates back to the 1930s which saw the highest levels of unemployment in most European countries this century (Bakke, 1933; Jahoda *et al*, 1933; Beales and Lambert, 1934). In a review of the literature, Eisenberg and Lazarsfeld (1938) listed over 100 references from Europe and America which had investigated aspects of unemployment. Most of the early literature constituted in-depth case studies of individuals or communities which had suffered unemployment. Many of the themes in these various studies coincided and have been actively pursued today. Two of the most important psychological effects of unemployment that were identified by nearly all the researchers were the sense of social stigma attached to being unemployed, and the suffering resulting from the lack of structure that people experience (Kelvin and Jarrett, 1985).

The most celebrated research in the 1930s is probably the study of Jahoda *et al.* (1933) on a small Austrian village, Marienthal. Although an unrepresentative town (it was a one-factory village in rural Austria) the study is worth considering in some detail for three reasons. First, it is a surprisingly detailed sociography of an unemployed community which has never been repeated since. Secondly, the basic findings from this study were found in other studies in the 1930s (Komarovsky, 1940) and the 1970s and 1980s (Marsden and Duff, 1975). Thirdly, it demonstrated quite clearly a perhaps counter-intuitive finding that has emerged from studies ever since—namely that unemployment leads more to personal apathy and disintegration than political insurrection or organised revolution.

Fraser (1980) has admirably summarised the findings of Jahoda *et al.* (1933) which are worth repeating. He lists the findings under seven headings:

1. *Finances.* Despite the fact that wages in the area had already been low, unemployment brought consistent reductions in income. The system of paying unemployment relief and assistance made this a necessity. Unemployment relief was payable for a period of about 6 months, then discretionary emergency assistance could be provided for a further period of up to a year. The maximum relief permissible was 80 per cent of wages in the last week of work; in turn, the maximum emergency assistance possible was 80 per cent of the relief.

   There were numerous ways in which families failed to be eligible for maximum benefits, but even if they were eligible, within 6 or 7 months of unemployment the most they could receive was slightly less than two-thirds of their previous, generally low, wages. Many families were even worse off. From the figures in the report I estimate, in a necessarily rough and ready way, that the plight of an unemployed Marienthal family of, say, two parents and three children might be compared with that of a similar British family having to live, in 1979, on less than £20 per week, i.e. between one-half and two-thirds of the weekly maintenance grant of a university student.
2. *Material aspects of life-style.* Obviously drastic economies of all sorts were absolutely essential. Standard items of food, such as coffee and butter, were replaced by cheaper alternatives. Carbohydrates dominated at meal times. Only 30 per cent of families had meat on at least two days per week, and over 90 per cent of that meat was either horse or rabbit meat. On the day before the fortnightly payments of

unemployment benefits, approximately half of the schoolchildren took either dry bread or nothing at all for their lunch at school. Even so, so much of a family's budget had to go on food (perhaps up to 90 per cent) that any other substantial item of expenditure, such as shoe repairs, became a major problem.

3. *Physical well-being.* There was evidence of an overall decline in health standards, despite the equally horrifying fact that there was actually improvement, at least in the short run, in the health of some adults, namely those who had been prone to tuberculosis as a result of their working conditions in the mill. Even the children suffered, despite the willingness of the unemployed families to spend a disproportionate amount of their income on milk for their children. During the study, one-third of the children under 14 were rated as being in poor general health. Only 8 per cent of the children had teeth unaffected by caries. There were signs of an inverse correlation between ill-health and family income.
4. *Emotional state.* There were many specific reports of emotionality, upsets, fearfulness, and the like. Many of the men in particular manifested a blunted sense of time relations. 'Apathy', 'despair', 'depression' were terms frequently used to describe the unemployed. The investigators attempted to classify the overall state of the 100 families for whom they had detailed information. They concluded: 16 families were 'unbroken', i.e. they remained positive, even optimistic, in attitudes and emotions; 48 were 'resigned', i.e. they had accepted the realities of unemployment but were still coping well with organising the necessities of everyday life; 11 were 'in despair', i.e. although still attempting to cope with the necessities of daily living, emotionally they were 'broken'; 25 were 'apathetic', i.e. they had given up all attempts to cope either emotionally or practically. Over one-third of the families, then, were regarded as psychologically 'broken'. The emotional well-being of the families showed a positive correlation with the amount of weekly income.
5. *Personal relationships.* In some cases, the crisis appeared actually to have improved marital relations by, for example, leaving husbands free to help around the house or forcing them, through financial pressures, to give up drinking. But those were exceptions. The more general picture was one of an increase in minor quarrels and of reports of withdrawal from social relations and friendships. So there was some, though by no means dramatic, evidence of increased interpersonal strains and difficulties. In fact, close personal relationships appear to have held up more effectively than many other facets of individual and family life.
6. *Social interests and activities.* In general, these decreased markedly. Clearly, some of the decrease, such as visits to Vienna or to the theatre,

reflected financial pressures. But almost all formal social organisations experienced a decline in membership and participation, even when financial outlay was not involved. Inexpensive or free informal activities, such as visiting friends or going for walks, also declined in popularity.

The fate of the village library is instructive. Just before the factory closed, the library, fortuitously, had expanded considerably, and its small borrowing charges were abolished. Yet borrowing dropped markedly, mainly in terms of the number of borrowers, but even in terms of the number of books per remaining borrower. The unemployed did not even feel like reading.

7. *Political activities.* The unemployment, poverty and shattered lives led to no increase in political action. Quite the reverse. There had been a history of political involvement in Marienthal, but all three of the major political organisations suffered marked losses in membership. Since membership fees for the unemployed were nominal, it is unlikely that the primary reason for such loss was financial, a point supported by the fact that the cheaper but more political newspaper lost more readers in the village than the dearer but entertainment-oriented one. A striking demonstration of the fact that those who remained politically active tended to be from the minority of people still in work was provided by the Young Socialist Workers, who retained 37 members, of whom only 7 were unemployed. 'When one of their officers lost his job he resigned from his position and decided to give up politics entirely' (Jahoda *et al.*, 1933, p. 41).

Researchers and reviewers (Fraser, 1980; Furnham, 1982a; Kelvin and Jarrett, 1985) including Jahoda herself (Jahoda 1979, 1981, 1982) have been impressed more by the similarities than the difference in research findings on current unemployment. This is not to say that research is no different now—for instance, very little of the early work was concerned with how people explain the causes of unemployment, unemployment among women, youth unemployment, etc. Furthermore the early research was more concerned with physical deprivation and hardship consequent upon employment, whereas current research has focused more upon psychological (clinical, social) aspects of unemployment. Samples are more representative, methods more sophisticated, analyses more powerful, but the essential nature of the results remains the same.

NATURE AND FUNCTION OF EMPLOYMENT AND UNEMPLOYMENT

One way to attempt to understand why the experience of unemployment is so psychologically detrimental is to attempt to understand the motivational functions of work. The question posed is therefore, 'What are the beneficial aspects of work, the absence of which leads the unemployed to experience so much difficulty?' Jahoda (1979, 1981), following Merton (1957), distinguished between manifest and latent consequences of employment. The manifest aspects of work are simply earning a living, while the latent consequences are unintended by-products of the purposeful action that is necessary to achieve the manifest consequences. The distinction is not unlike that made by Herzberg (1966) in his two-factor theory of job satisfaction. Hygiene (maintenance or dissatisfaction) factors relate mainly to the extrinsic, manifest aspects of employment, while the motivating (satisfaction) factors relate to the intrinsic, latent aspects of employment. While the unemployed quite demonstrably miss the manifest consequences of work such as a (possibly) high standard of income, what is most distressing to them is the latent functions. The latent functions of work include:

1. Work Structures Time

Work structures the day, the week and even longer periods. The loss of a time structure can be very disorienting. Feather and Bond (1983) compared the structure and purposeful activity among employed and unemployed university graduates. They found, as predicted, that the unemployed were less organised and less purposeful in their use of time, and reported more depressive symptoms when compared to the employed.

2. Work Provides Regularly Shared Experiences

Regular contact with non-nuclear family members provides an important source of social contact. There is a vast literature on social-skills deficits which suggests that social isolation is related to disturbed mental states (Trower *et al*, 1978). There is now a growing interest in the social support hypothesis which suggests that social support from family and friends buffers the major causes of stress and increases coping ability, so reducing illness (Gore, 1978). If one's primary source of friends and contacts is work colleagues then the benefits of social support are denied precisely when they are most needed. There are also a wealth of studies in organisational psychology which suggest that one of the most frequently cited sources of job satisfaction is contact with other people (Argyle, 1983).

3. Work Provides Experience of Creativity, Mastery and a Sense of Purpose

'Both the organisation and the product of work imply the interdependence of human beings. Take away this daily experience that efforts must be combined, and the unemployed are left with a sense of uselessness, of being on the scrap heap' (M. Jahoda, 1979). Work, even not particularly satisfying work, gives some sense of mastery or achievement. Creative activities stimulate people and provide a sense of satisfaction.

A person's contribution to producing goods or providing services forges a link between the individual and the society of which he or she is a part. Work roles are not the only roles which offer the individual the opportunity of being useful and contributing to the community but, without doubt, for the majority they are the most central roles and consequently people deprived of the opportunity to work often feel useless and report that they lack a sense of purpose. (Jahoda, 1979; p. 313)

4. Work is a Source of Personal Status and Identity

A person's job is an important indicator of his personal status in society—hence the often amusing debates over job titles such as sanitary engineer for street cleaner! Furthermore it is not only to the employed person that the job gives certain status but also to his family. The employed person therefore is a link between two important social systems—family and home. An unemployed person has lost his employment status and hence identity. Not unnaturally there is a marked drop in self-esteem following unemployment.

5. Work is a Source of Activity

All work involves some expenditure of physical or mental effort. Whereas too much activity may induce fatigue and stress, two little results in boredom and restlessness, particularly among extraverts. People seek to maximise the amount of activity that suits them by choosing particular jobs or tasks that fulfill their needs. The unemployed however are not provided with this possibility and have consistently to provide stimulation to keep them active.

A number of points should be made about this list of the functions of work. First, it is not exhaustive and the functions are not mutually exclusive. Secondly, it is possible that other, even more obvious, functions could be mentioned, such as providing an income. Thirdly, these latent or manifest functions of work can be provided by other social institutions such as societies, clubs, etc., which provide a source of unpaid work. Finally, nothing actually prevents the unemployed from seeking out some of the benefits of work, such as creating a stable time structure to their day, though this may be difficult particularly for those most likely to be unemployed (school-leavers, unskilled labourers).

Another way of understanding the benefits of employment—and by implication the frustrations of unemployment—is to look at the extensive and exhaustive literature on job satisfaction. There are, of course, a number of theories of job satisfaction (Herzberg *et al.*, 1959; Vroom, 1964; Maslow, 1970), but all have focused on certain specific factors. The following list is not exhaustive, neither are the factors in rank order as these differ from one job to another.

Challenging work	Work should be interesting, but not fatiguing.
Rewards for good performance	Clear contingencies between performance and rewards are very desirable.
Verbal recognition	Most persons enjoy praise and positive feedback.
Good working conditions	Physical working conditions should be comfortable and facilitate attainment of work goals.
Concerned supervision	Supervisors should demonstrate their concern with helping employees to attain important goals.
Positive interpersonal relations	Satisfaction is strongly enhanced by friendly relations with co-workers and supervisors.
Effective company policies	These should be designed to aid employees in attaining important work goals.
Job security	Employees should feel that if they perform adequately, their jobs are secure.
Pay	Absolute level is important, but the belief that such benefits are fairly distributed may be even more crucial.
Participation in decision-making	Employees generally feel that they know much about their jobs and should be consulted about them.
Degree of autonomy and responsibility	The greater these are, the higher satisfaction tends to be.
Role ambiguity	Individuals wish to know just what is expected of them; ambiguity should be avoided.

Source: From Baron (1983, p. 214).

Argyle (1983) has divided the causes of job satisfaction into a number of categories: intrinsic (variety, autonomy, use of skills and abilities); hours of work; incentive conditions (pay, occupational status, promotion prospects, security); work group (cohesiveness, popularity, size, opportunities for interaction); supervision (consideration, participation in decision-making); the company (size and structure, participation in management); and individual differences (age, intelligence, personality, orientation to work). Some of these sources of satisfaction apply only to the employed but others equally to the unemployed, to the extent that they do not have them.

Although it has been challenged (Hulin and Blood, 1968; Guion and Landy, 1972) Herzberg's two-factor theory perhaps gives the best insight into the sources of job satisfaction (as opposed to dissatisfaction) which are denied to the unemployed. These look very much like the list of the functions of work given above but include others as well: opportunity for achievement; opportunity for recognition; the work itself, responsibility; advancement; and personal growth. It is the consistent emphasis on intrinsic factors associated with job satisfaction, rather than extrinsic factors, that suggests that the unemployed are likely to suffer most from not being in work.

However the work on job satisfaction has one more important feature of relevance to unemployment. Jobs that lead to a high degree of dissatisfaction may be more unpleasant or unhealthy for the individual than unemployment under good conditions. Warr (1983) has differentiated between 'good' and 'bad' jobs and 'good' and 'bad' unemployment in terms of nine variables that have proved discriminating in previous research (Table 7.1). Thus it may be that if a person leaves a bad job he or she may adapt well to good unemployment. There are many examples of this. The point made here is that just as not all jobs are satisfying, so not all unemployment is unsatisfying. Depending on the job, the person and the society's reaction to unemployment it may be possible to experience beneficial aspects of unemployment. Indeed some have argued that the central ethic must move away from work to post-industrial self-fulfilment through the growth of the informal or free economy (Pym, 1980).

Table 7.1: Factors discriminating between jobs

	'Good' jobs have	'Bad' jobs have	'Good' unemployment has	'Bad' unemployment has
1. Money	more	less	more	less
2. Variety	more	less	more	less
3. Goals, traction	more	less	more	less
4. Decision latitude	more	less	more	less
5. Skill use/ development	more	less	more	less
6. Psychological threat	less	more	less	more
7. Security	more	less	more	less
8. Interpersonal contact	more	less	more	less
9. Valued social position	more	less	more	less

Source: Warr, 'Work, jobs and unemployment', *Bulletin of the British Psychological Society*, 1983, *36*.

The importance of the nature of the job, or organisational climate, was demonstrated in a study by Friedlander and Greenberg (1971) of the hard-core unemployed in a period of low unemployment. They examined 478 hard-core (people who find it difficult to hold down a job) unemployed people's biographic and demographic background, their attitudes to work, the organisational climate in which they were placed, and the effect of a two-week intervention programme. The only correlate of work effectiveness and behaviour was the degree of supportiveness of the organisational climate in which the person was placed. Hence the authors concluded that the social structure or climate in most organisations may be more a cause than a cure for the hard-core unemployeds' work behaviour.

Most of the work on people's actual reactions to unemployment is speculative. However Warr and Payne (1983) have looked at actual changes in behaviour following job loss. These authors looked at social class differences in specific behaviours after job loss which were grouped as: domestic work (household chores, shopping, cooking), domestic pastimes (radio, television), other pastimes (smoking, window shopping), book reading (library visits, extra-mural classes), recreations (sports, hobbies), entertainment through money (drinking, cinema), and social contacts (church, political meetings). Apart from entertainment through money (a set of behaviours which declined), many forms of behaviours appeared, not unnaturally, to increase after job loss. The middle-class group tended to report a significantly greater increase in book reading, and the working-class a greater increase in other pastimes, but a greater reduction in entertainment through money. Furthermore several significant associations between change in behaviour and general health were noted; for instance, a reduction of entertainment through money was moderately associated with lower well-being for the middle class, but not the lower-class respondents. Many of these results are in accordance with other studies, such as a reduction of drinking (Smart, 1979) but, contrary to older studies which found that apathy associated with unemployment led to a reduction in church and political party attendance (Bakke, 1940), there was no reduction (or increase) in this study.

In another study with a larger population, Warr (1984) focused on age and length of unemployment as mediating variables in self-reported behaviour after job loss. The same 38-item scale subdivided into seven categories was used. Just over a third of the activities changed with length of unemployment: all forms of domestic work increased as did other pastimes and social contacts. Entertainment through money however declined. Nearly half of the behavioural changes were age-related, particularly domestic work, other pastimes and recreations, many of which were curvilinear. Predictably, sitting around at home and watching television (not for study) were highly correlated with mental maladjustment. Warr does point out that the results probably illustrate that there is no overall difference in the *amount* of a person's social contact between periods of employment and unemployment, but that the *content* and *location* of encounters and the *range* of people met are reduced after becoming unemployed.

Warr and Jackson (1984) examined the age and length correlates of unemployment among nearly 1000 men. Psychological distress, financial strain and labour-market commitment were greatest amongst the middle-aged men. There was a positive relationship between length of unemployment and mental and physical illness; and the probability of having an unemployed wife was found to be negatively associated with the length of unemployment. They conclude: 'Age and duration are themselves not causal variables; they stand as proxies for processes and states which require elucidation'. (p. 84).

STAGES AND CYCLES OF REACTIONS TO UNEMPLOYMENT

A number of attempts have been made to understand the way in which the unemployed adjust over time to their new circumstances. Because so little research in this area is longitudinal (it is nearly all cross-sectional) there is more speculation than research with regard to transitional stages or phases for the unemployed. Those longitudinal studies which do exist (Warr *et al.*, 1982) have not investigated the reactions of the unemployed over a very long period (being usually less than one year) hence the long-term effects of unemployment are not clear.

There is, however, no shortage of theories concerning how the unemployed may react to unemployment (Hopson and Adams, 1976; Harrison, 1976). Because unemployment involves the reactions to *loss*, the extensive literature on grieving and bereavement (Parkes, 1975), divorce (Levinger and Moles, 1979) and migration (Furnham and Bochner, 1985) has been seen to be relevant. Researchers in all these areas have relied on early neo-psychoanalytic researchers (Bowlby, 1969) for their ideas.

Before examples of these stage-wise descriptions are considered it is perhaps worth noting that all stage-wise descriptions have their problems. First, stage-wise models are descriptive rather than explanatory—they simply describe the typical pattern of response over time. Secondly, they

Table 7.2: Stage-wise theories of reactions to unemployment.

Hopson and Adams (1976)	*Harrison (1976)*	*Hill (1977)*	*Briar (1977)*
1. Immobilisation	1. Shock	1. Trauma/denial	1. Shock
2. Minimisation	2. Optimism	2. Depression	2. Optimism
3. Depression	3. Pessimism	3. Adaptation	3. Self-blame
4. Acceptance of reality	4. Fatalism		4. Depression
5. Testing			5. Inertia
6. Search for meaning			
7. Internalisation			

Source: Hayes and Nutman, *Understanding the Unemployed*, Tavistock Publications, 1981.

rarely specify what factors determine that a person moves on from one stage to another or remains fixated in one stage. All stage-wise models are linear, but it is quite possible that patterns of reactions are cyclical: that is, there are erratic progressions and regressions. Further crucial individual differences and moderating variables are ignored in these descriptions which are by definition general. Finally, the more stages a theory has the more vulnerable it is to disproof.

Hayes and Nutman (1981) have reviewed a number of stage-wise, approaches. These include Hopson and Adams' (1976) seven-stage approach, the four stages of Harrison (1970), three of Hill (1977) and five of Briar (1977).

Clearly, although there are some obvious similarities between these theories, there are also important differences. Hayes and Nutman (1981) summarise their review thus:

> It appears that the transition can be viewed in terms of three broad stages. Within the first of these is an initial phase of shock and immobilization, followed by a phase characterized by renewed hope, optimism and a tendency to minimize or deny that there has been a change. The second broad stage seems to include a period in which the idea that 'things will turn out all right in the end' is shaken and the individual's identity comes under pressure. This stage often appears to be associated with depression and withdrawal. The onset of this stage is characterized by an acceptance that there has been a change and by a 'letting go' of the past, and during this second stage the individual gradually begins to search for and test out new relationships between self and situation. If unemployment is prolonged and if re-call to the lost job fails to materialize then the individual must find and internalize a new identity. This process of readjustment is characterized in the third and final broad stage irrespective of whether the individual successfully re-enters the world of work in a new work role or continues in a state of unemployment.
>
> It is as though the period of disorganization and crisis unfreezes both the individual and his or her family and helps them to search for and find new values and standards better suited to the present (pp. 18–19)

UNEMPLOYMENT AND HEALTH

For over a decade a considerable amount of research has been done on life changes and discontinuities in experience and their effects on mental and physical health. A vast literature surrounds the relationship between life events and illness which has shown that a range of physical illnesses are related to social stress. Many scales have been developed to measure these life events which include the Social Readjustment Rating Scale (Holmes and Rahe, 1967) which ranks both being fired at work and retirement highly, and the Cochrane and Robertson (1973) Life Events Inventory which ranks unemployment and retirement amongst the most stressful of items.

The work on life stresses is extensive yet equivocal. The exact nature of the causal link between personal distress and psychological disturbance is however unclear and many intervening variables have been hypothesised. There are also widely different models and explanations for the relationship, including Rahe's Optical Analogy (Rahe *et al.*, 1974) which posits a series of filters and lenses which are between exposure to stress and the reporting of symptoms, and Robertson and Cochrane's (1976) value change model which suggests that people with the new as opposed to the traditional value systems will be more aware of and sensitive to social stresses and pressures and less able to cope with them.

Yet researchers have noted that as unemployment is a major life event, it may explain the fact that unemployed people are by and large less healthy, well adjusted and happy than their employed peers. There are three sorts of data which show this relationship:

(1) There are a number of archival studies which have looked at such things as the relationship between unemployment and social problems over a specific period. For instance, Boor (1980) examined the relationship between unemployment rates and suicide rates in eight countries between 1962 and 1976. The question that was addressed was whether social and psychological conditions associated with relatively high suicide rates were also associated with relatively high suicide rates in these countries during these years (*not* whether unemployed persons were more likely to commit suicide than employed people). There were significant positive between 0.53 and 0.79 correlations between annual variations in suicide and unemployment rates for the USA, Canada, Japan and France, but no significant relationship for Germany, Sweden and Italy. Great Britain however showed the opposite pattern (–0.59). Annual variations in the suicide rates of females and males were highly intercorrelated but not associated differentially with unemployment rates, and showed similar patterns within the various age sub-groups, thus indicating that cultural factors associated with levels of unemployment had similar effects on the suicidal behaviour of male and females.

Boor explained the unpredicted British findings thus: The rate of unsuccessful suicides did actually increase during this period primarily due to the reduction of carbon monoxide in the domestic gas supply. Similarly, Schapiro and Ahlburg (1983) found a significant positive relationship between unemployment and suicides for males in America over the period 1946–76. That is, a 1 per cent point increase in the unemployment rate precipitates over 300 additional suicides per annum. In Britain Krafchik (1983) found a strong positive correlation between unemployment and vagrancy (measured by admissions to the poor law casual wards) in the 1930s.

(II) There is extensive research on macroeconomic factors and mental health at the University of California (Catalano and Dooley, 1977, 1979; Dooley and Catalano, 1977, 1980). Catalano and Dooley (1979) argued that recent analyses of annual archival data suggest that admission to mental hospitals is significantly associated with previous macroeconomic changes, but that this relationship is modified by two important intervening variables: stress in day-to-day life and mental depression, both of which vary with economic change. However, as they point out, it is not clear whether economic changes serve to uncover existing untreated cases or to provoke symptoms in persons previously normal. Their results however indicate that the relationship between economic change and recourse to inpatient mental health facilities was due more to the uncovering, than to the provocation, of behavioural disorders. Their other research in metropolitan communities has found significant time-series associations of monthly unemployment rate with depression (Catalano and Dooley, 1977), of absolute change in employment in the basic economic sector with stressful life events (Catalano and Dooley, 1979) and various psychophysiological symptoms associated with low-income respondents (Dooley and Catalano, 1979).

In a review paper Dooley and Catalano (1980) propose a model (given in Figure 7.1) that attempts to explain economic change as a cause of behavioural disorder. They believe that this model may help mental health planners to anticipate increases in economically-caused symptoms and to identify the sub-populations most likely to be affected.

The life event hypothesis has also been supported by work on low-income families. Thoits and Hannan (1979) compared an income-maintenance and

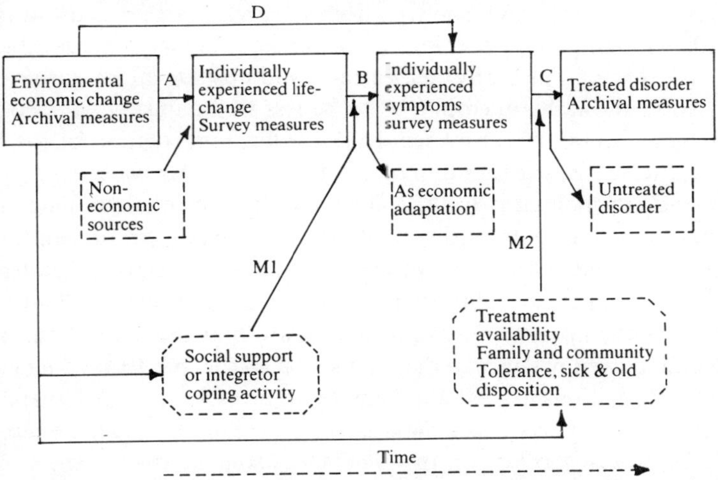

Figure 7.1: Hypothetical intervening variables between environmental economic change and treated disorder

Key:

A = Cause of life-events by economic change.
B = Cause of symptoms by stressful life-events.
C = Translation of experienced symptoms into demand for service.
D = Possibility that economic change might affect individual symptoms without mediating life change.

Reprinted by permission of the publisher and authors from Dooley/Catalano: 'Economic change as a cause of behavioral disorder', *Psychological Bulletin 87*, copyright 1980 by the American Psychological Association.

a control group's psychological distress. One hypothesis was that increase in or stabilisation of income would facilitate the experimental subjects' ability to cope with life crises, which in turn would reduce their psychological distress relative to the distress levels of the control subjects (resources hypothesis). The second hypothesis was that readjustments following from a change in income will raise the psychological distress levels of experimental rather than control subjects (life event hypothesis). Their results were consistent with the latter life event hypothesis, namely that *any* change (positive or negative) in life circumstances is distressing. Thus promotion as much as unemployment may be seen as leading to psychological problems.

(iii) There are studies concentrated exclusively on the mental/physical health and psychological well-being of unemployed people (Kasl and Cobb, 1970). Banks *et al.* (1980) compared the mental health (as measured by the General Health Questionnaire) of employees in an engineering firm, recent school-leavers and a group of unemployed men. They found, as predicted, that the unemployed group (and women more than men) had scores indicating lower mental health, but that these scores were unrelated to age, job level or marital status. Similarly Warr (1981) has suggested that the unemployeds' mental health deteriorates because they are denied many of the positive features of work (money, activity, variety, temporal structure, social contacts, status and identity within society). Warr notes that a variety of studies looking at such things as depression, anxiety, life satisfaction, minor psychiatric morbidity, self-esteem, and positive and negative effect, consistently show the unemployed to be less well adjusted. However this research has, so far, not answered the following important problems. What other features influence the strength of the association between employment status and psychological health? What is the sequential or longitudinal pattern of reaction to unemployment over time? What sort of people thrive in unemployment? Others (Liem and Rayman, 1982) have suggested that researchers need to concentrate more on mediating *processes* than on the outcome of unemployment: 'We need to know how the costs of unemployment are incurred, what material, and social factors moderate their effects, and what conditions exacerbate them' (p. 1122). One area of research that they note is the effects of unemployment on children—e.g. the effects of a family history of job loss on the child's adjustment, view of the world of work, and so on.

Furnham (1983a) looked at the mental health (as measured on the Langner index) of five groups depending on their employment status: full-time employed, part-time employed, unemployed, retired and students. Although there was no age or sex differences in the total mental health score, there was a significant difference between the five employment groups' total score with the full-time employed having the lowest (best-adjusted) score, the retired and students having moderately high scores, and the unemployed and the part-time the highest scores.

On the basis of previous findings, one might have expected the part-time employeds' adjustment score to be higher than that of students, which in turn would possibly be higher than that of retired people. Yet the part-time employed people's score was almost as high, and not significantly different from that of the unemployed. There could be many reasons for this. First, people seeking full-time work may take a part-time job which they do not like and which is not well paid, simply as an interim measure. Secondly, people with other commitments (family, handicapped relatives, etc.) may only be able to take a part-time job which, because of travelling and other stress, is too much for them and leads to mental distress. Thirdly, some part-time work is very casual in that it is for very short periods only, thus instead of giving the benefits of work, it does the precise opposite. Certainly future studies on the part-time employed would do well to tease apart these various hypotheses by asking subjects to stipulate clearly why they have chosen part-time employment, how long they intend to be in the job, and what the hours are. With the prospect of increased job-sharing, the importance of part-time employment is likely to rise.

The importance of longitudinal studies cannot be ignored. To establish a relationship between unemployment and psychological distress tells one nothing of causation, merely correlation. It is possible that the less psychologically adjusted are prone to unemployment or are indeed unemployable! Only careful longitudinal research can decide whether and how unemployment leads to psychological problems.

The social and private costs of unemployment naturally lead to various social policy considerations. The financial, psychological and medical costs of unemployment are borne not only by individual workers but also by their families and communities. Liem and Rayman (1982) have suggested a statutory minimum period of notification before workers can be laid off and the creation of a system of medical insurance which is not tied solely to current employment, 'nevertheless the primary assumption informing overall policy on unemployment should be that job loss brings costs to personal health and the quality of family and community life. This premise, together with the social ethic of "the right to work" should figure centrally in the formulation of unemployment policy'. (Liem and Rayman, 1982, p. 1121). They also note that one of the most important policy recommendations arising from their own work is to create a medical insurance scheme *not* tied solely to current employment.

Liem and Atkinson (1982) have noted that joblessness should be thought of not only as happening to individuals, but also to families. In their research they found that two or three months after their husbands became unemployed, wives in families with continuing unemployment were significantly more depressed, anxious, phobic and sensitive about their interpersonal relationships than their counterparts in employed (control) families. They conclude:

Consequently, to the familiar criticisms of official Bureau of Labor Statistics procedures for estimating the nation's unemployment rate we would have to add the short-sightedness of assuming that joblessness only happens to individuals. In terms of serious consequences of being without work the impact of unemployment probably exceeds by a factor of two or three that group of Americans who are counted as unemployed. (Liem and Atkinson, 1982, p. 19)

Other social policy implications may be found in studies concerning unemployment and the handicapped which shows that unemployed handicapped people suffer more problems than employed handicapped people (Markova *et al.*, 1980), and that in times of high unemployment the handicapped are *more* likely to be unemployed—that is, employers discriminate against them.

Another important source of data on the relationship between unemployment and health concerns studying the characteristics of unemployed people admitted to mental hospitals because this helps to unravel the direction of causality. Fruensgaard *et al.* (1983a) investigated the psychosocial characteristics of a group of unemployed patients consecutively admitted to a psychiatric emergency clinic in Denmark. They found that alcohol abuse was registered in two-thirds of their sample of 70, and about half were found to be habitual neurotics with a tendency to antisocial behaviour while intoxicated. However only 4 per cent had *never* suffered from a mental disorder requiring treatment prior to their unemployment. Indeed, 41 per cent had previously been admitted to a mental hospital, and 60 per cent were on sick leave prior to unemployment. Despite the fact that this sample was hardly typical and that there were other potential causal factors giving rise to mental disease in addition to unemployment, it was noted that anxiety, depression, neuraesthenic and psychotic illnesses were accentuated by or commenced with unemployment.

In a follow-up study Fruensgaard *et al.* (1983b) found that in most of the sample there had been a drop in alcohol and drug abuse and an improvement in mental health. Most importantly they found that those who succeeded in getting work and/or those who had favourable employment experiences were 'stronger' than those who did not get employment, and had had a significantly lower frequency of previous admission to the psychiatric department and of sick leave prior to unemployment: 'In addition, the duration of their actual unemployment was shorter and therefore probably less of a strain. . . . Furthermore, there was an extremely significant correlation between a favourable course with regard to employment and both improvement of the general mental condition and improvement of the interpersonal relations' (p. 135). Thus it seems that the relationship between mental health and unemployment is bi-directional. The mentally unstable are less likely to find employment than the mentally stable, but lack of employment accentuates the problem, whereas employment does the opposite.

Other attempts to understand the relationship between unemployment and health have been phenomenological. Fineman (1979) has looked specifically at psychosocial stress induced by managerial unemployment. He interviewed 25 unemployed managers and also gave them a battery of tests. Predictably they had high GHQ (General Health Questionnaire—a measure of mental health) scores indicating psychological disturbance almost twice the national average, yet their 16PF (a measure of personality with sixteen dimensions) scores fell within the normal range. Whereas some managers seemed highly stressed by unemployment others seemed to enjoy it. What appeared to characterise the high-stress group was prior high personal involvement in the job, belief in personal competence, domestic problems, symbiotic failure in job applications and learned helplessness. Low-stress cases, on the other hand, perceived their problem in low-threat terms, had previous low job involvement, strong belief in personal worth and a direct, confronting (as opposed to avoidance, passive) approach to problems. From his rich but unquantifiable data Fineman draws a number of conclusions. Stress in unemployment arises from the interaction of four factors: (I) an individual's perception of the environment; (II) personality, experienced threat and behaviour in response to threat; (III) direct confrontation is the only form of behaviour which can involve mastering the problem of stress; and (IV) a stressed person needs to be encouraged to examine his perception of environmental demands.

Swinburne (1981) also attempted to look at the psychological impact of unemployment on managers and professional staff. In the interview study she questioned subjects on their feelings about being unemployed, the problems of structuring time, and their job-search process. She found that although the experience of unemployment varied according to individual circumstances, certain trends were apparent. Many (50 per cent) reported initial shock and fear/uncertainty about the future, but as few as 10 per cent reported shame, or loss of status and self-respect. Although the negativity of their initial reactions appeared less than reported elsewhere, they appeared to pass through the various hypothetical stages much more slowly.

In a study of the effect of social support in moderating the health consequences of unemployment Gore (1978) interviewed 100 married men who previously had been regularly employed but had suddenly been made redundant. The men were interviewed five times over a two-year period. She was particularly interested in the effect of supportive and affiliative relations with wife, friends and relatives on the unemployed man's illness symptoms. She found that the rural unemployed, because of the ethnic ties and concern in a small community, had a higher level of support than the urban unemployed. In addition the unsupported unemployed had significantly greater levels of cholesterol illness symptoms and emotional response than did the supported. The author argued that these results demonstrate not so much that support buffers the effects of life stress, but rather a low sense/level of social support exacerbates life stress. Unemployment, in large part, means the inability to make instrumental accomplishments. Thus it might be interpreted that this loss in the absence of a continuing sense of self-worth maintained through supportive relationships contributes to negative health responses. In this research, it is impossible to point to specific behaviours of others which ameliorate life stress, i.e. the buffering effect. It thus makes more sense to explain the more negative responses of some terminees as the exacerbation of the unemployment experience by a low sense of social support.

Finally, it should be pointed out that not all studies on unemployment and health are retrospective. Jenkins *et al.* (1982) carried out a prospective study to examine the effects of the threat of journalists promised redundancy on minor psychiatric morbidity. Each subject was tested three times: 2 months prior to closure (1 month after receiving notice of redundancy), immediately after redundancy notices were revoked and work continued under a new proprietor, and then 3 months after the threat of redundancy had been removed. Despite various methodological problems it was unambiguously demonstrated that subsequent to the withdrawal of redundancy notices, there was a considerable reduction in minor symptomatology.

Hepworth (1980) looked at moderating factors in the relationship between unemployment and mental health. She found that length of unemployment was inversely correlated with mental health and well-being; semi- and unskilled men were less well adjusted than those of higher occupational status and that the best predictor of the unemployed's mental health was whether or not they felt their time was occupied. In a re-analysis of this data Brenner and Bartell (1983) found that with the passage of time a reciprocal process takes place in which mental health affects subjective well-being and the proportion of time occupied. The authors suggest that there may well be a 'critical period' immediately following job loss in which time adaptation may or may not occur. Poor adaptation leads to a vicious circle which results in increased negative effects with time.

Many writers have noted a change in the self-concept and identity in the unemployed. In their review of the psychological effects of unemployment in the 1930s Eisenberg and Lazarsfeld (1938) note the development of apathy, depression, fatalistic beliefs, lowered self-esteem, resignation and self-doubt among the unemployed.

As Kelvin and Jarrett (1985) have noted, in a society whose socio-economic structure is defined in terms of its divisions of labour, the unemployed are defined by what they are *not*—not integrated within that structure. This means that the unemployed person's position is highly ambiguous as saying what a person is *not*, and does not tell us much of what he is. It is only on the explicit and often unjustifiable assumption that once they find work that they will once again have an identifiable place in society.

It has been argued that the self-concept is a schema which locates the individual within the social environment and shapes his interaction with it. Hence becoming unemployed causes psychological dislocation and disorientation which induces a modification of the self-concept. Tiffany *et al.* (1970) administered the Tennessee Self-Concept Scale to two comparable groups, one in work and one not, and found that the profile of the unemployed group reflected a lower level of self-esteem. The unemployed had significantly less faith or confidence in themselves, and saw themselves as less desirable, doubted their worth more, and felt more anxious, depressed and unhappy than the employed group. This pattern has been studied by Allerhand *et al.* (1969), Hodgson and Brenner (1968) and Teahan (1969), all of whom found lower self-esteem in the previously unemployed compared with the previously employed. Briar (1977) has also noted a desire for secrecy and a distancing in the unemployed which appears to be a means of protecting themselves against being labelled failures and 'welfare-dependent'.

Of course one problem plagues the self-esteem and unemployment literature, and that is correlation and cause. It is possible that those with low self-esteem and a poor self-concept are more susceptible to unemployment rather than unemployment reducing self-esteem. Of course, what is more probable is that both occur together, exacerbating each other. Only longitudinal work can actually determine the direction of causality.

YOUTH UNEMPLOYMENT

Since the early 1970s when the problem became most acute there have several important studies of youth unemployment (Baxter, 1975; Fowler *et al.* 1976; Roberts *et al.* 1982; Mair and Raffe, 1983). Many of these have looked at the same factors (health, self-esteem, causal explanations) that have been investigated in the adult population, but some have been quite specific to young people.

The underlying causes of increased youth unemployment are of course manifold. They include demographic factors (change in the birth rate and an extension of the school career), micro- and macroeconomic changes (change in technology, different productivity agreements), and educational and training factors (the relevance and appropriateness of education). Changes in youth unemployment are naturally associated with changes in adult unemployment but move with a greater amplitude. It has been calculated that if the unemployment rate for males rises by 1 per cent, the unemployment rate for males under 20 (excluding school-leavers) rises by 1.7 per cent (Makeham, 1980). Compared with other groups, young people change jobs more often or start without jobs, hence as the recession deepens and recruitment is cut, young people are among the most vulnerable.

1. Psychological Adjustment

Some studies have looked at the emotional, social and psychological adjustment of unemployed school-leavers. Using a questionnaire developed from the ideas of the neo-psychoanalytic thinker Erikson, Gurney (1980) looked at over 400 unemployed Australian school-leavers. It was hypothesised that having a job helps school-leavers to clarify their perception of their identity, and not being able to get work leads to a confused perception of self or no change due to a moratorium. The hypothesis was confirmed for females but not for males. Furthermore the unemployed males showed a significant shift towards the mistrust pole of the first dimension of *trust–mistrust*, and the employed of both sexes shifted significantly on the *industry–inferiority* sub-scale. He concludes, it seems reasonable to conclude that unemployment has the effect of inhibiting development in school-leavers, rather than inflicting trauma as is sometimes popularly supposed' (p. 212). Gurney (1980b) also found that over a 4-month period after leaving school, self-esteem increased only for those young people who obtained work.

More recently Donovan and Oddy (1982) investigated the social and emotional development of a small, but carefully matched group of employed and unemployed school-leavers. They found that school-leavers who were unemployed were more depressed and anxious, had lower self-esteem and poorer subjective well-being, were less well socially adjusted and showed a higher incidence of minor psychiatric morbidity than school-leavers who had acquired jobs. They also found a significant interaction between employment status and gender on the locus of control scale: unemployed males tend to be more external than employed males, whereas these differences were minimal for females. They write, 'Certainly the apathy and hopelessness frequently associated with unemployment could be linked to an increased tendency to attribute events to uncontrollable forces' (p. 24). Similarly Feather (1982a,b) found both male and female young unemployed people had higher depression scores, lower self-esteem and Protestant work ethic scenes, and reported that good and bad outcomes to everyday events were less important to them compared with employed male subjects. He notes:

> These results therefore indicate that both lower self-esteem and less effort to find a job were associated with increasing time out of work. They also show that the active pursuit of employment tended to be more frequent among those with higher self-esteem, stronger Protestant ethic values and higher levels of concern about positive and negative events (Lower apathy). But frequency of job search was lower among those unemployed who reported more depressive symptoms. These findings may imply a sort of reciprocal determinism in which the state of continued unemployment has effects on the person, and the person, so modified by his or her experience, begins to behave in ways that alter the probability of finding a job. (p. 320)

Stafford (1982) examined the impact of the Youth Opportunities

Programme, devised to offer 16–18-year-olds opportunities for training and work experience to increase employment prospects, on young people's employment prospects and psychological well-being. She found a significant improvement in employment prospects after participation in the scheme, which also acts as a buffer against any detrimental effects of unemployment. However the beneficial effects of the programme do not last, and the detrimental effects of unemployment return for those ex-trainees who remain unemployed.

Other studies have noted the medical and psychological health costs of being unemployed. In Britain, Banks *et al.* (1980) gave 647 recent school-leavers the General Health Questionnaire (a self-administered screening test for detecting minor psychiatric disorders). There was a large significant difference between those unemployed (3.78) and those employed (1.27), but no significant sex differences. Further analysis showed that although the unemployed scored higher on the GHQ this relationship was moderated by their motivation to work, such that unemployed with a high motivation to work scored higher than those with lower work motivation. Similarly in an American study, Greenberger *et al.* (1981) compared the health and behavioural consequences of 16–18-year-old school children who had part-time jobs compared with those who had never worked. Although they recognised the potentially positive influence on adolescents, their work focused on the costs of job stress. Their study focused on self-reported frequency of psychological and physical health symptoms, school absence, and the use of cigarettes, alcohol, marijuana, and other things. The results indicated that the working youths (especially boys) reported fewer somatic symptoms than the non-working youths, and that even boys who worked under stressful job conditions report fewer somatic and psychological symptoms than do boys who hold less stressful jobs. However the results did show that exposure to job stress is related to alcohol and marijuana use for both boys and girls.

The authors proposed four explanations for their finding that work is associated with fewer symptoms in boys but more in girls: differential selection (hardier boys are likely to take more stressful jobs); differential attributes (hardier boys are likely to remain at stressful jobs while those less sturdy are likely to leave); differential reporting about health (boys who work under stress are less likely to report health problems than are girls); sex differences in socialisation (boys are led to expect more stress than girls).

Other studies have been concerned with the effect of youth unemployment as rapid labour turnover and deliquency. For instance Baxter (1975) studied chronic job changes in the early 1970s. Job-changers tended to be less intelligent, more neurotic, from poorer homes and less socially and occupationally skilled than their counterparts who did not change jobs so rapidly. However Raffe (1983), in a study of employment instability in young people, found that although instability was generated more by occupational than personal factors (unstable jobs not unstable workers) their chances of finding new employment depended on personal factors more than on their earlier occupational experiences. Similarly Raelin (1981) found that early career unemployment is not a critical factor in retarding personal economic growth, relative to educational background and first job experience, but does have negative job attitudinal consequences. Young males who are early entrants in the labour force and who spend the bulk of their work in part-time employment do as well economically and better occupationally in their later work experience than full-time youth.

Milham *et al.* (1978) in a study of over 1000 boys in approved schools found that employment experiences were a crucial factor in promoting economic and social well-being. Though the authors were careful not to draw causal links between unemployment and delinquency they did find that regular work did build up offending boys' confidence, changed their job aspirations, enhanced their self-perceptions and remotivated their interest in numeracy and literacy.

The problem with nearly all the studies on youth unemployment and psychological adjustment is that one cannot infer cause only correlation. That is, it is quite possible that poor psychological adjustment leads to a young person being unemployed rather than the other way around. The only study that attempted a longitudinal analysis of the problem however yielded ambiguous results. Warr *et al.* (1982) interviewed two cohorts of recent school-leavers over a two-year period, but measures of psychological stress and self-esteem were found to be correlated with the duration of unemployment for young men. In one cohort of women the young people appeared to be better adjusted the longer they were unemployed, apparently because of their reduced commitment to the labour market along with a stronger personal involvement in family matters. The authors offer two compatible explanations for their puzzling findings—the association between well-being and length of unemployment may differ between age groups (older people with more commitments may experience greater distress), and secondly that longer periods of unemployment than those studied in this study (over a year) lead to distress.

Similarly Banks and Jackson (1982) interviewed two age cohorts of young people up to 2½ years after leaving school to investigate the association between unemployment and risk of minor psychiatric morbidity. They found a positive relationship between unemployment and morbidity after controlling for sex, ethnicity and educational qualifications. Further longitudinal analyses showed that the experience of unemployment was more likely to create increased psychological symptoms, rather than the reverse. More recently Jackson *et al.* (1983) studied longitudinally two cohorts of young people in the first three years of their working lives. They found, as predicted, that psychological distress is higher for the unemployed than for the employed and that changes in employment status lead to changes in distress score. Furthermore this relationship is moderated by the person's commitment to work: the more committed suffer more from the experience of unemployment.

2. Attribution and Expectation about Employment and Unemployment

Although there have been some studies of adult explanations of unemployment (Furnham 1982c, 1983b), considerably less work has gone into establishing young people's beliefs about, and actual attempts at, getting a job. Feather and Davenport (1981) tested their expectancy valence theory on young people. A person's actions are seen to be related to the expectations that a person holds *and* to the subjective values of the outcomes that might occur following the action. They found, as predicted, that higher motivated, more depressed unemployed youths blamed stable external factors for unemployment and rated the attractiveness of work more highly than less depressed youths. Although incompatible with learned helplessness theory, the results supported their theory which assumes that positive motivation to seek employment is identical to the multiplicative combination of expectancy of success in getting a job *and* the perceived net attractiveness of unemployment. They note,

> One might assume that work will have stronger positive valence for individuals with strong Protestant ethic values than for those people for whom these values are weaker. If this assumption is valid, then it follows that people with a strong Protestant ethic value will be more persistent in their efforts to get a job and that they will suffer more negative effects if they fail to obtain employment. (p. 337)

Gurney (1981) in fact examined the attributions for the causes of unemployment in both employed and unemployed groups of school-leavers. In a first study he attempted to discover, among a population of Australian school-leavers, whether the unemployed differed in their attributions of employment from those who succeeded in getting work; and secondly, whether any differences were antecedent to, or consequent upon, unemployment. Subjects were asked to ascribe the ability to get work either to internal or external factors to the job-seekers, and to fill out a simple 8-item scale devised by the author. He found that unemployed males attributed both getting *and* not getting work significantly more to external factors as has been found previously, but there were no differences in the female groups. Gurney suggested that the lack of differences among the female groups may be due to their lesser defensiveness and need to blame external factors for being unemployed. In a second longitudinal study students were given a 12-item attribution for getting jobs questionnaire prior to leaving school, and then approximately four months later. He suggested that:

> The unemployed may believe themselves powerless to change the circumstances of their lives (external locus) but the fact that they are without work whereas others are not and that they remain so, may lead them eventually to see themselves as responsible for their condition (internal attribution) with consequent self-blame and self-derogation. (Gurney, 1981, p. 34)

The results showed that prior to leaving school the groups did not differ, yet later it was not the unemployed who changed their attributions, but the employed who shifted significantly toward a more internal set of causal ascriptions. Overall Gurney (1981) seemed unable to account for his 'counter-intuitive and unexpected' findings suggesting perhaps that subjects of this age have their self-esteem based on numerous other things such as parental evaluation and peer-group approval, rather than exclusively on work which is more often the case with adults.

In a rather different study Dayton (1981) looked at the way in which young people looked for a job. He set out to determine what job-seeking approaches were being used by young people and what factors they found positive and useful (aids) and what negative and worthless (barriers) in a job search. Using a population of 250 young Americans, Dayton found they regarded their own positive personal attributes (personality, flexibility, academic ability) as the most important aids in their job, and external factors (labour unions, welfare and unemployment insurance, government-training programmes) as least important. Employment success and satisfaction was correlated with careful analysis of which job suited them best, the assemblance of a placement file, letters of recommendation, and a CV, combined with persistence in the job search.

Research, within the framework of attribution theory, would however lead one to make a number of predictions about school childrens' expectations and beliefs about getting a job (Furnham 1982 a and c, 1983e). For instance people more prone to unemployment, and the unemployed themselves, tend to make more external attributions for the causes of unemployment in contrast to those in jobs and unlikely to become unemployed. Furthermore studies have shown that external attributions are to some extent protective of self-esteem in the context of achievement. (Harvey *et al.*, 1975). Hence Furnham (1984c) predicted that females more than males and working-class subjects more than middle-class subjects (for whom unemployment is statistically more probable) will be prone to make more external attributions about getting a job. Further it was suggested that these attributions will also be reflected in the number and type of job-search strategies adopted by young people and the barriers and aids that they consider operate in job-hunting success. In this study Furnham set out to examine sex and class differences in 240 British school-leavers' attributions about unemployment, the most and least useful job-search strategies, and which school course they believed most and least useful in getting a job. The results of the four different parts of this study suggest that, overall, attributions about getting a job are frequently internal (that is, to personal attributes or abilities) rather than environmental or societal factors. Confidence, perseverance and qualifications were all considered to be primary factors responsible for success in finding employment, yet this is moderated by the belief that jobs are not currently available (a fact which is attributed to the government). Yet failure to get a job was rarely attributed to the personal shortcomings of the job-seeker himself. Thus these results tend to support the well-established, attributional finding that success is attributed to internal factors and failure to external factors.

Where there were significant sex differences it was found that females were more external in their attributions than males. This conflicts with Gurney (1981) who found that unemployed males were more external in their attributions about employment than employed males, but that there were no differences between employed and unemployed females. However, the extensive locus of control literature has shown that where sex differences exist in generalised locus of control beliefs, females are more external than males. Similarly class differences tended to show that working-class subjects tend to place more emphasis on structural or external factors (Furnham, 1982c). Again this is to be expected and is in accordance with previous literature on the topic (Furnham and Gunter, 1984).

The results on the aids and barriers confirm the findings of Dayton (1981), who found that the subjects saw their own personal attributes as the greatest aids and external factors as the biggest hindrances. Similarly regarding strategies, class and sex differences showed that the middle class tended to rate all job-hunting strategies as more useful than the working class, and girls showed less faith in following up specific job choices than boys. The subjects all stressed the importance of summer and after-school work for experience, but tended to rely on personal contacts rather than direct approaches to employers. It would be interesting to compare these beliefs with those of employers who may have quite different beliefs concerning which factors make an applicant more employable.

The belief in the usefulness of 'A' level courses revealed that both males and females believed science courses (and English) were the most useful in getting a job, although females tended to opt for arts courses and males for sciences at 'A' level. Females also believed that arts courses were more useful than science courses, so providing a rationalisation for the choice. However a study such as this was unable to determine whether females chose arts subjects and then felt it necessary to justify their choice, or whether they actually believed them to be most useful *per se* and hence selected them accordingly. It is of course also possible that when candidates select a particular course they do so for many reasons only one of which is its usefulness for getting a job. Further, the believed importance of science courses may reflect recent government pronouncements and support for the 'hard' sciences, rather than the arts or social sciences. These results also indicate that attributions are to some extent a function of the expectation of work.

More recently Feather (1983c) examined causal attributions and beliefs about work and unemployment among Australian adolescents in state and independent schools. The results were analysed for school and sex differences. State school children tended to blame economic factors, physical appearance and interview inadequacy more than independent school children, 80 endorsing societal or external explanations. As predicted children from the independent schools (of higher socioeconomic status) as opposed to those from state schools had higher expectations of obtaining employment, higher internal attributions of controllability over their own lives, and were more likely to see work as attractive. Also female students tended to have lower expectations about finding employment, when compared with their male peers. These results were explained in terms of the current economic situation in Australia, socialisation forces in the family, the schools and in peer groups (middle-class children have experience of reward for effort and individual competition; working-class children have lower expectations).

In a more detailed study, Feather and Barber (1983) investigated correlates of depressive reactions associated with unemployment in a sample of young unemployed male and female Australians. From studies on depression and attributions three hypotheses were tested and some support was found for each. They were: depressive effect about unemployment is associated with high job expectations, with the rated importance of having a job and with external attributions for the causes of unemployment. General depressive symptomatology is associated with low expectation of getting a job, low self-esteem, internal attributions about the causes of unemployment, and perceived uncontrollability or helplessness about changing things. Depressive symptoms are associated with an unsuccessful employment history. Overall, the findings indicated that attributional variables accounted for only a relatively small proportion of the variance in depression: 'In future investigations of the psychological damage that unemployment may cause, it is important to assess a range of other variables as well, especially those that relate to the personal and social costs of not having a job and the different ways in which people learn to cope with negative outcomes' (Feather and Barber, 1983, p. 193).

3. Education about Unemployment

Because it has become so widespread, various researchers have argued for some sort of education about the problems and prospects of unemployment. Some (Stirling, 1982) have gone so far as to suggest that we need to prepare school-leavers for unemployment, arguing that because as many as a third of school-leavers in Britain (in 1982/83) may experience unemployment they need to know what to anticipate and how to cope. Furthermore high levels of youth unemployment have produced a questioning of and disenchantment with the whole education system (Hargreaves, 1981).

Dancy (1978) argued that young people need to be educated in all aspects of job-sharing and to be encouraged to have a new definition of work, to include not only paid employment but a variety of other activities. To this end he believes a careers education programme should involve such topics as the mechanics of collecting benefits, the acquisition of job-seeking skills, the experience of unemployment, leisure and community roles, the politics of the right to work.

Watts (1978) also considered the implications of school-leaver unemployment for careers education in schools. He argues that careers educators have not seriously dealt with the problem of unemployment because they do not feel competent to tackle it effectively; they are aware of its highly political and emotional overtones; it might affect deletariously the work ethic within and outside the school; and the teachers feel instinctively hostile to the concept of preparation for unemployment. A number of possible curricular objectives are listed including equipping children with employability, survival and leisure skills. Four alternative aims are described depending on whether one is focusing on change in society (to help students see unemployment as a phenomenon resolved by social and political measures); change in the individual (to maximise students' chances of finding meaningful employment); *status quo* in the society (to reinforce students' motivation to seek work) and status in the individual (to make students aware of the possibility of unemployment and how to cope best with it). Much of the educational responses and strategies are dependent on whether one believes unemployment to be voluntary (aversion to the will to work), cyclical (cycles of recession and expansion) or structural (a major change in the relationship between capital and labour). These solutions may include a deeper inculcation of the work ethic, job creation schemes, etc. Careers education is seen as the education of central life interests and personal growth and development, rather than the matching of people to (non-existent) jobs.

As a practical measure Lavercombe and Fleming (1981) attempted to identify (by using attitude measures) school children at risk of longer periods of unemployment and hence in particular need of support, information and skills. Although they found that their measures did not predict which pupils would take longest to find jobs, they believed all pupils should be prepared for unemployment. Their results suggested that employers have little confidence in what teachers report concerning expected examination results, attendance records or attitudes to school, authority or work when selecting among young applicants.

Fleming and Lavercombe (1982) in a study of 29 professionals working with young people found that they varied considerably in their topics and approaches. The sort of topics discussed by the professionals in schools were: whether work itself is the major basis of self-respect and how the unemployed can compensate; how to spend one's leisure/free time; the mechanics of claiming supplementary benefit; possibilities of continuing education; and the politics of unemployment. In talking with unemployed school-leavers after school the professionals believed their primary role was giving support while being as honest as possible. They also believed that their activities helped combat boredom and anxiety, to help them get a job; and to facilitate personal development. The professionals who believed that there was a chance of returning emphasised job-seeking and keeping skills, while those who were more pessimistic about the future of work concentrated on developing survival skills for the unemployed. This seemed a basic division among the professionals, some of whom believed their job was primarily to help young people get a job, while others believed it was to help young people cope and amuse themselves because they would never have a job. Not surprisingly many of the professionals seemed depressed and exhausted by a job that confronted so starkly the discrepancy between young people's aspirations and the lack of jobs available.

More recently Coffield (1984) has considered the future for the whole of education in a world without jobs. He suggests that young people are learning to live with unemployment, with moving in and out of jobs, and with government schemes. Furthermore he notes how the education system and particular schools should be willing to adapt their curriculum for new circumstances. He proposed a new organisation formed by schools, universities and colleges of education that would translate research findings into industrial terms, and vice versa; give educational institutions rapid and reliable feedback on the general and specific skills needed by young workers at the beginning of their careers; and use latest research findings to update educational curricula. Thus 'a return for a steady stream of articulate, literate and numerate young workers and managers with the appropriate skills, local industry would pay to keep both the university and local schools in the vanguard of progress' (p. 41).

EXPLAINING THE CAUSES OF UNEMPLOYMENT

A number of writers have suggested that people out of work for long periods of time tend to offer fatalistic explanations for the causes of their own and others' unemployment (M. Jahoda, 1979b; O'Brien and Kabaroff, 1979; Hayes and Nutman, 1981).

Furnham (1982c) set out to examine differences in the explanations for unemployment in Britain as a function of whether people were employed or unemployed as well as their age, sex, education and voting pattern. It was hypothesised that more unemployed people would find societal (external social, economic and political factors) and fatalistic (luck, chance, fate) explanations important for unemployment than employed people, who

Table 7.3: Means and F levels for the explanations for unemployment offered by employed and unemployed subjects

Explanations	*Employed*	*Unemployed*	*F level*
A. *Individualistic*			
Unemployed people can earn more money on social security	5.21	5.31	0.17
Lack of effort and laziness among unemployed people	5.13	4.81	1.72
Unemployed people don't try hard enough to get jobs	3.15	4.21	13.22[a]
Unemployed people are too fussy and proud to accept some jobs	4.89	4.57	1.67
Poor education and qualifications among unemployed people	4.40	3.55	12.94[a]
Unwillingness of unemployed to move to places of work	4.32	5.51	10.60[a]
Inability of unemployed people to adapt to new conditions	4.77	4.38	3.44[c]
Lack of intelligence or ability among the unemployed	5.46	4.76	9.70[b]
B. *Societal*			
The policies and strategies of the present government	2.05	2.33	1.48
The policies and strategies of previous British overnments	2.82	2.85	0.06
Inefficient and less competitive industries that go bankrupt	3.38	3.45	0.10
An influx of immigrants have taken up all available jobs	5.32	3.92	29.09[a]
Trade unions have priced their members out of a job	4.37	3.85	4.83[c]
Overmanning in industry which has occurred for too long	3.53	3.93	2.93
Incompetent industrial management with poor planning	2.94	3.46	5.98[b]
Weak trade unions that do not fight to keep jobs	4.80	3.58	26.05[a]
C. *Fatalistic*			
Sickness and physical handicap among unemployed people	5.14	3.74	29.32[a]
Just bad luck	5.73	5.27	4.63[c]
World-wide recession and inflation	2.19	2.57	3.69[c]
The introduction of widespread automation	3.70	3.09	6.14[b]

Note: [a] $p < .001$ [b] $p < .01$ [c] $p < .05$

Following scale: Important, 1; *Unimportant,* 7.

Source: Furnham, 'Explanations for unemployment in Britain', in *European Journal of Psychology* 1982, *12*, 335–52. Reprinted by permission of John Wiley & Sons, Ltd.

would find individualistic explanations (internal dispositional and personality factors) more important. It was also hypothesised that Conservative (right-wing) voters would find individualistic explanations for unemployment more important than employed Labour voters, who would find societal factors more important. The results showed a predictable pattern of differences between the employed and unemployed, the former believing more in individualistic explanations and less in societal explanations than the latter.

However whereas there were few sex and age differences, education and vote revealed numerous differences in explanations for unemployment. As is the case with explanations for poverty (see Chapter 5), Conservatives found individualistic explanations for unemployment more important than Labour voters, who in turn found societal explanations more important than Conservative voters. It was suggested that the results confirm the theses of a number of writers in the field (Tiffany *et al.,* 1970) that unemployed people will be more external in their attributions for the causes of unemployment than employed people, though this is only a matter of degree. Furthermore, according to Hayes and Nutman (1981) and others, this pattern should increase the longer a person remains out of work. Yet the overall national unemployment figures would probably affect this relationship. As unemployment grows, even employed people tend to offer societal and fatalistic (external) explanations for unemployment partly as a defence against becoming unemployed themselves.

More recently Furnham (1982a) looked specifically at the relationship between Protestant work ethic beliefs and attitudes towards and explanations for unemployment. Most of previous research concerned the relationship between work ethic beliefs and paid work. However Furnham (1983a) looked at the relationship between work ethic beliefs and unemployment. As predicted, subjects who strongly endorsed the work ethic endorsed negative individualistic explanations for unemployment and were, by and large, more against welfare payments than subjects who did not strongly endorse these beliefs. This confirms MacDonald's (1971) finding that Protestant work ethic believers were proponents of the ethics of social responsibility which tend to blame people rather than 'the system' for the source of their difficulty. It also confirms other findings which suggest that these beliefs (as measured by any of the Protestant work ethic scales) are part of a general conservative attitude pattern. These results are also in accordance with studies of lay beliefs about economics (poverty, wealth unemployment, taxation, social security, etc.), which suggest that there are coherent lay 'theories' about such matters. Thus a high Protestant work ethic scorer is likely to explain poverty in terms of idleness and poor money management, wealth in terms of hard work, honesty and saving unemployment in terms of laziness and lack of effort, and he is likely to be against both taxation and social security (Furnham, 1982a, p. 283).

Although most of the research on explanations for unemployment has been stimulated by other work within an attribution theory context, other conceptual frameworks have been put forward. Moscovici (1981) has argued that social representations (set of concepts, statements and explanations originating in daily life in the course of inter-individual communication) in fact determine people's attribution about such things as unemployment benefits. Whereas attribution theory is concerned with the way individuals attribute causes to events that belong to their experience, the theory of social representations concerns how groups or individuals create a stable world in which diverse, unfamiliar or unpredictable behaviours are given meaning and become familiar and predictable. He maintains that people gather information, classify it into certain categories *and then* attempt to explain it. He believes that attributions follow from social representation and not the reverse.

I am convinced that the theory of attribution will become more fruitful and less mechanical as soon as it recognizes the importance of the content of representation and its social character. Any reduction to cognitive patterns and constructs, by eliminating the extraordinary richness of collective thought, its rootedness in a well defined setting, and by flattening all social relation into interaction between two individuals, converts an important problem into a mere academic exercise. (p. 208)

He in fact illustrates his point by reference to unemployment:

Some think of the unemployed person as lazy, unlucky or as incompetent in looking for work; others consider him to be the victim of economic downturn, of social injustice and the contradictions of the capitalist regime. The former attribute the cause of unemployment to the individual, to his way of facing the world, and the latter to the general situation, to the individual's class affiliation and to the way in which the world treats him. Obviously this divergence is due altogether to their respective social representations. One representation gives precedence, under all circumstances, to personal responsibility, individual effort, and individual solutions to the problems of society; the other leads to a sharp awareness of social injustice and social responsibility, contemplating collective solutions to individual problems.' (pp. 107–8)

La France and Cicchetti (1979) were concerned with social-class and employment-status determinants of the perceived responsibility and blame for economic success and failure. Four groups of subjects (middle-class employed, middle-class unemployed, working-class employed, working-class unemployed) were asked a series of questions about a stimulus figure that they had read about. They found that subjects were more concerned with praising the successful job-seeker than with blaming the unsuccessful. The middle-class subjects distinguished significantly more between success and failure than working-class subjects, assigning more responsibility to the former and less to the latter. The middle class also believed personality to be more influencial than the working class. Overall employed subjects assigned more responsibility to the stimulus person and saw luck as being less influential in the successful outcome than did the unemployed. Nearly all of the studies in this section on explanations for unemployment used a limited and unrepresentative sample and a structured questionnaire. However more recent studies have considered a free-response interview format with large, representative samples.

In a free-response study Lewis and Furnham (1984) asked 450 people how they believed unemployment could be reduced. Many different answers were given, such as lowering the retirement age, increasing job-creation schemes, increase public spending, etc. Most people gave answers which implied a stimulation of the economy, a number for the redistribution of jobs, yet about 15 per cent could provide no answer at all. When given six closed questions it was found that over 90 per cent of the sample believed that the level of unemployment in Britain was unacceptably high, while 66 per cent argued that the government should spend more money in order to reduce unemployment. There were some interesting and predictable sex, age and employment history differences: e.g. women were against sacrificing their jobs if their husbands were unemployed but did favour job-sharing and reducing working hours; similarly younger people seemed more liberal than older people in that they did not believe in curbing immigration or in women giving up jobs.

Using a large and representative sample, Lewis *et al.* (1984) asked 900 British people to explain the causes of unemployment. Content analysis using 13 economic codes revealed that 28 per cent of the explanations concerned falling demand for goods, 23 per cent the rate of inflation 18 per cent government policy and 17 per cent high wage demands. Curiously, there were very few demographic differences, though many were investigated (sex, class, age, housing, trade union membership). These explanations (many of which defied coding) were reclassified into the three categories used by Furnham (1982c): 78 per cent of the explanations were societal, 24 per cent fatalistic and only 7 per cent individual. What was particularly striking about the explanations offered for unemployment was the fact that so few were purely economic—that is, lay explanations for economic phenomena are often normative, moralistic, and sociopolitical as well as economic.

WOMEN'S UNEMPLOYMENT

Even less research has been devoted to unemployment among women than to the effects of employment on well-being, self-esteem, etc. (Spitze and Waite, 1981; Faver, 1982).

In a review of work and well-being in women, Warr and Parry (1982) found that the association between employment status and psychological well-being is mediated by a woman's occupational status, the quality of her non-occupational environment, and the quality of her employment relationship. In certain circumstances psychological well-being is significantly associated with having paid employment—in single rather than married, and working-class rather than middle-class women. Although there appears to be a paucity of good research in this area, the results seem to indicate that work outside of the home is not generally as important to the well-being of women as it is of men. Indeed various studies have shown deleterious effects of work on physical and psychological health (Zimmerman and Hartley, 1982). In a study of the lives of women managers, Cooper and Davidson (1982) found that compared with men, women have major additional stresses to cope with, and that often their home life obstructs rather than supports their careers. Similarly Faver (1982) found that a women's labour force participation is partially a function of the interaction between career and family task demands and values.

Almost no work has been done on unemployed women. An exception is Warr and Parry (1982) who looked at depressed mood in working-class mothers with and without paid employment. They compared the depressed mood scores for matched full-time employed, part-time employed and non-employed mothers, and they found a large significant difference indicating that the former were least depressed and the latter most depressed. They also looked at various other variables such as their attitude to employment, strain in coping with domestic and paid work duties, the amount of social support they received, and their child-care demands. Overall the strain in coping variable was the most predictive of depressed mood in that employed mothers with high interaction strain have mood scores similar to those without paid employment and part-time employees with high strain have particularly high depressed mood scores. The smallest associations with depressed mood were child-care demands. The authors are conscious of the experimental shortcomings of their and others' work, especially in the need to control for various important demographic variables.

CONCLUSION

This chapter has attempted to review the now voluminous literature on unemployment under selected headings. Of course, there are others topics; for instance, there have been a few studies on personality differences between the employed and the unemployed. Hartley (1980) set about exploring the popular myth that unemployed managers possess fewer characteristics traditionally associated with managerial ability than employed managers. Contrary to this belief, a group of unemployed managers were significantly more outgoing, conscientious and imaginative than a group of matched employed managers. There was no evidence that the unemployed were more shy, tender-minded, forthright, apprehensive, conservative, tense or anxious that the employed managers. There are of course macroeconomic and organisational factors associated with unemployment and the author concludes from her data that researchers need to get away from conceptualising the 'problem' of unemployment strictly in individualistic terms.

Finally, there has also been some work on value systems of the unemployed which deserve mention. Penner and Rokeach (1969) hypothesised that there would be certain changes in salient variables as a result of changes in employment conditions. They contacted four groups: temporarily unemployed subsequently employed; actually unemployed subsequently employed; temporarily unemployed still unemployed; and actually unemployed still unemployed. For the first group the value 'broadminded' became significantly more important and 'polite' less important, which was also true of the second group. For the unemployed groups the terminal value 'equality' became less important especially for the third group, possibly because they were more concerned with their own well-being. The fourth hard-core group rated 'salvation', 'tender' and 'polite' as more important and 'patient' as less important over time. In Australia, O'Brien and Kabaroff (1979) found that compared with employed workers the unemployed had poor physical health, lower work values and higher external control orientation, and made more use of community helping agencies. The work value differences showed that the unemployed tended to desire less influence, interaction and pressure in their work compared with the employed.

Research on unemployment is scattered across a wide number of disciplines: economics, education, psychiatry, psychology (clinical, educational, occupational and social) and sociology. Although some results are equivocal and others contradictory, various themes and established findings emerge. For instance, studies on the psychological consequences of unemployment tend to point in the same direction, namely that unemployment causes stress, a lowering of self-esteem and a change in expectations. Similarly the work on attributions and explanations has revealed consistent findings. Taken together they show a vicious circle for those who are unemployed. Loss of work leads to lowered self-esteem, and possibly mental and physical illness and low expectations for getting work. These in turn lead to poor or maladaptive job-search strategies, so confirming beliefs. Hence we find self-fulfilling prophecies or reciprocal determinism (Feather, 1982).

Although research in this area is comparatively recent, difficult and expensive, there is no excuse for poor research which only leads to unreliable, unconfirmed and ambiguous findings. Researchers need to be more specific in the individual difference, organisational and macroeconomic factors which together influence unemployment. For instance three categories of individual difference factors need to be considered: (i) psychological differences in personality, self-concept, beliefs, and skills prior and subsequent to unemployment; (ii) there are demographic differences in age, sex, religious and ethnic group, schooling, class, etc, which condition expectations and coping strategies; and (iii) there are work experience differences in that some people have had some or all or none of the work experiences possible: full-time, part-time, voluntary, none. Similarly there are a number of organisational differences which have to be considered such as its size, structure, social support, manning levels, etc. Finally, gross macroeconomic factors, such as the inflation and unemployment rate, levels of social security and unemployment benefit, must be taken into consideration.

The problem with a lot of research is that, in that it has concentrated on a few specific variables, others have been ignored or at worst confounded. The reactions and hardship of people who are jobless seem sufficiently severe and important to merit good research for only sensible policy decisions can be made on the basis of good research findings.

8 The Protestant Work Ethic: Work Beliefs and Habits

INTRODUCTION

It has long been pointed out that psychology has two rather different traditions: *experimental*, which is concerned with general laws of behaviour, and *correlational*, which is concerned with individual differences in behaviour. One of the most interesting questions for the psychologist interested in economic behavour concerns which individual factors determine economic beliefs and behaviour. Traditionally psychologists have considered different types of individual difference factors: demographic (age, sex, class), personality (introversion, anxiety) and belief (political, social) variables, attempting to explain how, which and when individual differences are important in explaining and describing economic behaviour.

What is clearly important in this area is to delineate which of the myriad of possible variables explains most of the variance. This chapter is a review of the psychological literature on a concept that has been described as one of the most parsimonious for predicting economic behaviour (Furnham, 1984d). It is furthermore a concept that straddles all the social sciences and one which has commanded an extensive literature—the Protestant work ethic (PWE) as specified by Weber (1905).

Weber's theory was introduced into psychology by McClelland (1961) who offered a social-psychological explanation for the link between Protestantism and capitalism. The theory is simply that PWE ideas and values determine child-rearing practices of independence, procrastination of gratifications and mastery training, which in turn leads to the children acquiring strong achievement motivation. These high achievers in turn become successful entrepreneurs and create an expansion of business. In doing so McClelland extended previous research on individual achievement to the macro-societal level. In a lengthy historical and conceptual review he found relationships between the achievement level of a society (as measured by the content of children's literature) and the subsequent growth or decline in capitalism and industrialisation in that society. For instance he found that from 1500 to 1800 achievement motivation in England rose and fell with the level of coal imports. In a further study of 40 nations, he found a correlation of 0.53 between achievement motivation in 1925 and the growth in the electricity supply. Recent cross-cultural work in 30 cultures has documented the relationship between PWE type beliefs and achievement (Fyans *et al.*, 1983).

McClelland has subsumed the PWE concept into the need for achievement (nAch) concept which he saw as a basic dimension of personality. Indeed, results from studies on high achievers are similar to those from studies on people with high PWE beliefs—high achievers tend to do their best to obtain monetary and other rewards in laboratory games and tasks; they set themselves high but realistic targets; and are optimistic about the outcome, etc. More recent work on A-type behaviour would suggest that PWE beliefs, need for achievement and control, and A-type behaviour patterns are all linked (Furnham, 1983d).

Despite the fact that McClelland's work has spawned a great deal of research on nAch it has been criticised for having very poor measurement techniques, and equivocal findings. Furthermore, the nAch concept has concentrated on only some aspects of the PWE belief such as hard work, productivity and frugality, while ignoring others such as asceticism. Nevertheless the suggestion that nAch is a stable disposition resulting from early socialisation in the PWE probably encouraged other researchers to operationalise and attempt to measure PWE beliefs as an important individual difference variable in its own right.

However it has not been until comparatively recently that psychologists (primarily occupational and social psychologists) have actively pursued research using the PWE concept. Although psychologists have been interested (and probably ignorant) in the origins of PWE and of the criticism of Weber's thesis, they have recognised the behaviour pattern of the typical high PWE believer. However it is quite possible that PWE behaviour, as described by psychologists, has become independent of PWE beliefs as described by Weber. Scholars conversant with Weber's original thesis may however take issue with psychologists for not having read thoroughly or understood the PWE concept. That is, it may be argued, that scales devised to measure the PWE might measure some aspect of a person's belief system and behavioural patterns but definitely not what Weber himself had in mind. Hence the use of the term PWE by psychologists may be challenged.

Most of the research on the PWE has been concerned with devising a valid and reliable measure of PWE beliefs, and seeing how these beliefs related to variable aspects of work and non-work. Some work has however also been done on demographic attitudinal and personality determinants of PWE beliefs.

MEASUREMENT OF THE PROTESTANT WORK ETHIC

A number of self-report scales have been devised to measure the extent to which a person believes in the Protestant work ethic. Those not often used in research include the pro-Protestant Ethic Scale (Blood, 1969), the Survey of

Work Values (Wollack *et al.*, 1971) and the Protestant Work Ethic Scale (Mirels and Garrett, 1971). Furthermore other self-report scales concerning beliefs about work have sub-scales measuring such things as the work ethic (Buchholz, 1976). A problem with all these scales is that they are derived from either divergent interpretations or a very narrow reading of Weber's original works. Where high intercorrelations exist between scales they may simply be due to extensive item overlap between the different measures. Thus although they may all be measuring much the same thing, it may be inaccurate to describe it as PWE belief in the Weberian sense.

Perhaps the first attempt to devise a self-report measure for PWE beliefs was the work of two sociologists, Goldstein and Eichborn (1961), who used a simple 4-item scale which had been used earlier in unpublished work and shown to have a coefficient and reproducability of 0.91. In their research using this measure they found that high PWE beliefs were found to be related to individualism and asceticism, but no longer necessarily productive of systematic, rational, economic behaviour. The sociologists Hammond and Williams (1976) also developed a PWE scale (unworldly ascetic and spirit of capitalism) but provide little evidence of the validity or reliability.

Another short measure is the Pro-Protestant ethic scale (Blood, 1969) which has two 4-item sub-scales (pro- and non-Protestant ethic). The scale was initially tested on a group of over 400 airmen and passengers and appeared to show a reasonable factor structure and validity statistics. Later research by Wanous (1974) showed that the scale had a reasonable reliability coefficient, while Greenberg (1978) found evidence of the scale's construct validity. Cook *et al.* (1981) report on four recent studies which used this measure.

The survey of Work Values scale (Wollack *et al.*, 1971) is the longest, but perhaps the least used of these measures, though it has been used by Stone (1976, 1978). It is a 54-item scale, with 9 times covering each of six areas: activity preference, job involvement, pride in work, social status of job, upward showing and attitude toward earnings. The first three sub-scales supposedly measure intrinsic aspects of the Protestant ethic, while the latter three sub-scales measure extrinisic aspects. A correlational, discriminant and factor analysis all lend support to the various components of the scale

A similar multidimensional scale is the long questionnaire measuring Beliefs about Work, Buchholz (1976) developed a scale which has five indices: the work ethic, the leisure ethic, the organisational belief system Marxist-related beliefs and the humanistic belief system. Although some factor analytic work was done on the original item pool, no descriptive statistics have been provided. The scale has been used by Dickson and Buchholz (1977, 1979) and Buchholz (1978).

The Protestant Ethic Scale (Mirels and Garrett 1971) is perhaps the best known and most widely used of the three scales. It is a 19-item scale developed on three large student samples, and it appeared to correlate in a logical manner with a number of other measures. Later work by Kidron (1978) revealed reasonable reliability coefficients, while Lied and Pritchard (1976) report five recent studies which have used this measure though there are many more (Furnham, 1982a).

More recently Ray (1982) has developed an 18-item Eclectic Protestant Ethic scale, which was constructed 'to give some alternative to the rather pugnacious tone of the Mirels and Garrett items and because that scale has virtually no control against acquiescent response set' (p. 131). The author also attacks the Blood (1969) scale, as he found no significant negative correlation between the two sub-scales. He found that his new scale was significantly correlated with church attendance, religious belief and the Mirels and Garrett (1971) and Ray (1970) scales, and in a number of studies he demonstrated its reliability.

Few attempts have been made to compare these scales. An exception is Waters *et al.* (1975) who administered the Blood (1969), Wollack *et al.* (1971) and Mirels and Garrett (1971) scales to 165 students. All of the six sub-scales from the Wollack *et al.* (1971) scale correlated with the other scales, though they ranged from 0.24 to 0.49. The Blood (1969) scale correlated 0.70 with the Mirels and Garrett scale (1971), which is encouraging. A factor analysis of the Protestant ethic scale yielded two factors—intrinsic (work-related) and extrinsic (reward-related)—and the Blood (1969) and Mirels and Garrett (1971) scales loaded substantially on both factors.

Although there has not been a great deal of psychometric assessment on these self-report measures they appear to be moderately reliable and valid measures of the same thing. Certain criticisms may be levelled at them however: they may have more items in favour of the work ethic than against it; all the scales appear sexist in their language; many appear to be multi-dimensional but provide only one total score; too often they have been validated on students alone; and the extremeness of many of the items may induce various artificial response sets. Nevertheless it should be pointed out that they are probably no better or worse than numerous other measures in this area of work—beliefs, attitudes and behaviour.

THE PROTESTANT WORK ETHIC AND WORK

Most studies using the PWE concept have not unsurprisingly looked at the relationship between the PWE and paid employment/work. Most of these have looked at the relationship between the PWE and job satisfaction, but some have looked at actual work behaviour. For example, Blood (1969), using his own scale, found that the more a worker agreed with the ideals of the PWE the more he will be satisfied in his paid work and life in general.

Aldag and Brief (1975) also looked at the relationship between the PWE (as measured by the Blood scale) and certain work values (affective responses, perceived task dimension, perceived leader behaviour, and higher order need strength). The results confirmed the findings of Blood (1969). The pro-Protestant scale was positively correlated with internal work motivation and growth satisfaction as well as higher order need strength. On the other hand the non-Protestant scale was negatively correlated with general satisfaction, external work motivation, supervisory satisfaction, growth satisfaction, skill variety, task identity, task significance, autonomy, feedback from job, leader consideration and high order need strength. Certainly the results supported the hypothesis that adherence to the PWE is associated with strong higher order needs, which are perhaps the main alternatives of work attitudes.

Similarly Kidron (1978) found as predicted a positive relationship between the PWE and moral and calculative commitment to the work organisation. This relationship held over all three organisations tested—an insurance company, a hospital and a personnel department. He concluded that although the PWE is associated with stronger moral identification with the organisation for which one works, it need not necessarily indicate a willingness to remain in a given system.

Others however have found that this relationship is by no means clear, in that other variables are more powerful moderators of this relationship. Armenakis *et al.* (1977) attempted to identify whether the PWE or an individual's need strength would be most useful in identifying those textile workers who demonstrate a positive relationship between job characteristics and job satisfaction. Strong endorsers of the PWE showed positive correlations between job satisfaction and the job characteristics of autonomy, task feedback and friendship. Yet weak endorsers also showed the same positive correlations:

> It may be concluded then, that the moderator variable individual need strength is more discriminating than is PWE. . . . Therefore, being able to identify individuals as being strong PWE does not enable one to predict satisfaction any more accurately than being able to identify individuals as being weak PWE. (p. 1153)

Stone (1975, 1976) also found a positive relationship between job scope and job satisfaction, but neither the PWE nor any of its sub-scales (as measured by the Wollack *et al.* (1971) scale) appeared to moderate the job scope/satisfaction relationship. Ganster (1980) also found no direct relationship between PWE beliefs and job satisfaction. He attempted to test the moderating effects of the PWE, growth need strength, nAch and arousal-seeking tendency on task design relationships on 190 college students. He found that none of the individual difference variables moderated the objective scope/satisfaction relationship, althougth nAch did moderate the perceived scope/satisfaction relationship.

Earlier studies too found the PWE to be only a moderately useful predictor variable of job attitude. Wanous (1974) found higher order need strength, followed by the PWE and lastly urban-rural backgrounds are good predictors of reactions to job characteristics. However, as he noted;

The fact that higher order need strength yielded the clearest results seems reasonable because it is closest to the employee reactions it moderates. Thus, it is also not surprising that the PWE showed moderate usefulness as a moderator and urban/rural background the least because each is increasingly farther removed from on-the-job attitudes and behaviour. (p. 622)

Other studies have looked at the relationship between PWE and actual work behaviour. Merrens and Garrett (1975) suggested that as the PWE holds that hard steady work is itself worthy, and unwillingness to work is seen as a symptom of absence of grace or as sinful, high PWE scorers would perform better on tasks designed to provide low motivation and interest levels. As predicted they found high PWE scorers spent significantly more time participating in a boring repetitive task than low PWE scorers. Ganster (1981) however failed to replicate this result and concluded that Merrens and Garrett's task was not representative of real jobs and that their experiment may well have induced apprehension, evaluation and hence blessed the results.

Greenberg (1977) found that high PWE scorers' performances improved and low PWE scorers' performances declined when given negative performance evaluation. He also found that, when told a co-worker was superior to them at a task which brought them unearned rewards, high PWE scorers performed at a high level and felt neutral about the task, whereas low PWE scorers performed poorly but liked the task. In a later study Greenberg (1978) found that belief in the PWE among train commuters correlated positively with the relative frequency of working compared to not working while commuting, perception of commuting as an extension of work rather than leisure, and a preference for working rather than commuting. More recently Greenberg (1979) has shown that endorsing of the PWE is related to perceived fairness in using various equity inputs. In one experiment high PWE scorers were shown to distribute money to hypothetical workers in proportion to their total productivity by taking into account both the quantity and duration of work, while low PWE scorers paid only according to duration ignoring quantity. It was also found that high PWE scorers believe it fairer to base reward on performance when differences were attributed to internal rather than external causes, while the reverse was found for low PWE scorers.

The literature on the PWE and work belief and behaviour is therefore inconsistent. The PWE does not appear to be the major determinant of job satisfaction, though it does appear to predict certain quantitative and qualitative aspects of work behaviour. By and large, PWE believers had to work harder and be more satisfied with extrinsic aspects of their work and PWE beliefs appear to be closely associated with strong higher order needs. However considerably more and better research needs to be done in this area if firm conclusions about PWE beliefs as measured by self-report inventories and work behaviour are to be established.

THE PROTESTANT WORK ETHIC AND UNEMPLOYMENT

Whereas most of the previous studies have concerned the relationship between the Protestant work beliefs and paid work, some studies have looked at the relationship betwen these beliefs and unemployment. Furnham (1982a) asked subjects to rate the importance of various explanations for unemployment in Britain, as well as their agreement with various statements about social security (welfare) payments to the unemployed. As predicted, subjects who strongly endorsed the Protestant work ethic belief stressed negative individualistic explanations for unemployment and were by and large more against welfare payments than subjects who did not strongly endorse these beliefs. This confirms MacDonald's (1971) finding that PWE believers were proponents of the ethics of social responsibility which tend to blame people rather than 'the system' for the source of their difficulty. It also confirms other findings which suggest that the PWE is part of a general conservative attitude pattern (Mirels and Garrett, 1971; MacDonald, 1972; Beit-Hallahmi, 1979; Furnham, 1984d). These results are also in accordance with studies of lay beliefs about economics (poverty, wealth, unemployment, taxation, social security, etc.) which suggests that there are coherent lay 'theories' about such matters (Feagin, 1972; Feather, 1974; Forgas *et al.*, 1982; Furnham 1982a, b, c). Thus a high PWE scorer is likely to see poverty in terms of idleness and poor money management; wealth in terms of hard work, honesty and saving; unemployment in terms of laziness and lack of effort; and is likely to be against both taxation and social security (Furnham, 1983f). Nearly all of the analysis in Furnham's (1982a) study confirmed this view. The only exception being that of two fatalistic explanations for unemployment which, contrary to expectation, high PWE scorers endorsed more than low scorers. Research into locus of control and the PWE (Mirels and Garrett, 1971; Waters *et al.*, 1975) would suggest that they are related, yet as MacDonald (1972) has found this is only true for males and not females.

Further, in a study of the unemployed themselves Feather (1982a) found that young unemployed Australians had lower PWE scores than a comparable employed group. His results also showed that the active pursuit of employment tended to be more frequent among those unemployed with strong PWE values. He also found a confirmation of the results of Furnham (1982a and c)—a difference in attributional style of unemployed compared with employed people in that the former tend to blame bad events on stable recurrent aspects of the self that are outside the personal world and to externalise good events by attributing them to certain external factors that might not occur again (e.g. interaction of others, etc.).

Kelvin (1980) has set the relationships between PWE beliefs and unemployment in temporal perspective: 'What is happening in our time is precisely such a shifting of the attribution of responsibility for being unemployed from an internal personal level to the exterior situational level, this is not so much a cause as a manifestation of the end of the Protestant Work Ethic' (p. 309). However the studies of Feather (1982ab) and Furnham (1982a) would suggest that this is only true of the unemployed and/or those with low PWE beliefs. Thus, because of the stress on the virtue of hard work (doctrine of calling) and personal control over one's life (doctrine of sanctification) PWE believers are intolerant of, and unsympathetic to the poor, the unemployed and the disadvantaged. They are seen as non-elect, idle and damned, rather than the hard-working successful and elect. The unemployed, however, or those less concerned with PWE, tend to be sympathetic to the unemployed simply because they believe and attribute the causes of their plight to external social factors, rather than lack of individual effort.

THE PROTESTANT WORK ETHIC AND INDIVIDUAL DIFFERENCES

The way in which the various Protestant work ethic scales have most often been validated is by correlating them with numerous personality and individual difference measures. It has been suggested that PWE beliefs are closely related to a number of other psychological variables. These can be divided into two groups: personality and belief variables, and demographic variables, the former having received more attention than the latter.

1. Personality Variables

Since Mirels and Garrett (1971) suggested that PWE beliefs may be considered a personality variable (that is, a stable disposition) a number of studies have correlated individual difference measures with one or other measures of the PWE. A wide variety of personality measures have been used, but in different studies (with different populations, and often different PWE measures) the results have been remarkably similar. For instance when comparing the locus of control scale with the PWE, Mirels and Garrett (1971) found a significant correlation of –0.30; Waters *et al.* (1975)

–0.35, Lied and Pritchard (1976) –0.41; and McDonald (1972) –0.23. Similarly two studies which have used the California F scale found similar positive correlations between it and PWE beliefs: Mirels and Garrett (1971), 0.51 McDonald (1972), 0.44 and Joe (1974) 0.38.

Other related measures have shown a similar pattern. Mirels and Garrett (1971) found a significant correlation between the PWE and morality conscience and guilt, while Lied and Pritchard (1976) found a significant correlation between the PWE and restraint. McDonald (1971) found that endorsement of the ethics of social responsibility correlated with the PWE indicating that proponents of the ethics of social responsibility tend to blame people rather than the 'system' for the source of their difficulty.

In a later paper MacDonald (1972) looked at the relationship between the PWE, beliefs about the poor and human values. He found as predicted that the PWE was significantly related to negative attitudes towards the poor and opposition to a guaranteed minimum annual income. Further he found that such values as 'comfortable life, equality, an exciting life and pleasure were negatively related, and ambition, self-control and salvation, positively related to the PWE'. He suggests that the construct of the PWE may 'be valuable to those who are concerned with identifying and subsequently altering the attitudes and dispositions that militate against the success of our nation's poverty programs' (p. 121).

In a study comparing PWE beliefs with established measures of personality, Rim (1977) found that men whose PWE scores were above the median tended to be more intelligent, less extravert and less neurotic than those below the median though the very opposite was true for women. He offers no theoretical interpretation of these results. Few other studies in this area appear to exist.

Despite the variety of measures correlated with the PWE beliefs there appears to be coherence to these results. Studies on the psychology of conservatism (Wilson, 1973; Joe *et al.*, 1981) have noted a number of characteristics of the conservative person which are strikingly similar to those with PWE beliefs: religious fundamentalism, pro-establishment politics, insistence on rules or punishments, pro-militarism, preference for conventional art and institutions, an anti-hedonistic outlook, an intolerance of minority groups and a superstitious resistance to science. Indeed Furnham and Bland (1983) have demonstrated that PWE beliefs are consistently significantly related to more general conservative social attitudes and conclude that it would be unlikely that PWE beliefs would change without the other beliefs doing likewise.

The high PWE believer then is likely to be conservative in his views, have an internal locus of control, and to be concerned with self-control. He is likely to hold values that are concerned with achievement and ambition, but be against pleasure and relaxation. The PWE believer thus favours an ascetic rather than an aesthetic life-style.

2. Demographic Variables

A number of studies have attempted to establish demographic determinants of current beliefs in the PWE. Beit-Hallahmi (1979) found that PWE scores were significantly related to religious self-identification (Catholics and Protestants had higher scores than Jews and agnostics), ethnic background (white groups had higher scores than black groups), political self-identification (Conservatives had higher scores than Liberals and Leftists) and religious beliefs (people with conventional beliefs and high church attendance figures scored more highly than those with unconventional beliefs or poor attendance figures) but not to socioeconomic status. He concluded:

> The results may be interpreted as indicating that the PWE is separate from what is commonly referred to as 'achievement motivation' and that the PWE can be more correctly regarded as an attack towards work. ... The Protestant Ethic should be regarded as an orientation, toward the place of work in one's life and society, which is related to a great extent to social background variables. (p. 266)

Ray (1982) found that his PWE scale predicted both church attendance and religious belief but was not related to education or self-assigned social class. As Beit-Hallahmi (1979) had found, PWE beliefs did *not* discriminate between Protestants and Catholics

> We now have some reason to believe that the Protestant ethic as such has perhaps run its course, in any way to say that the spirit of enterprise or the worship of work is now dead it is only to say that all religions have come to share these attributes to an equal degree. The Protestant ethic in substantive terms is certainly not yet dead, it is just no longer Protestant. (p. 135)

Some studies have found that PWE beliefs are related to age—e.g. Aldag and Brief (1975) found a significant correlation between PWE beliefs and age. But neither Buchholz (1978) nor Furnham (1982a) found a significant relationship. Similarly there appears to be no sex differences in PWE belief (Furnham 1982a).

Thus there are no simple patterns in the relationship between demographic variables such as age, sex and class and PWE beliefs. Although there is a tendency for older, lower-middle-class people with a Conservative outlook to endorse PWE beliefs more than younger, middle-class or radical people, many other variables mediate this relationship. Most importantly perhaps is the feeling that the PWE does not now discriminate between Protestant and other Christian believers. Hence one finds some writers who have dropped the term Protestant and simply talk of the work ethic.

THE FUTURE OF THE PWE

Kelvin (1980) has recently considered the future of the PWE and its relevance to social psychology. With the inexorable decline of the PWE, rising unemployment and a decline in the central significance of work, Kelvin sees major cultural changes.

> The outcome of that change will be the acceptance of being unemployed as an essentially normal rather than deviant condition, like maternity or retirement rather than like poncing or recidivism. With this will come financial provision for the unemployed at comfortable levels of subsistence and the acceptability of unemployment and the provisions for the unemployed will greatly reduce the significance and status attached to work. (p. 306)

However Kelvin (1980) does not see the complete disappearance of the PWE but its transformation. Examples of this are cited such as the enthusiasm for do-it-yourself and home improvements literature which are seen as late twentieth-century descendants of Victorian working and lower-middle-class self-improvement literature. The do-it-yourself enthusiasts favour economy, work and independence all of which are core values of the PWE. Further the distinction between work and leisure will no doubt be softened. Thus for Kelvin there will be a steady decline in the PWE (at least in richer, western countries) though it may go through a number of transformations. Whereas religious beliefs may have been seen to lead to the development of the PWE, changes in the economy and the rise of structural unemployment are seen to lead to its decline and transformation. Indeed there are numerous popular calls for the end of the PWE which is seen at best to be inappropriate and at worst malicious in its consequences.

However Furnham and Bland (1983) are not as convinced as Kelvin regarding the future of the PWE. They argue that because PWE beliefs are such an integral part of general conservative beliefs and values in general one can only expect them to decline, if conservative beliefs do likewise. As there is no reason to suppose conservative beliefs will go into decline, there is no reason to suspect PWE beliefs also to do so. Though these beliefs may not change, their manifestations in such things as do-it-yourself, professional and trades work may undergo some change. Following from McClelland's analysis therefore if people still socialise their children in the traditional middle-class values of independence, mastery training, saving and achievement they will develop as adults beliefs that are similar to PWE beliefs. Unless of course their early primary socialisation experiences are changed by later secondary socialisation experiences in school or ordinary life, there can be no reason to expect the decline of the PWE.

However if indeed social welfare, taxation and other social benefit policies change radically in a country it is possible that the experience that people have as a result of these changes will lead them to alter their PWE beliefs (in either direction).

THE WEALTH ETHIC

In a lengthy and scholarly consideration of the PWE Kelvin and Jarrett (1985) argue that the PWE is a myth historically but presently evoked as an explanation which has no real basis.

> In effect, the Protestant Work Ethic is no longer just an idea discussed by academics, it has become part of public opinion: it has become so mainly because those who write and talk about 'Public Opinion' regularly explain that opinion in terms of the Work Ethic; and in doing so they have disseminated the *concept* of this Ethic. Repeated recourse to the Protestant Work Ethic as an 'explanation' has thus made it into a self-fulfilling prophesy: it has become a generally accepted way of looking at the unemployed and their problems. (p. 157)

Later they argue that the ethic which has truly been dominant and pervasive is not the work but the wealth ethic:

> Wealth is (quite correctly) perceived as the basis of economic independence; that is the key issue, and has been so for centuries. The 'ethic' is to make or to have sufficient wealth not to have to depend on others; work is only one means to that end and certainly not the one universally most esteemed; not in any class. Provided that one has money enough to be independent, there is no great moral obligation to work, certainly not in the sense of gainful, productive employment . . . The rest, even if they *also* gain numerous other satisfactions from work, work for the money, and the things which money enables them to have and to do. Within *this* ethic, the problem of the unemployed is not that they are 'idle' but that they are poor. The difference matters, especially from a psychological standpoint, and the myth of the Protestant Work Ethic has obscured it. In the final analysis, explanations in terms of an ethic rest on the distinction between the 'good' and the 'bad'. . . We have a psychologically vested interest in explanations in terms of the Protestant Work Ethic. Given our picture of ourselves as fundamentally moral, it is much more congenial to us to attribute our attitudes to the unemployed as 'conditioned' by an ethic, than as motivated by meanness. (pp. 158–9)

In their critique therefore Kelvin and Jarrett (1985) attack not only modern psychological and 'lay' interpretations of the PWE but also beliefs analysis itself. Their evidence is conceptual and not empirical but no less worthy of attention. If they are correct that the PWE is not so much a work as a wealth ethic, the social psychological understanding of Weber's thesis and its resultant meanings may be seriously deficient. As they argue work is the norm, not an ethic: it is expected with good statistical reasons, not on the basis of its moral significance. Kelvin and Jarrett (1984) are then much more materialistic in their understandings of current and past work attitudes, beliefs and behaviour and less metaphysical. Certainly it may be argued that PWE scales seem excessively concerned with work and not its fruits (such as wealth).

The work of Kelvin and Jarrett (1985) highlights in a sense the problem with the ahistorical nature and conceptually naive approach of empirical psychologists who, on a preliminary reading of a complex sociological and historical thesis, blandly set out to 'measure' it. What is needed before empirical work proceeds is a careful conceptual analysis of the origin and maintenance of work beliefs and attitudes.

CONCLUSION

More than a decade of intensive work on the PWE beliefs construct has confirmed its place as an important individual difference variable related to human motivation. Psychologists have chosen to conceive of and measure the PWE as a coherent, bi-polar belief system similar to the locus of control or just world belief constructs. Indeed there is a striking similarity between PWE and other individual differences (rather than dispositional) variables such as locus of control and just world belief systems both in their antecedents and determinants. However, as in the above two related concepts no attempt has been made to delineate the aetiology of the beliefs in individuals or the socio-cultural specificity of these beliefs.

Considerable effort has gone into devising valid, reliable and robust self-report questionnaires that measure PWE beliefs, and many exist. However, as in the locus of control construct it is probable that PWE beliefs are multidimensional as Weber (1905) initially suggested—including beliefs about work and leisure, pleasure and indulgence, success and failure, control and fate. Yet the present scales appear to concentrate on only a few of these dimensions and provide a simple single score. This may account for the fact that studies on the PWE and beliefs are equivocal as beliefs need to be subdivided into their various components.

Most of the research on the PWE has concerned PWE beliefs and work, where it has been found to be an only moderately useful predictor of behaviour, values, job satisfaction, etc. However where the PWE beliefs have been examined in relation to poverty, unemployment or mental illness, it has also been shown to be a more useful discriminatory variable. Perhaps the fact that the construct has been called the *Protestant work* ethic, has led psychologists to concentrate on the relationships between PWE beliefs and aspects of work, rather than looking at a range of related areas such as leisure, economic behaviour, health, etc.

The research relating PWE beliefs to other personality variables has been limited but is encouraging. However little or no work has looked at the aetiology and determinants of these beliefs, their stability over time or their cultural specificity. If the PWE beliefs are to be conceived of as a personality dimension as Mirels and Garrett (1971) suggest there is room for a great deal of further empirical and theoretical research in this field.

Finally there remains some confusion as to whether one should talk about the PWE, the work ethic (Buchholz, 1976) or the Protestant ethic (Ray,

1982). The term PWE implies that the concept has been borrowed from the writings of Weber which is clearly not the case, as few psychologists appear to have read his many works in detail or paid much attention to the metaphysical aspects of PWE beliefs. The PWE beliefs and behaviours as defined and measured by the many PWE scales appear to be concerned with work values, beliefs and needs and more particularly 'a person's continuing commitment to paid employment' (Cook *et al.*, 1981, p. 132). Just as it was pointed out that the Holy Roman Empire was neither Holy, nor Roman nor Empire, so it could be claimed that the PWE is neither exclusively Protestant, about only work nor exclusively concerned with ethics. It may therefore be more accurate to talk about work values and beliefs rather than the PWE itself.

In that the PWE seems such a good predictor of work, non-work, and socioeconomic beliefs and behaviours it seems that economic psychologists would do well to concentrate on it as an individual difference variable of great importance and relevance.

Part IV:
Saving, Spending and Gambling

9 The Psychology of Saving, Spending and Gambling

INTRODUCTION

This chapter is about saving, and one particular type of spending—gambling. Spending money is dealt with more specifically in the chapter on consumer behaviour.

However it should be pointed out that spending and saving are often in conflict as they represent the conflict between two types of expenditure. This is based on the simple idea:

Income earned + Amount borrowed = Discretionary and other spending + discretionary and contractual saving.

However, as it will be argued, this idea may be too simplistic particularly as it is often difficult to separate spending from saving. Also it is possible that both discretionary spending and discretionary saving increase because they are desired, while everyday expenditure might decrease.

The juxtapositioning of two rather different forms of economic behaviour—saving and gambling—may not be as odd as one may first think. Although it may be suggested that whereas saving is a rational cautious form of behaviour, and gambling irrational and risky, some might argue the precise opposite for economic as well as psychological reasons.

For instance psychiatrists have described the compulsive saver for whom saving is not a means to an end, it is an end in itself. Saving is its own reward. It has been suggested that compulsive savers have had anxious and insecure childhoods and that saving represents security. It would of course be misleading to suggest that all or indeed even most people are compulsive or irrational savers. (The same may also be true of gamblers.) However it should not be forgotten the motives individuals have for these behaviours are often complex and multifaceted. Furthermore they may not always be logical or rational but perfectly understandable within psychological theorising.

SAVING

One area of concern to both economists and psychologists is *why, how, where* and *how often* people save money, yet the latter have devoted almost no attention to this area. Economists on the other hand have long been interested in this topic though there appears to be more conceptual work than data in this area. Saving for the economist is a decision to refrain from consumption and therefore represents a reduction in demand.

For economists saving consists of earned income left over after consumption and may be held in many forms: cash, in bank accounts, in securities, stocks and bonds or in terms of valuable goods like precious metals, art and real estate. However the distinction between saving and consumption is far from clear and it is only convention that determines that durable goods and art purchases are labelled as consumption while bank accounts are savings. That is, some forms of behaviour can be seen as both saving and investment. Indeed factors that determine the flow of investment—expectations, interest rates, government legislation, technological change—may be equally important in saving. However since Keynes it has been pointed out that investment does not always equal saving.

For many years economists have been interested in the relationship between consumption and income and the average *propensity to consume* which is a ratio of consumption to income, and the *propensity to save* which is a ratio of saving to income. Because disposable income is the total of saving plus total of income, the propensity to consume plus the propensity to save equals one. Much work has gone into attempts to predict the marginal propensity to consume and save as a consequence of fluctuations of income. This becomes extremely important when governments attempt to determine the level of government spending and tax policy. Hence econometricians are employed to plot the saving and consumption function.

Of course economists are also interested in people's motives for saving. Keynes (1936) lists eight main motives or objectives that people have for saving money, though he provides no data in support of his categories. The eight motives were:

1. *Precaution:* To build up a reserve against unforeseen contingencies.
2. *Foresight:* To provide for an anticipated future relation between the income and needs of the individual or his family different from that which exists in the present (old age, education).
3. *Calculation:* To enjoy interest and appreciation—because larger real consumption in the future is preferable to a present smaller consumption.
4. *Improvement:* To enjoy a gradually increasing expenditure since most people look forward to a gradually improving standard of living.
5. *Independence:* To enjoy a sense of independence and the power to do things, though without a clear idea of definite intention of specific action.
6. *Enterprise:* To secure a capital mass to carry out speculative or business enterprise.
7. *Pride:* To bequeath a fortune to others.
8. *Avarice:* To satisfy pure miserliness.

In a famous passage Keynes notes,

> These considerations will lead, as a rule, to a greater proportion of income being saved as real income rises ... We take it as a fundamental psychological rule of any modern community that when its real income is increased it will not increase its consumption by an absolute equal amount, so that a greater amount must be saved. (Keynes, 1936, p. 96)

Keynes' ideas have however been challenged by economists as well as by sociologists. For instance Duesenberry (1949) proposed a sociological theory which separated the propensity to save from the absolute level of income relating it more directly to social factors such as the relative position of the consumer in the income distribution of his population. Therefore, over a period of rising income the savings ratio should remain approximately constant. Hence, a person on a high income will be able to satisfy all the basic living requirement put upon him and will have a residue for saving, while the low-income consumer will never have enough to save as all the money is consumed by meeting basic demands.

More recently Friedman (1957) has proposed a permanent income saving theory which is purely economic and rational. It is assumed that savings are provisions for the future not a residual phenomena. The 'actuarial' consumer saves to even out his income over the lifespan to ensure a permanent income though the time considerations may be longer for some categories and shorter for others. Of course aggregated data can be provided to support or refute these theories, yet it cannot be shown by economic or statistical analysis whether the motives that people have for saving are indeed those proposed by economists.

There has been some limited work in psychology on saving behaviour. Katona (1975) has been the leading researcher in this field. He has pointed out two major items that are usually included under personal saving: *contractual* saving such as mortgages which are fixed, regular obligations which require no new decisions but are not always regarded by the individual as saving *per se*; and *discretionary* savings which are deposits of income in various places and seen as a means of accumulating reserve funds. Discretionary saving may be subdivided into *residual* saving (money in banks, and the like) and *financial* saving, such as investment in property. He notes that in American surveys done over a number of years, there was a consistent pattern in the reasons people gave for saving. Most commonly people mentioned emergencies (illness, unemployment) because they felt the future to be uncertain and hence reserve funds were necessary. A second major concern was retirement (old age) expressed by comparatively young people (in their thirties). The other reasons were children's needs (primarily education) and the buying of a house (and to a lesser extent durable goods). Katona noted:

First of all references to savings for the purpose of later consumption or improving one's standard of living at a later date are infrequent ... Secondly, hardly any consumers mentioned saving for the purpose of earning additional income in the form of interest of dividends or in order to bequeath money to their heirs ... On the whole, surveys revealed that the accumulation of savings constitutes a highly valued goal. Savings are associated with important values and are seen as a goal for which it is worthwhile to strive. Not saving is regretted and sometimes considered morally wrong. The high value attached to thrift has puritan undertones that persist among many people despite the much-lamented 'thing-mindedness' of our age. (p. 234–5)

Katona noted that the demographic characteristics of the savers depends to some extent on the definition of saving. Discretionary saving is mainly done by middle-aged people with relatively high incomes. From his extensive surveys Katona was able to devise a scheme to predict spending and saving:

Table 9.1 Assumptions about changes in personal saving in good and bad times

Factor	*During a recession*	*During an upswing*
1. Instalment buying	Net saving grows because not reduced by extensive credit incurrence	Net saving declines because reduced by extensive credit incurrence
2. Unusual cash expenditures	Net saving grows because not reduced by extensive withdrawals from bank accounts	Net saving declines because reduced by extensive withdrawals from bank accounts
3. Frequency and size of income increases	Net saving declines because income increases less frequent and less substantial	Net saving grows because income increases frequent and substantial
4. Strength of saving motives	Net saving grows because people strongly motivated to save	Net saving declines because people less strongly motivated to save

When income

in the preceding *period has gone*	in the next period *is expected to go*	Then discretionary spending *is*
Up	Up	Unusually high
Same or down	Same or down	Unusually low
And discretionary saving is		
Up		
Up	Down	Unusually high
Down	Up	Unusually low

Source: Katona: *Psychological Economics*, North-Holland Publishing Company, Amsterdam, 1975.

He did however note that 'The scheme presented provides no definite answer to whether we save more during a period of upswing or of downswing.... Yet, at any given time, knowing the circumstances then prevailing, it is possible to derive definite answers from the scheme' (pp. 240–1). He does however note that inflation and interest rates being offered do affect saving.

Gianotten and van Raaij (1982) examined consumer credit and saving as a function of income and confidence. They found that the expectation to be able to save remains relatively stable over time, while the utility of saving shows a cyclical pattern. The young and the wealthy respondents in this Dutch survey have greater expectations to be able to save but the latter have a low saving motivation (and may prefer bonds, shares and real estate to a savings account). Generally the more optimistic one is about the general economic situation, the more one expects to save, but the utility of saving is unrelated to general economic expectations. The Katona model that saving is determined by income and saving expectation/motivation applies only to savings institutions.

More recently Lindqvist (1981) investigated determinants of household saving behaviour in Sweden. Independent variables included socioeconomic characteristics (household income, stage in family life-cycle, educational level of husband and wife, type of residence), attitudes and expectations, economic activity (planning of finances) and economic satisfaction. He found intervening behavioural variables significant particularly in explaining bank funds.

Furnham (1985c) set out to establish the determinants of people's attitudes towards and habits of saving money in Britain. Although people save through a variety of means (such as shares, investments, property speculation) the focus of his paper is the saving of *money*. Attitudes towards saving are assumed to be deeply rooted and connected with upbringing and life-style (Olander and Seipel, 1970). The study had a number of aims: (i) to determine the structure of beliefs about saving and whether, as Keynes (1936) and Katona (1975) imply, nearly everyone has positive attitudes and beliefs towards saving. (ii) The study set out to investigate the demographic and psychological determinants of these beliefs and habits in order to determine whether income or some other set of variables are the most powerful determinants of saving habits and values. (iii) The study set out to determine the range of people's motives for saving, which is partly revealed in where they save, in order to compare the ideas of Keynes, Duesenberry, Friedman and Katona.

First, it was demonstrated that attitudes towards saving are by no means unidimensional and involve such factors as beliefs about the benefits vs. the pointlessness of saving, how one should save, whether saving secures wealth and the self-denial implicit in saving. Katona's (1975) early work seems to imply that saving money was universally considered a positive goal, possibly linked to the Protestant work ethic. Furnham's (1985c) study has demonstrated that both these assumptions do not necessarily hold in current Britain as some people appear to believe the saving of money to be pointless and that overall Protestant work ethic beliefs are not strongly related to saving habits and beliefs. The reason for this difference may be in a number of areas: the current depressed economic climate in Britain vs. the comparatively well-off early 1960s in America; the different political and welfare arrangements in the two countries, sampling differences, and so on. Suffice to say, there do not appear to be universally positive beliefs about the benefits of traditional forms of saving money, even when inflation is comparatively low.

In Furnham's (1985c) study some factors did not (e.g. sex) and some did (e.g. education) discriminate between the various saving attitudes. Whereas age was directly and linearly related to saving (older people are more positive to saving) education was curvilinear with the most and least educated being negative about saving as such, but not investments (no doubt for quite different reasons). Income did not discriminate between saving beliefs much except that as income increased beliefs about the pointlessness of saving decreased. Overall the psychological belief variables did not discriminate money-saving attitudes concerning the benefits of saving, beliefs in the way in which saving leads to wealth accumulation or self denial required for saving. However whereas alienation was positively correlated with beliefs about the pointlessness of saving the opposite was true of conservative beliefs—the more conservative one is in social attitudes the less pointless (more important) one sees saving to be.

The canonical correlation showed a further important point. Although older, left-wing, lower-income, more alienated people believed saving to be pointless, they did recognise its benefits. That is, people's attitudes to *their* saving of money probably reflect their ability to save more than their beliefs about saving. Furthermore this apparent paradox may occur only in times of economic depression. Because this is a cross-sectional rather than a longitudinal study it is not possible to determine the effect of the economy on saving attitudes.

There were practically no differences (age being the only exception) in how *regularly* or what *percentage* of their income people saved. Income revealed *no* significant differences, so invalidating the speculations of Keynes (1936) but not that of Friedman (1957) or Duesenberry (1949). These results do not suggest that higher-income people save less than lower-income people but rather that the percentage of money saved is the same hence casting doubt on the discretionary concept. It is possible that people will forgo certain goods in order to save a constant percentage of their income.

Psychological studies on saving are in their infancy. Much more research needs to be done on where and why people save, and what determines their patterns of saving. More importantly perhaps, rational economic theories for how and why people save need to be put to the test not only through examining aggregate econometric data but also by large-scale representative surveys and small-scale studies of particular groups.

GAMBLING

Despite a fairly considerable effort devoted to attempting to measure the real expenditure on gambling on a national basis, figures are unreliable and probably grossly underestimate the actual amount gambled in any one year. Various commissions have attempted a fairly objective assessment of the economic significance of gambling monitoring how much is waged. For instance Cornish (1978) has noted that the total expenditure for gambling in 1975 in Britain was £581 million—a 45 per cent increase on 1972 figures, but a downturn in real financial terms. However most attention has been paid to a limited number of types of gambling: football pools, horse racing, gaming clubs and bingo.

Attempts to understand how and why people gamble have been limited and partisan. The literature is poor and diffuse and few good reviews exist. Cornish's (1978) Home Office Research study is however an exception. Cornish's review of the literature on gambling is important for a number of reasons. First, gambling is a highly emotive topic with strong moral overtones and opinions are expressed that do not accord with facts. Secondly, the review is eclectic in that he considers the sociological, psychological, psychiatric, psychoanalytic and experimental work on gambling without being partisan. Thirdly, the review is critical. For instance, the point is made that three assumptions are often made by both theorists and researchers which are both erroneous and obfuscatory:

1. By reason of their behaviour alone, gamblers may be distinguished from non-gamblers. This both ignores the quantitative and degree of participation aspect which tends to lead researchers to look for one or two motivations common to all members of either group.
2. People who gamble can be regarded as engaging in the same basic activity. This ignores the fact that different types of gambling offer different experiences and rewards; involve more or less luck vs. skill; and are available to different groups in the community.
3. Explanations for the initial decision to gamble will be closely related to those used to explain persistent gambling. This assumption often arises from the individualistic person-centred approach which erroneously assumes that the motives which explain the continuance of gambling also accounts for its initiation.

Finally the review considers implications for policy and research. However it is maintained that what is most essential is a better information base and means of monitoring gambling and the gambling industry. Only poor policy-making can result from decisions made on weak, unrepresentative data.

THEORIES OF GAMBLING

Although compulsive gambling has been fairly extensively studied from a number of perspectives, very little work has been done on 'normal' non-compulsive gamblers (Bolen and Boyd, 1968; Greenberg, 1980). Most of the existing literature attempts to explain what motivates people to gamble though there are some psychological studies on people's perceived probabilities of winning and losing at gambling (Cohen, 1970; Halliday and Fuller, 1974).

Compulsive gambling (which is defined as a chronic and progressive preoccupation with gambling and urge to gamble, and gambling behaviour that compromises, disrupts or damages personal, family and/or vocational pursuits) has received a great deal of interest. Descriptions of chronic gamblers are remarkably similar to those of alcoholics. Extensive biographical, social and psychological data have been gathered on a very limited number of individuals (Lesieur, 1977). All studies show a prevalence of male over female compulsive gamblers (Custer, 1976). There are no reliable data to show how social class, occupational or religious differences affect the evidence of compulsive gamblers, but the literature suggests that the compulsive gambling syndrome affects all types of people (Greenberg, 1980).

1. Psychoanalytic Theories

Psychoanalyists have long been interested in gambling (Simmel, 1920; Bergler, 1958). Freud (1928) himself examined the case of Dostoyevsky, who was a pathological gambler, and linked pathological gambling to other compulsive neurotic traits especially the Oedipus complex. Later research has shown that Freud's insights could be generalised to other gamblers. (Lindner, 1950; Harris, 1964). Central to psychoanalytic thought is the idea that the complusive gambler is driven by an overwhelming desire to lose—to savour victimhood and injustice and to revel in remorse and self-pity (Bergler, 1958; Mynott, 1979). For Bergler (1958) six features characterise the 'pathological' gambler:

1. The gambler *habitually* takes every chance to gamble.
2. The gambler's game precludes *all* other interests.
3. The gambler is full of optimism and apparently never learns from defeat and loss.

4. The gambler never stops when winning.
5. Despite initial caution, the gambler eventually risks too much.
6. Tension and thrill is experienced during the game.

Whether normal gamblers are qualitatively or quantitatively different from pathological gamblers is not made clear. Psychoanalytic writers place a great deal of emphasis on clinical observations and attempt to typologise them. Bergler offered a typology of six distinct types of neurotic gamblers:

1. The 'classic' gambler whose 'neurosis centers around infantile omnipotence and its masochistic elaboration. Characterologically, he is distinguished by the mechanism of orality, made up of the three parts previously described: unconscious construction of defeats; retaliative fury, seemingly for the purpose of self-defense; and finally, self-commiseration' (p. 83).
2. The passive-feminine male gambler who has a tendency towards unconscious feminine identification which makes it possible for him to enjoy the feeling of being overwhelmed in defeat.
3. The defensive pseudo-superior gambler who manifests a strong defence against the wish to be overwhelmed and believes that the stronger personality is bound to win.
4. The gambler motivated by unconscious guilt 'originating in psychic masochism is shifted to later masturbatory fantasies that have an edipal content' (p. 96).
5. The unexcited gambler who is usually a professional gambler who only occasionally makes dramatic gestures and decisions.
6. Female gamblers who are 'typical psychic masochists fighting their "battle of injustice" with the unconscious image of the "cruel" mother' (p. 98).

Custer (1976) found less than 20 per cent of a large American population of compulsive gamblers revealed typical neurotic symptoms and argued that compulsive gamblers are more like addicts, becoming dependent on the arousing effects of gambling. There are also the many other consistent criticisms of psychoanalytic theory and research in general which may be applied to gambling as well.

2. Individual Differences (Personality Theory)

Others have argued that the compulsive gambler is psychophysically predisposed to self-arousal (Greenberg, 1980). Lozkowski (1977) exposed subjects previously classified on their preferences for stimulus levels to high and low-risk gambling situations. Subjects who preferred high environmental stimulus levels consistently preferred gambling with high risk, and vice versa. This is clearly linked to the extensive psychological literature on extraversion (Eysenck, 1967; Mehrabian, 1978; Zuckerman, 1979). Indeed Hataro and Inagaki (1977) found significant differences between extraverts and introverts in betting situations. Yet Cornish (1978) has noted:

> But although hypothesised differences in stimulus-seeking might be put forward to account for individual differences in the riskiness of gambling behaviour, or in the decision to gamble at all, it would be difficult on any particular occasion, given only behavioural evidence, to identify this disposition as an important causal factor. As mentioned earlier, objectively risky behaviour may equally be the result of individual differences in the perception of the probabilities or pay-offs involved, or in terms of other factors operating in the gambling situation. There is evidence that the situation itself may also, on occasion, encourage riskier behaviour than an individual might otherwise take. (p. 151)

Goffman (1967) also supported the hypothesis that gambling is a surrogate for the risk-taking which has been removed from everyday life. He also believed that occupation was related to gambling: both those with very high and very low-risk jobs would indulge in high risk gambling while those in middle-risk jobs would take part in low risk.

Other individual difference variables have been mentioned either from studies that attempted to test the extent of a particular trait in a gambling population or from studies simply comparing matched groups of gamblers and non-gamblers. Many of these studied were seriously defective both because of the sampling policy and the measures used. Apart from variables associated with risk or sensation-seeking, others have also been considered such as 'need for achievement' and 'locus of control beliefs'. It has been hypothesised and demonstrated that people with high internal locus of control scores and with high need for achievement tend to prefer intermediate rather than high or low probabilities. However, not only have replicative studies failed to establish these findings, it may equally be argued that these beliefs and needs are a consequence, rather than a cause of gambling (Cornish, 1978).

3. Evaluations of Probabilities and Pay-offs

A third approach has considered gambling from a mathematical or cognitive viewpoint (Cohen, 1960; Liverant and Scodel, 1960; Strickland *et al.* 1966). This has primarily been concerned with how and why individuals choose *between* gambles not with why they gamble at all. Furthermore, it assumes that individuals both know and understand all the relevant information (probabilities, pay-offs) required in making a logical decision. Yet it attempts to provide a systematic treatment of the cognitive variables involved. These studies have demonstrated that gamblers are by no means logical or rational in their gambling in an objective sense. For example, if roulette players were rational they would play in such a way as to maximise their gains or to minimise their losses but this does not happen (Edwards, 1953). Simple expectation theories based on the idea that people bet to maximise expected gain do however hold up in some situations. More complex models have been proposed which provide reasonable explanations in terms of economic motivation for some forms of gambling (e.g. lotteries) but cannot account for other types of gambling or individual variation. Cohen (1972) has noted that most experimental studies on gambling rest on two assumptions: the worth of a bet to the gambler is the product of the utility of each outcome and its corresponding probability summed over all outcomes; and that the gambler chooses that gamble which yields the maximum sum of products of utility and probability. Yet these ideas have been criticised primarily because they neglect so many obvious salient psychological variables such as the belief in luck and skill, the subjective nature of risk-taking, etc.

More intelligent people tend to prefer gambling games where the element of choice is minimised (e.g. some card games) while less intelligent people tend to prefer games of chance where the outcome is beyond their control (e.g. lotteries). Schoemaker (1979) examined the role of statistical knowledge in gambling decisions which is central to this approach to gambling. He found that statistically untrained subjects tended to simplify judging gambles by focusing more on certain risk dimensions than others. The price of the strategy is to reduce consistency and confidence in the resulting decision. More recently Gilovich (1983) examined biased evaluations and persistence in gambling. As predicted, subjects spent more time explaining their losses than their wins—they described their losses but bolstered their wins. There is a growing and very interesting literature on judgemental heuristics and illusion of control all of which stress the problems in conceiving of the rationality of gambling behaviour in economic terms.

4. Sociological Theories

There are numerous sociological theories of gambling. Devereux (1968) developed a structural-functionalist theory which saw gambling as the perfect scapegoat for the contradictions of capitalism. Capitalism seeks to encourage economic self-interest of a 'rational' kind; competition with a visible correlation between effort and reward; institutional mechanisms of banking and credit which service both producers and consumers and the Protestant work ethic which stressed rationality and avoidance of reliance on risk and luck. Gambling survives and flourishes because it meets personal and social needs frustrated in capitalist societies, or acts as a protest against budgetary constraints, rationality and ethics, while providing thrills, aggression behind a playful façade, and artificial and short-time problem-solving issues differentiated from real life. More importantly, gambling is counter-religious because it stresses ultimate ignorance and helplessness over luck which has to be constantly tested. This, according to sociologists, accounts for the many contradictory and ambivalent attitudes to gambling in the West where it is tolerated in practice and yet often illegal in principle. this ambivalence is strongest in the middle class where Protestant work ethic values are at their strongest. Downes *et al.* (1976) have suggested that gambling is deeply rooted in working-class culture with its limited deferment of gratification and strong beliefs in luck, fate and destiny. Evidence for this is found in the Gallup (1974) survey which found that lower socioeconomic class people predominated in the major forms of gambling.

Downes *et al.* (1976) tested various theories of gambling. As independent variables they included 38 measures including socioeconomic characteristics (age, education), beliefs, leisure activities, political beliefs, etc. Large samples in three areas in Britain were used to test eight theories:

1. *Anomie.* The more people experience anomie the more they gamble (propensity to gamble is inversely related to socioeconomic level).
2. *Alienation.* The more people experience alienation the more they gamble as an expression of self-assertion.
3. *Working-class culture.* The working class gamble more than the middle class because they believe more in luck, fate and destiny.
4. *Structural-functional theory.* Certain middle-class groups gamble least but encourage or tolerate gambling since its elimination would leave the contradictions of capitalism untouched and exposed.
5. *Decision-making.* People who have no scope for decision-making in their work gamble more than those who have opportunities to make decisions.
6. *Risk-taking.* Those whose jobs are most hazardous (action-oriented) and those whose are least action-oriented gamble most.
7. *Home-Centredness.* Those people who are most home-centred gamble least.
8. *Work-Centredness.* Those people whose leisure is work-centred get satisfactions that are at odds with gambling activities and hence do not partake.

Though the authors appreciate the limitations of their study for assessing the total merits of these sociological theories, they do believe their results a useful ground for better theory testing. Suffice to say no support was found for anomie theory, alienation, working-class culture ideas or risk-taking, yet there was equivocal support for structural-functionalist theories, risk-taking, and home- and work-centredness. They did however find a strong intergenerational pattern of gambling which exists irrespective of class suggesting 'that broad, class-based theories of gambling are ill founded, and that the factors making for variations in involvement and gambling, whatever they are, are permeated throughout the social structure rather than localized in one sector' Downes *et al.* (p. 77).

Like Cornish (1978), Downes *et al.* (1976) explored social variations in gambling activity as well as describing the distribution of gambling for their entire sample. They conclude making statements in support of the structuralist-functionalist and decision-making viewpoint. They stress that all macro- and micro-sociological theories of gambling implicitly or explicitily rely on a functional analysis, and that one needs to make sense of gambling in sociological terms. Yet they do acknowledge that these theories cannot provide an adequate explanation for the variability in different forms of gambling in smaller-scale contexts. Furthermore many myths surround the increase and decline of gambling which need to be examined empirically and historically. Finally, they consider the social policy implications of gambling.

> Social objectives—the goal of minimizing criminal entrepreneurship—clashes with fiscal ends—the goal of drawing in some revenue for the state from gambling profits: the larger the revenue drawn from gambling, the greater the inducement to make illegal books. The overall trend, however, is towards gambling as a key component in large-scale, interlocking 'leisure' industries. (p. 212)

5. Social Psychological Studies

Although few studies appear to have been done in the area social psychological concepts and measures appear to be particularly appropriate to the study of gambling.

Furnham (1985d) set out to examine the determinants and structures of people's attitudes to gambling as well as their gambling habits. Because the motivation for and satisfaction that people derive from gambling are diverse, and the fact that gambling is related to other economic and work beliefs, it might be expected that attitudes to gambling are multidimensional. (This has been suggested by Downes *et al.*, 1976.) Furthermore these attitude dimensions are probably related to other beliefs such as conservatism (Wilson, 1973) and the Protestant work ethic (Mirels and Garrett, 1971).

Secondly, although some work has gone into social variations and gambling activity they have tended to look at only limited demographic determinants of this behaviour such as class, income or religion rather than at psychological variables (Downes *et al.*, 1983). Furnham (1985d) also aimed to investigate the relationship between people's attitudes to and habits of gambling. As predicted he found attitudes towards gambling are far from unidimensional or even bi-polar (pro- vs. anti-gambling). Two factors concerned clinical aspects of gambling while one was economic factors (losses) and another about morals. Clearly people have complex attitudes towards gambling in general. As regards the determinants of these attitudes, age and general conservative beliefs tended to discriminate more than the other demographic or other belief variables. This result was confirmed in the canonical correlation which also suggested that alienation was an important factor. Older, alienated and conservative people tend to be more against all forms of gambling than younger, less alienated, liberal subjects. Factors which did not discriminate extensively with regard to gambling attitudes included sex, education and income.

Table 9.2: Factor Analysis (Varimax) of the attitude to gambling scale (from Furnham, 1985d)

	Factors 1	2	3	4	5
1. All forms of gambling should be made illegal	.02	.66	–.14	–.17	.33
2. The taxes on all forms of gambling are too high	–.25	.12	.66	–.01	.19
3. Gambling is an innocent social activity	.09	–.13	.67	–.15	–.31
4. Compulsive gamblers are psychologically ill & in need of treatment	.16	.00	.01	.63	.03
5. People who gamble regularly never really win money in the long run	.36	.26	.22	.58	.02
6. Children should be prevented from gambling (eg fruit machines)	.05	.19	.07	.21	.76
7. People should be freely allowed to gamble with their money if they wish to	.04	–.37	.49	.26	–.23
8. The odds against winning much money on most forms of gambling are very high	.02	–.09	–.15	.78	.12
9. Gambling satisfies the attraction for danger which is present	.35	–.15	.52	.06	.13
10. All gamblers are cheats at heart	.06	.72	–.16	–.02	.11
11. Gambling represents the abandonment of reason and giving oneself up to superstition	.27	.60	.08	.15	–.04
12. Few people are better able to size-up others as gamblers	.04	.18	.22	–.02	.03
13. People would still gamble even if legal forms of gambling were made illegal	.35	–.51	–.10	.21	.20
14. Many families suffer because of the compulsive nature of some gamblers	.56	–.16	–.04	.07	.15
15. Men are more likely to become hooked on gambling than women	.23	.04	.08	.02	.09
16. Gamblers usually have very few other interests	.59	.32	–.08	–.04	.14
17. Gamblers are usually absurdly optimistic	.60	.22	.16	.20	.01
18. Most gamblers are unable to stop when winning	.74	.06	–.05	.23	–.09
19. Most gamblers inevitably risk more than they can afford	.72	.22	–.06	.10	.07
20. Gambling divides the working class against itself	.22	.54	–.02	.18	.16
21. Paradoxically, most people gamble to lose money	.13	.25	.29	–.01	.21
22. Even inexpensive forms of gambling become addictive	.38	.06	–.15	–.02	.58
Eigenvalue	4.14	2.45	1.77	1.34	1.15
Variance	18.8%	11.2%	8.1%	6.1%	5.2%

Reprinted with permission from *Personality and Individual Differences*, 1985, Furnham, 'Attitudes to, and habits of, gambling in Britain', Pergamon Press.

Table 9.3: Analysis of variance (one-way) for the eight independent variables on the factors arising from the attitude to gambling scale

Factor	Sex	Age	Education	Vote	Income	Alienation	PWE	Conservatism
			Independent variables					
1. Pathology	2.92	6.68$_a$	1.76	1.09	1.23	2.33	5.58$_b$	21.88$_a$
2. Illegality	0.00	1.81	1.08	0.78	2.19	11.17$_a$	1.48	4.54$_c$
3. Pro-gambling	8.69$_a$	3.98$_b$	1.71	0.43	1.44	1.94	0.31	4.76
4. Losses	0.40	8.40$_a$	7.32$_a$	2.51	2.02	0.28	1.06	2.89
5. Addictiveness	0.16	2.45	0.91	4.31$_b$	4.01$_b$	4.56$_c$	2.49	12.29$_a$

$_a\,p < .001$, $_b\,p < .01$ $_c\,p < .05$.

Reprinted with permission from *Personality and Individual Differences*, 1985, Furnham, 'Attitudes to, and habits of, gambling in Britain', Pergamon Press.

Furnham (1985d) argued that the types of, motivation for, satisfaction derived from, attitudes to and habits of gambling are interrelated and multidimensional. In most western countries gambling takes many forms which are favoured by some members of society more than others and which are considered more or less acceptable by them. The motivation for gambling—ranging from social contact through psychophysical arousal, to the desire to lose and punish oneself too—are as varied as the satisfactions derived from gambling. Hence attitudes to gambling are manifold: some concern the psychopathology of this possibly irrational activity; others the moral and legal aspects of gambling; while others the financial possibilities. - Any attempt to measure gambling beliefs and attitudes needs to take this complexity into consideration. Furthermore, as one might expect, gambling attitudes are not independent of gambling habits. Those who gamble frequently and in a variety of ways find the activity harmless and exciting and resist legal or financial restraints, whereas the opposite is true of those who rarely if ever gamble.

6. Other Approaches

It should be pointed out that there are other approaches to gambling which have been mentioned. *Structuralists* or *situationists* attempt to describe and identify key environmental features which stimulate, maintain or suppress the incidence of gambling. Factors which have been considered include:

1. The frequency of opportunities to gamble such as the regularity of lotteries, the number of betting shops, fruit machines, etc. and the number of horse/dog race meetings.
2. The pay-out interval which refers both to how long people have to wait before they know of the result of the bet and how long they have to wait for their winnings.
3. The range of odds and stakes available which may be quite variable.
4. The degree of personal participation and the exercise of skill as gamblers feel more active when present at the gambling event and when they are able to select the odds of the bet.
5. Probability of winning an individual bet and pay-out ratio.

Another approach is based on classic learning theory and the principles of operant conditioning which stresses schedules of reinforcement. Gambling usually provides intermittent schedules of reinforcement (variable ratio) which, though not the best schedule for establishing a particular response pattern, is probably the most addictive—that is, maintaining the response pattern over long periods of time. Experimental studies have looked at resistance to extinction as a function of the duration of previous reinforcement with mixed results. But there are very wide differences in behavioural terms between different forms of gambling such as event frequency, expected values, etc. Thus it may be that the reinforcers differ from person to person, and from one type of game to another. Precisely what is reinforcing (feedback, exercise of skill, excitement, etc.) is extremely important.

Clearly, as Cornish (1978) stresses, both personal (psychoanalytic), individual difference (trait) and situational (sociological learning theory) factors are important in understanding the development of all forms of gambling behaviour. Personal factors are important as they attempt to isolate which demographic and psychological difference (cognitive, belief and personality) accounts for the fairly large behavioural variance noted in all forms of gambling. Situational characteristics are relevant as they limit the range, frequency, type and amount of reinforcement available as well as the social and economic consequences of gambling. An eclectic approach does not however necessarily mean an uncritical acceptance of all aspects of all approaches. What needs to be done is to attempt to delineate which theory best accounts for either or both the initiation *or* maintenance of which type of gambling with which particular group of people.

PROBLEMS WITH GENERAL THEORIES OF GAMBLING

Many of the very different gambling theories and approaches above, even the most disparate, share similar problems. Though they may be elegantly and persuasively described with supporting evidence, events reconcile apparently paradoxical problems which are often difficult to test. That is, some do not make clear, testable. falsifiable hypotheses which may be used to test their usefulness (see Downes *et al.*, 1976).

Secondly, many are very similar and may be seen as complementary rather than contradictory so that the same evidence may be used to support (or refute) more than one approach at the same time.

Thirdly, many studies have simply not provided supporting evidence. Some studies have failed to support predictions or even provide evidence against the theory. Furthermore it is never difficult to cite a range of examples that contradict any one theory. This is particularly true of psychodynamic approaches.

Fourthly, because these are mostly general theories (with the exception of psychoanalytic approaches) it is not always easy to make specific predictions about individuals' gambling behaviour. The theories attempt to explain people's motives for gambling inferred from their social or demographic backgrounds. Yet these inferred motives nearly always are unable to explain why an individual chooses or prefers one particular style of gambling above others.

Fifthly, there appears to be some vagueness about motives that account for people beginning gambling and those that continue at it. Because individual differences are ignored it is not clear why some people from much the same background are heavy, others moderate, and still others infrequent gamblers. That is, either the theories fail to account for individual variation within socioeconomic classes, for instance (treating it as error variance), or else they neglect important structural variables like income differences.

Finally, and perhaps most importantly, many theories have been derived from, and hence are applicable to, specific (and very different) types of gamblers or types of gambling. Hence studies of compulsive roulette players may not provide useful insights into football lottery gamblers. As Cornish (1978) has elegantly noted, it is true that general accounts can offer broad explanations for the prevalence and social distribution of gambling, in terms of social structures and socioeconomically-determined expressive needs, which can complement or compete with simpler accounts in terms of economic motivation. But they are neither suited, nor intended to provide more detailed information about the relationship between particular motives and particular types of gambling. Where they occasionally appear to provide such information it is either because they are particular accounts masquerading as general ones, or general accounts which offer so many possible motives for gambling as to be consistent with virtually any explanation for any form.

Nevertheless, general accounts do offer the important recognition that gambling behaviour does not take place in a social vacuum. Gambling, like other entertainments and pastimes, merits consideration as expressive behaviour which may be quite closely related to and indicative of important features of the social structure within which it occurs. In this sense general theories provide a way of discussing gambling seriously. They rehabilitate it sufficiently for it to be placed into its cultural context, though at some risk of exaggerating the social significance of the needs for which it caters or the uniqueness of its contribution to their satisfaction. At their best they provide a structure or formula within which values corresponding to particular expressive needs or particular forms of gambling can be substituted for more general terms. But beyond this they rarely go except, perhaps, to indicate (not always correctly) the direction in which more particular explanations should be sought.

THE PSYCHOLOGY OF DECISION-MAKING

Saving, spending and gambling all involve prediction and investment—that is, making probabilistic judgements and inferences. Will the interest rate in this savings account allow one to keep up with (or exceed) the probabilistic rate of inflation over the next three years? What is the probability of winning a certain gamble? Are gilts a good investment given the way the market is moving?

A great deal of cognitive psychological research has been devoted to the ways in which individuals process information. Most of this research has shown that people adopt strategies to cope with complex information which lead to marked errors, particularly in probabilistic judgements and inferences. The best research has been done by Kahneman and Tversky (Tversky and Kahneman, 1974; Kahneman, Slovic and Tversky, 1982) who have noted three very common heuristics of judgement. The first is *representativeness*, which refers to a tendency to judge the probability that a stimulus belongs to a particular class or group while ignoring base-rate probabilities. This bias tends to occur even when people are given incentives for accuracy and are told about base-rate probabilities. The *availability* heuristic refers to the tendency for an event to be judged more probable simply according to the extent to which it could be easily imagined or recalled. Where dangers, for example, are explicit and comprehensible will be overestimated, where not they will be underestimated. Associated with this phenomenon is the idea of illusory correlations—the overestimation of the co-occurence of natural associates. The *anchoring* bias refers to people's failure to revise their estimates adequately even when new information is presented. That is, early predictions in some sense anchor later predictions irrespective of the evidence presented.

Although these various heuristics may be both economical and often effective, they can and do lead to systematic and predictable errors. What the psychological literature has demonstrated is that people in general—indeed, all except those with a fairly sophisticated statistical knowledge—are prone to errors, biases and fallacies in judgements of inductive reasoning.

Much of this work is, of course, applicable to economic judgement. Indeed Kahneman and Tversky (1979) have applied their research specifically to economic decision-making. Kahneman and Tversky (1979) have argued that expected utility theory is not an adequate description of economic behaviour especially when it comes to gambling. They found in their research that with positive bets or prospects (those that involve gains) people are risk-averse. That is, people seem to prefer a sure gain over the probability of gaining, even if the expected value of the probability prospect is slightly higher. Yet with negative bets or prospects (those that involve losses) people are risk-seekers and prefer a small probability of not losing over a sure loss. Thus it appears that certainty increases the aversiveness of losses as well as the desirability of gains. Kahneman and Tversky contrast their prospect theory with utility theory, the former of which shows that the aggravation of losing a sum of money is greater than the pleasure of gaining the same amount of money. One's current assets act as an anchoring-point such that gains and losses may be considered relative to an expectation or aspiration level that differs from current assets.

CONCLUSION

This chapter has covered two rather different forms of behaviour—saving and gambling—the former of which has been of great interest to economists but of little interest to psychologists, while for the latter psychologists have been fairly interested and economists very little interested.

Although the similarity between these topics—how people save and spend their money—are not necessarily very striking, there appear to be two similar conclusions that one might draw from the scattered and patchy literature in both fields.

First, there is a distinct lack of good information. There are few reliable statistics that accurately reflect the amount or type of money saved or gambled. Though these figures may be of more interest to economists, policy planners and sociologists than psychologists, they provide an important source of hypotheses and data against which some theories may be tested. Taboos concerning both activities (saving and gambling) as well as possible fears about tax (avoidance and evasion) mean that these figures may be extremely difficult to obtain. As a result it is difficult to refute moralist scaremongery about such things as the decline in saving, the increase in gambling, etc.

Secondly, both topics have been dealt with in a rather too simple, undimensional way. Asking naive individualistic motivational questions such as why do people save/gamble will not do. Clearly different groups save and gamble differently for different reasons. Their motives are manifold, complex and changing. They are determined by individual and demographic differences as well as economic, political and social constraints. Hence no one theory, or theoretical approach, can on its own account for much of the variation found. Numerous distinctions need to be made at the outset before any useful theoretical or empirical work can be done.

Finally recent, widely applauded work on individual decision-making would seem to have numerous important applications for economic psychology.

Part V:
Consumer Choice and The Public Sector

10 Consumer Choice in the Private Sector

INTRODUCTION

How do people make economic choices? What encourages people to buy a Ford car rather than a Chrysler? Butter rather than margarine?

There are at least four major approaches to the investigation of consumer choice relevant to our present discussion. These are (i) The economic theory of consumer demand; (ii) Katona's use of 'consumer sentiments' in aggregate demand; (iii) consumer behaviour as studied in the marketing literature; and (iv) economic psychology—a selective synthesis of the first three.

Work has been done by Anderson *et al.* (1981) who have provided a useful sourcebook of concepts in judgement and decision research, both in psychology and economics. Eight major groups of references are identified: Game and utility theories (von Neumann and Morgenstern, 1944; Arrow, 1963); decision theory (Raiffa, 1968); preference theories (Coombs, 1975); attribution theory (Heider, 1958; Kelley, 1967); information integration theory (Anderson, 1981); psychological decision theory (Tversky and Kahneman, 1977); behavioural decision theory (Edwards, 1954; Lichtenstein *et al.*, 1977); and social judgement theory (Brunswick, 1955; Hammond, 1976). The academic and related literature on choice, judgement and decision research is genuinely vast (as for that matter is the literature on consumer behaviour generally). Given our limited space we have to be highly selective.

It will become clear that the differences between our four sections is methodological. In short the approaches differ in what they set out to do, and in their aims and purposes. The economic approach sets out a theoretical analysis of consumer demand based on the familiar concept of rationality, and is interested in how consumer demand may rise or fall according to fluctuations in 'objective' economic criteria such as the relative price of goods and income. Katona's approach differs in that he believed 'subjective' expectations and economic optimism have an influence on aggregate consumer demand, and can be measured. The marketing literature, not surprisingly, is partly aimed at ways of increasing sales for particular products using various psychological techniques. Finally, the aspirations of an economic psychology are legion and not a little confused; an effort is being made to explore what consumers actually do at the micro-level while at the same time attempting to improve economic predictions and marketing efficiency.

ECONOMICS AND CONSUMER BEHAVIOUR

The economics of consumer demand is quantitative rather than qualitative, 'hard' rather than 'soft'. The emphasis is placed on theory construction and deduction. 'Objective' factors such as the price of goods and the income of consumers are major components (consumer psychologists have been criticised for underestimating the importance of budget constraints). Consumers are clearly constrained; there is a limit to the quantity of a good or combination of goods they can purchase. Budget constraints are determined by the price of goods and the income of the consumer. Neoclassical economists accept that purchasing decisions are also influenced by preferences, but have no account of how preferences are formed or how they change. Their understanding of preferences is axiomatic; optimising consumers are assumed to want more rather than less and to exercise choice in a systematic manner given the constraints.

Note, the model or theory is not usually dependent on the observation or questioning of even a single consumer. Although the aggregated data to which it is applied may be derived from a diary of purchases kept by consumers accompanying income and personal details of consumers (see for example the *Family Expenditure Survey in Britain*), no individual consumers are asked why they purchased what they did or how they arrived at their decisions.

The basic theory can be treated with varying degrees of sophistication and can be modified to allow for the presence of uncertainty or lack of information (Deaton and Muellbauer, 1980). Generally economists are seeking the minimum of complication in their models and are reluctant to build additional elements unless they significantly add to the range of events explained or predicted by the models. A rational maximiser is always at the heart of the analysis. A modern neoclassical theorist is not interested in how choosers 'make up their mind'.

KATONA'S CONTRIBUTION

In contrast, George Katona was interested in how choosers choose, and was in many ways successful in bridging the gap between economists and psychologists. He was directly interested in consumers' 'expectations', 'attitudes', 'levels of aspiration', 'social learning' and 'cognition' (Katona 1975, 1977). He was keen to prove that psychological knowledge could improve economic predictions of consumer demand. He placed consumer choice in a social context: people do not make choices in isolation, their choices are dependent on the choices of others. Katona also believed that the picture of the consumer rationally deliberating between alternatives was misplaced. Consumers have cognitive limitations and are creatures of habit. Katona's crucial point was that economic behaviour is not the simple consequence of economic stimuli, especially in the short term and in periods of frequent economic fluctuation. There are mediating variables between stimulus and response, namely the perceptions of consumers. It is the empirical pursuit and measurement of these perceptions which is the central aspect of Katona's approach.

'Expectations' have more commonly been incorporated in economic approaches to consumer demand in recent years. However, the so-called 'rational expectations' model is different from what Katona means by the term. In the economic approach people are assumed to have certain notions about the future based on recent economic changes and the constraints of search and information costs, etc. (Deaton and Muellbauer, 1980). For Katona (1980) people's economic expectations are not necessarily what you would expect them to be. Consequently Katona feels that there is no adequate substitute for direct examination of 'consumer sentiment', consumers' expectations, their optimism and pessimism. We cannot assume that consumers' implicit economic theories are the same as those held by professional economists, or what professional economists expect them to be—for example, between the rate of inflation and 'rational' behaviour in terms of the influence this should have on consumption and saving. For Juster (1981), the 'rational expectations' model is more appropriate for commodity markets and other markets where professional speculative activity is the dominant force.

Juster has suggested that varying reactions to inflation cannot be understood without recourse to consumer knowledge. Why did US consumers react with speculative buying in response to the inflation of 1978/79, while they failed to react in this way to the inflation of 1973/74? The likely answer is that consumers learnt from experience.

Katona's index of 'consumer sentiment', in its original form was based on only five interview questions. These questions cover whether respondents considered themselves financially better off or worse off than a year ago, whether they think they will be financially better off in a year from now, whether it is a good time for buying things, and whether the next 12 months and the next 5 years will be better or worse for the economy as a whole.

The index of 'consumer sentiment' has proved a success in short-term forecasts. For the years 1952–66, Katona (1967) was able to record some impressive results from regression studies of time-series data. The index, combined with income level, explained 91 per cent of the variance in consumer expenditure on durables. (For a review of the success of the index of 'consumer sentiment', see Schapiro, 1972.)

Naturally economists have wished, wherever possible, to do without this kind of survey evidence, preferring instead more 'objective' economic criteria. A way forward may be in the combination of so-called quantitative and qualitative evidence. (Qualitative evidence referring, for the economist, to 'subjective' attitude and expectation data.)

Williams and Defris (1981), combined qualitative and quantitative measures of inflation, unemployment and 'consumer sentiment' in traditional models of the allocation of consumers' income. Using survey data collected by the Melbourne Institute of Applied Economic and Social Research, equations were estimated for expenditure on motor cars, and household durable and non-durable goods. The study by Williams and Defris therefore not only included measures of 'consumer sentiment' and expectations of future increases, but perceptual data on the seriousness of inflation and unemployment levels. The results showed that both quantitative and qualitative measures are of importance. In particular the factors influencing non-durable consumption are diverse but relate particularly to how consumers perceive their present and future economic well-being. For motor vehicle consumption, actual inflation levels performed much better than qualitative measures of inflation. This said, for other kinds of consumption both qualitative measures of unemployment and inflation were superior to their quantitative counterparts.

Finally, the consumer attitude surveys conducted by the Commission of the European Communities deserve mention. The questions asked in these surveys cover attitudes to the general economic situation, prices, unemployment, the household's financial circumstances, saving and durable purchasing expectations. Ward and Pickering (1981) have reported on the explanatory power of this survey data (1975–79) in the British context. Although this appraisal is a preliminary one only, Ward and Pickering, like Williams and Defris, conclude that qualitative measures are important predictors of consumer expenditure on consumer durables. 'Expectations' variables were predictively superior over this period to measures of personal income, and perhaps surprisingly, were broadly independent of real personal disposal income (RPDI), seasonally adjusted.

CONSUMER BEHAVIOUR IN THE MARKETING LITERATURE

Engel and Blackwell (1982), Howard and Sheth (1969) and Nicosia (1966) have produced highly influential models of consumer behaviour in the marketing literature. The formation of consumer preferences and how they change is the meat and drink of consumer psychology and consumer studies. Engel and Blackwell (1982), in their widely read *Consumer Behaviour* (now in its 4th edition), discuss social and cultural factors in consumer decisions, the psychological foundations of consumer behaviour, examples of high and low-involvement decision processes and the wider issues of the ethical and political considerations of consumerism and consumer protection.

The Social and Cultural Environment

Consumer demand and changes in consumer demand are dependent upon changes in income levels, rates of inflation, and so on. Equally demand is affected by what Engel and Blackwell refer to as the 'economic demographics' of a population, i.e. changes in income distributions, and varying government provisions for education, health and other social benefits. The twentieth century has witnessed an increase in affluence in western capitalist countries and a substantial growth in both the number and variety of consumer goods. At the same time there has been a reduction in working hours and an increase in leisure time—macroeconomic factors of paramount importance. There has been an increase in urbanisation and a fall in the birth and death rates. New markets have been created to accommodate the demands of new groups of consumers. (Younger readers may forget that the 'teenager' and the 'teenage market' were largely inventions of the 1950s.) The structure of households has altered, as has the role of women in society; social mobility is less restricted; travel is more widespread; communications ubiquitous. The list of changes is a long one, all have economic consequences, whether or not they have straightforward economic antecedents leads us into mists of grand theory and undoubtedly would raise the hackles of historians, anthropologists and sociologists if it were pursued exclusively. We take the view that the structure, function and behaviour of society (and consequently of consumers) is not only determined by the wealth of nations, their use of resources and the nature of production, but by the cultural values, norms and traditions of that society.*

The importance of cultural values is a central theme of economic anthropology, (Herskovits, 1952). Cultures not only differ in their economic organisation and complexity, but also the 'value' attached to money, wealth and the acquisition of consumer goods. Goods may be acquired for religious purposes, or given away in order to increase prestige. Economists may feel this is all very interesting but largely irrelevant to economic concerns. This view can be countered on many grounds, not least among them being that consumer demand is dependent on consumer preferences and that these can be culturally determined.

In complex societies predicting these preferences is of great importance to marketers. Similarly the changing proportions of individuals from varying cultural backgrounds can have a substantial influence on the pattern of aggregate consumer demand.

Social class is an important variable in consumer behaviour, and while notoriously difficult to define and measure there are good grounds for supposing different social classes have systematically varying preferences. Some aspects of the influence of social class on consumer behaviour is extremely difficult to explain in direct economic terms and is more easily

* It is also affected by various biological factors, and those interested in this theme of economic psychology should consult Lea, Tarpy and Webley (1985).

understood when viewed through sociological or social-psychological spectacles. A good example is 'complaining behaviour'. A working-class couple, where one member works in a department store and the other is a builder, may easily be sitting in the same restaurant as a couple where one member is an accountant and the other a lecturer in fine arts. Let us assume the builder is a successful one and the incomes of the couples are similar. Let us further assume that both couples notice something is wrong with the meal. The difference is the middle-class couple return the meal and make a complaint and the working-class couple do not. How can this be? One hypothesis is that the inconsistencies of the meal are more upsetting to the middle-class pair than the working-class. A more central argument to our thesis is that the middle-class couple are less intimidated by the waiter, are more 'at home' in the atmosphere of the restaurant, and are less constrained by the pressures of conformity. The working-class couple are less skilled in complaining and fear that any complaint might turn into an unpleasant confrontation and they don't want to 'make a scene that would ruin our evening'. Neither could they forget the expression on the waiter's face when one of them spread the pâté with the fruit knife, and were relieved when the wine waiter pronounced the name of the wine they tentatively pointed to on the wine list.

Le Grand (1978) and others have made the point that working-class National Health Service patients may demand and consequently receive less from the service; they are less likely to be critical of doctors; and less inclined to exercise positive choice in the manner in which they are treated, preferring a more passive role where the responsibility for the patient's health is handed over to the medical profession rather than remaining with the patient.

Marketers often pay close attention to market segmentation by social class. Advertising is frequently couched to appeal to one social class or another, and especially to those who aspire to 'higher' things. The magazine *Country Life* depicts the life-style of English country gentlefolk; articles may cover the joys of fox-hunting in Berkshire; two pages on the engagement of the Honourable Georgina Horrocks to a Captain Gregory De'Ath; an article on gardening with such sentiments as 'no garden (however small) should be without an acre or two of uncultivated woodland'; as well as reams of property pages with photographs of magnificent Georgian and Tudor mansions with their outhouses, stables and grounds. The readership of *Country Life* far exceeds those who could actually afford to buy these houses or share the life-styles of those depicted.

What one wears and what one buys can communicate information about social class and values, but unlike some of the writings on conspicuous consumption what is communicated about the person is much subtler than the price of the good displayed alone (cf. Veblen, 1953). Consumption which is too conspicuous identifies the *nouveaux riches*; there are times when it is much more sophisticated to wear a well-tailored suit and drive a Bentley, than brandish a mink coat from the seat of a Rolls-Royce.

Social psychologists differ from sociologists in that psychologists tend to talk in terms of socialisation, of personal and social identification rather than about social class, but the two sets of concepts have much in common.

The pervasiveness of the media, whether of film, television, magazine or newspaper, is unavoidable save in a few religious and similar retreats. Readers, listeners or mere bystanders are bombarded with the norms and expectations of their culture—how women, men, families should behave, think and dress.

The influence of socialisation is complex and continuous. It begins in the earliest periods of life and follows us to our deaths. It is sustained and perpetuated in families from brother to sister, from mother to son, from father to daughter, from generation to generation. All of this influence consumer choice and consumer behaviour: the consumer behaviour of bachelors differs from married men—bachelors spend a higher proportion of income on alcohol. Among married couples in the USA husbands are more likely to make purchasing decisions on behalf of the household about insurance and motor cars; wives on food and kitchenware, and strangely, joint decisions are more common when it comes to the husband's clothing! (Davis and Rigaux, 1974). Advertisers are usually well informed as to which family member their publicity should be channelled.

We have said little about the personality of consumers. Do extraverts have different preferences from introverts? The evidence for the influence of personality variables on purchasing decisions is on the whole rather poor (see Engel and Blackwell, 1982) and of very minor importance when compared with demographic and income factors.

General Psychological Foundations

How consumer behaviour arises is usually dealt with in terms of learning theory, socialisation and information processing. There are several reductionist learning theories which have been developed from experimental psychology and animal work. The theories include classical, instrumental and basic drive theories and these will be alluded to only briefly here. Those interested in a more detailed and up-to-date appraisal of the relevance of these theories to consumer behaviour and other aspects of economic psychology should consult Lea, Tarpy and Webley (1985). In classical conditioning it has been shown how new responses from new stimuli can be produced because of their juxtaposition with basic stimulus—response patterns. Put an appetising meal in front of a hungry hound and the dog will salivate. The food is referred to as the unconditioned stimulus (US) and the salivation as the unconditioned response (UR). Introduce a bell or buzzer at the same time as the food (the conditioned stimulus, CS), and after a number of repetitions, the dog will salivate to the sound of the bell or buzzer alone (conditioned response, CR) (Pavlov, 1928).

In a similar fashion to Pavlov's dogs, consumers may learn to associate novel product stimuli with pleasure or satisfaction. The job of the advertiser is to bring about this learned association. John Watson was foremost in his time in applying lessons gained from animal experiments to advertising practice. In particular he preached the advantages of frequency and recency; the more an advertising slogan is repeated and the more recently it has been repeated the better. The practices of many advertisers seem to accord with this 'wisdom', and it has particular relevance to low-involvement purchasing behaviour (Watson, 1930).

Operant (or instrumental) conditioning as described by Skinner (1953) differs from classical conditioning because of the former's theoretical use of reinforcement principles and its emphasis on the 'active' (rather than passive) aspects of the learner and the learning process. 'Reinforcement' is a reward for a given behaviour: 'shaping' is the process whereby behaviour is selectively reinforced as it approximates to the desired response. Operant principles are commonly employed in commercials. The reward for buying a sleek sports car is the adoration of a beautiful and sophisticated member of the opposite sex. The reward for purchasing a bright pink dessert called 'Heavenly Delight' is happy, smiling obedient children. Notice the reinforcement need not be in the form of a saccharine tablet given to rats in animal experiments: human beings are reinforced by less specific but extremely potent social reinforcers, such as praise and social recognition.

Drives and motives are considered by many to form an integral part of the learning process. Drive refers to an increased readiness to respond, while the concept of motivation is more specifically defined as the purposeful pursuit of a particular goal. Drives and motives are commonly differentiated into primary, secondary and higher categories. Primary drives are physiological and refer to hunger and thirst for example; secondary drives are learnt drives, such as the pursuit of money, which can aid the satisfaction of primary drives but can have a motivating effect in their own right; higher order motives include the quest for social recognition and esteem, and, using Maslow's terms, has 'self-actualisation' at the pinnacle (Maslow, 1954). Borrowing from Fromm (1976), self-actualisation is the recognition of the difference between 'being' and 'having'; it is the antithesis of Oscar Wilde's definition of a cynic as someone who 'knows the price of everything and the value of nothing' (*Lady Windermere's Fan*, Act III).

Advertisers are cognisant of the importance of drives, and schedule commercials for cooling drinks and ice-creams for summer days.

When things are learnt they are in some sense remembered. The learning may be very specific, or general: one's initiation and enjoyment of a bottle of Bordeaux may mean that you will continue to buy a particular wine and no other, alternatively it may generalise to a liking of all red wines from the Bordeaux region, all French red wines, or even all red wines. Marketers often want customers to be able to discriminate between their product and similar others, whereas the owners of a chain of supermarkets may wish consumers to generalise about the quality and competitive prices of all the products sold in their shops.

The experimental literature concerning memory is vast (Estes, 1976). Some of the most basic distinctions of this literature are alluded to in marketing texts. The first of these is the distinction between short-term and long-term memory. It is precisely because low-involvement purchases are often determined by preferences in consumers' short-term memory that the frequency and recency of advertisements becomes so important. Preferences safely ensonced in long-term memory are less open to such vagaries but take much longer to be secured in the first instance. There is also a connected difference between recognition and recall. In the first case, customers may recognise and choose goods when seen or conspicuously displayed, whilst 'recall' without this stimulus may encourage a prospective purchaser to seek out a desired product even when tucked in a corner, or request its ordering when it is not in stock.

Learning theory is experimental psychology's major contribution to knowledge. Yet much of what we have so briefly described has been an attempt to define and experimentally test the building-blocks and fundamental aspects of behaviour; but knowledge of the stone can never describe or comprehend the magnificence of the cathedral. To Gestalt psychologists the whole is greater than the sum of its parts. And cognitive learning theories come closer to this whole and are more sympathetically dealt with in the present volume. It is an approach which stresses the importance of socialisation and the uniquely human ability of an elaborate language.

Herbert Simon (1976ab) has consistently stressed the information processing limitations of human beings in economic decision-making. It would be quite impossible for a consumer to gather all the relevant information about a group of related goods in order to make a 'rational' choice between them. Human beings do not weigh up all the alternatives Initially economists and psychologists do not differ about this, it is their interpretations that differ. Psychologists would be more likely to stress the cognitive limitations of consumers; economists the search costs of gathering information which outweighs the importance of the good purchased. It may be quite irrational to spend time and effort in the deliberation of the purchase of a pound of butter; alternatively much more information is likely to be brought to bear on the decision to purchase a motor car. Similarly there is much more at stake and the risks are consequently higher in the car purchase. There is a major difference in our example, namely that between durable and non-durable goods. Consumer psychologists appear to accept part of the economic argument in this context in their distinction between high and low-involvement decision processes—high-involvement decisions often referring to durable goods with relatively high prices, and low-involvement decisions to non-durable goods with relatively low ones.

Before we leave the discussion of information processing it is worthwhile to recall one of the central notions of Gestalt psychology, that of perceptual 'set' (Miller, 1968). 'Set' describes the tendency selectively to perceive only part of the environment, to pick out from it, if you like, the sounds that one is attuned to hear, the sights to which we have attached particular meaning and to which other sight and sounds and meanings are anchored. Perceptual 'set' is rarely if ever a conscious process and is the result of past learning. The purchase of inexpensive items often involves behaviour which may be attributed to habit but can also be usefully viewed in terms of 'set': the consumer 'shields out' the stimuli provided by alternative products and brands. Part of the marketers' job is to break this 'set', to encourage the consumer to attend to new stimuli.

Problem Recognition and Satisfaction in High Involvement Consumer Decisions

Psychologists and economists apparently agree that goods are purchased in pursuit of the satisfaction of some need or want. So under the heading 'problem recognition' it is assumed that a prospective consumer has a 'problem' which the consumption of a certain good or combination of goods assuages. Throughout, high-involvement decisions are treated as though they are a conscious and deliberate process with recognisable elements. A concrete example would be where an individual perceives that he is hungry, seeks out a pâtisserie, selects a chocolate éclair, leaves the shop and nibbles at the delicacy whilst promenading along the pavement. This is all pretty straightforward. Hunger is a basic physiological need, given enough money and available food, people will buy food to satisfy their hunger. Whether we could predict the purchasing of chocolate éclairs and furthermore whether this really matters is another question. Physiological needs are also straightforward. What about other types of need including 'social' needs? (recalling Maslow's (1954) hierarchy). You cannot, for instance, say that the purchase of many durable goods satisfies physiological needs. What physiological need does the purchase of a car satisfy? Even some very imaginative reductionist thinking would be unlikely to lead to an answer to this question. An economic approach would point to the relative costs of running a car and available public transport. The mental equation may be a complicated one: there are benefits associated with the convenience of ownership both in terms of time saved in travelling between home and work, and in the pleasure gained through the use of a car at weekends, on holidays, and so forth. A commodity which saves time, is convenient and pleasurable, is clearly satisfying needs and wants beyond the purely physiological. Problem recognition is also social. One may not appreciate the benefits of car ownership until it is pointed out to you by friends, neighbours and relatives. In an era when car ownership is common this social influence is more likely to take the form of preference for one make over another, of Ford over Chrysler, of Jaguar over BMW, of Mini Metro over Fiat 127. So how does one explain these preferences? One possibility is that different cars satisfy different wants.

Information Sources and the Search Process

The consumer is not an entirely passive recipient of information. Attention to information is selective. There are also many circumstances where the active pursuit of information is advantageous, this is especially true in the purchase of one's first car, where there is no direct knowledge based on previous purchases that can be called upon. Nevertheless, the prospective purchaser will have certain attitudes and beliefs about the relative merits of American or British compared with German or Japanese cars. These predispositions may have been built up from such diverse sources as friends, relatives, neighbours, newspaper and magazine articles, advertisements, or even from a cheap comedian's repertoire of jokes. The actual specification of the car, and the relatively 'objective' information available from standard testing and the articles of consumer association publications and the better motoring magazines, may not influence our rational consumer quite as much as one might at first suppose.

A highly influential book on the flow of communications remains Lazarsfeld, Berelson and Gaudet's *The People's Choice* (1948). It is a communication hypothesis of two major steps: information from the mass media is envisaged to filter down to 'opinion leaders', who then influence the rest of us. Word-of-mouth communications are seen as much more influential in themselves than mass media communications and the claims of advertisers. If this research is valid any marketer who could somehow manipulate word-of-mouth communications, or who could significantly influence the so called 'opinion leaders', might even transcend the dizzy heights of a J. Walter Thompson!

Much of the research and knowledge gained about the effectiveness and flow of persuasive communications has come from the political science literature and other related sources (Greenstein and Polsby, 1975). Clearly the two-step communication hypothesis is a simplified but useful one. There can be little doubt that the media is both influential towards and influenced by the public (Key, 1965); so whether the communication flow from the mass media to the public is a two-step one or not, it must be remembered in any evaluation that counter-currents are a natural part of the process. But as we have discussed elsewhere, advertisers and other media sources may not respond to recipients in a direct manner, but alter the form of their campaigns because of what they *think* the recipients think of it. Those advertisers with the most accurate perceptions may be among the most successful. Even this analysis underestimates the strengths of the links between media presentation and consumer and other preferences: successful advertisers not only respond to consumer preferences they actually mould them.

One of the major reasons given for the highly influential effects of personal communications is comparative disinterest. Those who are professionally employed to market a product are extremely unlikely to compare and contrast their product with others in a balanced way!

Much of the relevant social psychological literature on persuasive communications has concerned itself with the analysis of five elements, namely (a) the influences of the 'sources' of information; (b) the 'message', (e.g. is the information content of the advertisement high, or is its intention the communication of an insistent catch-phrase?); (c) the 'channel' in which the information is transmitted (e.g. television, in the newspapers, or word-of-mouth); (d) the nature and characteristics of the 'recipients' of the communication, (are they young or old? are they prospective purchasers of refridgerators or life insurance policies?); and (e) the 'effects' of the communication, (are the attitudes and beliefs of consumers altered? do sales of the advertised product increase? are the effects persistent over time?) (McGuire, 1969).

Much of the pertinent work done in experimental social psychology in the 1960s and 1970s tended to underestimate the dynamic nature of the communication process as well as the interaction between 'source' and 'recipient' among other interactions between the elements of this framework. The bombardment of advertising campaigns has altered recipients' susceptibility—some of the communications which were highly effective 20 years ago would be unlikely to have the same impact now. Furthermore 'sources' and 'recipients' have knowledge and suspicions of one another, and messages sometimes reflect the reciprocity of this relationship (Lewis, 1976). Marketers are opportunistic sources of information, recipients know this, marketers know that recipients know this. (This can become as entangled as Laing's *Knots*, 1970.) A good example from a travel brochure where the marketer attempts to take the recipient's negative perceptions into account follows:

> We go to extraordinary lengths with our brochure, not just to get the facts right, but to present each holiday exactly as it is, with the bias towards undersell. It is not that we are holier than our competitors, it's just good business sense in as much as that way we get a very low level of complaints, and a high level of repeat business. Yes, you've guessed our secret—we're in it for the money. (*Sun Med Holiday Brochure*, Summer 1983, p. 124)

It is like a game where the 'source' and 'recipient' attempt to get one step ahead of the other. For the source to deny any ulterior motive would be an absurdity, few if any recipients would accept such a message. The source however may gain by admitting to a pecuniary motivation, thereby gaining in perceived sincerity, and pointing toward potential mutual benefits.

Assessing the comparative influence of information sources is immensely difficult; it is rather like attempting to grasp fog. Imagine the following decision. You have a choice between three cars, x, y and z. They are of similar price and specification but have a different country of origin. You are requested to rank them according to which car you would expect to break down the most and which the least frequently. In some ways the actual answers to this question are immaterial. What matters is that so many people will be prepared to reply, albeit some with more confidence than others. Where did they get the information from? You could try asking them: (a) 'a friend', (b) 'relations or neighbours', (c) 'from a magazine or newspaper', (d) 'from TV or radio' or (e) 'from some statistical or other "official" source'. Any suitable sample will provide replies in all the categories. Any concentrated quizzing of respondents will reveal that many of them would wish to tick several and in some cases all the alternatives provided. A more qualitative approach would turn up the fact that people felt they have 'heard it somewhere' or 'read it somewhere' or 'seen it somewhere' and were unable, quite reasonably, to be more specific.

The subtlety of the communication process is partly recognised by Everett Rogers' work on the diffusion of innovations (Rogers, 1971). The diffusion approach stresses the social structure and networks of communication and as a consequence has many overlaps with social psychology. It is concerned less with the personality and social characteristics of innovators and more with how innovation is communicated, how it spreads, how it relates to later adoption and the purchasing of products over time. When one thinks of the diffusion and flow of political communication the 'opinion leaders' that come to mind are appointed leaders of trade unions, commercial organisations, banks, pressure groups, and so forth. Similarly innovators and those influential in the diffusion of information about new products may take this role because of the position they hold in society and in the communication network as a consequence—e.g. teachers, broadcasters, those who hold chairs and influential positions in the golf club, the Women's Institute, and many other associations in the local community.

At a more micro-analytic level an appreciation of the diffusion process can be gained by studies in sociometry, interpersonal and inter-group relations. Major studies of communications in groups have pointed to the disproportionate contribution and influence of group members (Bales, 1950; Janis, 1972). There are good grounds for supposing that influential product innovators may be among the most well-liked 'social leaders' (Arndt, 1968).

The diffusion process may also be thought of in terms of geographical factors although these are certainly associated with social-structural and economic ones. Take clothes as an example. The new fashions worn in London will take a while to diffuse to the provinces, which is determined not only by the relevant goods appearing in the local shops but by the gradual imitation and comparison with those 'trend-setters' 'down from town' for the weekend.

The diffusion process is plainly of great importance to market strategists, and because of its potential in predicting aggregate demand rather than the behaviour of individuals it has an attraction for economists as well. This is nowhere more apparent than in the penetration model of Kelly (1967) and the so-called epidemiological models of Bass (1969) and Midgley (1976). These are stochastic models using regression analysis. The simplest, the Kelly model, is especially notable for its parsimony employing only the ratio of 'triers' to 'repeat purchasers' and a 'ceiling proportion' pertaining to the theoretical maximum number of purchasers of a new product in determining the slope of a curve with time on the X axis and number of customers on the Y. The slightly more complicated Bass model has met with some predicitve success and evisages the influence of innovators declining monotonically over time and uses a coefficient of imitation determined by the number of previous buyers.

Choice, Attitudes and the Evaluation of Alternatives

It is assumed by many researchers in consumer psychology that high involvement purchasers have a number of criteria in mind when making a

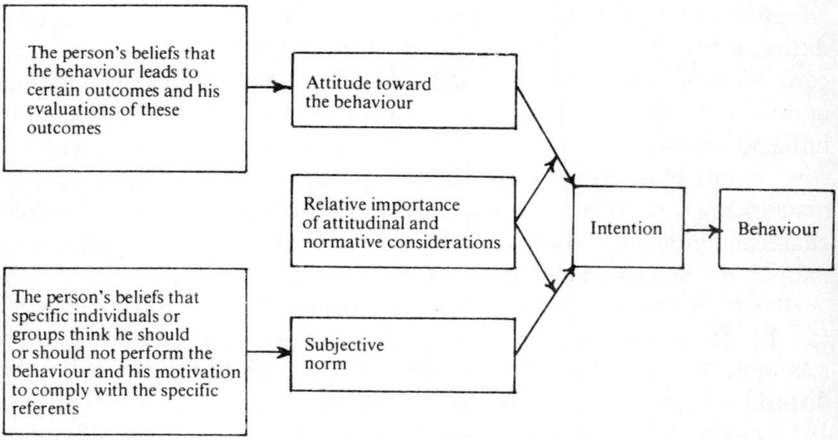

Figure 10.1: Factors determining a person's behaviour.

Note: Arrows indicate the direction of influence

Source: Icek Ajzen, Martin Fishbein: *Understanding Attitudes and Predicting Social Behavior*, 1980, p. 8. Reprinted by permission of Prentice-Hall, Inc., Englewood Cliffs, New Jersey.

choice. These criteria are likely to include the price of the good, its reputation, and in the case of footstuffs, its taste, texture, and so on. It is also largely agreed that there are cognitive limitations on the number of choice criteria that can be employed at any given time, of the relative importance of each and of combinations.

When we make choices or take decisions there are a number of different outcomes that are possible from such a choice or decision. Edwards (1954) has not unreasonably assumed that people attempt to maximise their utilities in the choices they make. The outcomes of choices are uncertain. Therefore each choice is made up of subjective probabilities about various outcomes each of which also has a subjective utility attached to it. If you have grasped this really quite straightforward and acceptable idea it is only a relatively short step to Fishbein's expectancy value theory of attitudes (Fishbein and Ajzen, 1975). An outline of the approach is presented in Figure 10.1. In Fishbein's framework it is asserted that prospective purchasers evaluate the outcomes of their purchase (e.g. satisfaction with a car's reliability) and have varying belief strengths that the behaviour (buying a car) will actually lead to these outcomes. So this is really very similar to subjective expected utility theory (SEU) where 'belief strengths' replace subjective probabilities, and 'evaluation of outcomes', the utility of outcomes. The Fishbein model becomes more social psychological in that it includes the influences of norms. Individuals are asked about the beliefs of important others and whether they feel motivated to comply with them.

The Fishbein model also incorporates attitudes towards the purchase, an assessment of the relative importance of attitudinal and normative components, and a specific reference to purchasers precise behavioural intentions. The theory is formally presented as a regression equation:

$$B1 = A_{act/w1} + SN_{w2}$$

where $B1$ = behavioural intention; A_{act} = attitude to act; SN = subjective norm; and w_1 and w_2 = the regression weights of the equation to be empirically arrived at. Fishbein and his associates have gone some way to operationalising attitude and beliefs components for use in predicting consumer behaviour. It must be remembered however that Fishbein takes a rather restricted unidimensional view of the nature of attitudes, one that undoubtedly simplifies the relationship between attitudes, beliefs and behaviour.

An obvious marketing strategy is to increase favourable attitudes and beliefs about the products that one is promoting; but it would be wrong to envisage attitudes merely as precursors of behaviour, they are also altered as a consequence of behaviour (see, for example, dissonance theory, Festinger, 1957). If I buy a Japanese car and it breaks down soon after I have spent a lot of money on it, this is unlikely to sway my positive attitude both towards the car and my decision to buy it. Speculating for a moment, dissonance theory and economic theory have something in common: purchasers may be less prone to question the wisdom of their purchasing decision the more they have spent on the car; in other words the psychological 'costs' rise in relationship to the size of the 'economic' and 'psychological' investment.

Low-Involvement Decision Processes

Low involvement often accompanies the purchasing of goods with relatively low prices, e.g. non-durable rather than durable goods. The economic and psychological approaches again have much in common here. If economic theory is extended to interpret subjective processes it follows that as the price of the goods falls people will deliberate less as there is less at risk. One would deliberate more about the purchase of a car than one would about a box of matches: so much is obvious.

Psychologists would particularly point to the likelihood that attitudes, in the sense of relatively enduring predispositions, would take a lesser role in the low-involvement process. Rather, decisions may be made on relatively 'superficial' criteria such as the packaging or the way goods are presented in a supermarket display.

This said, brand loyalty and repeat purchasing behaviour are aspects of low-involvement decisions of considerable economic importance. A rational consumer may well stick to the brand he likes thereby avoiding the risk of trying new ones which are not as good. So an appreciation of brand loyalty could well aid in the prediction of the market share of new products, or the continuing market share of existing ones. It is the contention of many consumer psychologists and economic psychologists that there are other processes at work in brand loyalty, including the tendency consumers have for 'habitual' purchases (Katona, 1975) which may persist long after higher quality and lower priced alternatives become available. Katona (1975) has also stressed the importance of learning in consumer purchases; a consumer gains information from past purchases which in turn affects future ones. The influence of marketers must not be underestimated either: goods of long standing are likely to have more developed and sophisticated marketing strategies which would sustain demand in the face of opposition from new brands, and especially those introduced by fresh (and perhaps even green!) companies where the 'back-up' is less well organised. Brand loyalty may also be due to some kind of 'psychological' commitment, but this all sounds rather vague, especially as it is difficult to argue that low-involvement decisions make a contribution to social identity: my social identity may partly rest on the car I drive and the clothes I wear but hardly on my choice of tissues or brand of disinfectant! This said, some minor goods related to appearance are often marketed as though they offered an irresistible opportunity for self-proclamation; examples are scents associated with middle-class 'tweedy' English country-folk, and the aftershave for men who don't have to try too hard to have their shirts unbuttoned at the neck by strange and alluring women. Vague as the notion of psychological commitment might be, people do become attached to the most trivial of goods, or so it would seem from the use of personalised pronouns when referring to 'my' shampoo and 'my' washing-up liquid.

The Consumer Movement

Consumer rights were itemised in J.F. Kennedy's famous and oft-quoted speech to Congress on 15 March 1962, which plainly states the rights of consumers of both public and private goods. These rights are: (1) the right to safety; (2) right to be informed; (3) right to choose; and (4) right of redress. If you buy a children's toy you have a right to assume that it is safe for children to play with: a consumer could reasonably expect a manufacturer to alter the way a teddy bear is made if a child could easily remove its eyes exposing a long, sharp, securing pin. It is reasonable to expect that a child's nightdress will not ignite on the slightest exposure to a naked flame. You have a right to know the constituents of foodstuffs—how much preservative and colouring they contain, what proportion of the ingredients are 'natural' or the result of chemical manufacture. The right to choose restricts the development of monopolies and cartels. And finally the right of redress legitimises a proper complaints procedure.

Legislation in many countries has curbed the claims of advertisers in an attempt to protect the consumer and to make advertisements more truthful. (To the cynic the latter aim is nothing but a contradiction in terms!) Unperturbed, the makers of a well-known lager in Britain tell us only that their beverage is *probably* 'the best in the world', a slogan that has become so well known that just the word 'probably' stimulates recognition of the product.

Values in society change and commercials reflect those values and contribute to or inhibit social change. The women's movement have perennially challenged marketers' presentation of middle-class housewives smiling their way through detergent commercials, immaculately dressed and soothingly articulate in their conversation, and quietly adorned with irreproachable children. The marketers' reply is that they are simply providing what the punters want, it is not their job to change the world! They bear neither responsibility nor blame.

But values have changed: talk of the unacceptable face of capitalism and the naked self-interest of businesses is commonplace (Galbraith, 1958), and the larger firms are aware of this. Imperial Chemical Industries in Britain (ICI) conduct an annual opinion survey of attitudes towards ICI and their products, their perceived civic responsibility, ethical reputation, reputation as an employer; as well as general attitudes towards industry and nationalisation (Worcester and McIntyre, 1982). ICI also poll 'special publics' such as members of parliament, the business and financial press, trades unions, their own employees, and so on. One consequence of these surveys has been an advertising campaign explaining how ICI's profits are distributed. The campaign specifically stresses the reinvestment of profits (contributing to the growth and stability of British industry), countering the public's 'misconception' that profits largely only benefit the select band of ICI directors.

So, effective consumer feedback can work to the advantage of industry, making it more responsive and successful to changing consumer attitudes and values, and in a broader sense highlights the pertinence of attitudes and values in understanding consumer behaviour.

ECONOMIC PSYCHOLOGY AND CONSUMER BEHAVIOUR

In an earlier section we suggested that the economic theory of consumer demand tells us little about the economic mind of the consumer. This is a view which can be strongly challenged. If neoclassical choice theory works then it certainly looks 'as if' consumers are behaving rationally given the constraints. An economic psychology must recognise this. If improved economic prediction is the aim there seems little point in investigating the minutiae of human social interaction. What is required is some simple tool for measuring cognitive mediating factors which have a tangible effect on aggregate consumer demand. As we have mentioned, the work of Katona and others has shown some success in this regard. But is this all there is to be done? Many think not, advocating instead more micro-analytic experimental studies of consumer choice under controlled conditions. Furthermore, some economic psychologists do not see their emerging discipline as a branch of economics. They are interested in the economic acts and their cognitive antecedents rather than in the consequences of economic acts alone. Prediction of economic behaviour is not their only idol. The comprehension of human behaviour and thinking and, in this case, human economic behaviour, is the major motivating force for the research.

The main strength of the economic approach to consumer choice is also its main weakness. The deductive methodology employs a convincing and relatively reliable theory, but with little or no direct exploration of economic behaviour. Alternatively our review of the market research literature has suggested the reverse: the inductive evidence and speculation is interesting and plausible but the field is relatively atheoretical. Engel and Blackwell's model (involving stimulus factors, and background variables, information processing, personality and environmental factors, search behaviour and outcomes) has intuitive appeal but falters, as do other models, because they are extremely difficult to confirm or falsify (see Figure 10.2). In addition positivist economists would question their excessive complexity (Zaltman, Pinson and Angelmar, 1973). The Howard-Sheth (1969) model is somewhat simpler than Engel and Blackwell's. There are just four components: inputs, perceptual constructs, learning constructs and outputs (see Figure 10.3).

Inputs are characteristics of individual and reference groups, and the characteristics (in terms of stimuli) of the product. Perceptual constructs involve aspects of search and attention. Learning constructs are concerned with motivation, satisfaction and feedback from purchasing. Outputs concern the actual purchase.

One of the main problems with the Howard-Sheth approach, is that the link between product stimuli and observed purchasing behaviour is hypothetical and unobservable (Zaltman, Pinson and Angelmar, 1973).

The model proposed by Nicosia (1966) is perhaps the most complicated encountered so far (see Figure 10.4). The model includes marketing factors as well as consumer decisions. Essentially, Nicosia describes four fields: (1) external factors of the buyer and seller and the nature and organisation of marketing and advertising; (2) buying behaviour and personal environmental factors relevant to search activity; (3) act of choice and outcomes thereof; and (4) function and results of the purchase, the storing of information, and so on.

This model, like the others described above, is difficult to test overall, although hypotheses can be derived from its many subsections. The model gains as it stresses the interaction between marketing and buyer behaviour.

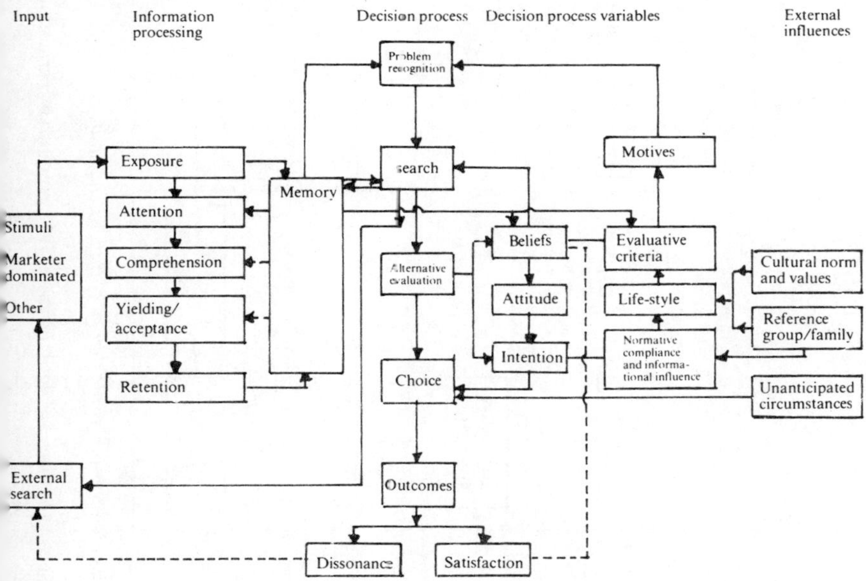

Figure 10.2: The EKB Model

Source: CONSUMER BEHAVIOR, Fourth Edition by James F. Engel and Roger D. Blackwell. Copyright © 1982 CBS College Publishing. Reprinted by permission of The Dryden Press, CBS College Publishing.

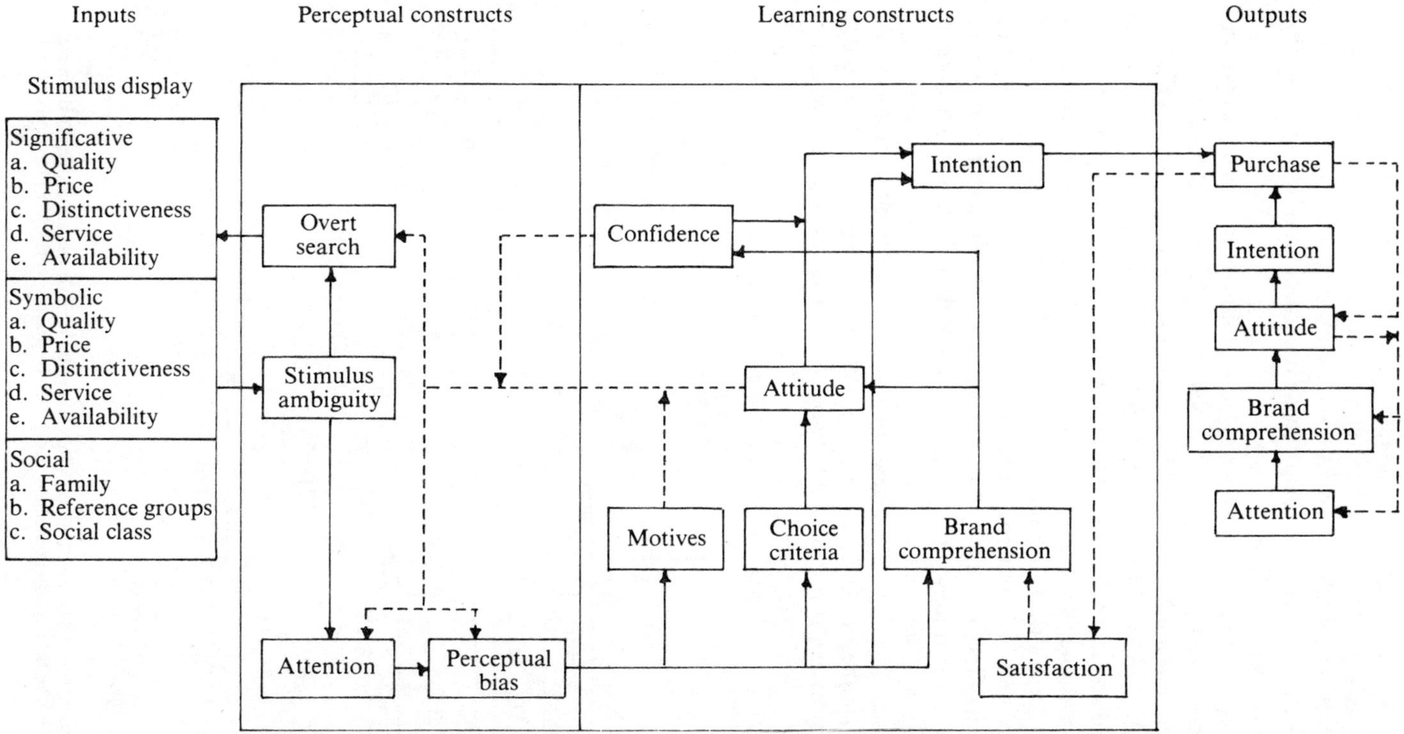

Figure 10.3: Simplified description of the theory of buyer behaviour.

Source: Howard and Sheth: *The Theory of Buyer Behavior*, 1972, reprinted by permission of John Wiley & Sons, Inc.

Generally, Nicosia offers a decision-making orientation; Howard and Sheth, an orientation based on learning theory.

Any evaluation of the relevance of these models to an understanding of the economic mind must pose questions. What are the models for? Is the purpose of research to improve marketing? To improve predictions of consumer demand? Or to increase our understanding of people's thinking about economic matters? Much of the psychological literature is normative and concerned with marketing. This in itself need not hinder our investigation of economic thinking. This said, we do not wish to appear to support the view that economic thinking is independent of what we as researchers think of it. The economic ideology of a society and its researchers frames economic thinking.

For the academic the quest for knowledge is sufficient justification and reward. For practitioners, quite understandably, what counts are results. It would be quite wrong to ignore the insights provided by marketing strategies, given that these strategies clearly influence consumer demand (Tuck, 1976).

Some Experiments

While some of the general marketing texts have been criticised because of their vagueness (Zaltman *et al.*, 1973; Tuck, 1976), a body of rigorous research has developed in empirically-based marketing and consumer behaviour journals. Some of the experimental methods and forms of analysis that have been used involve conjoint measurement, discriminant analysis, factor analysis, multidimensional scaling, cluster analysis, multiple regression and analyses of variance (Jain, Pinson and Ratchford, 1982). Some selected examples employing experimental methods are presented below.

Verhallen (1982) has used a factorial design and conjoint measurement in his experiment on scarcity and consumer choice behaviour. The experiment set out to test commodity theory (see Brock, 1968), the main premise of which is that a commodity is valued to the extent that it is unavailable. The more restricted and less available a good is, the more it will be valued. In Verhallen's first experiment 111 subjects were asked to choose between three recipe books of varying availability (high: 30 copies available; medium: 16 copies available; and low: 6 copies available). In the limited availability conditions, one of four reasons were given: accidental circumstances, popularity of the books in earlier product tests (of which the experiment was described as one), limited supply, or both popularity and limited supply. The experimental design is a $(3 \times 3) \times 4$ nested factorial design: 3 recipe books, 3 levels of availability and 4 causes for limited availability.

The initial results showed that the experimental treatments had no significant effects. However when the subjects were subdivided into a group of respondents who considered recipe books attractive and those who did

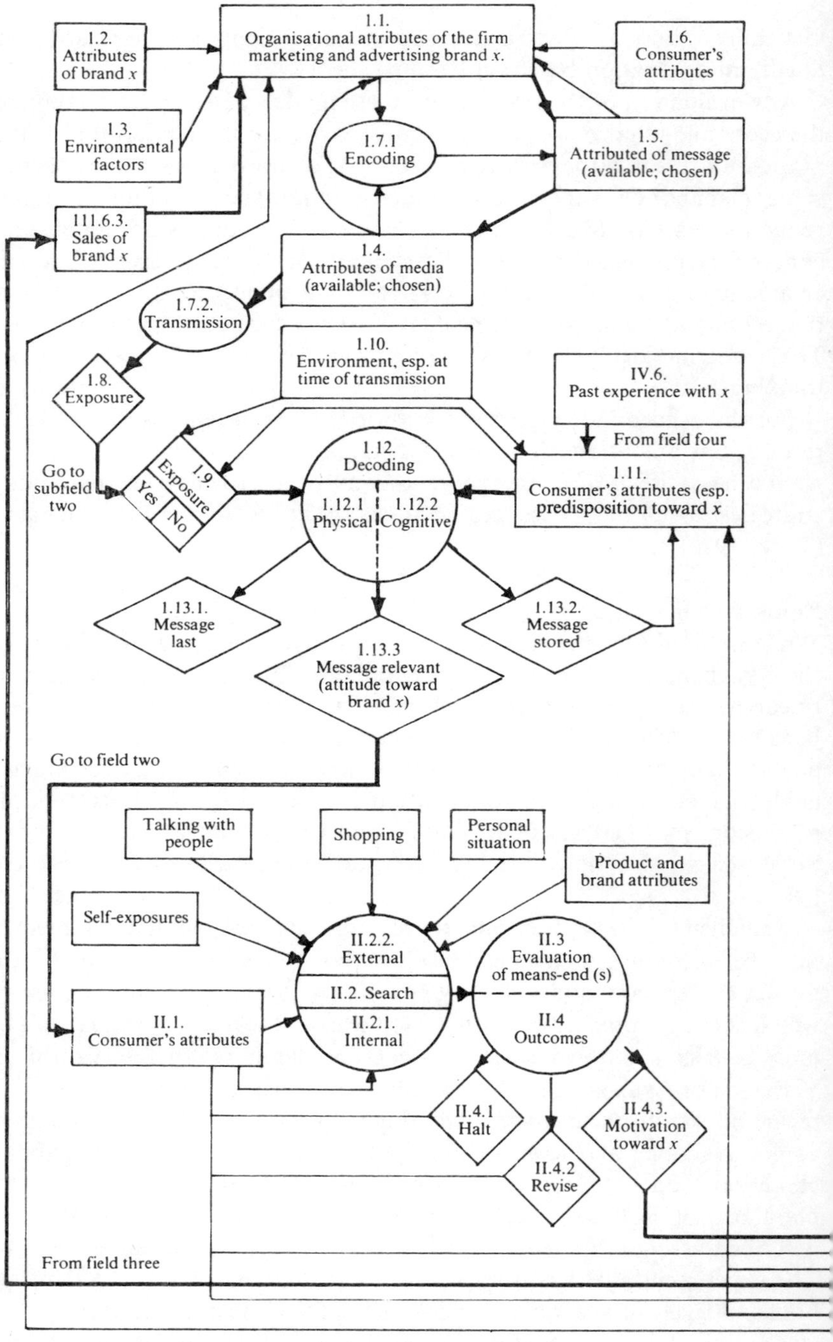

Figure 10.4: The Nicosia model of consumer decision processes.

Source: Nicosia (1966), reprinted by permission of the author.

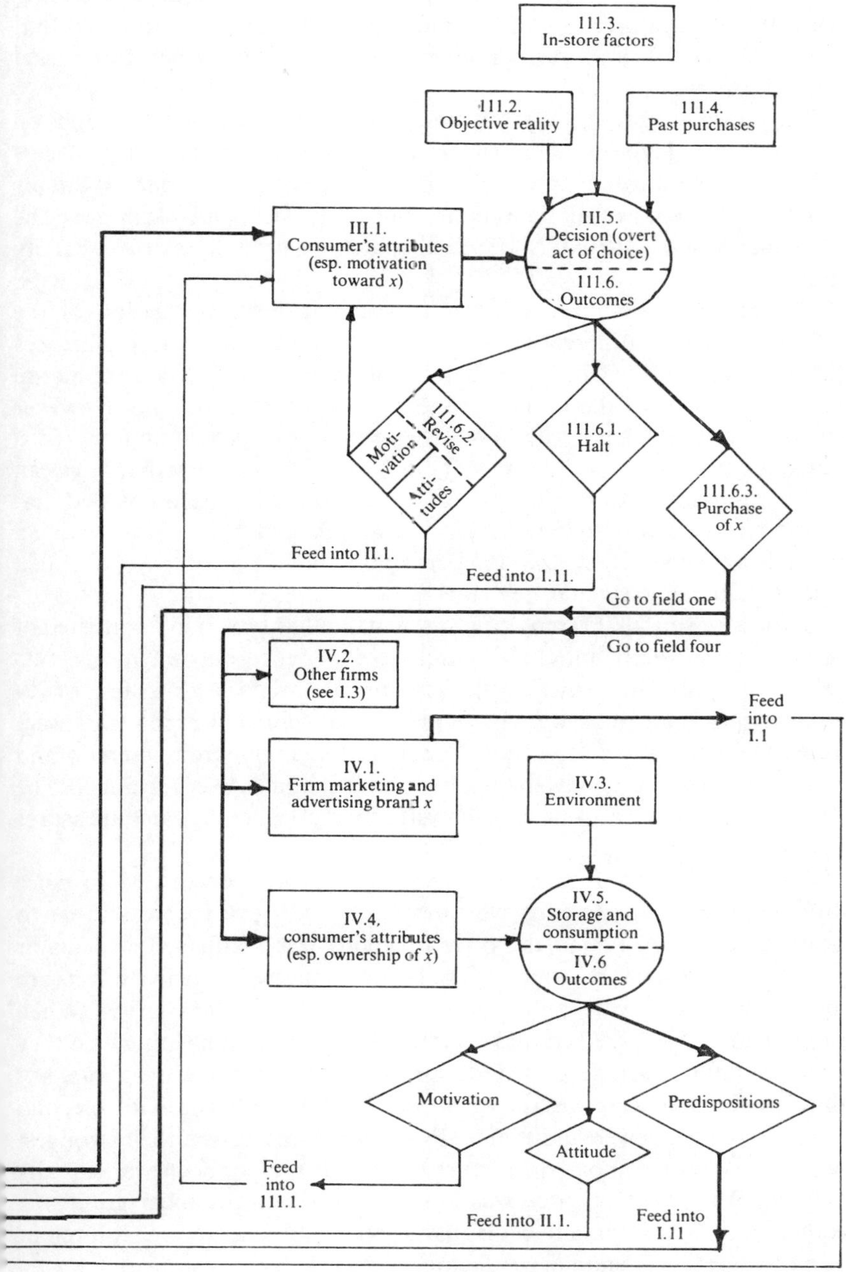

111.3.
In-store factors
111.2.
Objective reality
111.4.
Past purchases
III.1.
Consumer's attributes (esp. motivation toward x)
III.5.
Decision (overt act of choice)
111.6.
Outcomes
111.6.2.
Revise
Moti-vation
Atti-tudes
111.6.1.
Halt
111.6.3.
Purchase of x
Feed into II.1.
Feed into 1.11.
Go to field one
Go to field four
IV.2.
Other firms (see 1.3)
Feed into I.1
IV.1.
Firm marketing and advertising brand x
IV.3.
Environment
IV.4.
consumer's attributes (esp. ownership of x)
IV.5.
Storage and consumption
IV.6
Outcomes
Motivation
Attitude
Predispositions
Feed into 111.1.
Feed into II.1.
Feed into I.11

not, significant and informative results were obtained. For the 'attractive' group availability treatments had a significant effect on product preference for all but the accidental availability condition. It appears that unavailability affects product preference only when it is attributed to market conditions.

The results suggest the effect of scarcity of supply on demand depends on the number and type of other product cues. This is one of the main problems with the experimental approach—limited numbers of variables can be examined in controlled conditions, but it is far from clear how the combinations of attributes of goods, their price and relative scarcity interact.

Monroe has also used a factorial design in his investigation of the influence of price differences and brand familiarity on brand preferences (Monroe, 1976). It will be remembered that price and budget constraints are the cornerstones of the economic theory of consumer demand. However some economists have questioned these simplifying assumptions. In a seminal paper Gabor and Granger (1966) were able to show that price can act as an indicator of quality. In related research it has been revealed that consumers have both upper and lower price limits in mind when making a purchasing decision (Stoetzel, 1954), even that there may be 'psychological' price thresholds (Reynaud, 1981).

In the Monroe (1976) study a purchasing familiarity variable consisted of three degrees (recent purchase, purchase experience but not in last two years, no purchase experience). The price variables consisted of 19 comparisons, and there were three product categories. Respondents were asked to compare two brands on 7-point scales ranging from 'prefer brand A to brand B very strongly' to 'prefer brand B to brand A very strongly'. The results were analysed using the analysis of variance for repeated measures factorial designs.

Overall Monroe's results show asymmetric preferences due to price differences. Brand preferences were more sensitive to price decreases than to price increases. Although the price of goods was reaffirmed as a major variable in consumer decisions by the Monroe study its principal effects are in collaboration with other ones, such as brand familiarity. When respondents were asked to make choices between brands with which they were unfamiliar, people preferred brands that were cheaper it is true, but these preferences were weaker when price was the only cue available, and many respondents were indifferent. Price differences were at their strongest when goods were compared with those with which respondents were equally familiar. The effect of price was again weak when a familiar good was compared with an unfamiliar one; large price differences were required in order to override the familiarity factor.

Multiple comparisons reach a high level of sophistication in conjoint measurement (Green and Wind, 1975; Green and Srinivasan, 1978). For example how do people choose between a Goodyear tyre, which is long-lasting, expensive and where there is a garage nearby, and a Dunlop tyre of average durability and price and where the nearest garage is a mile away? A choice has to be made, but clearly complex trade-offs could arise between attributes. Conjoint measurement decomposes the global judgement, say, the preferences of Goodyear over Dunlop into constituent parts so that the relative importance and sensitivity of price changes and durability can be assessed.

Some Related Work by Economists

Conjoint measurement (and discriminant analysis) bears a resemblance to the 'characteristics' approach of Lancaster (1971) in his book on consumer demand. For Lancaster the purchasing of goods is not a straightforward function of the good but of its characteristics. The assumptions that Lancaster makes are similar to those in the neoclassical theory of consumer demand. It is assumed that the decision-making process itself is not open to observation but the 'characteristics' on which consumers base their decisions, he argues, can be objectively arrived at. Furthermore while market research is often highly specific and normative Lancaster attempts to devise a universal and generally applied theory based on 'objective' criteria. There is no departure from the assumption of rationality—if people generally choose car A over car B, and car B costs less, the consumer is not being irrational, it simply means that car A has a desirable characteristic that the purchaser cannot buy for less. One simply has to discover what the characteristics are that the good possesses and which the consumer values.

Lancaster has met with some success in mapping efficiency frontiers for car sales using only a small number of 'objective', physical characteristics (sometimes as few as five). The efficiency frontier defines feasible trade-offs between prices and characteristics and replaces the budget constraint in the traditional neoclassical model. In conclusion Lancaster makes it clear that his method, although allowing for the multi-attribute characteristics of goods, has no need of 'psychologising': 'Our analysis suggests that the automobile market is readily available to rational analysis in terms of straightforward physical characteristics of cars, without using such imponderables as "style" or any sex at all' (Lancaster, 1971, p. 174).

Earl's *The Economic Imagination: Towards a Behavioural Analysis of Choice* (1983) offers a much more integrated product of the two disciplines of economics and psychology. The book provides a comprehensive methodological critique of neoclassical economics. In particular, issue is taken with the neoclassical theory's tendency towards reductionism at the expense of holism and structuralism—a failing to see 'the wood for the trees'.

Earl has some sympathy with the work of Lancaster and with expectancy/value theories (e.g. Fishbein and Ajzen, 1975) and with multi-attribute analyses generally. However (referencing Simon, 1959), the complexity of the mental calculations required in multi-attribute considerations is called into question given the cognitive limitations of a bounded rationality. Earl instead prefers a 'lexicographic' or non-compensatory analysis: goods may not be chosen because they have the best mix of characteristics, in that the comparative lack of one characteristic can be compensated for by the abundance of another, but because certain 'target' qualities of specific attributes are reached. Earl also attempts to integrate Kelly's (1963) theory of personality and the application of the 'repertory grid' as a research tool. It is stressed that choices are made in social context and have a social function. And in Kelly's terms, that choices take place in a context where consumers are actively attempting to make sense of the world and to anticipate events.

CONCLUSIONS

The marketing and consumer behaviour literature varies in quality and purpose. Katona's research has provided ways of anticipating aggregate consumer demand using subjective measures and is of considerable interest to economists as a consequence. In comparison the general marketing texts attempt to describe processes inherent in consumer decisions, how choices develop and how they can change. The general texts are readable, have intuitive appeal, but lack scientific rigour. Alternatively articles published in modern consumer behaviour and marketing journals are frequently sophisticated in their design and statistical analysis yet the generality of the findings, given that many are experimentally based, is in question. At least two major areas of research require development. The first requires a concerted effort to gain access to marketing campaigns used in private industry; to analyse systematically the data, to offer a rigorous analysis for appraisal by the academic public. If such campaigns are shown to work in practice they have important lessons for researchers seeking to understand the process of consumer choice and the mechanisms of consumer demand.

Economists are generally uninterested in the actual process of individual consumer decisions, and while market researchers profess to be interested in this process accounts by consumers of their own behaviour are comparatively rare visitors to the pages of academic journals. It can be argued that a second area of research that needs to be developed requires a genuine inquiry into the economic mind of the consumer; what people actually do and what they are thinking. It would be informative for the reader to recollect their thinking and behaviour the last time, for example, they purchased a car. Were compensatory trade-offs made between multi-attributes? Or was the choice non-compensatory or 'lexicographic'? What was the influence of financial constraints, attitudes and beliefs about the make of car, towards the car trader, and so forth? What other social influences and time constraints were there? In short, research in this area needs to be supplemented by qualitative data.

11 Taxation and Public Expenditure

INTRODUCTION

How much should the government spend on schools and hospitals? And how should the money be raised to pay for these services? These are the kinds of questions that are considered in this chapter.

When we speak of the public sector we refer to a range of services that governments provide through public expenditure. These can vary enormously, and some are more direct than others: defence expenditure provides benefits of a kind for all citizens, while unemployment benefits are paid directly to those who are eligible. The public sector obviously has to be financed—the money does not materialise out of thin air—yet people often talk colloquially of getting something 'free on the National Health', of 'free school milk', and so forth. A certain amount of finance is obtained through government borrowing, but the majority depends on what the government can raise in revenue from taxes on income and goods and services in particular.

The size of the public sector differs from country to country; for example, it is proportionally larger in Sweden than in the UK where in turn it is a larger part of the economy than in the USA. It also follows that, on average, people pay less tax in the USA than in the UK. Sweden is one of the highest taxed nations in the world (see Table 11.1).

Just how important the public sector is is sometimes forgotten; people simply become accustomed to state provision. In Britain at least, it would seem a very radical proposal indeed to privatise the supply of gas, electricity and coal, and the increased privatisation of health services (to understate the case) has been greeted ambivalently.

A fundamental question becomes 'Just how big should the public sector be?' 'And what is it for anyway?' We find ourselves, inevitably, grappling with moral, political and economic issues. Social security payments, for example, involves the consideration of all three. Morally the government may appear to feel that poverty is unacceptable and that cash and other benefits should be provided for those in need. Politically they decide to act as a kind of 'benevolent dictator'—there can be no guarantee that sufficient provision for those in need can be provided solely through voluntary or charitable means, so the government makes it a legal requirement for citizens to make appropriate contributions through taxation. Economically we may want to examine the efficiency of the distribution to those in need,

Table 11.1: Total tax revenue as percentage of gross domestic product at market prices

	1981
Sweden	51.31
Norway	48.49
Netherlands	45.47
Belgium	45.44
Denmark	45.26
France	42.95
Austria	42.54
Ireland	38.44
United Kingdom	37.35
Germany	37.32
Finland	36.82
Canada	34.74
Luxembourg	34.12
Italy	33.74
New Zealand	32.78
Australia	31.55
United States	31.24
Portugal	31.11
Switzerland	30.28
Greece	29.22
Japan	26.86
Spain	25.24
Turkey	19.29
Unweighted average	
OECD. Total	36.16
OECD. Europe	37.47
EEC	38.93

Source: OECD, (1982, p. 68).

and the effects taxation and social security benefits may have on the incentive to work and the supply of labour.

In democratic states the fiscal policies of governments are not truly dictatorial: the political party in power can be voted out of office at the next election. Fiscal policies are partly dependent upon the attitudes and preferences of taxpayers, citizens and voters; loosely speaking they are influenced by 'public opinion'.

Economics has paid little direct attention to fiscal preferences and attitudes, relying instead on familiar maximising assumptions and rational economic man. Because social psychologists and market researchers have developed an expertise in the measurement and assessment of attitudes and preferences an obvious link is forged for the advancement of an economic psychology (Lewis, 1982a).

Similarly social psychologists' interest in the link between attitudes and behaviour, compliance with rules, motivation, communications and values all have relevance to the study of the public sector. The link between attitudes and behaviour is pertinent in the study of tax evasion behaviour. Does increased antipathy towards taxation increase the likelihood of tax evasion? Can tax evasion be successfully reduced by tightening up on enforcement procedures? Or does the literature on compliance with rules suggest otherwise? Given what we know about motivation, is taxation likely to act as a disincentive to work effort? What is the communication system between government departments and citizens really like? Is it all bureaucratisation and gobbledegook? And finally an examination of the role of the state and its perceived legitimacy is intertwined with the value systems beliefs and ideological perspectives of citizens. Does a bloated state undermine individuals' ability to look after themselves and their right to privacy? We cannot of course fully answer these questions but we can examine new sources of evidence and evaluate them in a new context.

The social psychological literature is based mainly on attitude surveys and opinion polls and as such we are aware that this is rather a restricted interpretation of 'public opinion'. In the concluding sections, therefore, we offer a brief methodological critique, the implications of the results reviewed for policy-making, and some suggestions for future research.

PERCEPTIONS AND OPINIONS ABOUT PUBLIC EXPENDITURE AND TAX

Public Expenditure

What do people think the government spends its money on? This is the kind of question posed in a national quota sample of the UK conducted by Marplan Ltd in 1981. The precise question read as follows.

All governments spend money on a variety of different things. What are the main things governments spend money on?

Respondents were given a free choice and were unprompted. This gives some information about the comparative 'visibility' of government expenditure (Jones and Cullis, 1984). The most mentioned expenditure (53 per cent) was defence and the armed forces. This was closely followed by 'hospitals and the health service' (51 per cent) and 'schools and education' (44 per cent). There was then a gap until we come to the 'social security' (26 per cent), 'roads' (21 per cent), 'unemployment benefits' (19 per cent) and the 'nationalised industries' (19 per cent). There were a number of interesting differences between sub-groups, most notably between the sexes and social classes. Men were much more likely to think of defence and the armed forces (62 per cent of men vs. 43 per cent of women) and the police and law courts (16 per cent vs. 10 per cent). On the other hand, women seemed marginally more aware of welfare issues such as hospital care, care for the elderly, and schools and education.

There was proportionally more awareness of public expenditure among respondents in professional occupations (social class AB). Awareness of hospitals and the hospital service, schools and education and defence declined in a more or less linear fashion from social class AB, to C1, through C2 to DE. As an example, awareness of defence expenditure was as follows AB, 64%; C1, 56%; C2, 51%; DE, 44%. Social class by occupation can act as a proxy for years in education. It seems likely that fiscal awareness (or 'civic consciousness') is related to education, and this has important implications both in the qualitative interpretation of fiscal preferences recorded in polls and referenda (to be covered in more detail later); and implications for those advocating a more participative role for the public in policy-making (David, 1980).

Clearly awareness is not very great overall, even in the case of defence only just over half the respondents mentioned it.

The next logical step is to find out how much people think the government spends on particular macro-items—e.g. how much does the government spend on, say, social insurance compared with health? As one might predict from previous results, misperceptions are rife. In a study by Auld (1978), 1294 individuals from Ontario were interviewed about their awareness of the size of the provincial budget and the estimated share of the budget of a number of public expenditure items such as social welfare and health. Only about 20 per cent of those asked had even a rough idea of the answer to either of these questions.

Having painted a rather gloomy picture of people's knowledge about public expenditure this is not to say that people do not have preferences. When asked, in general over 90 per cent of the public are prepared to state that they would like to see more, less or about the same spent on various items. Furthermore, results based on simple questions about public expenditure conducted in the UK have shown a remarkable consistency in recent years (Lewis and Jackson, 1985) which is commensurate with preferences having a certain salience for respondents. In a small study of 200 electors selected at random from the electoral register of the City of Bath, the majority favoured increased spending on the National Health Service (59.5 per cent) and on education (53.5 per cent) (Lewis, 1980). Edgell and Duke (1982), in a 10 per cent sample of two parliamentary wards in Greater Manchester (N = 948), recorded similar results, but with evidence of stronger support for increased public expenditure: 78 per cent wanted more spent on health and 73 per cent wanted more spent on education.

In the intervening years between the two studies both Margaret Thatcher in the UK and Ronald Reagan in the USA have pursued fiscal policies aimed at reducing the size of government, and of reducing both public expenditure and taxation. Yet support for public expenditure seems to have grown. This is of interest both to political scientists and psychologists in attempting to understand how preferences and opinions are formed and how they change over time. Some useful information is provided by a disaggregation of the overall survey results. In the studies of Lewis (1980), Edgell and Duke (1982) and in a national survey of the UK conducted by Marplan (Lewis and Jackson, 1985) the most important differences were those recorded between supporters of differing political parties. Furthermore, respondents revealed preferences which closely reflected the fiscal policies of the party to which they felt some allegiance. In the national MORI sample (N = 900), for example, Labour Party supporters favoured increases in 6 of 14 items mentioned in the questionnaire—namely, health, help for the old, schools, housing, roads, and assistance to industry; while Conservative supporters favoured increases on only three—health, help for the old, and on police and the law courts. Conservative supporters called for cuts in social security and the nationalised industries, while Labour supporters felt they would like to see expenditure remain much as it is at present for these three items (Lewis and Jackson, 1985).

That these results should be so consistent is something of a mystery since few of the respondents were party members, or highly committed politically. How did they know what the fiscal preferences of their favoured party were? Does one's party political allegiance shape expenditure preferences? Or can expenditure preferences themselves have an influence on voting behaviour? The evidence is not sufficiently clear to answer these questions (and where have you heard that before?), but we can offer some suggestions. First of all, because fiscal policy in both USA and the UK has been so plainly stated the issue has become more pertinent and salient to the electorate. Furthermore, fiscal matters have received considerably more coverage in the press and the media generally—and the USA is a few years ahead of the UK: Proposition 13, the Californian fiscal referendum, was big news in the summer of 1978 and tax limitation proposals have been news ever since. (Californians voted almost 2:1 in favour of reductions in property tax (the state's rates) for over 50 per cent of business and home owners.)

Philip Converse has written widely on the political knowledge of electors (Converse 1964, 1975). He explains the relative 'ignorance' of the electorate with reference to information costs. (Why bother to find out things which have no immediate effect on you?) It would follow, if indeed the consistent preferences revealed in surveys are a consequence of the increased salience of the issues, that public expenditure policies are perceived as something that affects people personally. Edgell and Duke report evidence in support of such a notion: 94 per cent of their respondents said they had heard about spending cuts and 50 per cent reported that they personally, and/or someone in their household had been affected by the cuts.

We would not want to argue that public expenditure preferences are a major influence on forming party political allegiances. However it seems probable that expenditure preferences are having an increasing effect on the voting patterns of so-called 'floating voters'. Again we turn to Edgell and Duke (1982). They found that 'Conservative defectors' (i.e. people who voted for the Conservative Party in 1979 but would not do so if there was an election 'tomorrow') exhibited preferences for the welfare state and law and order which were different from stable Conservative voters in that they preferred more spent on the former and less on the latter. There is reasonable evidence too that people can accurately link expenditure policies with the relevant political parties. In the Edgell and Duke study one of the largest differences between Conservative and Labour supporters' preferences related to expenditure on schools and education. A study of undergraduates at Exeter University has shown that 79 per cent of people who did not identify with the Conservative Party (and 83 per cent of those who did) accurately associated the 'restoration of grammar schools' with Conservative Party policy, of whom 79 per cent of Conservative identifiers supported the restoration of grammar schools as against 56 per cent of non-identifiers (Holland and Moon, 1982).

It also seems possible that expenditure preferences are organised even before people become regular voters or have experience of paying tax. In a small study of 50 Bath University undergraduates Lewis (1983) was able to show that both perceptions, and particularly preferences for a series of seven macro-expenditure items were significantly different from one another and broadly predictable from individuals' self-reported positions on 'Left/Right' scales—and this from a sample where almost 50 per cent said they did not support any political party.

Taxation

In the national sample conducted by Marplan mentioned earlier, which investigated economic beliefs among the British electorate, the specific question was asked: 'Do you know where governments get the money to pay for services we've just been talking about?' (This question followed one about knowledge of, and preferences for, public expenditure.) Over 93 per cent of the sample mentioned income taxation, 56 per cent taxes on goods, and over 30 per cent named taxes on vehicles, tobacco, petrol and alcohol. Only 21 per cent mentioned rates (which are similar to property taxes in the USA), and only 11 per cent, customs and excise revenue (e.g. VAT). When the results were disaggregated there were few differences between groups in their comparative awareness of income tax. For taxes other than income tax there was a tendency for men to be more aware than women; for professional and clerical workers more than manual workers; and for Conservative voters more than Labour. Although many more working women deal with their own tax affairs and those of their families than previously, the burden still falls more often on the male: thus, to a certain extent knowledge of taxation is a function of familiarity with it. As before, we suspect that social class acts as a proxy for years in education and thus to 'fiscal awareness'.

Comparative data have become available from a study reported by Beedle and Taylor-Gooby (1983) of 240 respondents from eight census enumeration districts in the Medway towns of Kent. Unlike the Marplan study people were not given a free choice. Instead, respondents were shown a card displaying in random order five ways of financing services. People were asked in which way 'most money is raised at present?': the five choices were income tax, VAT, National Insurance contributions, rates and other charges. As before income tax is perceived as the most salient: overall 75 per cent mentioned this, against 9%, VAT; 9%, national insurance; 6%, rates; and 0.4% other charges. (In this latter study it must be remembered that respondents were limited to one choice only.) In 1980, at the time of the survey, the actual amount of revenue raised by each source was income tax, 34%; VAT and other indirect taxes, 41%; insurance contributions, 16%; and rates, 9%. The comparative 'visibility' of taxes is clearly at odds with the facts.

'Visibility' may have important consequences for tax attitudes— i.e. the taxes one notices may be those where the burden is perceived to be highest and antipathy most pronounced. The so-called 'fiscal illusion' is also of wide interest to public sector economists as it may aid in the explanation of growing government spending (see, for example, Wagner, 1976; Goetz, 1977). The survey evidence we have reviewed so far certainly suggests that people favour increased public expenditure and are comparatively unaware of so called 'indirect' taxes. It follows that people may underestimate their true tax burdens, especially where the tax system is complex and tax collection disseminated (Wagner, 1976). Consequently benefits from expenditure may seem to have a small price in terms of tax revenue. Wagner's approach is a persuasive one, but there appears to be no systematic evidence that people do consistently underestimate their tax burden overall. Studies in Britain have concentrated on marginal income tax rates—Brown's (1968) results pointed towards overestimation, Enrich's (1963) and Lewis's (1978) to underestimation.

In a study of 200 voters in the City of Bath, Lewis (1978) asked respondents how much they would lose in income tax if they earned an extra pound (£1). Thus the question related to income tax—the most 'visible' of taxes as our Marplan results showed—and the question concerned the marginal rather than the average rate of tax. It seems reasonable to expect that people would be more knowledgeable about the marginal rate as, unlike the average rate, complicated mental arithmetic is not required. Furthermore if tax really is a disincentive to work effort people should be cognisant of how much pay they would be losing if they worked longer hours in order to see whether it was 'worth their while'. The results showed consistent underestimation of the marginal rates of taxes.

Economists, in their theories concerning the relationship between taxation and labour supply, have pointed out that logically taxation can just as readily act as an incentive for work effort as an disincentive (Brown, 1981). In the hypothetical trade-off between work and leisure an individual may choose more leisure in the face of high marginal tax rates as leisure becomes less expensive as income forgone (because the individual is not working) is reduced. Alternatively the individual may choose to work more; as tax reduces income, individuals may feel they need to work more in order to pay for things.

The idea that taxation may be an incentive for work effort may not have occurred to many readers not familiar with economic theory. Certainly, policy-makers, as do many other people, tend to talk as though the disincentive effects of taxation were a matter of fact. Katona (1977) has argued that cuts in income taxation frequently fail to have the desired effect on work motivation and job-creation, concluding that people persist with habitual forms of economic behaviour as though they were ignorant of fiscal changes. Much of the interview and survey evidence too fails to settle the argument between the relative strengths of incentive and disincentive effects. In fact in both the USA and the UK the majority of respondents report that taxation has no effect on their work effort (for the USA, see Sanders, 1951; Barlow, Brazer and Morgan, 1966; Holland, 1969; for the UK, Break, 1957; Fields and Stanbery, 1970). The results are remarkably consistent—70 per cent of respondents say tax has no effect on hours worked, and among the rest replies are evenly split between incentive and disincentive effects (Lewis, 1982a Ch. 12).

There are considerable methodological problems in this kind of research. A concentration on aggregate labour supply data can only attempt to make the link with taxation via rather gross statistical means. Survey and interview data can be criticised because of the questions used, the nature of the sample, and the problem that the interview requires an explanation or an interpretation from the respondent which he may not previously have considered. Work effort is also an extremely difficult dependent variable to define either quantitatively or qualitatively. To make matters even more complicated work or production can take place in at least three economies: the official economy recorded in national income statistics; the cash-only 'shadow economy'; and in the cashless domestic economy (see Rose, 1983).

The question of work motivation provides one of the most potentially productive liaisons between economists and psychologists. Economists have become more interested in the use of survey and interview techniques and disaggregating data to take into account age, sex, family size and occupational factors (Brown *et al.*, 1984). Occupational psychologists have argued that pay (and presumably therefore tax) are not always the sole or even primary motive for work, concentrating instead on aspects of work satisfaction and fulfilment (Warr and Wall, 1975). In conclusion it seems likely that the effects of tax are largely generated through perceptions, attitudes and feelings rather than having a direct influence on working behaviour. The relationship between taxation and work effort is a simple explanation that may be considered appropriate in the interpretation of another's behaviour but rarely one's own (cf. attribution theory; see Kelley and Michela, 1980 for a review). The Royal Commission of the Taxation of Profits and Income (1954) reported that three-quarters of the sample thought that income tax was a deterrent to work effort, yet less than 30 per cent of people claimed that tax had any effect on their own behaviour.

There has been agreement among economists about 'tax principles', namely, 'efficiency', 'ability to pay', 'equity', 'simplicity', 'flexibility', 'compatibility' and 'certainty' (Brown and Jackson, 1978; Sandford, 1978). In the present section we pay particular attention to the first four. 'Ability to pay' is concerned with the equality of sacrifice—Should tax payments be proportionate to income, or should wealthier individuals pay a higher proportion in tax (progressive taxaton)? 'Equity' is concerned with 'fair' treatment for people with similar taxable capacities (horizontal equity) and differing ones (vertical equity). 'Efficiency' relates to the way that taxation may distort the supply of labour. 'Simplicity' relates to the principle that the basics of a tax system should be understood by the majority of citizens. We have touched on the topic of efficiency when discussing work motivation; simplicity and comprehensibility will be discussed in a later section; for the time being we concern ourselves with the perception of fairness.

Karlyn Keene (1983) has reviewed public opinion data conducted in the USA between 1978–83 on the perceived fairness of income taxation. The point is made (which will be elaborated on in our critique at the end of this chapter) that answers to survey questions depend both on how they are phrased and the knowledge of respondents. On this basis Keene criticises the conclusions by the pollster Louis Harris that a flat-rate income tax that eliminates deductions from taxable income is supported by the majority of the electorate. But support for progressive taxation among the general public does not appear to be particularly strong to say the least. Before we ask respondents to reveal their preferences we first need to know whether people perceive the system is progressive in the first instance. There is even disagreement among economists, given the imaginative and legal tax avoidance schemes available to taxpayers, whether the acutal incidence of income tax is genuinely progressive.

Lewis (1978), in a study of 200 electors in the UK, attempted to compare perceptions with preferences. He showed, unsurprisingly perhaps, that people would like to pay less in income tax than at present, feeling in particular that their personal tax burden was too high. (A result which is internationally consistent: Keene (1983) reports that nearly every survey conducted in the USA since the second world war has a majority view that taxes are too high. One should not lose touch with the well-founded and the obvious.) Continuing, Lewis also found that individuals felt others with different incomes should pay less as well. Income taxation was perceived as being progressive, preferences were progressive—but at lower rates; a progressive tax system was perceived as being the most fair. These results may be particularly British—economic history and tax structures clearly differ from country to country. The results could be interpreted as showing that electors share notions of social justice which they apply to fiscal matters. More likely perhaps is the explanation that perceptions and especially preferences merely reflect the *status quo*. If respondents were asked whether they supported a flat rate income tax (as in some of the surveys received by Keene, 1983) it seems likely that many UK respondents would support such a scheme. This is quite different from respondents putting forward such an idea of their own accord.

Support for the finding that taxpayers have some idea of the structure of income tax in the UK also comes from Beedle and Taylor-Gooby (1983). Overall half of their sample believed that income tax took more from the better off both in absolute and relative terms. People with higher incomes were more likely to state this view however.

Schmölders (1970) has speculated about the nature of 'tax-mentality' (individuals' perceptions of fairness, purposes of taxation and tax morale) and how 'tax mentality' may relate to compliance with the tax system or propensity to evade tax illegally. We shall pursue this in later sections, nevertheless it is timely to consider how various tax perceptions and preferences may fit together. The first of these must be the link between taxation and public expenditure itself.

Fiscal Preferences

The majority of individuals are relatively unaware of what we can term the 'fiscal connection' between taxes paid and benefits received from government spending. This lack of awareness can be crucial when interpreting survey evidence. The mass of results from the UK, USA, France, Germany and Denmark over the last 15 years (and before) show majority preferences for reductions in taxation but increases in public expenditure especially on favoured items such as provisions for the sick, the old and for schools (Lewis, 1982a; Coughlin, 1980). Over 20 years ago Mueller (1963) pointed out this 'fiscal incongruity' yet surveys are still conducted which fail to take the 'fiscal connection' into account. Seldon (1980) has referred to it as 'price-less' opinion research—people favour increased expenditure because they do not adequately consider the 'tax price'. Put another way, people are antipathetic towards taxation because they do not consider what it pays for.

Certainly the results from surveys which make the fiscal connection, either in the phrasing of the question or in a preamble, produced preferences which are moderated in the predicted direction—i.e. antipathy towards taxation is reduced when it is linked with favoured items of expenditure; enthusiasm for expenditure increases are tempered by mention of the tax price.

Fiscal preferences have changed in recent years as fiscal issues have become more salient. Probably the most important influence on this raised fiscal consciousness in the USA and the UK has been the much publicised economic policies of President Reagan and Margaret Thatcher. Both are pledged to a reduction in the size of government, cuts in taxation and public spending. Tax limitation referenda held in the USA, and especially Proposition 13 in California in 1978, caught many people's imagination. Referenda flourished in many US states, but over time the popular pressure for radical change has dwindled; tax cuts at the expense of reductions in services are rarely favoured by a majority. In a review of contemporary survey results in the USA Keene (1983) has shown that the largest percentage of voters have returned to sustaining the *status quo* by keeping the level of taxaton and expenditure at much the same levels as at present. In some senses, of course, California was a special case because of the massive size of surplus reserves (Levy, 1979; Goodenough, 1982). Large-scale public expenditure reductions have also been avoided in California by raising various changes such as those for licences, permits, and by raising fines and other penalties. Goodenough concludes, 'if government is to hold down taxes and decrease spending, then the taxpayers must ultimately lower their expectations and demands in relation to public services' (Goodenough, 1982, p. 456). There is little evidence to suggest that expectations have been lowered.

Tax referenda have not met with political approval in the UK, although there was some support for them among senior ministers within the Conservative government, and non-legislative 'referenda' have been held (Lewis, 1982b). The Conservative central government has reduced provisions (via the rate support grant) for local authorities who 'overspend'. The local authority is faced with the prospect of reducing expenditure to save money or to raise local rates. Labour-controlled local authorities have generally resisted expenditure cuts, and the lack of enthusiasm for cuts has been widespread. As in the USA recent UK evidence suggests that the majority favour keeping the levels of taxation and expenditure much the same as those in operation at the moment, whilst being prepared to increase their tax contributions to see expansion of services, particularly for health (Beedle and Taylor-Gooby, 1983). In Britain the salience of fiscal issues is further revealed in the preferences of floating voters (see Bristow, 1982; Edgell and Duke, 1982). Bristow, in a study of electors in the Oxley ward of Wolverhampton, recorded that four out of five people who changed their vote between 1979 and 1980 said it was something to do with the rates issue. Cuts are generally not favoured. The economic mind seems set against them—at least for the time being.

TAX EVASION

If a person reduces his tax bill by illegal means that person is a tax evader. (The line between tax evasion and tax avoidance, which is legal, is a blurred one and we shall not pursue it here.) Our task is to speculate about the mind of evaders and those who may seek to understand or curb their activities.

The economic approach to tax evasion activity has concentrated on utility maximisation under uncertainty (Allingham and Sandmo, 1972). Briefly, people are assumed to want to reduce their tax bill to a minimum and are only deterred from doing so because of detection by the authorities and the imposition of fines.

The psychological approach makes no such assumptions and concentrates instead on perceptions and attitudes. We would not want to take issue with the notion that evasion is a function of opportunity, probability of detection, and size of fine; instead, the influence of these factors is mediated through perceptions and attitudes and these deserve attention. One's reluctance to evade is a function of what one perceives the likelihood of detection by the authorities to be, not what they actually are. Compliance is affected by people's attitudes to taxation and tax authorities as all tax systems require, to a greater or lesser degree, the cooperation of taxpayers.

Tax evasion is considered to be of major economic importance. It has even been argued that the loss of revenue in North America and Europe may be as much as the equivalent of 10 per cent of GNP (*Newsweek*, 1983). The extent of tax evasion, partly because of its covert nature, has proved extremely difficult to measure (Guttman, 1977; O'Higgins, 1981a, b; Lewis, 1982a). In the light of this difficulty survey results hold a certain attraction. Direct questions about tax evasion are likely to produce evasive answers. Researchers have attempted to get round this problem in varying ways: by assessing people's disapproval of tax crimes; by asking individuals what they consider the extent of tax evasion to be or how many tax evaders they know of; or by enquiring about an individual's own evasion behaviour, describing it in the question posed more as a momentary oversight than as a premeditated and regular act.

A most imaginative approach was used in a survey of 4888 individuals conducted for the Internal Revenue Service (IRS) in the USA, and reported by Aitken and Bonneville (1980)—namely, the 'locked-box' and 'randomised response' techniques. As the names imply, in the 'locked-box' example respondents completed self-administered questionnaires and placed them in a box similar to a ballot box so as to reassure respondents about confidentiality. The results revealed that 13 per cent said they sometimes under-reported income on their tax returns; 4 per cent said they listed more tax deductions than they were entitled to; and 3 per cent made illegal claims for dependants. These results closely resemble some earlier ones derived from 800 Oregon adults and reported by Mason and Calvin (1978) where 14 per cent admitted under-reporting, and 5 per cent overstatement of deductions.

In the randomised response technique respondents answered either questions about tax cheating ('A') or other questions ('B') at random. Which questions were answered was not known directly by the researchers but replies to the cheating questions could be assessed by taking a sub-set of people who were required to answer 'A' questions only and comparing the results. This technique proved particularly successful. Those admitting under-reporting rose to an estimated 21 per cent of the sample; 11 per cent said they misled the tax authorities about deductions; and 16 per cent mentioned inappropriate dependants (a suspiciously high figure this).

People can feel confident about under-reporting income by the way they run their affairs; so-called 'cash in the hand' transfers are commonplace and extremely difficult to trace by tax authorities. In a study of 426 Swedish male taxpayers reported by Warneryd and Walerud (1982), fully 42 per cent of sample admitted paying 'black money' to traders which they suspected was untaxed. These results suggest that estimates of the size of the tax evasion problem may not be as inflated as one might at first suppose.

Perceptions and Ethics

Widespread ignorance of tax enforcement procedures was found in the Internal Revenue Survey of 4888 individuals throughout the United States (Aitken and Bonneville, 1980). Generally people tended to overestimate the number of audits and investigations that took place. This implies that if people had a better idea of their true chances of detection, evasion might be even more rife than at present. Indeed Warneryd and Walerud's (1982) study of 426 Swedish male taxpayers revealed that people who admitted to tax evasion thought their chances of evading tax successfully were better than did other people; i.e. they had more realistic perceptions of their chances of getting caught and were more likely to know other people involved in tax evasion.

It seems probable that the adjudged 'rightness' or 'wrongness' of tax evasion has an influence on tax evasion behaviour. In a small study conducted in Scotland (Dean, Keenan and Kenney, 1980) 26 per cent of all respondents felt they would be able to evade a small amount of tax without being caught. A further question revealed that 66 per cent of the respondents agreed that almost all taxpayers would evade small amounts if they thought they would not get caught. The fact that this figure is not 100 per cent suggests that people believe there is something else in the equation, which could be tax ethics, tax morals, or people's basic honesty.

One way of progressing is to examine people's hypotheses about why others cheat and whether the reasons given can be justified (cf. Vogel, 1974; Aitken and Bonneville, 1980; Keenan and Dean, 1980; Kemp, 1980). In

Vogel's (1974) survey of 1769 Swedish taxpayers less than 30 per cent felt the perceived unfairness of the tax system was sufficient justification for tax evasion. Similarly, Keenan and Dean (1980) found that justifications concerning poor fiscal exchange rates, the burden of taxes, equity considerations and the misuse of taxpayers' money were deemed adequate only by a minority. The only action that merited some approval in this Scottish study was evading tax on part-time earnings, given that full-time income was fully declared to the authorities, and there was a feeling that the rich and famous had many more ways of cheating the government compared with others. The IRS study showed that over 42 per cent of respondents identified high-income families as receiving more lenient treatment from tax enforcement agencies. There is also a feeling, given that people on lower incomes tend to receive almost all their earnings in salaries and wages taxed at source, that tax evasion is the poor man's tax avoidance.

Kemp (1980), reporting a survey of over 1000 Australian taxpayers, found no obvious relationship between approval of tax evasion (in terms of understatement of income) and the feeling that the tax system is unfair. We cannot rule this relationship out however as the more direct questioning used in Warneryd and Walerud's (1980) study showed that people who admitted evading tax were more likely to see the tax system as unjust and something to exploit. Kemp did report correlations between the view that tax evasion was justified with the income of respondents, lack of confidence in government and politicians, and belief that 'unjust' laws need not necessarily be obeyed. More specifically, on the ethical side, tax evasion approval was negatively correlated with belief in God and frequency of church attendance. (Rather curiously tax evasion approval is positively correlated to belief in life after death! Although this could be a 'typo'.) On a more down-to-earth level, Aitken and Bonneville (1980) found 55 per cent of their respondents said the reason that people do not cheat is because of their basic honesty.

Another way of investigating tax ethics is to ascertain how serious a crime tax evasion is perceived to be. In our earlier review of the IRS survey results it was ascertained that many more people mentioned under-reporting of income than claiming for non-existent dependent relatives. Using Sandford's (1979) terms the former is evasion by omission and the latter evasion by commission. Commission is viewed as more unacceptable by respondents—it is as though people make an ethical distinction between lying and failing to tell the whole truth. (An alternative explanation is that evasion by commission is more likely to get you into trouble—you either have a dependent relative or you do not, while the truth or falsity of your exact income can be fudged.)

Further evidence that there are 'degrees of wrongness' comes from Warneryd and Walerud's (1982) Swedish study where it was found that claiming a false deduction was viewed as more serious than receiving 'black money'. Paying 'black' money to others was seen as the least unacceptable behaviour and indeed is probably the most common.

Aitken and Bonneville (1980), Vogel (1974) and Lewis (1979a) have all illustrated, in various ways, that people view evasion of small amounts quite differently from the evasion of large amounts. Evasion of large amounts is considered to be ethically wrong and a serious offence warranting heavy fines, even imprisonment—e.g. 58 per cent considered evasion of $500 a very serious offence (Aitken and Bonneville, 1980). On the other hand, while evasion of small amounts is still considered wrong by the majority, it is viewed as comparatively trivial, in fact, about as serious as stealing a bicycle (Song and Yarbrough, 1978) and less serious than pilfering at work, not paying a friend or fiddling social security (Keenan and Dean, 1980). Sociologists and criminologists have consistently shown that cheating individuals is seen as far worse than cheating large organisations, firms and, in this case, government organisations (Sutherland, 1949; Ditton, 1977; Henry, 1978). It is therefore particularly interesting to see that distinctions are made by the economic mind between the unacceptability of cheating different government departments: cheating the Revenue is seen as less serious than cheating on welfare payments (Aitken and Bonneville, 1980). In Britain, at least until very recently, so-called 'welfare scroungers' were pursued with a good deal more zeal than tax-evaders by the relevant authorities, a campaign arguably fuelled by the popular press and popular opinion (see Golding and Middleton, 1982).

Models

The models of tax evasion behaviour proposed in greater or lesser detail by Strumpel (1969), Lewis (1982b), Groenland and van Veldhoven (1983) and Warneryd and Walerud (1982) bear many similarities and can be described as 'psychological', in the sense that they place emphasis on the mediating effects of tax attitudes and perceptions—what might be termed 'tax mentality'.

Major influences on tax evasion are the fiscal policies of the country concerned, the tax structure and the constitutional structure. Is the tax structure progressive? What is the proportion of 'direct' to 'indirect' taxes? Is tax administration centralised? What is the system of 'exchange' between tax paid and services received? What say do individuals have in fiscal policy-making, or in how they manage their personal tax affairs? While the psychological models include these factors they are not given as much credence as would be given them by economists (particularly political economists) and sociologists. However an advantage of the psychological models may be in including perceptions of these political and economic components, and attitudes towards governments and fiscal policy—an empirical approach also of some value to political scientists.

Clearly tax enforcement structure and policies influence the incidence and extent of evasion. And this is in part a technical matter.

Again the psychological models stress the mediating effects of the perceptions of enforcement and the perceived equity of its application. Although psychological models stress the mediating influence of preceptions and attitudes the link between attitudes and behaviour is a troublesome one (for a discussion in the context of tax, see Lewis, 1982a, Ch. 9) for example, studies of general tax attitudes (e.g. Lewis, 1979a) have tended to suggest they are multidimensional with no obvious general factor. This may be interesting in itself and we pursue this further in a later section on attitudes, values and ideology, in the meantime positivist economists might reasonably be asking, 'All this about attitudes and perceptions seems reasonable to me, but does it improve our predictions?' The authors would like to argue that the study of these attitudes certainly improves our comprehension but the case still has to be made for its improving predictions of evasion trends and the influence of mediation as opposed to the direct effect of economic variables. For those who are interested, one way forward may be to adopt a more restricted interpretation of attitudes portrayed in the work of Ajzen and Fishbein (1980). In this case demographic variables and attitudes towards fiscal authorities are treated as external variables. Specific behaviourial intentions, attitudes towards tax evasion, subjective norms and the relative importance given to attitudinal and normative components are the mainstays of the approach (Lewis, 1982a, p. 172).

Warneryd and Walerud (1982) and Vogel (1974) have both produced results which could be interpreted as supportive of the Ajzen and Fishbein model of attitude/behaviour links. Warneryd and Walerud found that their general tax attitude measure was not as good a predictor of admitted tax evasion behaviour as a more specific measure of attitudes to tax evasion. Furthermore both Warneryd and Walerud (1982) and Vogel (1974) have underlined the importance of perceived opportunities (included in Ajzen and Fishbein's notion of outcome evaluation) and normative influences (subjective norm—Ajzen and Fishbein). Tax evaders think the chances of getting caught (probably rightly) are less than other people do, and are more likely to have friends and acquaintances who are tax evaders themselves.

The importance of normative influences has methodological consequences for future investigations. As de Braak (1983) has intimated, psychological models are sociologically naive. There is a kind of cultural atmosphere and acceptance of tax evasion which is difficult if not impossible to understand purely by aggregating individuals' opinions gathered in surveys. De Braak (1983) has also criticised psychological models because of their apparent lack of theory; it is argued that self-interest assumptions and interpretations based on the income of respondents are still the best predictors. The present authors would want to point out that the important influence of normative factors cannot easily be derived from self-interest assumptions, and that furthermore age, fiscal education and social-class variables are good predictors in their own right. For example, Kemp (1980), Keenan and Dean (1980), Warneryd and Walerud (1982) and Vogel (1974) have all reported major age differences where younger people seem more approving of tax evasion practices, a result that can be considered to be of long-term importance and one that stresses divergences in behaviour caused by cultural, historical and attitudinal changes rather than simply by changes in constraints on behaviour.

Experimental simulation studies are more closely allied to economic theory, in that they concentrate on tax rates, probability of detection, size of fines, and where these factors are made 'objective' by informing subjects of the 'facts' before the simulation begins (cf. Friedland, Maital, and Rutenberg, 1978; Spicer and Becker, 1980; Friedland, 1982). Simulations have obvious weaknesses not least being the relationship between a simulation and reality, and more specifically the small sample sizes employed, and the fact they are more often than not students rather than long-standing taxpayers. In general the simulation experimenters are aware of these limitations and intriguing and extremely valuable experiments could be devised with larger samples, where both 'objective' and 'subjective' (including attitudes and perceptions) variables are included and where respondents are asked to behave as they themselves might do in the circumstances constructed rather than being asked to maximise their utilities.

Clearly model-building in this area is in its early stages. Future models should include attitudinal and perceptual components but these need to place greater stress on objective and cultural factors and the link between mediating variables and behavioural constraints.

Reducing Tax Evasion

When we begin our methodological critique of this review one of the debating points will be whether research in this area should be merely descriptive or whether it should have prescriptive elements as well. With our knowledge of the economic mind should we be recommending to policy-makers ways of reducing tax evasion? Leaving this question aside for a moment, we can see that different approaches taken by economists and psychologists may lead to varying recommendations. Because economic models pay next to no attention to mediating factors recommendations might include reducing tax rates and increasing the probability of detection. Alternatively psychological approaches would stress the need to improve tax attitudes, and point out that an increase in the probability of detection might actually make tax attitudes more negative and increase tax resistance (Strumpel, 1969; Schmölders, 1970).

Guidance can be gained from deterrence theory outlined in sociological and criminological literature (Silberman, 1976), and from the more psychological literature concerned with compliance with rules (Thibaut, Friedland and Walker, 1974). Generally, deterrence theory makes a distinction between legal sanctions (punishments imposed by the state), social stigma (normative effects) and guilt feelings (self-imposed). Clearly all these factors have an influence. In a field-study by Schwartz and Orleans (1967) in conjunction with the IRS, taxpayers were approached a month before filing their tax returns. One group was visited by an agent who stressed, by implication from the questions asked, legal sanctions. A second group received appeals to conscience and responsibility in the same manner. There was a third 'control group'. When tax records were examined there was a mean increase in income declaration of $181 in the 'sanctions' group. Better still, the 'conscience' group showed a mean increase of $804. (The control group showed a decrease of $87).

The importance of guilt feelings and compliance has also been underlined in a survey of 400 people from a metropolitan area of the USA by Grasmick and Scott (1982). Their results showed that guilt feelings were a stronger deterrent for tax evasion than threat of punishment. In conclusion however the authors remark:

> Perhaps to a considerable degree, the government-taxpayer relationship is inevitably an adversary relationship. While governments often lack the ability to increase the public's sense of moral duty to pay, they usually have the capacity to increase the threat of legal sanctions for evasion, and this might be the only feasible mechanism for increasing taxpayers' compliance with the law. (Grasmick and Scott, 1982, p. 228)

In some ways this is a sobering and disappointing conclusion but a realistic one in the short term. Grasmick and Scott suggest that moral appeals by governments may themselves backfire, increasing cynicism among taxpayers and criticisms of government expenditure. More positively however such a move may increase public participation and support for the state as they become more aware of its purposes and functions. In a democracy we prefer to think that the state is supported by the electorate and, in this case, fiscal policy by taxpayers. If this is an illusion it may explain why fiscal authorities prefer to maintain a relatively low profile.

It must be pointed out that the Schwartz and Orleans (1967) 'conscience' manipulation stressed the 'fiscal connection', purposes of taxation and the importance of the relationship between citizen and government, as well as other aspects of moral obligation. It is this raising of fiscal consciousness and knowledge which may have been particularly influential and leads us on naturally to the next section dealing with the simplicity and comprehensibility of government documents and leaflets distributed to the general public.

SIMPLICITY AND COMPREHENSIBILITY

Public opinion about the public sector is crucially affected by communications and interactions between citizens and government. Among the most important communications are those which arise when, for example, individuals need to visit a Department of Health and Social Security office in Britain in order to claim social security or other benefits, or when taxpayers communicate with or are in receipt of documents from the Inland Revenue. A folk wisdom may build up on the basis of the feelings or experiences of a minority in such a way that individuals gather more information as to their rights and responsibilities from friends and neighbours than from official sources. While these informal networks are frequently extremely influential in many communication systems the information imparted is often inaccurate and can help to sustain negative attitudes towards officialdom.

Olive Stevenson in her book *Claimant or Client* has shown, through case studies, how the experiences, behaviour and language of the encounter between official and consumer can contribute to shared beliefs and perceptions, even stereotypes (Stevenson, 1973). The social security 'claimant' treated as 'client' is an altogether healthier and more equal encounter. The consumer movement, the emphasis on consumer rights and fair play, have at long last penetrated the public sector.

In addition to direct face-to-face interaction, there are letters, telephone calls, forms and leaflets to be considered. Are the public happy with the information they receive, and do they understand it?

In response to these questions both the IRS in the USA and the Inland Revenue in Britain have conducted surveys (Aitken and Bonneville, 1980; Inland Revenue, 1980). And in recent times studies of relations between taxpayers and tax administrations is a continuing aspect of research of the OECD (see Delormé, 1980).

Both the IRS and IR studies showed widespread (if mild) satisfaction with the services and explanations provided by tax authorities in the two countries. In both countries however only a minority contacted the official tax authorities for advice during the tax year (or in the self-assessment 'tax-season' in the USA). In the USA approximately 50 per cent of taxpayers rely on others to complete their tax forms for them; 44 per cent of whom use a lawyer or an accountant, 32 per cent a commercial tax firm, and 16 per cent a friend or relative. Under the PAYE system in the UK a much higher proportion fill in tax forms themselves, however many prefer to gain advice from such 'unofficial' sources as Citizens Advice Bureaux (CABs) or through the letters columns of newspapers (see Sandford, 1973; Allison, James and Lewis, 1985). It has been found that those most in need of help are among the least likely to contact the official tax authorities. Generally a higher proportion of professional, well-educated people contact the official sources. People who know least about tax tend to have less positive feelings about the Revenue and are more likely to use 'unofficial' sources of information.

There has been prolific growth of academic literature concerned with document and form design, much of which is relevant to the improvement in the design of tax forms (Felker *et al.*, 1981; Allison, James and Lewis, 1985). This has coincided with the introduction of special form and leaflet design units within, for example, the IRS in the USA, and the IR and DHSS in Britain and the RSV in Sweden. Aitken and Bonneville (1980) in their IRS report show that the most frequently occurring reason for not completing a tax return was that the forms were considered too complicated.

There are at least two sets of 'economic minds' that we need to consider: the minds of 'consumers' and the minds of bureaucrats and administrators—it must be remembered that communication is a two-way process. The simplification of forms and leaflets can have benefits on both sides. By reducing the time, effort and anxiety of form-fillers, this not only reduces taxpayers' so-called tax compliance costs (Sandford, 1973), it could improve their attitudes towards Revenue authorities as well. Simplified forms would help administrators too. The number of errors made by form-fillers would fall, reducing the amount of tedious checking, correcting and correspondence. In addition many different kinds of forms circulate within bureaucracies—internal memoranda, points of procedure, and so forth. While old hands get used to those documents, simplified material would reduce staff training time and the tendency for bureaucrats to develop specialised or archaic language when this is not really required.

So surely simplification is a good idea—or is it? As senior administrators and policy analysts will point out to you, how can you have simple forms for a complex system? Principles of 'simplicity' and 'equity' can be at odds. At the most extreme a flat-rate tax, with few or no tax allowances, would be extremely cheap and simple to administer, but would it be fair?

There are employment consequences as well. A simplified system incorporating simplified procedures and forms could lead to job losses: one can hardly criticise bureaucrats for protecting their own. Large organisations and bureaucracies are conservative by nature, in that they are resistant to change however desirable that change may appear to an outsider. And there can be very good reasons for this. Present practices in some senses work, but what guarantee is there that new procedures are not prone to greater errors in their actual practical operation than present systems?

The main relevant academic literature has concerned 'readability' measures, syntactics, semantics, typography and layout (Felker *et al.*, 1981; Allison *et al.* 1985). 'Readability' measures attempt to assess the difficulty of prose using 'objective' techniques. As an example, the Flesch reading ease formula (Flesch, 1948) requires the assessment of the average number of syllables per 100 words and the average number of words per sentence. (For a review of the wide range of available reading formulae, see Klare, 1976, 1982.) The readability measures provide a 'reading age', grade or degree of difficulty for the sample of prose chosen. The reading grade refers to the years of study in the educational system of the USA; the reading age to the age at which a child could reasonably be expected to read the material. These reading measures are widely used in government departments, insurance companies and other large organisations. An Assistant Secretary of the British Board of the Inland Revenue has reported that reading measures are now applied as a matter of course to all new Inland Revenue leaflets.

Preliminary published research has shown that tax forms and leaflets used in Britain, as well as in USA, Australia, Sweden, Canada, South Africa and New Zealand generally record a reading age of 15 or 16 years (James and Lewis, 1977; James, Lewis and Wallschutzky, 1981; Lewis and James, 1981). Some literature that has been used by the Department of Health and Social Security in the past has recorded even higher scores, (see Lewis, 1979b). As a benchmark it has been estimated that 2 million adults in Britain have a reading age of less than 9 years.

It must be pointed out that reading measures are not prescriptive, they do not in themselves provide guidelines as to how prose is to be rewritten. Furthermore, reading measures ignore difficulties caused by such varying factors as the size of print, the presentation of headings, matters of style, and semantics. Reading measures do not take motivation into account. Quite difficult prose can be deciphered if the reader has the will to do so. Improvements to the design and presentation of tax forms have a good chance of reducing errors, administration and compliance costs but, if the form-fillers' attitude remains negative the gains will not be as substantial as they may otherwise have been. Certainly the self-assessment procedures in the USA increase compliance costs, but the form-fillers have the incentive that many of them will receive tax rebates soon after their completion. On a more positive note, reading measures are relatively easy to take and are a useful preliminary stage in the design process.

Manuals of 'do's' and 'don'ts' for document designers are now available which deal with many of the problems reading measures ignore. The advice in these 'cook books' is based largely on experimental studies conducted by psychologists, educationalists and typographers. We will not deal with this literature here and interested readers are referred to *Guidelines for Document Designers* by Felker *et al.* (1981). To offer a flavour, the guidelines cover such diverse aspects as the temporal sequence of forms and leaflets, the use of flow charts and algorithms, the tenses of verbs, personal vs. impersonal references, conditional sentences, the size and use of answer boxes, the length of lines, width of margins, the number of headings, and the size of print.

These guidelines are extremely useful but should not be slavishly adhered to. Neither reading measures nor manuals can circumvent the need for feedback information gained from testing forms and revisions with the audience for whom they are intended.

Redesigning forms and improving written communications not only has a direct practical appeal, it can provide material of relevance to the advancement of cognitive psychology and information theory. In particular future research may do well, in pursuit of knowledge of the economic mind, exploring the familiar linguistic expressions of the target population (form-fillers) and the way perceptions and expectations of what is required of them are structured.

ATTITUDES, VALUES AND IDEOLOGY

Earlier we introduced the notion of 'tax mentality'. In this section we examine the concept more closely by looking at the possible structure and domain of attitudes to the public sector.

Lewis (1979a) asked 200 Bath electors to complete 16 Likert items about taxation and related matters and the results were later factor analysed. Five factors emerged which largely reflected the subject-matter of the items, namely an 'avoidance' factor, which concerned the ethics and justification for tax avoidance; a 'personal tax' factor, relating to the incidence and fairness of individual contributions; an 'evasion' factor relating to the punishment of evaders; a factor dealing with the fairness and purposes of progressive taxation; and a grouping dealing with the level of taxation and the frequency of evasion, the 'justification for evasion' factor. The main result shows that, for these items at least, there is no general factor of tax mentality, rather it may best be measured on a series of sub-scales. The second main result was that the most salient items by far related to personal tax payments.

Furnham (1983f, 1984b) has used the same Likert measure for two separate populations, replicating the factors as described. Furnham (1983f) extended the study from a preliminary one looking at tax attitudes and their relationship to background variables to a study relating tax attitudes to the Protestant work ethic (Mirels and Garrett, 1971) and a measure of values (Rokeach, 1973). And in a second study Furnham (1984b) investigated the relationship between tax attitudes and the Protestant work ethic as before but also to a measure of conservatism (Wilson and Patterson, 1968) and alienation (Srole, 1956). Overall in the two studies the finding that Furnham stresses the most is the way that measures of the Protestant work ethic, of alienation, of values and of conservatism differentiate between tax attitudes in a predictable and related fashion. In the 1983 study people who scored highly on the Protestant work ethic measure tended to have poorer tax attitudes as recorded on the items relating to personal contributions, again pointing to the salience of these items. Looking at values next, those holding anti-tax views are more likely to endorse the 'instrumental' values of ambition, cleanliness and independence and again using Rokeach's terms, the 'terminal' value of freedom. Those holding pro-tax views were more likely to endorse love and helpfulness, a comfortable life and equality as important values. These same items were recorded by Rokeach (1973) as differentiating between favourable and unfavourable attitudes towards the poor; and values associated with anti-tax attitudes have also been shown to be related to conservatism (Feather, 1975) and authoritarianism (Rim, 1970).

Preferences for public expenditure appear to form predictable structures as we have discussed in earlier sections. But a central question becomes whether people have a general and integrated conception of the 'public sector' as a whole. And the picture is a somewhat confused one. In replies to open-ended questions about what would constitute an ideal taxation and welfare system, Beedle and Taylor-Gooby (1983) report that those favouring an indirect taxation system are more likely to think welfare is expensive, unfair and working-class-oriented. Those favouring income tax explained their choices in terms of fairness. In the public mind National Insurance payments are most closely linked with welfare. Put another way, the fiscal connection is more in evidence when incorporated with notions of insurance.

Taylor-Gooby (1982, 1983) has attempted to describe the structure of attitudes to welfare, arguing that while they may not always be related to tax preferences they are informative in their own right. Earlier, when discussing the values of individuals with pro- and anti-tax attitudes, we recorded that notions of 'equality' were associated with the former, and freedom and self-help with the latter. Taylor-Gooby, taking a more sociological perspective, examines how the values are reflected by the welfare state and market capitalism generally: where the welfare state stresses cooperation, altruism and equality, market capitalism stresses self-help, freedom, individualism and competition (for details, see George and Wilding, 1976; Coughlin, 1980). It is no surprise then that people's views are a mixture of ambivalence and altruism, of support for universal services and the ideology of the market. In a complex and sometimes bewildering presentation Taylor-Gooby concludes that attitudes towards welfare are affected by values, political allegiances and background variables such as age and family composition. However people's evaluations are frequently dictated by their own interest and experience with welfare services and the implications of services from their own perspective. (Taylor-Gooby is careful however to make a distinction between 'felt interest' as we have described it and 'self-interest'.) Taylor-Gooby makes apt use of quotes from Mann (1970) in his general conclusions. For Mann value consensus (among the working class) may be a myth. Support for values is more likely to relate to concrete everyday life or to vague populist concepts than to abstract political philosophy. There are normative pressures too. For Mann social cohesion depends primarily on the lack of consistent commitment to general values of any sort, or the 'pragmatic acceptance' by subordinate classes of their limited roles in society (Mann, 1970, p. 423).

A METHODOLOGICAL COMMENTARY AND CONCLUSION

Attempting to assess the structure and domain of attitudes to the public sector is a daunting task; results are highly dependent on the method and intensity of the inquiry and the academic expertise and interests of the researcher. Political scientists and sociologists may variously wish to link these attitudes to voting intention, the influence of the media and pressure groups, and more generally the perceived legitimacy of governments and the structure of society. A comprehensive appraisal of these links is beyond our present brief. We must mention however problems associated with explanations in the social sciences. Is public opinion on the public sector determined by voting preferences, income, age, occupation, contact with services, or economic and fiscal knowledge? The answer to all these questions must be yes. Is opinion about the public sector associated with other attitudes and values? The answer again must be yes. Is opinion dependent on the political structure? The answer still must be yes. Our task has been to say something about the 'economic mind'—what people think and believe about economic issues. If we were to attempt to explain where economic consciousness comes from, were are in, as the Americans say, another ball game. It is part of that all-embracing term 'socialisation', and we have attempted to look at aspects of economic socialisation in an earlier chapter. Productive future research should be aimed at examining the development of views and attitudes towards the state and its provisions. Again referring to earlier chapters in the present volume, this time on poverty and wealth, it is also important to trace the development and presentation of lay explanations in everyday life. Support for government fiscal programmes depends (among many other things) on whether you think governments can actually do something about poverty or the distribution of wealth generally. If you believe poverty is the fault of the individual then you would be disinclined to praise the welfare state.

The findings we have reported throughout this chapter are not independent of the methods used to collect them. Primarily we have reported replies to closed and open-ended questions on questionnaires and information from interviews. All the findings must be interpreted carefully in terms of the questions asked, as we underlined in our discussion of fiscal preferences.

A more qualitative interview approach may prove informative when investigating lay explanations and attitude structure. But the present authors would not want, in general, to put forward the view that qualitative methods are in any way superior, only that quantitative evidence is in relative abundance in this field and qualitative evidence is not.

Public opinion, as assessed by public opinion polls, social surveys and social investigation, is a special type of public opinion (Key, 1960; Hodder-Williams, 1970; Nisbett, 1975). Results from public opinion polls and surveys are often treated by politicians and others as if they are true 'public opinion'. Public opinion has even been described as those aspects of opinion which politicians feel it expedient to heed. The measures we have reported have a series of important faults which need to be rectified in future research. First of all, they often fail to take into account the knowledge of respondents and the importance and salience of opinions sought. Second, they tend to imply that the aggregation of individual preferences in itself constitutes public opinion. Such an atomistic view should be anathema to social psychologist and sociologist alike. In particular it ignores the influence of normative pressures, of conformity, social cohesion, and the power and influence of social identity and pressure groups. Gestaltists rightly view the whole as more than the sum of parts. While difficult to grasp and explore, attitudes need to be examined in a social context, and social attitudes may even have a life of their own quite different from individual preferences. Public opinion is not only partly constructed by individual preferences, public opinion actually influences those preferences.

We also need to make a distincton between public and popular opinion. To quote Nisbett (1975):

> Public opinion is given its character by genuine consensus, by unifying tradition by what Edmund Burke called 'constitutional spirit'. Popular opinion is by contrast shallow of root, a creature of the mere aggregate or crowd, rooted in fashion or fad and subject to caprice and whim, easily if tenuously formed around a single issue or personage, and lacking the kind of cement that time, tradition and convention alone can provide. (p. 168)

In our discussion we have also been vague about the terms 'perceptions', 'beliefs' 'attitudes' 'opinions' 'values' and 'ideology'. Any discussion of attitude structure must concentrate on the links between these concepts Again this should be the focus of future research. Generally the differences and links can be described as in Figure 11.1.

In our mapping of the 'economic mind' we have mostly concentrated on comprehension, an exception being our brief discussion of models for tax evasion. By 'ideology' we refer to a kind of fundamental belief system used by social groups to interpret their social world. 'Attitudes' have traditionally

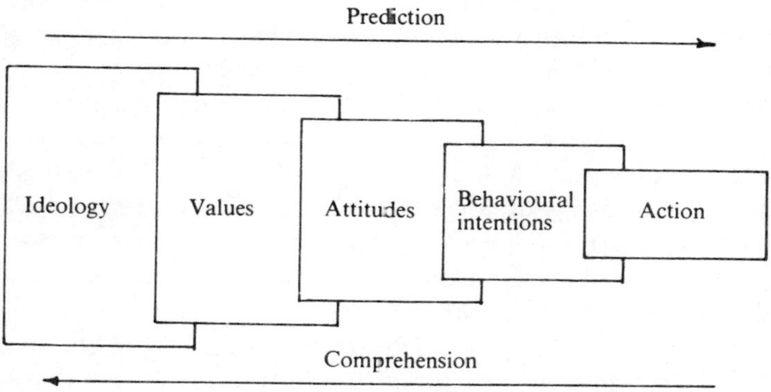

Figure 11.1: The link between attitudes and other concepts and their role in comprehension and prediction

Source: Lewis: *The Psychology of Taxation*, 1982, Blackwell, Oxford. Reprinted with permission.

been thought of as comprising three elements: cognitive, affective and conative (Rosenberg and Hovland, 1960; Newcomb, Turner and Converse, 1964; Triandis, 1971). Briefly cognitive aspects constitute beliefs and perceptions; the affective component comprises emotional responses; and the conative describes overt action and verbal statements concerning behaviour (and in this sense is similar to 'behavioural intentions'). Attitude theorists and those who attempt to measure attitudes have differed; rarely do attitude measures reflect all three components. Often attitude measures analyse the links between a set of 'opinions', attitudes being assumed to be more stable over time. A small amount of research has begun attempting to link perceptions about public expenditure with preferences (see Lewis, 1983). Clearly much of the evidence we have reported begs for more integrated research of this kind.

Finally, as we have stated 'ideology' is clearly a cognitive phenomenon. So how does it differ from the cognitive component of attitudes? There are two main distinctions. The first is that the cognitive component of attitudes is that which is directed towards a specific attitude object or set of objects. Ideological belief systems are much broader than this, they provide the structure and foundation for the interpretation of the social world as a whole. The second distinction, as we have already mentioned, is that ideologies are regarded as reflecting the belief systems of social groups rather than the beliefs of individuals.

In this chapter we have dealt lightly with the differing fiscal and political structures and cultural variations in our international comparisons. And these of course should not be underestimated. Most of the results come from western capitalist countries, but it can be seen, in this context at least, there is a great deal of consistency in the findings reported.

The political context requires that the reader considers the proper role of public opinion in policy-making. If it is agreed that fiscal policy should reflect what people want, how should these preferences be measured? Are legislative referenda a good idea? A note of caution comes from Taylor-Gooby (1982)—given that people favour universal service *and* support the ideology of the market, opinion may be vulnerable to swift changes depending on the salience of either aspect.

In conclusion, interesting research has begun relating to the so-called 'tragedy of the commons', a central issue in this debate (see Poppe and Utens, 1984, after Hardin, 1968). The equitable provision of public goods is a kind of social dilemma and can be examined experimentally in the laboratory. In a village there is a pasture for common use by the herdsmen of the village. The pasture available is sufficient for the total number of animals the herdsmen have on the pasture. An individual herdsman may want to increase his stock and profits but the pasture will consequently be depleted and bring in less financial return. Usually if a single herdsman adds one animal this will outweigh his loss for his other animals. If every individual maximises his immediate personal gain in little time at all the pasture will be no more.

This little fable suggests that goods have to be administered by benevolent authorities for the general good. But who should these people be and who should appoint them? The 'tragedy of the commons' may be part of the abstract political philosophy missing in public opinion about the public sector. We do not know. The question becomes *should* they become part of public consciousness? We are moving from the realm of the descriptive to the prescriptive, and we have set our task as describing the economic mind alone. For Marxists, social scientists should not merely describe the world, but change it. But that is another story.

Part VI: Conclusion

12 Economic Psychology and Psychological Economics

It is too easy to conclude glibly that new research needs to be done. We need to question why there is such a requirement and in which areas. We have made a distinction between 'economic psychology' and 'psychological economics'—the former referring to the extension of the investigation of social behaviour into the economic realm, and the latter the employment of psychology to expand and aid the discipline of economics. We offer some speculations for the future of each of these interdisciplinary themes in turn.

ECONOMIC PSYCHOLOGY

Social psychology is concerned with people's values and attitudes and how people interact with one another. An extension of this interest naturally leads to the exploration of economic values and attitudes and how people interact in these contexts. In Chapter 3 of the present volume we examined aspects of economic socialisation. This is of particular value to developmental psychologists. It is also of importance as it illuminates the process whereby notions of exchange, the value of ownership, profit and saving are formed and passed from one generation to another. These lessons can have such affective strength that subsequent economic and later political judgements made by adults can be extremely difficult to change. Longitudinal studies could provide particularly fruitful insights. The process of economic socialisation may be changing in such a way that so-called post-materialistic values are more common and where notions of profit are emphasised less and ecological and redistributive notions more. But at this stage this is no more than speculation. More effort is required in pursuing the differing socialisation of varying social classes and socioeconomic groups, as this underlies the divergent ways separate groups view the world. And more generally it provides information concerning social structure and the likelihood of social change. Are, for example, the expectations of working-class children purposely restricted so that their aspirations of social mobility are narrowed? On a grander scale this leads to the need for research which examines the radically different processes of economic socialisation in socialist countries as compared with capitalist countries.

A concern with socialisation also points to the development of notions of fairness, equity and just deserts and the perceived causes of wealth and poverty. The chapters on poverty, wealth and unemployment have shown how values, and in particular political values, shape both people's perceptions of the importance of these issues and how anything could or should be done about them. Future research would do well to place attribution theory within its proper political and economic framework. The attribution of causality is not only a function of stimulus conditions but how the stimuli themselves are perceived. A more qualitative approach is required whereby the contradictions and ambivalence of a range of beliefs and attributions are integrated as this illustrates the multi-casual nature of many attributions and the contradictions of the society of which individuals form a part. Furthermore work is required in examining the beliefs and attitudes of opinion leaders, e.g. politicians, newspaper editors, employers' organisations and trade unions—and influential economists—given their disproportionate influence in the formation and solidification of these beliefs among the general public. It is a preference for examining the process from the 'top-down' rather than just from the 'bottom-up'.

The literature on consumer choice is voluminous and our review has shown how important social aspects of choice can be. Again we find ourselves questioning the quality of the research findings in the extent to which they really tell us how choosers choose. There are, of course, many methodological problems both here as elsewhere, but there are next to no case studies which examine how individuals actually make a choice. Difficulties arise as interviews conducted after a choice is made often reveal more about people's rationalisations of their choices than about what led to the choice in the first instance. In a rather bizarre example whereby people are asked to explain their choices between two pairs of tights which differ only in that one pair smells of oranges and the other does not, people explain their choices in terms of differences in quality and durability rather than fragrance alone. This is of course of interest in its own right as it stresses the importance of the cognitions of the perceiver and chooser rather than the 'objective' characteristics of the goods alone (see Cox, 1967; Grunert and Keller, 1984; and compare with Lancaster, 1966).

In considering consumer preferences in the public sector we again encounter a good deal of ambivalence and inconsistency of replies, when, for instance, attitudes towards taxation and preferences for public expenditure are placed side by side. An examination of these contradictions merits future research as people generally feel no apparant need to resolve them. Research on tax evasion behaviour also offers a challenge to those wishing to develop models of behaviour of the 'expectancy-value' type which incorporate social variables (e.g. Fishbein and Ajzen, 1975). In short, tax evasion behaviour is likely to be influenced not only by the expected utility, the probability of detection by the authorities and the size of fine, but also by people's attributes, moral values and the perceived approval or disapproval of important others. The example of tax evasion has important general implications for model-building in social psychology. Specifically it emphasises the need to incorporate opportunity variables and a proper analysis of the constraints on behaviour prescribed by the circumstances.

PSYCHOLOGICAL ECONOMICS

We have alluded to several developments within economics which have utilised a more realistic model of man, and the debate will continue as to the instrumental value of such an approach. We can however make some specific suggestions from the social psychological and related literature.

Economic socialisation has obvious importance for future economic behaviour. There are norms of exchange which are additional to narrow self-interest interpretations. People do not maximise profits in such exchanges, rather they behave in such a way which appears to them fair and reasonable. Notions of fair and reasonable behaviour differ between cultures and change over time. An examination of present-day economic socialisation could provide advance warning of how people may behave in the future. Budgeting will suffice as a specific example. Children learn to budget—how much to save and how much to spend, the value they are to attach to the accumulation of wealth and the proper management of money. It seems likely to us that people choose to spend or save not only as a function of interest rates and inflation, for example, but according to their beliefs and values. Even during periods where the economic conditions dictate that the most rational thing to do is to spend rather than save, people may have a reluctance to behave in this way as spending may seem squanderous, indisciplined, incautious or hedonistic. It is useful as well to speculate about differing socialisation patterns concerning debits. The banking and credit systems now make 'spending money one has not got' commonplace. The values of prudence and thrift inherent in the Protestant work ethic are replaced, perhaps with notions of the wisest ways to borrow money. Put simply, children and young people may be less concerned or anxious about loans and debits than their parents.

On reflection, speculations such as these question which forces (economic or sociological) are at the root of these changes. The changing economic socialisation of children could be viewed as a function of economic changes experienced by parents where credit and loan facilities have generally expanded. But values (in the sociological or sociopsychological sense) do not change so quickly—economic socialisation will always be out of phase with economic changes as it is overladen with these values. It will also be out of phase as the 'economic learning' of parents may prove inappropriate for a new generation.

The chapters on poverty, wealth and unemployment are of use and interest to those concerned with macroeconomic policy-making. Lay explanations and beliefs about these issues shape and limit the scope of policy-makers, especially as an election approaches. While a government in mid-term and with a large majority can afford—if not quite to ignore—public opinion, it can at least direct and lead it. In the recent past Public Enemy No. 1 in Britain was inflation, now it is unemployment. While lay opinion can be partly predicted from economic changes only research conducted at regular intervals can trace the salience and affective strength of opinion on these issues. Policy innovation can stand or fall depending on what is perceived as the electoral climate. Clearly politicians of all persuasions have an interest in educating voters. If lay opinion makes a connection between say inflation and unemployment levels, then high levels of unemployment may be accepted given the inflation rate is seen to fall. It would be informative to examine lay economic theories more carefully, althougth we suspect many of the lay explanations for economic relationships may not be 'economic' in the narrow sense at all.

The attribution framework becomes especially pertinent when examining support for government policy: the support is dependent upon what people believe the government is capable of doing. Individualistic as opposed to societal attributions lead people to believe that there is little the government can do about poverty and the redistribution of wealth ('the poor are always with us'; 'the cream will always come to the top').

Contemporary research should not only direct itself to the problems mentioned above but also to an examination of the formation of lay beliefs. And by this we mean not only the examination of early socialisation processes but also influences in later life. In an imaginative piece of research, Paul Mosley has analysed economic news coverage in the British popular press (see Mosley, 1984). This approach shows how the comparative visibility of economic problems changes over time and how sometimes contradictory economic relationships and theories are popularly espoused to explain them. Subsequent research should be directed more towards the sources of economic communications; mere aggregation of individuals' lay beliefs will not suffice alone. It should also not be forgotten that lay beliefs will systematically differ between socioeconomic groups.

Some encouraging modern research in macroeconomics has involved adaptations of game theory and the subjective perceptions of participating groups. In particular Shlomo Maital has alluded to the 'economic games people play' and macroeconomic conflict between competing groups in society (Maital 1984; Maital and Maital, 1984). It is useful to go into some detail about this potentially exciting programme of research.

Maital's major contention is that Keynesians, monetarists and neoclassical economists alike have provided inadequate models of recent macroeconomic changes. Maital's approach emphasises the macroeconomic relations among people, rather than among things. In a simplified form he constructs hypothetical games comparing the interests of capital and labour, and the choices that each group faces. These games are non-zero-sum, where large increments accrue to cooperative behaviour and large social costs (in the form of high inflation and employment rates) to competitive behaviour. Maital outlines scenarios where labour have the opportunity to choose wage moderation and employers and businessmen price moderation, and a 'social contract' where both wages and prices are moderated. He describes three games depicting the relationship between employers and labour, namely 'charity' games, the familiar 'prisoner's dilemma' game, and finally a game called 'chicken'.

In the 'charity' game choices are determined by perceptions of the choices of the other party. Both business and labour interests prefer a situation where both moderate their behaviour (i.e. where price rises and wage demands are limited). Yet if either group suspects the other will push for price rises or higher wage demands respectively they must themselves act in an immoderate fashion. In the 'prisoner's dilemma' mutual moderate behaviour on the part of interest groups is even more difficult. Here the game is constructed where labour prefer higher real wages to lower inflation and unemployment and where capital prefers higher growth and lower real wages to lower inflation and unemployment: an equally familiar and, for Maital, futile scenario. Finally the game of 'chicken' is a bluff. Labour threatens higher wages demands and business higher price rises. And a called 'bluff' results in disastrous outcomes; in addition an offer of a 'social contract' may lead to defections by either party.

The game of 'chicken' best characterises strikes. The 'prisoner's dilemma' typifies 'buy-in-advance' behaviour of consumers, who accelerate spending in anticipation of higher prices. 'Charity' typifies wage-price bargaining where both sides recognise moderation is beneficial to all. At any given moment in the economy all three 'games' may be being played simultaneously. As in earlier sections of our speculations much of Maital's work depends on the lay perceptions and beliefs of participants, as it is the participants who in some senses make the rules of the game or at least agree to play it.

In a Gallup poll of 1500 Americans conducted in 1979, respondents were asked to choose between four wage-price configurations. These were:

1. where prices rise at a faster rate than wages,
2. where wage and price rises are equal but small,
3. where wage and price rises are equal but large,
4. where wages rise faster than prices.

In addition respondents were asked which pair of alternatives was best for (a) 'people who work for a living', and (b) 'all Americans'. Generally the result showed that what was perceived as best for working people was best for all, although a sizeable minority did note a conflict of interest. Thus the most favoured combination in the interests of working people was a larger increase of wages compared with prices (48 per cent), followed by an equal and slower growth of both price and wage increases (33 per cent). This was reversed for combinations in the best interest of all Americans, where 46 per cent chose equal small rises in prices and wages first and higher comparative wage increases second (33 per cent).

Clearly perceptions of macroeconomic conflicts and their perceived resolution could be a fruitful area of future research. Similarly it would be interesting to evaluate the preferences for various macroeconomic policies and to link these preferences to germane background variables such as economic optimism, socioeconomic status and party political allegiance (Alt, 1979).

Maital's ideas, although well-worn in the conflict resolution literature, show considerable promise for macroeconomic research. However it must be underpinned by perceptual data of high quality. The 'games' are by necessity simplifications and it must be remembered that choices are dependent on the behaviour of interest groups such as trade unions and employers' organisations who subsume the preferences of individuals. Furthermore the choices of interest groups themselves may not be in harmony—there can be conflict between unions as well as between unions and employers.

The chapters on wealth and poverty are linked to questions in social policy and welfare economics. How do people define poverty? How should income be distributed? What are the needs of families of different sizes? The Leyden income evaluation project has used perceptual data in this context to some effect (Hagenaars and van Praag, 1984). Research of this kind is racked with normative problems; the authors side-step this by accepting the poverty-line definitions of respondents themselves. Interestingly aggregate responses reveal that perceptions rest somewhere between absolute and relative poverty definitions. Van Praag has used similar material from large data sets to examine people's perceptions of appropriate and sufficient incomes. Van Praag has argued that these data can be used to derive equivalence scales which circumvent the need for elaborate decision-making models.

It would not be difficult to speculate about many other productive research programmes in both economic psychology and psychological economics: Kahneman and Tversky's work (1979) on decisions under risk, and Akerlof and Dickens' (1982) use of cognitive dissonance theory in a modification of rational decision-making, readily spring to mind. For the most up-to-date references in this area interested readers should consult the *Journal of Economic Psychology* and the forthcoming *Handbook of Behavioural Economics* and *Handbook of Economic Psychology*. The future promises much of mutual benefit to both economics and psychology. And on an optimistic note we look forward to research in economic psychology and in particular psychological economics which places more emphasis on people. At a time when both leisure and long-term unemployment is increasing we look forward to more imaginative government policy and research, not least on the changing values that these long-term economic factors will entail if western capitalist society is to remain stable.

References

Abrahamson, A., 'Sudden wealth, gratification and attainment: Durkheim's anomie of affluence reconsidered', *American Sociological Review*, 1980, *45*, 49–57.

Adams, J., 'Inequality in social exchange', in *Advances in Experimental Social Psychology*, vol. 2, ed. Berkowitz, L., New York: Academic Press, 1965.

Aitken, S. and Bonneville, L., *A General Taxpayer Opinion Survey*, Washington, D.C.: CSR, 1980.

Ajzen I. and Fishbein, M., *Understanding Attitudes and Predicting, Social Behaviour*, Princeton, N.J.: Prentice-Hall, 1980.

Akerlof, G. and Dickens, W., 'The economic consequences of cognitive dissonance', *The American Economic Review*, June 1982, 307–19.

Aldag, R. and Brief, A., 'Some correlates of work values', *Journal of Applied Psychology*, 1975, *60*, 757–60.

Allen, V., *Psychological Factors in Poverty*, Chicago: Markham, 1970.

Allerhand, M., Friedlander, F., Malone, J., Meadow, H. and Rosenberg, M., *A Study of the Impact and Effectiveness of the Comprehensive, Manpower Project of Cleveland*, Dept. of Labor, 1969.

Allingham, M. and Sandmo, A., 'Income tax evasion: a theoretical analysis', *Journal of Public Economies*, 1972, *1* (34), 323–38.

Allison, F. James, S. And Lewis, A., forthcoming, 1985.

Alt, J., *The Politics of Economic Decline*, Cambridge: Cambridge University Press. 1979.

Alves, W. and Rossi, P., 'Who should get what? Fairness, judgements of the distribution of earnings', *American Journal of Sociology*, 1978, *84*, 541–63.

Anderson, B., Deane, D., Hammong, K., McClelland, G. and Shanteau, J., *Concepts in Judgement and Decision Research*, New York: Praeger, 1981.

Anderson, N., *Foundations of Information Integrating Theory*, New York: Academic Press, 1981.

Antaki, C. (ed.), *The Psychology of Ordinary Explanations of Social Behaviour*, London: Academic Press, 1981.

Argyle, M., *The Social Psychology of Work*, Harmondsworth: Penguin Books, 1983.

Argyle, M., Furnham, A. and Graham, G., *Social Situations*, Cambridge: Cambridge University Press, 1981.

Armenakis, A., Fields, H., Bederan, A. and Ledbetter, B., 'Human resource considerations in textile work redesign', *Human Relations*, 1977, *30*, 1147–56.

Armistead, N. (ed.), *Reconstructing Social Psychology*, Harmondsworth: Penguin Books, 1974.

Arndt, J., 'Selective processes in word-of-mouth', *Journal of Advertising Research*, June 1968, 19–22.

Arrow, K., *Social Choice and Individual Values*, New York: Wiley, 1963.
Auld, D., *Public Awareness and Preferences in Ontario*, Ontario: Department of Economics, University of Guelph, 1978.
Ayllon, T. and Azin, N., *The Token Economy: A motivational system for therapy and rehabilitation*, New York: Appleton-Century-Crofts, 1968.
Ayllon, T. and Roberts, M., 'Eliminating discipline problems by strengthening academic performance', *Journal of Applied Behaviour Analysis*, 1974, *7*, 71–6.

Bakke, E., *The Unemployed Man*, London: Nisbett, 1933.
Bakke, E., *Citizens Without Work*, New Haven: Yale University Press, 1940.
Bales, R., *Interaction Process Analysis*, Cambridge, Mass.: Addison-Wesley, 1950.
Banks, M. and Jackson, P., 'Unemployment and risk of minor psychiatric disorder in young people: Cross-sectional and longitudinal evidence', *Psychological Medicine*, 1982, *12*, 789–98.
Banks, M., Clegg, C., Jackson, P., Kemp, N., Stafford, E. and Wall T., 'The use of the General Health Questionnaire as an indicator of mental health in occupational studies'. *Journal of Occupational Psychology*, 1980, *53*, 186–94.
Barclay, W., *Ethics in a Permissive Society*, London: Fontana, 1971.
Barlow, R., Brazer, H. and Morgan, J., *Economic Behavior of the Affluent*. Washington, D.C.: Brookings Institution, 1966.
Baron, R., *Behaviour and Organization*, Boston, Mass.: Allyn & Bacon, 1983.
Bass, F., 'A new product growth model for consumer durables', *Management Science*, January 1969, 215–27.
Baxter, J., 'The chronic job changer: A study of youth unemployment', *Social and Economic Administration*, 1975, *9*, 184–206.
Beales, H. and Lambert, R. (eds.), *Memoirs of the Unemployed*, London: Gollancz, 1934.
Becker, S., *The Economic Approach to Human Behavior*, Chicago: University of Chicago, 1976.
Beedle, P. and Taylor-Gooby, P., 'Ambivalence and altruism: public opinion about taxation and welfare', *Policy and Politics*, 1983, *II*, no. 1, 15–39.
Beiser, M., 'Poverty, social disintegration and personality', *Journal of Social Issues*, 1965, *1*, 56–78.
Beit-Hallahmi, B., 'Personal and social components of the Protestant ethic', *Journal of Social Psychology*, 1979, *109*, 263–7.
Bellack, A. and Hersen, M., *Introduction to Clinical Psychology*, Oxford: Oxford University Press, 1980.
Beloff, H., 'The structure and origin of the anal character', *Genetic Psychology Monograph*, 1957, *55*, 141–72.
Bergler, E., *The Psychology of Gambling*, London: Harrison, 1958.
Berk, R., Lenihan, K. and Rossi, P., 'Crime and poverty: Some experimental evidence from ex-offenders', *American Sociological Review*, 1980, *45*, 766–86.

Berlyne, D., *Conflict, Arousal and Curiosity*, New York: McGraw-Hill, 1960.
Bernstein, B., 'Social class and linguistic development: A theory of social learning', In A. Halsey (ed.), *Education, Economy and Society*, New York: Free press, 1961.
Berti, A. and Bombi, A., 'Where does money come from?', *Archivio di Psicologia*, 1979, *40*, 53–77.
Berti, A. and Bombi, A., 'The development of the concept of money and its value. A longitudinal study', *Child Development*, 1981, *52*, 1179–82.
Berti, A., Bombi, A. and Lis, A., 'The child's conception about means of production and their owners', *European Journal of Social Psychology*, 1982, *12*, 221–39.
Biggart, N., 'Rationality, meaning, and self-management: Success manuals, 1950–1980', *Social Problems*, 1983, *30*, 298–311.
Billig, M., *Ideology and Social Psychology*, Oxford: Basil Blackwell, 1982.
Blood, M., 'Work values and job satisfaction'. *Journal of Applied Psychology*, 1969, *53*, 456–9.
Bolen, D. and Boyd, W., 'Gambling and the gambler', *Archives of General Psychiatry*, 1968, *18*, 617–30.
Boor, M., 'Relationships between unemployment rates and suicide rates in eight countries, 1962–1976', *Psychological Reports*, 1980, *47*, 1095–101.
Boulding, K., 'Economics as a moral science', *American Economic Review*, 1969, *59*, 1–12.
Bowlby, J., *Attachment and Loss*, London: Hogarth, 1969.
Braak van de, H., 'Taxation and tax resistance', *Journal of Economic Psychology*, 1983, *3*, no. 2, 95–111.
Break, G., 'Income taxes and incentives to work: an empirical study', *American Economic Review*, 1957, *47*, no. 5, 529–49.
Brenner, S. and Bartell, R., 'The psychological impact of unemployment: A structural analysis of cross-sectional data', *Journal of Occupational Psychology*, 1983, *56*, 129–36.
Briar, R., 'The effect of long-term unemployment on workers and their families', *Dissertation Abstracts International*, 1977, *37*, 6062.
Bristow, S., 'Rates and votes—1980 district council elections', *Policy and Politics*, 1982, *10*, no. 2, 163–80.
Brock, T., 'Implications of commodity theory for value change', in *Psychological Foundations of Attitudes*', ed. A. Greenwald, T. Brock and T. Ostrom, New York: Academic Press, 1968.
Brown, C., 'Misconceptions about income tax and incentives', *Scottish Journal of Political Economy*, 1968, *15*, 1–21.
Brown, C., *Taxation and the Incentive to Work,* Oxford: Oxford University Press, 1981.
Brown, C. and Jackson, P., *Public Sector Economics*, Oxford: Martin Robertson, 1978.
Brown, C., Levin, E., Rosa, P., Ruffell, R. and Ulph, D., *Direct Taxation and Short-Run Labour Supply*, Scotland: Working Papers, Dept. of Economics, University of Stirling, 1984.
Bruce, V., Gilmore, D., Mason, L. and Mayhew, P., 'Factors affecting the

perceived value of coins', *Journal of Economic Psychology*, 1983a, *4*, 335–47.

Bruce, V., Howarth, C., Clark-Carter, D., Dodds, A. and Heyes, A., 'All change for the pound. Human performance tests with different versions of the proposed U.K. one pound coin', *Ergonomics*, 1983b, *26*, 215–27.

Bruner, J. and Goodman, C., 'Value and need as organizing factors in perception', *Journal of Abnormal and Social Psychology*, 1947, *42*, 33–44.

Brunswick, E., 'Representative design and probabilistic theory in a functional psychology', *Psychological Review*, 1955, *62*, 193–217.

Buchholz, R., 'Measurement of beliefs', *Human Relations*, 1976, *29*, 1177–88.

Buchholz, R., 'An empirical study of contemporary beliefs about work in American society', *Journal of Applied Psychology*, 1978, *63*, 219–27.

Burgess, M., 'Poverty and dependency: Some selected characteristics', *Journal of Social Psychology*, 1965, *47*, 231–40.

Burnis, V., 'Stays in the development of economic concepts', *Human Relations*, 1983, *9*, 791–812.

Burns, R., *The Self Concept: Theory, Measurement, Development and Behaviour*, London: Longman, 1981.

Campbell, A., *The Sense of Well-Being in America*, New York: McGraw-Hill, 1981.

Carlson, J., and Parkin, M., 'Inflation expectations', *Economica*, 1975, *42*, 123–38.

Carter, C., *Wealth: An Essay on the Purpose of Economics*. Harmondsworth: Pelican Books, 1971.

Catalano, R. and Dooley, C., 'Economic predictors of depressed mood and stressful life events', *Journal of Health and Social Behaviour*, 1977, *18*, 292–307.

Catalano, R. and Dooley, C., 'The economy as stressor: A sectoral analysis', *Review of Social Economy*, 1979, *37*, 175–88.

Coates, K. and Silburn, R., *Poverty: the Forgotten Englishmen*, Harmondsworth: Penguin Books, 1970.

Cochrane, R. and Robertson, A., 'The life events inventory. A measure of the relative severity of psychosocial stressors', *Journal of Psychosomatic Research*, 1973, *17*, 215–18.

Cochrane, R., *The Social Creation of Mental Illness*, London: Longman, 1983.

Coffield, F., 'Learning to live with unemployment: What future for education in a world without jobs?', Unpublished paper, 1984.

Cohen, J., *Risk and Gambling: The Study of Subjective Probability*. New York: Philosophical Library, 1956.

Cohen, J., *Chance, Skill and Luck: The Psychology of Guessing and Gambling*, Harmondsworth: Penguin Books, 1960.

Cohen, J., *Psychological Probability*, London: Allen & Unwin, 1970.

Collard, D., *Altruism and Economy*, Oxford: Martin Robertson, 1978.

Converse, P., 'The nature of belief systems in mass politics', in *Ideology and Discontent*, ed. D. Apter, New York: Free Press, 1964.

Converse, P., 'Public opinion and voting behavior', in *Handbook of Political Science*, vol. 2, ed. N. Polsby and F. Greenstein, Boston: Addison-Wesley, 1975.

Cook, J., Hepworth, S., Wall, T. and Warr, P., *The Experience of Work*, London: Academic Press, 1981.

Cook, V., 'A comparison of work values of disadvantaged black males, with work values of advantaged black males in an urban setting, unpublished Ph. D, Catholic University, Washington, D.C.

Coombs, C., 'Portfolio theory and the measurement of risk', in *Human Judgment and Decision Processes* ed., M. Kaplan and S. Schwartz, New York: Academic Press, 1975.

Cooper, C. and Davidson, M., *High Pressure: Working Lives of Women Managers*, London: Fontana, 1982.

Cornish, D., *Gambling: A review of the literature and its implications for policy and research*, London: HMSO, 1978.

Coser, L., *The Functions of Conflict*, New York: Free Press, 1964.

Coughlin, R., *Ideology, Public Opinion and Welfare Policy*, Berkeley: Institute of International Studies, University of California, 1980.

Coughlin, R., 'Payroll taxes for social security, in the United States: The future of fiscal and social policy illusions', *Journal of Economic Psychology*, 1982, *2*, 165–85.

Coward, B., Feagin, J. and Williams, J., 'The culture of poverty debate: Some additional data', *Social Problems*, 1974, *21*, 621–34.

Cox, D. (ed.), *Risk Taking and information Handling in Consumer Behavior*, Cambridge, Mass: Graduate School of Business Administration, 1967. Harvard University.

Crow, J., 'Do genetic factors contribute to poverty?', in *Psychological Factors in Poverty*; ed. V. Allen, Chicago: Markham, 1970.

Cullis, J. and Lewis, A., 'Some evidence on tax knowledge and preferences', submitted for publication, 1984.

Cummings, S. and Taebel, V., 'The economic socialisation of children. A neo-Marxist analysis', *Social Problems*, 1978, *26*, 198–210.

Custer, R., 'Description of compulsive gambling', unpublished paper, 1976.

Dalton, G., *Economic Anthropology and Development*, London: Basic Books, 1971.

Dancy, J., 'Education about unemployment: A reflective element', *Oxford Review of Education*, 1978, *4*, 289–94.

Danziger, K., 'Children's earliest conception of economic relationships', *Journal of Social Psychology* 1958, *47*, 231–40.

David, M., *The Use of Attitude Surveys in Determining Tax Policy*, University of Wisconsun: Institute for Research on Poverty, 1980.

Davidson, C. and Gaitz, C., 'Are the poor different? A comparison of work behaviour and attitudes among the urban poor and non-poor', *Social Problems*, 1974, *22*, 229–45.

Davis, E., Grube, J. and Morgan, M., *Attitudes Towards Poverty and Related Social Issues in Ireland*, unpublished report, Trinity College Dublin, 1984.

Davis, H. and Rigaux, B., 'Perception of marital roles in decision processes',

Journal of Consumer Research, June 1974, 51–61.
Davis, K. and Taylor, T., *Kids and Cash: Solving a Parent's dilemma*, La Jolla, Calif: Oak Tree, 1979.
Davol, S. and Reimans, E., 'The role of anomie as a psychological concept', *Journal of Individual Differences*, 1959, *15*, 215–25.
Dawson, J., 'Socio-economic differences in size-judgements of discs and coins by Chinese Primary VI children in Hong Kong', *Perceptual and Motor Skills, 41*, 107–10.
Dayton, C., 'The young person's job search: Insights from a study', *Journal of Counselling Psychology*, 1981, *28*, 321–33.
Deacon, A., 'The scrounging controversy: Public attitudes towards the unemployed in contemporary Britain', *Social and Economic Administration*, 1978, *12*, 120–35.
Dean, P., Keenan, A. and Kenney, F., 'Taxpayers' attitudes towards income tax evasion: an empirical study', *British Tax Review*, 1980, *1*, 28–44.
Deaton, A. and Muellbauer, J., *Economics and Consumer Behaviour*, Cambridge: Cambridge University Press, 1980.
Delormé, G., 'General report to the XXXIV Congrès International de Droit Financier et Fiscal 1980', *Cahiers de Droit Fiscal International*, 1980, *LXVA*, 43–67.
Devereux, E., 'Gambling in psychological and sociological perspective', *International Encyclopedia of the Social Sciences*, 1968, *6*, 53–62.
Dickson, J. and Buchholz, R., 'Managerial beliefs about work in Scotland and the USA, *Journal of Management Studies*, 1977, *14*, 80–101.
Dickson, J. and Buchholz, R., 'Differences in beliefs, about work between managers and blue-collar workers', *Journal of Management Studies*, 1979, *16*, 235–51.
Ditton, J., *Part-time Crime: An Ethnography of Fiddling and Pilferage* London: Macmillan, 1977.
Dohrenwend, B. and Dohrenwend, B., *Social Status and Psychological Disorder: A Causal Inquiry*, New York: Wiley, 1969.
Donovan, A. and Oddy, M., 'Psychosocial aspects of unemployment: An investigation into the emotional and social adjustment of school leavers, *Journal of Adolescence*, 1982, *5*, 15–30.
Dooley, D. and Catalano, R., 'Economic, life, and disorder changes: Time-series analyses', *American Journal of Community Psychology*, 1979, *7*, 381–96.
Dooley, D. and Catalano, R., 'Economic change as a cause of behavioural disorder', *Psychological Bulletin*, 1980, *87*, 450–68.
Douglas, M. and Isherwood, B., *The World of Goods: Towards an Anthropology of Consumption*, Harmondsworth: Penguin Books, 1980.
Downes, D., Davies, B., David, M. and Stone, P., *Gambling, Work and Leisure*, London: Routledge & Kegan Paul, 1976.
Duesenberry, J., *Income, Saving and the Theory of Consumer Behaviour*, Cambridge, Mass.: Harvard University Press, 1949.

Earl, P., *The Economic Imagination: Towards a behavioral analysis of choice*, New York: Sharpe, 1983.
Easterlin, R., 'Does money buy happiness?', *The Public Interest*, 1973, *30*, 3–10.
Edgell, S. and Duke, V., 'Reactions to the public expenditure cuts: Occupational class and party realignment', *Sociology*, 1982, *16*. 431–9.
Edwards, W., 'Probability—preferences in gambling', *American Journal of Psychology*, 1953, *66*, 349–64.
Edwards, W., 'The theory of decision-making', *Psychological Bulletin*, 1954, *51*, 380–417.
Edwards, W., 'Behavioural decision theory', *Annual Review of Psychology*, 1961, *12*, 473–98.
EEC Report, *The Perception of Poverty in Europe*, Brussels, 1977.
Eisenberg, P. and Lazarsfeld, P., 'The psychological effects of unemployment', *Psychological Bulletin*, 1938, *35*, 79–96.
Engel, J. and Blackwell, R., *Consumer Behavior*, Chicago: Dryden Press, 1982.
Enrich, N., 'A pilot study of income tax consciousness', *National Tax Journal* 1963, *16*, 169–73.
Epstein, Y. and Babad, E., 'Economic stress: Notes on the psychology of inflation', *Journal of Applied Social Psychology*, 1982, *12*, 85–99.
Estes, W., '*Handbook of Learning and Cognitive Processes*', vol. 4, Hillsdale, N.J.: Erlbaum, 1976.
Eysenck, H., *The Psychology of Politics*, London: Routledge & Kegan Paul, 1957.
Eysenck, H., *The Biological Basis of Personality*, Springfield, Ill.: Thomas, 1967.
Eysenck, H., *Psychology is about People*, Harmondsworth: Penguin Books, 1977.
Eysenck, M. and Eysenck, M., 'Effects of Incentive on cued recall', *Quarterly Journal of Experimental Psychology*, 1982, *34*, 489–98.

Farmer, M., 'Rational action in economics and social theory: some misunderstandings', *European Journal of Sociology*, 1982, *23*, 178–96.
Farr, R., 'Homo socio-psychologicus', in *Models of Man*, ed. A. Chapman and D. Jones, Leicester: British Psychological Society, 1980.
Faver, C., 'Achievement orientation, attainment values, and women's employment', *Journal of Vocational Behaviour*, 1982, *20*, 67–80.
Feagin, J., 'Poverty: we still believe that God helps them who help themselves', *Psychology Today*, 1972, *6*, 101–29.
Feagin, J., *Subordinating the Poor*, Englewood Cliffs, N.J.: Prentice-Hall, 1975.
Feather, N., 'Explanations of poverty in Australian and American samples: The person, society and fate', *Australian Journal of Psychology*, 1974, *26*, 199–216.
Feather, N., *Values in Education and Society*, New York: Free Press, 1975.
Feather, N., 'Unemployment and its psychological correlates: A study of

depressive symptoms, self-esteem, Protestant ethic values, attributional style, and apathy, *Australian Journal of Psychology*, 1982a, *34*, 309–23.

Feather, N., 'Unemployment and its psychological correlates: A study of depressive symptoms of self-esteem, Protestant ethic values, attributional style and apathy', *Australian Journal of Psychology*, 1982b, *34*, 309–23.

Feather, N., 'Some correlates of attributional style: Depressive symptoms of self-esteem, and Protestant ethic values', *Personality and Social Psychology Bulletin*, 1983a, *9*, 125–35.

Feather, N., 'Causal attributions and beliefs about work and unemployment among adolescents in state and independent secondary schools', *Australian Journal of Psychology*, 1983c, *35*, 211–32.

Feather, N. and Barber, J., 'Depressive reactions and unemployment', *Journal of Abnormal Psychology*, 1983, *92*, 185–95.

Feather, N. and Bond, M., 'Time structure and purposeful activity among employed and unemployed university graduates', *Journal of Occupational Psychology*, 1983b, *56*, 241–54.

Feather, N. and Davenport, P., 'Unemployment and depressive effect: A motivational and attributional analysis', *Journal of Personality and Social Psychology*, 1981, *41*, 422–36.

Felker, D., Pickering, F., Charrow, V., Holland, V. and Redish, J., *Guidelines for Document Designers*, Washington, D.C.: American Institute for Research, 1981.

Fenichel, O., 'The drive to amass wealth', in *The Collected Papers of Otto Fenichel*, ed. H. Fenichel and O. Rapoport, New York: Norton, 1947.

Ferenczi, S., *Further Contributions to the Theory and Techniques of Psychoanalysis*. London: Knopf, 1926.

Festinger, L., 'A theory of social comparison "processes"', *Human Relations*, 1954, *7*, 117–40.

Festinger, L., *A theory of Cognitive Dissonance*, Row, Illinois: Peterson, Evanston, 1957.

Fields, D. and Stanbury, W., 'Incentives, disincentives and income tax: further empirical evidence', *Public Finance*, 1970, *25*(3), 381–415.

Fineman, S., 'A psychological model of stress and its application to managerial unemployment', *Human Relations*, 1979, *32*, 323–45.

Fishbein, M. and Azjen, I., *Belief, Attitude, Intention and Behavior*, Reading, Mass.: Addison-Wesley, 1975.

Fleming, D. and Lavercombe, S., 'Talking about unemployment with school-leavers, *British Journal of Guidance and Counselling*, 1982, *10*, 22–33.

Flesch, R., 'A new readability yardstick', *Journal of Applied Psychology*, 1948, *32*, 221–33.

Forgas, J., Morris, S. and Furnham, A., 'Lay explanations of wealth: Attributions for economic success, *Journal of Applied Social Psychology*, 1982, *12*, 381–97.

Fowler, B., Littlewood, B. and Madigan, R., 'Immigrant school-leavers and the search for work', *Sociology*, 1977, *11*, 65–85.

Fox, K., 'What children bring to school: The beginnings of economic education', *Social Education*, 1978, *10*, 478–81.

Fraser, C., 'The social psychology of unemployment', in *Psychology Survey*, no. 3, Jeeves, M. (ed.), London: Allen & Unwin, 1980.

Freud, S., *Character and Anal Eroticism*, standard edn, London: Hogarth, 1908.

Freud, S., 'Dostoevsky and parricide', in J. Strachey (ed.) *Freud: The Collected Papers*, New York: Basic Books, 1928.

Friedland, N., 'A note on tax evasion as a function of the quality of information about the magnitude and credibility of threatened fines', *Journal of Applied Social Psychology*, 1982, *12*, (1), 54–9.

Friedland, N., Maital, S. and Rutenburg, A., 'A simulation study of income tax evasion', *Journal of Public Economies*, 1978, *10*, 107–16.

Friedlander, F., 'Importance of work versus non-work among socially and occupationally stratified groups', *Journal of Applied Psychology*, 1966, *50*, 437–41.

Friedlander, F. and Greenberg, S., 'Effect of job attitudes, training and organisation climate on performance of the hard-core unemployed', *Journal of Applied Psychology*, 1971, *55*, 287–95.

Friedman, M., *Essays in Positive Economics*, Chicago: University of Chicago Press, 1953.

Friedman, M., *A Theory of the Consumption Function*, Princeton, N.J.: Princeton University Press, 1957.

Frith, R., *Themes in Economic Anthropology*, London: Tavistock, 1978.

Fromm, E., *To Have or To Be*, New York: Harper & Row, 1976/Bungay: Abacus, 1980.

Fruensgaard, K., Benjaminsen, S., Joensen, S. and Helstrup, K., 'Follow-up of a group of unemployed patients consecutively admitted to an emergency psychiatric department', *Social Psychiatry*, 1983, *18*, 129–35.

Fuller, R. and Rice, B., *Christianity and the Affluent Society*, London: Hodder & Stoughton, 1966.

Furby, L., 'Sharing: decisions and moral judgements about letting others use one's possessions', *Psychological Reports*, 1978, *43*, 595–609.

Furby, L., 'Inequalities and personal possessions. Explanations for and judgement about unequal distribution', *Human Development*, 1979, *22*, 180–202.

Furnham, A., 'The Protestant work ethic and attitudes towards unemployment, *Journal of Occupational Psychology*, 1982a, *55*, 277–86.

Furnham, A., 'Why are the poor always with us? Explanations for poverty in Britain', *British Journal of Social Psychology*, 1982b, *20*, 311–82.

Furnham, A., 'Explanations for unemployment in Britain', *European Journal of Social Psychology*, 1982c, *12*, 335–52.

Furnham, A., 'The perception of poverty among adolescents', *Journal of Adolescence*, 1982d, *5*, 135–47.

Furnham, A., 'Mental health and unemployment status: A preliminary study', *British Journal of Counselling and Guidance*. 1983a, *11*, 197–201.

Furnham, A., 'Attitudes to the unemployed receiving social security', *Human Relations*, 1983b, *36*, 135–50.

Furnham, A., 'Inflation and the estimated sizes of notes', *Journal of Economic Psychology*, 1983c, *4*, 349–52.

Furnham, A., 'The A-type behaviour pattern, mental health and health locus of control beliefs', *Social Science and Medicine*, 1983d, *17*, 1569–72.

Furnham, A., 'Attributions for affluence', *Personality and Individual Differences*, 1983e, *4*, 31–40.

Furnham, A., 'The Protestant work ethic, human values and attitudes towards taxation', *Journal of Economic Psychology*, 1983f, *8*, 112–28.

Furnham, A., 'Many sides of the coin: The psychology of money usage', *Personality and Individual Differences*, 1984a, *5*, 95–103.

Furnham, A., 'Determinants of attitudes towards taxation in Britain', *Human Relations*, 1984e, *37*, 535–546.

Furnham, A., 'Getting a job: School-leavers' perceptions of employment prospects', *British Journal of Educational psychology*, 1984c, *54*, 293–305.

Furnham, A., 'Work values and belief in Britain', *Journal of Occupational Behaviour*, 1984d, *5*, 281–91.

Furnham, A., 'The perceived value of small coins', *Journal of Social Psychology*, 1985a, in Press.

Furnham, A., 'The determinants of attitudes towards social security recipients', *British Journal of Social Psychology*, 1985b, *24*, 19–27.

Furnham, A., 'Why do people save? Attitudes to, and habits of saving money in Britain', *Journal of Applied Social Psychology*, 1985c *15*, 354–73.

Furnham, A., 'Attitudes to, and habits of, gambling in Britain', *Personality and Individual Differences*, 1985d.

Furnham, A. and Bland, K., 'The Protestant work ethic and conservatism', *Personality and Individual Differences*, 1983, *4*, 205–6.

Furnham, A. and Bochner, S., *Culture Shock: Psychological Reactions to Unfamiliar Environments*, London: Methuen, 1985.

Furnham, A. and Gunter, B., 'Political knowledge and awareness in adolescents', *Journal of Adolescence*, 1983, *6*, 373–85.

Furnham, A. and Gunter, B., 'Just world beliefs and attitudes towards the poor', *British Journal of Social Psychology*, 1984, *23*, 265–69.

Furnham, A. and Thomas, P., 'Pocket-money: A study of economic education', *British Journal of Developmental Psychology*, 1984a, *2*, 205–12.

Furnham, A. and Thomas, P., 'Adults' perception of the economic socialization of children', *Journal of Adolescence*, 1984b, *7*, 217–31.

Furnham, A. and Weissman, D., Judging the value of British coins: A developmental and cross-cultural study, unpublished paper, 1985.

Furth, H., *The World of Grown-Ups*, New York: Elsevier, 1980.

Fyons, L., Salilli, F., Maehr, M. and Desai, K., 'A cross-cultural exploration into the meaning of achievement', *Journal of Personality and Social Psychology*, 1983, *44*, 1000–13.

Gabor, A. and Granger, C., 'Price as an indicator of quality: Report on an enquiry' *Economica*, February 1966, 43–70.

Galbraith, J., *The Affluent Society*, London: Hamish Hamilton, 1958.

Galbraith, J., *The Age of Uncertainty*, London: André Deutsch, 1977.

Gallup, L., *Gambling in Britain*, London: Gallup Social Surveys, 1976.

Gans, H., 'The positive functions of poverty', *American Journal of Sociology*, 1972, *78*, 275–89.

Ganster, D., 'Individual differences and task design: A laboratory experiment', *Organizational Behaviour and Human Performance*, 1980, *26*, 131–48.

Ganster, D., 'Protestant ethic and performance. A re-examination', *Psychological Reports*, 1981, *48*, 335–8.

George, V. and Wilding, P., *Ideology and Social Welfare*, London: Routledge & Kegan Paul, 1976.

Gianotten, H. and van Raaij, W., 'Consumer credit and saving as a function of income and confidence', Paper given at the Economic Psychology Colloquim, Scotland, 1982.

Gilovich, T., 'Biased evaluation and persistence in gambling', *Journal of Personality and Social Psychology*, 1983, *6*, 1110–26.

Goetz, C., 'Fiscal illusion in state and local finance', in *Budgets and Bureaucrats: The Sources of Government Growth*, ed. T. Borcherding, Durham: Duke University Press, 1977.

Goffman, I., *Interaction Ritual*, London: Allen Lane, 1967.

Goldberg, H. and Lewis, R., *Money Madness: The Psychology of Saving, Spending, Loving and Hating Money*, London: Springwood, 1979.

Golding, P. and Middleton, S., *Images of Welfare: Press and Public Attitudes to Poverty*, Oxford: Martin Robertson, 1982.

Goldstein, B. and Eichborn, R., 'The changing Protestant ethic: Rural patterns in health, work and leisure', *American Sociological Review*, 1961, *26*, 557–65.

Goodenough, R., 'Proposition 13 and its impact on local government programs in California', *Policy and Politics*, 1982, *10*, 4, 439–57.

Goodwin, L., 'Middle-class misperceptions of the high life, aspirations and strong work ethic held by the welfare poor, *American Journal of Orthopsychiatry*, 1973, *43*, 554–64.

Gordon, D., *Theories of Poverty and Underemployment*. Lexington: Lexington Books, 1972.

Gore, S., 'The effect of social support in moderating the health consequences of unemployment', *Journal of Health and Social Behaviour*, 1978, *19*, 157–65.

Grasmick, H. and Scott, W., 'Tax evasion and mechanisms of social control: a comparison with grand and petty theft', *Journal of Economic Psychology*, 1982, *2*, 3, 213–30.

Green, P. and Srinivasan, V., 'Conjoint analysis in consumer research', *Journal of Consumer Research*, 1978, *5*, 103–23.

Green, P. and Wind, Y., 'New ways to measure consumers judgments', *Harvard Business Review*, 1975, pp. 107–117.

Greenberg, J., 'The Protestant work ethic and reactions to negative performance evaluations on a laboratory task', *Journal of Applied Psychology*, 1977, *62*, 682–90.

Greenberg, J., 'Equity, equality and the Protestant ethic: Allocating rewards following fair and unfair competition', *Journal of Experimental Social Psychology*, 1978, *14*, 217–26.

Greenberg, J., 'Protestant ethic endorsement and the fairness of equity inputs', *Journal of Research in Personality*, 1979, *13*, 81–90.

Greenberg, H., 'Psychology of gambling', in Kaplan, J. *et al.* (eds), *Comprehensive Textbook of Psychiatry*, vol. III, London and Boston: Williams & Wilkins, 1980.

Greenberger, E., Stenberg, L. and Vaux, A., 'Adolescents who work: Health and behavioural consequences of job stress', *Developmental Psychology*, 1981, *17*, 691–703.

Greenstein, F. and Polsby, N., *Handbook of Political Science*, vol. 4, Reading, Mass.: Addison-Wesley, 1975.

Groenland, A. and van Veldboven, G., 'Tax evasion behaviour: a psychological framework', *Journal of Economic Psychology*, 1983, *3*(2), 129–44.

Grunert, K. and Keller, A., 'Cognitive determinants of attribute information usage: a pilot study', Paper delivered to IAREP, Tilburg, The Netherlands, 1984.

Grygier, T., *The Dynamic Personality Inventory: Manual*, Windsor: NFER, 1961.

Guion, R. and Landy, F., 'The meaning of work and the motivation to work', *Organizational Behaviour and Human Performance*, 1972, *8*, 308–39.

Gurin, G. and Gurin, P., 'Expectancy theory in the study of poverty', *Journal of Social Issues*, 1970, *26*, 83–104.

Gurney, R., 'Does unemployment affect the self-esteem of school-leavers?', *Australian Journal of Psychology*, 1980a, *32*, 175–82.

Gurney, R., 'The effects of unemployment on the psychosocial development of school-leavers', *Journal of Occupational Psychology*, 1980b, *53*, 205–13.

Gurney, R., 'Leaving school, facing unemployment and making attributions about the causes of unemployment', *Journal of Vocational Behaviour*, 1981, *18*, 79–91.

Guttman, P., 'The subterranean economy', *Financial Analysts's Journal*, 1977, *33*, 26–7.

Hagenaars, A. and van Praag, B., 'A synthesis of poverty line definitions', Paper presented to IAREP, Tilburg, The Netherlands, 1984.

Haire, M. and Morrison, F., 'School children's perception of labour and management', *Journal of Social Psychology*, 1957, *46*, 179–97.

Halliday, J. and Fuller, P. (eds.), *The Psychology of Gambling*, London: Allen Lane, 1974.

Hammond, G., McClelland, K. and Mumpower, J., *Human Judgement and Decision-Making*, New York: Praeger, 1980.

Hammond, K., 'Externalizing the parameters of quasi-rational thought', in *Multiple Criteria Decision-Making*, ed. M. Zeleny., New York: Springer-Verlag, 1976.

Hammond, P. and Williams, R., 'The Protestant ethic thesis: A social psychological assessment', *Social Forces*, 1976, *54*, 579–89.

Hardin, G., 'The tragedy of the commons', *Science*, 1968, *162*, 1243–8.

Hargreaves, D., 'Unemployment, leisure and education', *Oxford Review of Education*, 1981, *7*, 197–210.

Harris, H., 'Gambling addiction in an adolescent male', *Psychoanalytic Quarterly*, 1964, *33*, 515–25.

Harrison, R., 'The demoralizing experience of prolonged unemployment', *Department of Employment Gazette*, 1976, *4*, 339–48.

Hartley, J., 'The personality of unemployed managers: myths and measurement', *Personal Review*, 1980, *9*, 12–18.

Harvey, J., Ickes, W. and Kidd, R. (eds.), *New Directions in Attribution Research*, Hillsdale, N.J.: Erlbaum, 1975.

Hataro, G. and Inagaki, K. 'Behavioural differences between extraverts and introverts in betting situations', *Japanese Psychological Research*, 1977, *19*, 174–83.

Hayes, J. and Nutman, P., '*Understanding the Unemployed*' London: Tavistock, 1981.

Heath, A. and Clifford, P., The measurement and explanation of school differences', *Oxford Review of Education*, 1981, *1*, 33–40.

Hebb, D., 'Drives and the CNS', *Psychological Review*, 1955, *62*, 243–54.

Heider, F., *The Psychology of Interpersonal Relations*, New York: Wiley, 1958.

Henry, S., *The Hidden Economy*, Oxford: Martin Robertson, 1978.

Hepworth, S., 'Moderating factors of the psychological impact of unemployment', *Journal of Occupational Pyschology*, 1980, *53*, 139–45.

Herman, E., 'The institutionalization of bias in economics', *Media, Culture and Society*, 1982, *4*, 275–91.

Herskovits, M., *Economic Anthropology*, New York: Norton, 1952.

Herzberg, F., *Work and the Nature of Man*, Cleveland, Ohio: World Publishing Company, 1966.

Herzberg, F., Mausner, B. and Snyderman, B., *The Motivation to Work*, New York: Wiley, 1959.

Hess, R., 'The transmission of cognitive strategies in poor families', in V. Allen (ed.), *Psychological Factors in Poverty*, Chicago: Markham, 1970.

Hewstone, M. (ed.), *Attribution Theory: Social and Functional Extensions* Oxford: Basil Blackwell, 1983.

Hill, A., 'Methodological problems in the use of factor analysis: A critical review of the experimental evidence for the anal character', *British Journal of Medical Psychology*, 1976, *49*, 145–59.

Hill, J., 'The psychological impact of unemployment', *New Society*, 12 January 1978.

Hitchcock, J., Munroe, R. and Munroe, R., 'Coins and countries: The value-size hypothesis', *Journal of Social Psychology*, 1976, *100*, 307–8.

Hodder-Williams, R., *Public Opinion Polls and British Politics*, London: Routledge & Kegan Paul, 1970.

Hodgson, J. and Brenner, M., 'Successful experience: Training hard-core unemployed', *Harvard Business Review*, 1968, *46*, 148–56.

Holland, D., 'The effects of taxation on effort: some results for business executives', in National Tax Association, Proceedings of the 62nd Annual Conference, September 1969.

Holland, M. and Moon, J., 'A response to Lewis: partisanship and issue preferences', *Political Studies*, 1982, vol. XXX, no. 1, 102–6.

Hollis, M. and Nell, E., *Rational Economic Man*, Cambridge: Cambridge University Press, 1975.

Holmes, T. and Rahe, R., 'The social readjustment rating scale', *Journal of Psychosomatic Research*, 1967, *11*, 213–18.

Homans, G., *Social Behavior: Its Elementary Forms*, New York: Harcourt, Brace, Jovanovich, 1974.

Hopson, B. and Adams, J., 'Towards an understanding of transition', in J. Adams, J. Hayes and B. Hopson (eds.), *Transition*, London: Martin Robertson, 1976.

Howard, J. and Sheth, J., *The Theory of Buyer Behavior*, New York: Wiley, 1969.

Huber, J. and Form, W., *Income and Ideology*, New York: Free Press, 1973.

Hudson, J., *Inflation: A theoretical Survey and Synthesis*, London and Boston: Allen & Unwin, 1982.

Hulin, C. and Blood, M., 'Job enlargement, individual differences and worker responses', *Psychological Bulletin*, 1968, *69*, 41–55.

Hurlock, E., *Child Development*, New York: McGraw-Hill, 1972.

Hyman, H., 'The psychology of status', *Archives of Psychology*, 1942, *269*, 147–65.

Inland Revenue, *Survey of Attitudes to the Inland Revenue among PAYE Taxpayers*, London: Central Office of Information, 1980.

Irving, K. and Siegal, M., 'Mitigating circumstances of children's perceptions of criminal justice', *British Journal of Developmental Psychology*, 1983, *1*, 179–88.

Jackson, P., Stafford, E., Banks, M. and Warr, P., 'Unemployment and psychological distress in young people', *Journal of Applied Psychology*, 1983, *68*, 525–35.

Jahoda, G., 'A cross-cultural perspective on experimental social psychology', *Personality and Social Psychology Bulletin*, 1979a, *5*(2), 142–8.

Jahoda, G., 'The construction of economic reality by some Glaswegian children', *European Journal of Social Psychology*, 1979b, *9*, 115–27.

Jahoda, G., 'The development of thinking about economic institution: The Bank', *Cahiers de Psychologie Cognitive*, 1981, *1*, 55–78.

Jahoda, G., 'European "lag" in the development of an economic concept: A study in Zimbabwe', *British Journal of Developmental Psychology*, 1983, *1*, 110–20.

Jahoda, G. and Woerdenbagch, A., 'The development of ideas about an economic institution: A cross-national replication', *British Journal of Social Psychology*, 1982, *21*, 337–8.

Jahoda, M., 'The impact of unemployment in the 1930s and the 1970s', *Bulletin of the British Psychological Society*, 1979, *32*, 309–14.

Jahoda, M., 'Work, employment and unemployment: Values, theories and approaches in social research', *American Psychologist*, 1981, *36*, 184–91.

Jahoda, M., *Employment and Unemployment: A social-psychological analysis*, Cambridge: Cambridge University Press, 1982.

Jahoda, M., Lazarsfeld, P. and Zeisel, H., *Marienthal: The Sociography of an Unemployed Community*, London: Tavistock, 1933.
Jain, A., Pinson, C. and Ratchford, B. (eds.), *Marketing Research: Applications and Problems*, New York: Wiley, 1982.
James, S. and Lewis, A., 'Fiscal fog', *British Tax Review*, 1977, *6*, 371–8.
James, S., Lewis, A. and Wallschutzky, I., 'Fiscal fog: a comparison of the comprehensibility of tax literature in Australia and the UK', *Australian Tax Review*, 1981, *10*(1), 26–35.
Janis, I., *Victims of Groupthink*, Boston: Houghton Mifflin, 1972.
Jenkins, R., MacDonald, A., Murray, J. and Strathdee, G., 'Minor psychiatric, morbidity and the threat of redundancy in a professional group, *Psychological Medicine*, 1982, *12*, 799–807.
Jensen, A. and Reynolds, C., 'Race, social class and ability patterns on the WISC-R', *Personality and Individual Differences*, 1982, *3*, 423–35.
Joe, V., 'Personality correlates of conservatism', *Journal of Social Psychology*, 1974, *93*, 309–10.
Joe, V., Jones, R. and Miller, R., 'Value pattern of a conservative', *Personality and Individual Differences*, 1981, *2*, 25–30.
Jones, P. and Cullis, J., 'Fiscal preferences: some theory for some evidence and some evidence for some theory', submitted for publication, 1984.
Jundin, S., 'Children's economic socialization', Paper presented at the International Colloquium on Economic Psychology, Italy, 1983.
Juster, T., 'An expectational view of consumer spending prospects', *Journal of Economic Psychology*, 1981, *1*(1), 87–105.

Kahneman, D. and Tversky, A., 'Prospect theory, an analysis of decision-making under risk', *Econometrica* 1979, *47*, 263–92.
Kahneman, D., Slovic, P. and Tversky, A. (eds.), *Judgement under Uncertainty: Heuristics and Biases*, Cambridge: Cambridge University Press, 1982.
Kallen, D. and Miller, D., 'Public attitudes towards welfare', *Social Work*, 1971, *2*, 83–90.
Kasl, S. and Cobb, S., 'Blood pressure changes in men undergoing job loss', *Psychosomatic Medicine*, 1970, *32*, 19–38.
Katona, G., 'Anticipations statistics and consumer behavior', *American Statistician*, 1967, *21*, 12–13.
Katona, G., 'Consumer durable spending: Explanation and prediction', *Brookings Papers on Economic Activity*, 1971, 234–9.
Katona, G., *Psychological Economics*, Amsterdam: Elsevier, 1975.
Katona, G., *Psychological Analysis of Economic Behavior*, Westport: Greenwood Press, 1977.
Katona, G., *Essays on Behavioral Economics*. Ann Arbor, MA; Institute for Social Research, 1980.
Katz, J., 'A new approach to the study of school motivation in minority group children', in Allen, V. (ed.), *Psychological Factors in Poverty*, Chicago: Markham, 1970.
Keenan, A. and Dean, P., 'Moral evaluations of tax evasion', *Social Policy and Administration*. 1980, *14*(3), 209–20.

Keene, K., 'What do we know about the public's attitude on progressivity?', *National Tax Journal*, 1983, 371–6.

Kelley, H.H., 'Attribution theory in social psychology', *Nebraska Symposium on Motivation*, 1967, *15*, 192–238.

Kelley, H.H. and Michela, J., 'Attribution theory and research', *Annual Review of Psychology*, 1980, *31*, 457–507.

Kelly, G.A., *A Theory of Personality*, New York: Norton, 1963.

Kelly, R., 'Estimating ultimate performance levels of new retail outlets', *Journal of Marketing Research*, 1967, 3–19.

Kelvin, P., 'Social psychology 2001; The social psychology bases and implications of structural unemployment', In R. Gilmour and S. Duck (eds.), *The Development of Social Psychology*, London: Academic Press, 1980.

Kelvin, P. and Jarrett, J., *Social Psychological Consequences of Unemployment*, Cambridge: Cambridge University Press, 1985.

Kemp, D., 'Taxation: The politics of change', in *The Politics of Taxation*, ed. J. Wilkes, Sydney: Hodder & Stoughton, 1980.

Key, V., *Public Opinion and American Democracy*, New York: Knopf, 1965.

Keynes, J., *The General Theory of Employment, Interest and Money*, London: Macmillan, 1936.

Kidron, A., 'Work values and organisational commitment', *Academy of Management Journal*, 1978, *21*, 239–47.

Kim, H., 'Relationship of Protestant ethic value beliefs to achievement, *Journal for the Scientific Study of Religion*, 1977, *16*, 255–62.

Kinsey, A., Pomeroy, W. and Martin, C., *Sexual Behavior in the Human Male*, Philadelphia: Saunders, 1948.

Klare, G., 'A second look at the validity of readability formulas', *Journal of Reading Behaviour*, 1976, *8*, 129–52.

Klare, G., *Encyclopaedia of Educational Research*, Washington, D.C.: American Education Research Association, 1982.

Kline, P., 'The validity of the Dynamic Personality Inventory', *British Journal of Medical Psychology*, 1968, *41*, 307–11.

Kline, P., *Fact and Fantasy in Freudian Theory*, London: Methuen, 1972.

Kline, P., *Ai3Q Test*, Windsor: NFER, 1971.

Koch, S. (ed.), *Psychology: A Study of Science*, vol. 3, New York: McGraw-Hill, 1959.

Komarovsky, M., *The Unemployed Man and His Family*, New York: Dryden, 1940.

Kourilsky, M., 'The Kinder-economy: A case study of kindergarten pupils', acquisition of economic concepts, *The Elementary School Journal*, 1977, *77*, 182–91.

Kourilsky, M. and Campbell, M., 'Sex differences in a simulated classroom economy: Children's beliefs about entrepreneurship', *Sex Roles*, 1984, *10*, 53–66.

Krafchik, M., 'Unemployment and vagrancy in the 1930s: Deterrence, rehabilitation and the depression', *Journal of Social Policy*, 1983, *12*, 195–214.

La France, M. and Cicchetti, C., 'Perceived responsibility and blame for economic success and failulre: Social class and employment status comparisons', *Journal of Applied Social Psychology*, 1979, *9*, 466–75.

Laing, R.D., *Knots*, London: Tavistock, 1970.

Lakatos, I., 'Falsification and the methodology of scientific research programmes', in I. Lakatos and A. Musgrave (eds.), *Criticism and the Growth of Knowledge*, London: Cambridge University Press, 1970.

Lambert, W., Soloman, R. and Watson, P., 'Reinforcement and extinction as factors in size estimation, *Journal of Experimental Psychology*, 1949, *39*, 637–41.

Lancaster, K., *Consumer Demand*, New York and London: Columbia University Press, 1971.

Lane, R., 'Money and the varieties of happiness', Paper given at Oxford ISPP Meeting, 1983.

Langner, T., Herson, J., Greene, E., Janeson, J. and Goff, T., 'Children of the city: affluence, poverty and mental health, In Allen, V. (ed.), *Psychological Factors in Poverty*, Chicago: Markham, 1970.

Larwood, L. and Blackmore, J., 'Fair pay: field investigations of the fair economic exchange', *Academy of Management Proceedings*, 1977, 81–5.

Lavercombe, S. and Fleming, D., 'Attitudes and duration of unemployment among sixteen-year-old school-leavers', *British Journal of Guidance and Counselling*, 1981, *9*, 36–45.

Lazarsfeld, P., Berelson, B. and Gaudet, H., *The People's Choice*, New York: Columbia University Press, 1948.

Le Grand, J., 'The distribution of public expenditure: the case of health care', *Economica*, 1978, *45*, 125–8.

Lea, S., 'Inflation, decimalization and the estimated sizes of coins', *Journal of Economic Psychology*, 1981, *1*, 79–81.

Lea, S. and Webley, P., 'Théorie psychologique de la monnaie', Paper given at the Economic Psychology Conference, Paris, 1981.

Lea, S., Tarpy, B. and Webley, P., *The Individual in the Economy*, Cambridge: Cambridge University Press, 1985.

Leahy, R., 'The development of the conception of economic inequality: Descriptions and comparisons of rich and poor people'. *Child Development*, 1981, *52*, 523–32.

Leibenstein, H., 'Micro-micro theory, agent-agent trade and x-efficiency' in *Economics in the Future*, ed. K. Dopfer, Basingstoke and London: Macmillan, 1976.

Leibenstein, H., *Beyond Economic Man*, Cambridge, Mass.: Harvard University Press, 1978.

Leiser, D., 'Children's conceptions of economics. The constitution of a cognitive domain' *Journal of Economic Psycholiogy*, 1983, *4*, 297–317.

Lerner, M., *The Belief in a Just World: A Fundamental Delusion*, New York: Plenum Press, 1980.

Lesieur, H., *The Chase: Careers of the Compulsive Gambler*, New York: Anchor Books, 1977.

Levinger, G. and Moles, O., *Divorce and Separation: Context, Causes and Consequences*, New York: Basic Books, 1979.

Levy, F., 'On understanding Proposition 13', *Public Interest* 1979, *56*, 66–89.

Lewis, A., 'Experimental studies of reciprocal communications', unpublished Ph D thesis, University of Wales, 1976.

Lewis, A., 'Perceptions of tax rates', *British Tax Review*, 1978, *6*, 358–66.

Lewis, A., 'An empirical assessment of tax mentality', *Public Finance*, 1979a *2*, 245–57.

Lewis, A., 'The comprehensibility of government forms and pamphlets', *Policy and Politics*, 1979b, *7*(4), 377–85.

Lewis, A., Sandford, C. and Pleming, C., *A Survey of Attitudes towards Wealth, the Wealthy, and the Proposed Annual Wealth Tax*, Bath University Report, 1979.

Lewis, A., 'Attitudes to public expenditure and their relationship to voting preferences', *Political Studies*, 1980, vol. XXVIII, no. 2, 284–92.

Lewis, A., 'Attributions and politics', *Personality and Individual Differences*, 1981, *2*, 1–4.

Lewis, A., *The Psychology of Taxation*, Oxford: Martin Robertson, 1982a.

Lewis, A., 'Rate and fiscal referenda: The issues', *Political Quarterly*, 1982b, *53*(1), 73–7.

Lewis, A., 'Public expenditure: perceptions and preferences', *Journal of Economic Psychology*, 1983, *3*, 159–67.

Lewis, A. and Furnham, A., 'Reducing unemployment: lay beliefs about how to reduce current unemployment, submitted for publication, 1984.

Lewis, A., Furnham, A. and Snell, M., '*Homo psychologicus* and *Homo economicus*: Economic and psychological explanations for unemployment, submitted for publication, 1984.

Lewis, A. and Jackson, D., 'Voting preferences and attitudes to public expenditure: Some new data', forthcoming *Political Studies*, 1985.

Lewis, A. and James, S., 'Understanding tax forms', *Certified Accountant*, 1981, *78*(1), 49–52.

Lewis, O., *Life in a Mexican Village*, Urbana, Ill.: University of Illinois, 1951.

Lewis, O., *The Children of Sanchez*, Harmondsworth: Penguin Books, 1965.

Lewis, O. *La Vida*, London: Panther Books, 1968.

Lichenstein, S., Fishchhoff, B. and Phillips, L., 'Calibration of probabilities: The state of the art', in *Decision-Making and Change in Human Affairs*, Dordrecht, Holland: Reidel, 1977.

Lied, T. and Prichard, R., 'Relationship between personality variables and components of the expectancy-valence model', *Journal of Applied Psychology*, 1976, *61*, 463–7.

Liem, R. and Atkinson, T., 'The work and unemployment project: Personal and family effects of job loss', unpublished paper, 1982.

Liem, R. and Rayman, P., 'Health and social costs of unemployment', *American Psychologist*, 1982, *37*, 1116–23.

Lindner, R., 'The psychodynamics of gambling', *Annals of the American Academy of Political and Social Science*, 1950, 269, 93–107.

Linqvist, A., 'A note on determinants of household saving behaviour', *Journal of Economic Psychology*, 1981, *1*, 39–57.

Liverant, S. and Scodel, A., 'Internal and external control as determinants of decision-making under conditions of risk', *Psychiological Reports*,

1960, *1*, 59–67.
Lozkowski, T., *Win or Lose: A Social History of Gambling in America*, New York: Bobbs Merril, 1977.
Luft, J., 'Monetary value and the perceptions of persons', *Journal of Social Psychology*, 1957, *46*, 245–51.

MacDonald, A., 'Correlates of the ethics of personal conscience and the ethics of social responsibility', *Journal of Consulting and Clinical Psychology*, 1971a, *37*, 443.
MacDonald, A., 'Relation of birth order to morality types and attitudes towards the poor', *Pyschological Reports*, 1971b, *29*, 732.
MacDonald, A., 'More on the Protestant ethic', *Journal of Consulting and Clinical Psychology*, 1972, *39*, 116–22.
Machlup, F., *Methodology of Economics and Other Social Sciences*, New York: Academic Press, 1978.
Mair, B. and Raffe, D., 'The transition from school to work in 1980/81: A dynamic account', *British Educational Research Journal*, 1983, *9*, 57–70.
Maital, S., *Minds, Markets and Money*, New York: Basic Books, 1982.
Maital, S., 'The psychology of macroeconomic conflict', Paper delivered to the International Association for Research in Economic Psychology (IAREP). Tilburg, The Netherlands, 1984.
Maital, S. and Maital, S., *Economic Games People Play*, New York: Basic Books, 1984.
Makeham, P., *Youth Unemployment: An examination of evidence on youth unemployment using national statistics*, London: Dept of Employment, Reach paper no. 10, 1980.
Mann, M., 'The social cohesion of liberal democracy', *American Sociological Review*, 1970, *35*, 423–39.
Markova, J., Lockyer, R. and Forbes, C., 'Self-perception of employed and unemployed haemophiliacs', *Psychological Medicine*, 1980, *10*, 559–65.
Marsden, D. and Duff, E., *Workless*, Harmondsworth: Penguin Books, 1975.
Marshall, H. and Magruder, L., 'Relations between parent money education practices and children's knowledge and use of money', *Child Development*, 1960, *31*, 253–84.
Maslow, A., *Motivation and Personality*, New York: Harper, 1954/Harper & Row, 1970.
Mason, R. and Calvin, L., 'A study of admitted income tax evasion', *Law and Society Review*, Autumn 1978.
Matza, D. and Miller, H., 'Poverty and proletariat', in Merton, R. and Nisbet, R. (eds.), *Contemporary Social Problems*, New York: Harcourt, Brace, Jovanovich, 1976.
McClelland, D., *The Achieving Society*, Princeton, N.J.: Van Nostrand, 1961.
McClelland, D., Atkinson, J., Clark, R. and Lowell, E., *The Achievement Motive*, New York; Appleton-Century-Croft, 1953.
McCurdy, H., 'Coin perception studies and the concept of schemata', *Psychological Review*, 1956, *63*, 160–8.

McGuire, W., 'The nature of attitudes and attitude change', in *The Handbook of Social Psychology* vol. 3, ed. G. Lindzey and E. Aronson, Reading, Mass.: Addison-Wesley, 1969.

McGuire, W., 'The development of theory in social psychology', in *The Development of Social Psychology*, ed. R. Gilmour and S. Duck, London: Academic Press, 1980.

McKenzie, R. and Tullock, G., *The New World of Economics*, Homewood, Ill.: Irwin, 1978.

Mehrabian, A., 'Characteristic individual reactions to preferred and unpreferred environments', *Journal of Personality*, 1978, *46*, 717–31.

Merrens, M. and Garrett, J., 'The Protestant ethic, scale as a predictor of repetitive work performance', *Journal of Applied Psychology*, 1975, *60*, 125–7.

Merton, R., 'Social structure and anomie', *American Sociological Review*, 1938, *3*, 672–82.

Merton, R., 'The role-set: Problems in sociological theory', *British Journal of Sociology*, 1957, *8*, 106–20.

Merton, R., *Social Theory and Social Change*, New York: Free Press, 1968.

Merton, R. and Nisbett, R., *Contemporary Social Problems*, New York: Harcourt, Brace, Jovanovich, 1976.

Merton, R. and Rossi, A., 'Contributions to the theory of reference group behaviour', in Merton, K. (ed.), *Social Theory and Social Structure*, New York: Free Press, 1968.

Midgley, D., 'A simple mathematical theory of innovative behaviour', *Journal of Consumer Research*, 1976, 31–41.

Milham, S., Bullock, R. and Hosie, K., 'Juvenile unemployment: A concept due for re-cycling', *Journal of Adolescence*, 1978, *1*, 11–24.

Miller, G.A., *The Psychology of Communication*, Harmondsworth: Penguin Books, 1968.

Miller, L. and Horn, T., 'Children's concepts regarding debt', *The Elementary School Journal*, 1955, *56*, 406–12.

Mirels, H. and Garrett, J., 'The Protestant work ethic as a personality variable', *Journal of Consulting and Clinical Psychology*, 1971, *36*, 40–4.

Mischel, W., *Introduction to Personality*, New York: Holt, Rinehart & Winston, 1981.

Monroe, K., 'The influence of price differences and brand familiarity on brand preferences', *Journal of Consumer Research*, 1976, *3*, 42–9.

Moscovici, C., 'On social representation', in J. Forgas (ed.), *Social Cognition*, London: Academic Press, 1981.

Mosley, P., *The Making of Economic Policy*, Brighton: Wheatsheaf, 1984.

Mueller, E., 'Public attitudes toward fiscal programs', *Quarterly Journal of Economics*, 1963, *77*(2), 210–35.

Munroe, P., Munroe, R. and Daniels, R., 'Effect of status and values on estimation of coin size in two East African societies', *Journal of Social Psychology*, 1969, *77*, 28–34.

Mynott, C., 'The gambler's self-destructive drive', *American Medical Association* 1979, (Special Report).

Newcomb, T., Turner, R. and Converse, P., *Social Psychology*, New York: Holt, Rinehart & Winston, 1964.
Newson, J. and Newson, E., *Seven Year Olds in the Home Environment*, London: Allen & Unwin, 1976.
Newsweek, 'Europe's "Black Economy"', July 25 1983, p. 12.
Ng, S., 'Children's ideas about the bank and shop profit. Developmental stages and the influence of cogniture contrasts and conflict', *Journal of Economic Psychology*, 1983, *4*, 209–21.
Nicosia, F., *Consumer Decision Processes*, Englewood Cliffs, N.J.: Prentice-hall, 1966.
Nisbett, R., 'Public opinion versus popular opinion', *Public Interest*, 1975, *41*, 166–92.
Noble, T., *Structure and Change in Modern Britain*. London and Sydney: Batsford, 1975.

O'Brien, G. and Kabaroff, B., 'Comparison of unemployed and employed workers on values, locus of control and health variables', *Australian Psychologist*, 1979, *14*, 143–54.
OECD, *Revenue statistics of OECD Member countries 1965–82*, OECD, 1982.
O'Higgins, M., 'Aggregate measures of tax evasion: an assessment', *British Tax Review*, 1981a, *5*, 286–302.
O'Higgins, M., 'Tax evasion and the self-employed, an examination of the evidence', *British Tax Review*, 1981b, *6*, 367–78.
Ölander, F. and Seipel, C., *Psychological Approaches to the Study of Saving*, Urbana: University of Illinois, 1970.
Orford, J., *The Social Psychology of Mental Disorder*, Harmondsworth: Penguin Books, 1976.
Osgood, M., 'Rural and urban attitudes towards the poor', *Social Work*, 1977, *22*, 41–7.
Osgood, C. and Tannenbaum, P., 'The principle of congruity in the prediction of attitude change', *Psychological Review*, 1955, *62*, 42–55.
Osmond, M. and Grigg, C., 'Correlates of poverty: The interaction of individual and family characteristics', *Social Forces*, 1978, *56*, 1099–120.
Overlaet, B. and Lagrou, L., 'Attitude towards a redistribution of income', *Journal of Economic Psychology*, 1981, *1*, 197–215.

Pandey, T., Kakkar, S. and Bohra, K., 'The functional perception of poverty in India', *Journal of Social Psychology*, 1982a, *117*, 149–50.
Pandey, T., Sinha, T., Prakash, A. and Tripathi, R., 'Right-Left political ideologies and attribution of the causes of poverty', *European Journal of Social Psychology*, 1982b, *12*, 327–31.
Pareek, U., 'Poverty and motivation: figure and ground', in Allen, V. (ed.), *Psychological factors in Poverty*, Chicago: Markham, 1970.
Parkes, C., *Bereavement: Studies of Grief in Adult Life*, Harmondsworth: Penguin Books, 1975.
Patterson, J. and Locksley, G., 'How fifth formers see the unions', *Labour Research*, 1981, *11*, 23–25.

Pavlov, I., *Lectures on Conditioned Reflexes*, trans. W. Gantt, New York: International, 1928.

Penner, L. and Rokeach, M., 'The effects of employment condition on value systems', *Papers in Psychology*, 1969, *3*, 47–51.

Peterson, G., Southworth, L. and Peters, D., 'Children's self-esteem and maternal behaviour in three low-income samples', *Psychological Reports*, 1983, *52*, 79–86.

Polanyi, G. and Wood, J., *How much Inequality*?, London: Institute of Economic Affairs, 1974.

Pollio, H. and Gray, T., 'Change-making strategies in children and adults', *Journal of Psychology*, 1973, *84*, 173–9.

Poppe, M. and Utens, E., 'Effects of change in size of a common good on choice behaviour in a social dilemma situation',. Paper presented at the International Association of Researchers in Economic Psychology, Tilburg, The Netherlands, 1984.

Prevey, E., 'A quantitative study of family practices in training children in the use of money', *Journal of Educational Psychology*, 1945, *36*, 141–81.

Pym, D., 'Towards a dual economy and emancipation from employment', *Futures*, 1980, *6*, 223–37.

Raelin, J., 'A comparative study of later work experience among full-time, part-time, and unemployment male youth', *Journal of Vocational Behaviour*, 1981, *19*, 315–27.

Raffe, D., 'Employment instability among less-qualified young workers', *British Journal of Guidance and Counselling*, 1983, *11*, 21–34.

Rahe, R., Floistad, I., Bergan, T., Ringdal, R., Gerhardt, R., Gunderson, E., and Arthur, R., 'A model of life changes and illness research', *Archives of General Psychiatry*, 1974, *31*, 172–7.

Raiffa, H., *Decision Analysis: Introductory Lectures on Choices under Uncertainty*, Reading, Mass.: Addison-Wesley, 1968.

Rainwater, L., 'Neutralizing the disinherited: Some psychological aspects of understanding the poor', in Allen, V. (ed.), *Psychological Factors in Poverty*, Chicago: Markham, 1970.

Ray, J., 'Christianism ... The Protestant ethic among unbelievers', *Journal of Christian Education*, 1970, *13*, 169–76.

Ray, J., 'The Protestant ethic in Australia', *Journal of Social psychology*, 1982, *116*, 127–38.

Ray, J. and Kiefl, W., 'Authoritarianism and achievement motivation in contemporary West Germany', *Journal of Social Psychology*, 1984, 122, 3–19.

Reid, I., *Social Class Differences in Britain*, London: Open Books, 1979.

Reynaud, P.L., *Economic Psychology*, trans. S.E.G. Lea, New York: Praeger, 1981.

Rim, Y., 'Values and attitudes', *Personality*, 1970, *1*, 243–50.

Rim, Y., 'Significance of work and personality', *Journal of Occupational Psychology*, 1977, *50*, 135–8.

Rim, Y., *Personality and Attitudes Connected with Money*, Paper given at the Economic Psychology Conference, Edinburgh, 1982.

Rim, Y., 'Explanations for poverty: personality aspects', *Personality and Individual Differences*, 1984, *1*, 123–4.

Robbins, L., *The Nature and Significance of Economic Science*, London: Macmillan, 1935.

Roberts, K., Duggan, J., and Noble, M., 'Out-of-school youth in high unemployment areas, *British Journal of Guidance and Counselling*, 1982, *10*, 1–11.

Robertson, A. and Cochrane, R., 'Attempted suicide and cultural change: An empirical investigation', *Human Relations*, 1976, *9*, 863–83.

Robinson, R. and Bell, W., 'Equality, success and social justice in England and the United States, *American Sociological Review*, 1978, *43*, 125–43.

Rockwell, R. and Elder, E., 'Economic deprivation and problem behaviour; Childhood and adolescence in the Great Depression', *Human Development*, 1982, *25*, 58–63.

Rogers, E., *Diffusion of Innovations*, Glencoe: The Free Press, 1971.

Rokeach, M., *The Nature of Human Values*, New York: Free Press, 1973.

Rose, R., 'Getting by in three economies: The resources of the official, unofficial and domestic economies', Glasgow: University of Strathclyde, 1983.

Rosen, B., 'Race, ethnicity and the achievement syndrome', *American Sociological Review*, 1959, *24*, 47–60.

Rosenberg, M. and Hovland, C., 'Cognitive, affective and behavioral components of attitudes', in *Attitude Organization and Change*, ed. M. Rosenberg *et al.*, New Haven: Yale University Press, 1960.

Rowntree, B.S., *Poverty: A Study of Town Life*, London: Macmillan, 1901.

Rowntree, B. and Lasker, B., *Unemployment: A Social Study*, Toronto: Macmillan, 1911.

Royal Commission on the Taxation of Profits and Income, *PAYE and Incentives*, Cmnd 9150, London: HMSO, 1954.

Rubinstein, C., 'Your money and your life', *Psychology Today*, 1980, *12*, 47–58.

Rubinstein, W., 'Men of property: Some aspects of accommodation, inheritance and power among top British wealth holders', in P. Stanworth and A. Giddens (eds.), *Elites and Power in British Society*, Cambridge: Cambridge University Press, 1974.

Runciman, W., *Relative Deprivation and Social Justice*, London: Routledge & Kegan Paul, 1966.

Rushton, J., *Altruism, Socialization and Society*, New Jersey: Prentice-Hall, 1980.

Ryan, W., *Blaming the Victim*, New York: Partheon, 1971.

Sanders, T., 'Effects of taxation on executives', Cambridge, Mass.: Harvard University Graduate School of Business Administration, 1951.

Sandford, C., *The Hidden Costs of Taxation*, London: Institute for Fiscal Studies, 1973.

Sandford, C., *The Economics of Public Finance*, Oxford: Pergamon, 1978.

Sandford, C., 'Tax compliance costs, evasion and avoidance', in *Limits to Redistribution*, Colston Symposium, University of Bristol, 1979.

Schapiro, M. and Ahlberg, D., 'Income aspirations, unemployment and suicide: An analysis and forecast of US postwar suicides by age and sex', unpublished paper, 1983.

Schmölders, G., 'Survey research in public finance: a behavioural approach to fiscal policy', *Public Finance*, 1970, *25*(2), 300–6.

Schoemaker, P., 'The role of statistical knowledge in gambling decisions', *Organizational Behaviour and Human Performance*, 1979, *24*, 1–17.

Schwartz, R. and Orleans, S., 'On legal sanctions', *University of Chicago Law Review*, 1967, *34*, 274–300.

Scitovsky, T., *The Joyless Economy*, London: Oxford University Press, 1976.

Seldon, A., 'Price-less opinion research', *British Public Opinion*, 1980, *1*, 2, 8.

Semin, G. and Manstead, A., 'Social psychology: social or psychological?', *British Journal of Social and Clinical Psychology*, 1979, *18*(2), 191–202

Sen, A., 'Rational fools: a critique of the behavioural foundations of economic theory' *Philosophy and Public Affairs*, 1977, *6*, 317–44.

Shackle, G., *Expectation in Economics*, Cambridge: Cambridge University Press, 1949.

Shamir, B., 'A note on tipping and employee perceptions and attitudes', *Journal of Occupational Psychology*, 1983, *56*, 255–60.

Shapiro, H., 'The index of consumer sentiment and economic forcasting—a reappraisal', in *Human Behaviour in Economic Affairs*, ed. B. Strumpel, B. Morgan and E. Zahn, Amsterdam: Elsevier, 1972.

Shultz, T. and Coddington, M., 'Development of the concepts of energy conservation and entropy', *Journal of Experimental Child Psychology*, 1981, *31*, 131–53.

Siegal, M., 'Children's perception of adult economic needs', *Child Development*, 1981, *52*, 379–82.

Siegal, M. and Shwarb, I., 'Economic justice in adolescence: A cross-cultural analysis', Paper given at the SRCO Meeting, Detroit, 1983.

Silberman, M., 'Towards a theory of criminal deterrence', *American Sociological Review* 1976, *41*, 442–61.

Simmel, E., 'Zur Psychoanalyse des Spielers', *Internationale Zeitschrift für Psychoanalyse*, 1920, *6*, 397–412.

Simon, H., 'Theories of decision-making in economics and behavioral sciences'. *American Economic Review*, 1959, *69*, 253–83.

Simon, H., *Administrative Behavior: A study of decision-making processes in administrative organisation,* New York: The Free Press, 1976a.

Simon, H., 'From substantive to procedural rationality', in *Method and Appraisal in Economics*, ed. S. Latsis, Cambridge: Cambridge University Press, 1976b.

Simon, H. and Stedry, A., 'Psychology and economics', in *Handbook of Social Psychology* vol. V, ed. G. Lindzey and E. Aronson, Reading, Mass.: Addison-Wesley, 1969.

Simon, W. and Gagnon, J., 'The anomie of affluence: A post-Mertonian conception', *American Journal of Sociology*, 1976, *82*, 356–77.

Singh, S., 'Effect of motivation, values, cognitive factors and child-rearing attitudes on productivity among Punjabi farmers', *Journal of Social Psychology*, 1983, *120*, 273–8.

Singh, S. and Vasudeva, P., 'A factorial study of the perceived reasons for poverty', *Asian Journal of Psychology and Education*, 1977, *2*, 51–6.
Skinner, B.F., *Science and Human Behavior*, New York: Macmillan, 1953.
Smart, R., 'Drinking problems among employed, unemployed and shift workers', *Journal of Occupational Medicine*, 1979, *11*, 731–6.
Smith, H., 'Value and the perceptual judgement of magnitude', *Psychological Review*, 1957, *64*, 192–204.
Smith, S. and Razzell, P., *The Pools Winners*, London: Caliban Books, 1975.
Song, Y.D. and Yarbrough, T., 'Tax ethics and taxpayers' attitudes', *Public Administration Review*, 1978, 442–52.
Spicer, M. and Becker, L., 'Fiscal inequality and tax evasion: an experimental approach', *National Tax Journal*, 1980, *33*(3), 171–5.
Spitze, G. and Waite, L., 'Wives' employment: The role of husbands' perceived attitudes', *Journal of Marriage and the Family*, 1981, *12*, 117–24.
Srole, L., 'Social integration and certain corollaries: an exploratory study', *American Sociological Review*, 1956, *21*, 709–16.
Stacey, B., 'Economic socialization in the pre-adult years', *British Journal of Social Psychology*, 1982, *21*, 159–73.
Stafford, E., 'The impact of the Youth Opportunities Programme on young people's employment prospects and psychological well-being', *British Journal of Guidance and Counselling*, 1982, *10*, 12–21.
Steinberg, L., Catalano, R. and Dooley, D., 'Economic antecedents of child abuse and neglect', *Child Development*, 1981, *52*, 975–85.
Stevenson, O., *Claimant or Client?* London: Allen & Unwin, 1973.
Stigler, G., 'The intellectual and the market place', in *Price Theory*, ed. H. Townsend, Harmondsworth, Penguin Books, 1971.
Stirling, A., 'Preparing school leavers for unemployment', *Bulletin of the British Psychological Society*, 1982, *35*, 421–2.
Stoezel, J., 'Le prix comme limite', in *La Psychologie Economique*, ed. P.L. Reynaud, Paris: Rivière, 1954.
Stone, E., 'Job scope, job satisfaction, and the Protestant ethic', *Journal of Vocational Behaviour*, 1975, *7*, 215–24.
Stone, E., 'The moderating effect of work-related values on the job scope—job satisfaction relationship', *Organizational Behaviour and Human performance*, 1976, *15*, 147–67.
Stouffer, S. *et al.*, *The American Soldier*, vol. 1, Princeton, N. J.: Princeton University Press, 1949.
Strauss, A., 'The development and transformation of monetary meanings in the child', *American Sociological Review*, 1952, *17*, 275–86.
Strickland, L., Lewichi, R. and Katz, A., 'Temporal orientation and perceived control as determinants of risk-taking', *Journal of Experimental Social Psychology*, 1966, *2*, 143–51.
Stroebe, W. and Frey, B., 'In defence of economic man: towards an integration of economics and psychology', *Schweiz Zeitschrift für Volkswirtschaft und Statistik*, 1980, *2*, 119–48.
Strumpel, B., 'The contribution of survey research to public finance', in *Quantitative Methods in Public Finance*, ed. A. Peacock, New York: Praeger, 1969.

Sullivan, T., Thompson, K., Wright, R., Gross, G. And Spady, D., *Social Problems: Divergent Perspectives*, New York: Wiley, 1980.
Sutherland, H., *White-Collar Crime*, New York: Holt, Rinehart & Winston, 1949.
Sutton, R., 'Behaviour in the attainment of economic concepts', *Journal of Psychology*, 1962, *53*, 37–46.
Swinburn, P., 'The psychological impact of unemployment on managers and professional staff', *Journal of Occupational Psychology*, 1981, *54*, 47–64.

Tajfel, H., 'Value and the perceptual judgement of magnitude', *Psychological Review*, 1977, *64*, 192–204.
Tajfel, H. (ed.), *Differentiation between Social Groups: Studies in the Social Psychology of Intergroup Relations*, London: Academic Press, 1978.
Tajfel, H., *Human Groups and Social Categories*, Cambridge: Cambridge University Press, 1981.
Tan, H. and Stacey, B., 'The understanding of socio-economic concepts in Malaysian Chinese school children', *Child Study Journal*, 1981, *11*, 33–49.
Taylor, D. and Brown, R., 'Towards a more social social psychology', *British Journal of Social and Clinical Psychology*, 1979, *18*(2), 173–80.
Taylor-Gooby, P., 'Two cheers for the Welfare State: public opinion and private welfare', *Journal of Public Policy*, 1982, *2*(4), 319–46.
Taylor-Gooby, P., 'Moralism, self-interest and attitudes to welfare', *Policy and Politics*, 1983, *11*(2), 145–60.
Teahan, J., 'Future time perspective and job success', *A Group-Oriented Approach for Facilitating the Work Adjustment of the Hard Core Unemployed*, Department of Labor, Washington, D.C., 1969.
Thibaut, J., Friedland, N. and Walker, L., 'Compliance with rules: some social determinants', *Journal of Personality and Social Psychology*, 1974, *30*, 792–801.
Thoits, P. and Hannan, M., 'Income and psychological distress: The impact of an income-maintenance experiment', *Journal of Health and Social Behaviour*, 1979, *20*, 120–38.
Thurnwald, R., *Economics in Primitive Communities*, Oxford: Oxford University Press, 1932.
Tiffany, D., Cowan, J. and Tiffany, P., *The Unemployed: A Social-Psychological Portrait*, Englewood Cliffs, N.J.: Prentice-Hall, 1970.
Townsend, P., *Poverty in the United Kingdom*, Harmondsworth: Penguin Books, 1979.
Triandis, H., *Attitude and Attitude Change*, New York: Wiley, 1971.
Trower, P., Bryant, B. and Argyle, M., *Social Skills and Mental Health*, London: Methuen, 1978.
Tuck, M., *How Do We Choose?* London: Methuen, 1976.
Tversky, A. and Kahneman, D., 'Causal schema in judgments under uncertainty', in *Progress in Social Psychology*, ed. M. Fishbein, Hillsdale, N.J.: Erlbaum, 1977.

Vandenberg, S., Genetic factors in poverty: A psychologist's point of view', in Allen, V. (ed.), *Psychological Factors in Poverty*, Chicago: Markham, 1970.

van Praag, B., 'Linking economics with psychology: an economist's view', Paper presented to the International Association for Research in Economic Psychology (IAREP), Tilburg. The Netherlands, 1984.

van Raaij, F., 'Economic psychology', *Journal of Economic Psychology*, 1981, *1*(1), 1–24.

van Raaij, W.F., 'Attribution of causality to economic action and events', Paper given at International Association for Research on Economic Psychology. Tilburg, The Netherlands, 1984.

Veblen, T., *The Theory of the Leisure Class*, New York: Mentor Books London: Macmillan, 1953.

Vecchio, R., 'Workers' beliefs in internal versus external determinants of success', *Journal of Social Psychology*, 1981, 114, 199–207.

Verhallen, T., 'Scarcity and consumer choice behaviour' *Journal of Economic Psychology*, 1982, *2*(4), 299–322.

Vogel, J., 'Taxation and public opinion in Sweden: an interpretation of recent survey data', *National Tax Journal*, 1974, *28*(4), 499–513.

von Mises, L., *The Ultimate Foundation of Economic Science* Kansas: Sheed, Andrew & McKeel, 1978.

von Neumann, J. and Morgenstern, N. O., *Theory of Games and Economic Behavior*, Princeton, N.J.: Princeton University Press, 1944.

Vroom, V., *Work and Motivation*, New York: Wiley, 1964.

Wagner, R., 'Revenue structure, fiscal illusion and budgetary choice', *Public Choice*, 1976, *25*, 45–61.

Wagstaff, G., 'Attitudes to poverty, the Protestant ethic and political affiliation: A preliminary investigation', *Social behaviour and Personality*, 1983, *11*, 45–7.

Walker, K., *The study of primitive economics', Oceania*, 1943, *8*, 131–42.

Walls, Ltd., *Pocket-money Monitor, 1983: Annual Study by Birds Eye Walls Ltd*, Surrey, 1983.

Walster, E., Berscheid, E. and Walster, G., 'New directions in equity research', *Journal of Personality and Social Psychology*, 1973, *25*, 151–76.

Wanous, J., 'Individual differences and reactions to job characteristics', *Journal of Applied Psychology*, 1974, *59*, 616–22.

Ward, A. and Pickering, J., 'Preliminary testing of the explanatory power of the EEC consumer attitudes survey in the UK', *Applied Economics*, 1981, *13*, 19–34.

Warneryd, K.E. and Walerud, B., 'Taxes and economic behaviour: Some interview data on tax evasion in Sweden', *Journal of Economic Psychology*, 1982, *2*(3), 187–211.

Warr, P., 'Psychological aspects of employment and unemployment', *Psychological Medicine*, 1981, *11*, 125–36.

Warr, P., 'A national study of non-financial employment commitment', *Journal of Occupational Psychology*, 1982, *55*, 297–312.

Warr, P., 'Reported behaviour changes after job loss', *British Journal of Social Psychology*, 1984, *23*, 271–5.

Warr, P., 'Work, jobs and unemployment', *Bulletin of the British Psychological Society*, 1983, *36*, 305–11.

Warr, P. and Jackson, P., 'Men without jobs: Some correlates of age and length of unemployment', *Journal of Occupational Psychology*, 1984, *57*, 77–85.

Warr, P., Jackson, P. and Banks, M., 'Duration of unemployment and psychological well-being in young men and women', *Current Psychological Research*, 1982, *2*, 207–14.

Warr, P. and Parry, G., 'Paid employment and women's psychological well-being', *Psychological Bulletin*, 1982, *91*, 498–516.

Warr, P. and Payne, R., 'Social class and reported changes in behaviour after job loss', *Journal of Applied Social Psychology*, 1983, *13*, 206–22.

Warr, P. and Wall, T., *Work and Well-Being*, Harmondsworth: Penguin Books, 1975.

Waters, L., Bathis, N. and Waters, C., 'Protestant ethic attitudes among college students', *Educational and Psychological Measurement*, 1975, *35*, 447–50.

Watson, J., *Behaviorism*, Chicago: Chicago University Press, 1930.

Watts, A., 'The implications of school-leavers: Unemployment for careers education in schools', *Journal of Curriculum Studies*, 1978, *3*, 233–50.

Weber, M., *The Protestant Ethic and the Spirit of Capitalsim*, New York: Scribners, 1905.

Webley, P., Lea, S. and Portalska, R., 'The unacceptability of money as a gift, *Journal of Economic Psychology*, 1983, *4*, 223–38.

Wernimont, P. and Fitzpatrick, S., 'The meaning of money', *Journal of Applied Psychology*, 1972, *56*, 218–26.

Whiteley, P., 'Public opinion and the demand for social welfare in Britain', *Journal of Social Policy*, 1981, *10*, 453–76.

Williamson, J., 'Beliefs about the motivation of the poor and attitudes towards poverty policy', *Social Problems*, 1974, *18*, 634–48.

Williams, R. and Defris, L., 'The roles of inflation and consumer sentiment in explaining Australian consumption and saving patterns', *Journal of Economic Psychology*, 1981, *1*(2), 105–20.

Wilson, G., *The Psychology of Conservatism*, London: Academic Press, 1973.

Wilson, G. and Patterson, J., 'A new measure of conservatism', *British Journal of Social and Clinical Psychology*, 1968, *7*, 264–9.

Witryol, S. and Wentworth, N., 'A paired comparison scale of children's preferences for monetary and material researchs used in investigations of incentive effects', *Journal of Genetic Psychology*, 1983, *142*, 17–23.

Winocur, S. and Siegal, M., 'Adolescents' judgements of economic arrangements', *International Journal of Behavioural Development*, 1982, *5*, 357–65.

Wiseman, T., *The Money Motive*, London: Hodder & Stoughton, 1974.

Wollack, S., Goodale, J., Wilting, J. and Smith, P., 'Development of the survey of work values', *Journal of Applied Psychology*, 1971, *55*, 331–8.

Worcester, R. and McIntyre, I., 'Strategic decision research: its communication and use at ICI', in *Applied Marketing and Social Research*, ed. U. Bradley, Wokingham: van Nostrand Reinholt, 1982.
Wright Mills, C., *The Sociological Imagination*, New York: Oxford University Press, 1959.

Yamanchi, K. and Templer, D., 'The development of a money attitude scale', *Journal of Personality Assessment*, 1982, *46*, 522–8.
Younger, J., Arrowood, A. and Hemsley, G., 'And the lucky shall inherit the earth: Perceiving the causes of financial success and failure', *European Journal of Social Psychology*, 1977, *7*, 509–15.

Zaltman, G., Pinson, C. and Angelmar, R., *Metatheory and Consumer Research*, New York: Holt, Rinehart & Winston, 1973.
Zimmerman, M. and Hartley, W., 'High blood pressure among employed women: A multi-factor discriminant analysis', *Journal of Health and Social Behaviour*, 1982, *23*, 205–20.
Zinser, O., Perry, J. and Edgar, R., 'Affluence of the request value of donations and sharing behaviour in preschool children', *Journal of Psychology*, 1975, *89*, 301–5.
Zuckerman, M., 'Sensation-seeking and psychopathology', in R. Hare and D. Schalling (eds.), *Psychopathic Behaviour*, New York: Wiley, 1979.

Index